RESTAURANT MANAGEMENT
Customers, Operations, and Employees

Robert Christie Mill

School of Hotel, Restaurant, and Tourism Management
Daniels College of Business
University of Denver

Prentice Hall
Upper Saddle River, New Jersey 07458

Library of Congress Cataloging-in-Publication Data

Mill, Robert Christie.
    Restaurant management : customers, operations, and employees /
Robert Christie Mill.
      p.   cm.
    ISBN 0-13-201774-1
    1. Restaurant management.   I. Title.
TX911.3.M24M55 1998
647.95'068—dc21
                                    97-30345
                                          CIP

Dedication

*For Christian, Jordan,
and Mikayla*

Director of production and manufacturing: *Bruce Johnson*
Managing editor: *Mary Carnis*
Production coordinator: *Ed O'Dougherty*
Editorial/production supervision, interior design,
   art production, and page layout: *Julie Boddorf*
Creative director: *Marianne Frasco*
Cover design: *Maria Lange*
Cover illustration: *Lisa Henderling, Stock Illustration Source*
Acquisitions editor: *Neil Marquardt*
Marketing manager: *Frank Mortimer, Jr.*
Editorial assistant: *Rose Mary Florio*
Proofreader: *Susan Shakhshir*

© 1998 by Prentice-Hall, Inc.
Simon & Schuster / A Viacom Company
Upper Saddle River, New Jersey 07458

Printed in the United States of America
10 9 8 7 6 5 4 3 2 1

ISBN   0-13-201774-1

PRENTICE-HALL INTERNATIONAL (UK) LIMITED, *London*
PRENTICE-HALL OF AUSTRALIA PTY. LIMITED, *Sydney*
PRENTICE-HALL CANADA INC., *Toronto*
PRENTICE-HALL HISPANOAMERICANA, S.A., *Mexico*
PRENTICE-HALL OF INDIA PRIVATE LIMITED, *New Delhi*
PRENTICE-HALL OF JAPAN, INC., *Tokyo*
SIMON & SCHUSTER ASIA PTE. LTD., *Singapore*
EDITORA PRENTICE-HALL DO BRASIL, LTDA., *Rio de Janeiro*

CONTENTS

chapter   5
Pricing and Designing the Menu   **101**

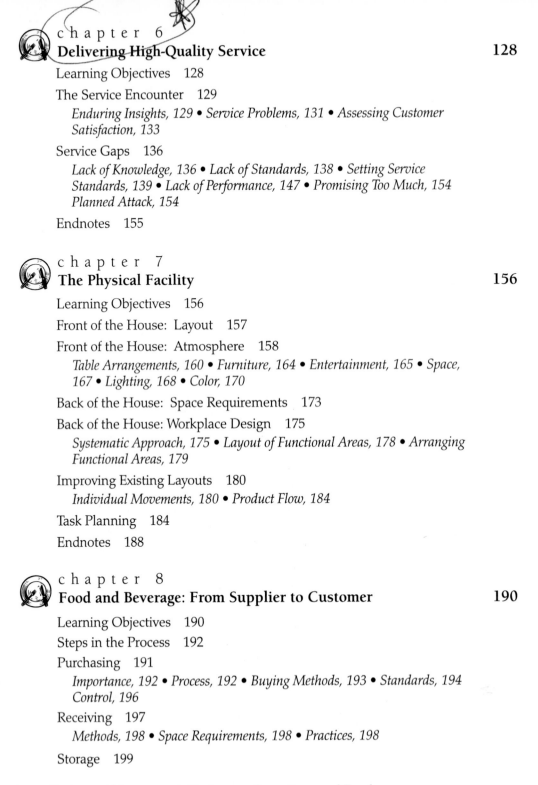

c h a p t e r   1 3
Training and Development   318

c h a p t e r   1 4
Motivating the Employee   339

PREFACE

In writing this book I wanted to identify the crucial elements involved in the successful operation of a restaurant and show their interrelationships. In providing what John Fuller, the former head of the Scottish Hotel School, called the "meal experience," the restaurant manager brings together three elements: customers, the operation (consisting of food and beverage items as well as the physical facility), and employees. The operator's task is to manage these elements to produce satisfied customers. How to do this is the thrust of this book.

In Chapter 1 we provide a financial overview of the restaurant industry while looking at the major factors affecting the growth of the business and considering the factors that make the difference between success and failure in running a restaurant.

In Chapters 2 through 6 we consider the first of the three elements of the meal experience: the customer. The eating habits of the various segments of the market are described in Chapter 2 and the major trends in customer behavior that affect the business are identified. Chapter 3 goes on to show how to develop a marketing plan to attract one or more of the segments identified in Chapter 2. The importance of promotion as a marketing tool is recognized in Chapter 4 as we consider how and when to use various types of advertising to bring people in the front door. The role of the menu as a crucial part of the marketing effort is covered in Chapter 5, with sections on pricing and design to develop the strongest possible promotional vehicle. The culmination of the marketing effort to the customer is the provision of high-quality service, the topic of Chapter 6. The features that make the service encounter unique are identified and strategies developed to provide service to the customer that will result in satisfied patrons who want to return and who will tell their friends to visit.

Chapters 7 through 11 deal with the physical facilities. In Chapter 7 we show how the front of the house can be designed to make a positive impact on the psychological needs and behavior of the customer. The effect on employee productivity of the design of the back of the house is also covered. Chapter 8 follows the flow of food and beverage items from supplier to customer through the various departments within the operation in developing procedures for effective purchasing, receiving, storing, and issuing of items used. The various production and service systems are compared within the context of developing effective cost control. Chapter 9 focuses on kitchen equipment and interiors. Guidelines are given on the proper procedures to follow in selecting, cleaning, and repairing kitchen equipment. Readers are shown how to develop a comprehensive energy management program. The importance of sanitation and food safety is stressed in Chapter 10. The major sanitation problems faced by restaurant managers are identified and procedures developed for preventing foodborne diseases. A program to build effective employee habits is presented. In the final chapter in this section, Chapter 11, we show how to analyze financial statements systematically to determine the profitability of the operation.

In the third section of the book we examine the role of employees. Chapter 12 deals with employee selection, identifying the work groups that managers will turn to increasingly in the next decade. The legal environment within which managers must operate is described and the steps involved in staffing the operation are noted and guidelines given on how to improve the quality of employees selected. The design of effective orientation, training, and development programs is covered in Chapter 13, together with tips on how to develop the skills necessary to be an effective trainer. The topic of employee motivation is dealt with in Chapter 14. Suggestions are given as to why employees behave the way they do, and techniques are developed that will allow managers to channel and maintain employee behavior through the implementation of various process theories of motivation. In the final chapter we examine the National Restaurant Association's report on the manager in the year 2000, indicating the major skills and knowledge that will be required of restaurant managers by the turn of the century.

ACKNOWLEDGMENTS

I am grateful to Professor John Fuller who, as head of the Scottish Hotel School, first brought the phrase "the meal experience" to my attention. Experiences with chefs and managers at Canadian Pacific, McTavish's Kitchens, Trust House Forte, and Intercontinental Hotel Corporation added practical examples of the concept.

While the layout for the book languished on a piece of paper for over twenty years it was Prentice Hall's Robin Baliszewski who believed in the idea sufficiently to push the idea into reality. I am also indebted to the reviewers who gave their experience and knowledge to suggest excellent improvements: Robert D. Buchanan, Purdue University; Matt A. Casado, Northern Arizona University; Richard J. Doyon, Quincy College; Fred T. Faria, Johnson & Wales University; Terence F. McDonough, Erie Community College/City Campus; David V. Pavesic, Georgia State University; Edward B. Pomianoski, County College of Morris; John Rousselle, Purdue University; and James R. Turley, New York Institute of Technology.

Last, but by no means, least, this book would not have been completed were it not for the heroic efforts of Sara M. Fontaine, my graduate assistant who oversaw final proofing while I was out of the country, and Julie Boddorf, Senior Production Editor at Prentice Hall, who polished this rough manuscript into what, I believe, is a gem of a book.

chapter one

INTRODUCTION

learning objectives

By the end of this chapter you should be able to:

1. Identify the major factors affecting the growth of the restaurant industry.
2. Identify the common denominators of restaurants.
3. Provide a financial overview of the restaurant industry in the United States.
4. Identify the reasons that restaurants fail.
5. Identify the major reasons contributing to the financial success of a restaurant.
6. Identify the skills necessary to manage a restaurant.

THE FOOD SERVICE INDUSTRY

The foodservice industry as a whole is made up of two major segments: commercial and noncommercial. The noncommercial part of the business accounts for 26 percent of total sales and includes catering operations in offices, factories, hospitals, and colleges. From 1991 to 1995 revenues in both segments of the foodservice industry grew from $260 billion to $307 billion [1]. The 1995 figures for the various segments of the commercial sector were as follows [2]:

Segment	Revenue (billions)	Percent Share
Quick-service restaurants	$ 96.9	43.6
Full-service restaurants	86.3	38.8
Recreation foodservice	10.1	4.5
Lodging	9.1	4.1
Supermarket delis	9	4.0
Cafeterias and buffets	4.8	2.2
Other retail hosts	4.1	1.8
General merchandise and drugstores	1.9	0.9
Total	$222.2	99.9[a]

[a]*Does not equal 100 percent because of rounding.*

The figures above were developed by Technomic Inc. for the International Foodservice Manufacturers Association. By contrast, the National Restaurant Association projected 1995 revenues of $93.4 billion for quick-service restaurants and $87.8 billion for full-service restaurants. Whichever figure is closer to the mark, the fact remains that these two sectors represent the dominant parts of the foodservice industry.

In this book we focus on the two largest segments of the commercial industry: quick- and full-service restaurants.

INDUSTRY TRENDS

The restaurant industry does not operate in a vacuum. Industry trends are a direct reflection of changes in the society within which the business operates. The manager who is aware of (and, better still, able to anticipate) these trends is in a position to take advantage of opportunities in the marketplace. This involves conducting a scan of the environment.

Environmental Scan

A situation analysis or environmental scan examines the external environment within which a business operates. Such an analysis will identify the constraints

In 1983, Nordahl Brue and Michael Dressell put together their own financial resources to open the first Bruegger's. Since then Bruegger's Bagel Bakery has expanded to 155 units in 16 states.

Looking for a low-ticket item in the fast-food segment, Dressell saw "more fresh bagels in supermarkets and more fresh whole-grained breads in restaurants. I felt we were becoming a wheat, not meat, generation." They prepare their bagels authentically, boiling and hearth-baking them on-site by a trained bake master to give them a crusty outside and chewy center. The regular menu consists of 10 varieties of bagel and 13 specialty cream cheese spreads, with an average check of $3.50.

To help them grow, they hired Stephen A. Finn from Burger King. Says Finn: "The biggest challenge now is to manage the explosive growth effectively. I need to develop a corporate structure to manage a strong concept."

Through franchising, the company intends to expand rapidly. To help ensure success, they will only recruit experienced foodservice franchisees who must first become owners in Bruegger's by buying preferred stock. The franchisees must commit to developing a minimum of 10 stores in markets where they are given sole rights. Startup costs are $275,000 per unit. Mature stores average $900,000 in annual volume.

Source: Robin Lee Allen, "Bruegger's Bagel Bakery," *Nation's Restaurant News*, May 22, 1995.

and opportunities facing the operation. A scan of the environment considers trends in the social, economic, technological, and political or regulatory arenas. These factors are uncontrollable in that the individual property cannot change them but must attempt to anticipate change and adapt the operation to it before it has an adverse impact on the business.

Key issues and trends can be scored on the basis of opportunities or threats and scored on the basis of +10 (opportunities) to −10 (threats). The National Restaurant Association offers periodic analyses of environmental trends as they affect the restaurant industry [3].

Social Environment. Studies of the social environment focus on demographic and cultural changes that affect the foodservice industry. Demographically, the U.S. population is getting older; there is continuing population growth in the south and west, and there are changes in the structure of the family. In the past two decades, there has been a growth in the number of single, unrelated, and single-parent households; a move back to the nest for children, and a leveling off of working mothers.

Between 1980 and 1990 the number of households made up of singles and unrelated roommates grew at a rate almost three times that of family households. The impact on restaurants is positive, as singles dine out more often,

Courtesy Bruegger's Bagel Bakery.

spend more per person, and use carryout and delivery more than do most other households.

Young people are also staying at home longer than they have in the past. In 1980, 3.2 million people between the ages of 25 and 34 lived with their parents. In 1990 the number was almost 5 million. It is likely that this group has more money available for—among other things—eating out.

The proportion of two-parent families has dropped from 40 percent of households in 1980 to 26 percent in 1990. Of all household types, married couples without children spend the most annually per person on food away from home. Single-parent households, which account for the least amount of money spent on food away from home, are also on the increase.

The number of mothers aged 16 and older with children under 3 years of age who are employed outside the home has increased steadily from 34 percent in 1975 to 54 percent in 1990. Recent indications, however, suggest that numbers could be leveling off as more and more people are placing an emphasis on family life over job commitment. This movement has meant increased time pressure on families and has added to increased sales in various sectors of the foodservice industry including takeout.

Picking up on customers' need for convenience, more restaurants are offering takeout and delivery service [4]. In 1990 almost half of adults under 55

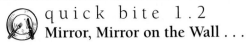

quick bite 1.2
Mirror, Mirror on the Wall . . .

Here is one well-qualified writer's viewpoint of upcoming trends in foodservice.

1. Growing mistrust over the content of food.
2. Incorporation of underused wild edibles and aquaculture into the diet.
3. Reduction of dietary fat, especially saturated fat.
4. Increased variety in diets by the addition of vegetables, fruits, and grains.
5. Demand for more detailed labeling and information on the nutritional content of menu items.
6. A movement away from the pursuit of new dining experiences, toward those we know.
7. An opportunity for restaurants to create vacation packages featuring at-home parties for family and friends.
8. A growing market of people working at home that can be serviced by food management contractors.
9. Small private family rooms in restaurants.

Source: Jane Young Wallace, "Gateway to the Millennium," *Hospitality Research Journal*, vol. 17, no. 1, 1993, pp. 59–65.

indicated that they would be willing to buy ready-to-eat takeout meals if offered at table service restaurants. In that same year 90 percent of operators with a check size of less than $15 offered ready-to-eat takeout meals.

Children are becoming increasingly important as a market segment for restaurateurs [5]. Children influence the amount spent on food away from home as well as where families eat. The NRA found that 35 percent of parents with one or more children younger than 6 years of age said that children were "very influential" in the decision to eat out. The proportion was similar for families with children aged 6 to 12. The U.S. population is becoming more diverse. In response, there is a greater demand for foreign and exotic fruits and vegetables.

Americans are becoming more concerned with health and nutrition. Overall grain consumption increased by almost 10 pounds per capita from 1989 to 1990, while for the first time since data have been recorded, per capita consumption of chicken and turkey matched that of beef. Additionally, the National Restaurant Association reports that over 90 percent of operators with a check average over $25 offer vegetarian entrees, as do 70 percent of operations with an average check below $25.

Health professionals are issuing specific guidelines for particular market segments. Specific attention has been given to those with low incomes, the elderly, and children. Recent figures from the National Cholesterol Education

Program, for example, suggest that children should get no more than 30 percent of their calories from fat. The National Restaurant Association projects that the nutritional needs of vegetarians will get more attention as numbers of people in these segments grow.

In response to this development, school menus and those of businesses aiming at children have been reevaluated. The beef industry has increased production of low-fat beef, and fast-food operations have added items such as salads and broiled chicken sandwiches to their menus. More and more chains are providing nutritional information to the customer, and "healthy" cooking methods such as stir frying, steaming, broiling, and grilling are on the rise.

On the other hand, there is some evidence that patterns of behavior are lagging behind the things that people say are important to them. More people say that they will change their eating habits to more nutritional items than actually do change.

Economic Conditions.   Both macroeconomic conditions and trends in consumer income are important to the restaurateur. The prime macroeconomic concern of business is whether the economy is inflationary or recessionary. For the customer, inflation means higher prices, reducing what a customer can afford to buy.

Businesses finance operations by borrowing money from banks. The interest rate charged banks' best customers is called the prime rate. All other interest rates are tied to the this rate. When a country experiences inflation, the prime rate rises, thereby increasing the cost of borrowing and the cost of doing business.

In recessionary times customers have less discretionary money—the amount left after taxes and necessities—and are more concerned with value. In the National Restaurant Association's 1992 forecast, only 20 percent of U.S. adults surveyed indicated that eating out is usually a necessity; 49 percent regarded it as a luxury. In inflationary times the people who consider eating out to be a luxury might be inclined to eliminate that activity.

Despite difficult economic times, only 29 percent of adults in 1992 were "brown bagging" lunch more than in the preceding year. However, more than half indicated that they were more price-conscious than in the preceding year. Almost half said that they are more inclined to eat at a restaurant offering a money-saving promotion.

Technological Trends.   Trends in changing technology and its ecological impact as it affects foodservice operations are of concern to business. Because technological change is brought about through research, the timing of new developments is difficult to predict. However, we can expect to see significant changes in microprocessors, telecommunications, robots, and materials technology. Technological innovations in aquaculture may lead to a controlled supply of such items as fish, lobster, oysters, and crawfish. Advances in technology give operators better ways to understand their customers. Arby's has used electronic maps in the placement of new restaurants, and others use maps to set up routes for their sales staff.

Regulatory Considerations.   The major areas that should be tracked in the regulatory arena are laws protecting competition, laws affecting marketing mix actions, self-regulation, and the issue of consumerism. Government has a major impact on how business is run. In 1992, under the Americans with Disabilities Act, public places had to provide access to customers and employees with disabilities. Operations must make "reasonable accommodation" to ensure that the disabled can enter and get around the property unless they can demonstrate that such changes would have an "adverse impact" on their business.

Health benefits will continue to become an even greater issue for businesses in terms of the respective roles of government, business, and the employee in financing such benefits. Family-leave provisions—some form of legislation allowing nonpaid time off to care for family members—will continue to be an issue. States are becoming more vigilant in enforcing child-labor laws that restrict the number of hours that teenagers can work during the school week. The National Restaurant Association continues to fight to overturn the provision whereby employers must pay FICA tax on tips to employees.

Competition. While a detailed study of competing facilities is a separate part of a marketing audit, the situation analysis considers such things as alterna-

---

 quick bite 1.3
Regulatory Issues

According to restaurant operators, the four major state issues they face in the regulatory arena are:

1. *Smoking.* Many states are debating a statewide ban on smoking in public places, including restaurants. In some states operators are backing state legislation that would require restaurants to reserve a proportion of their space for nonsmokers.

2. *Workers' compensation.* Workers' Compensation costs increased dramatically during the 1980s because of increases in medical costs and loose definitions of on-the-job injuries. Steps are under way in most states to reform the system.

3. *Music licensing.* While restaurateurs recognize the need to pay royalties on music played in their operations, they resent the tactics used by music-licensing organizations. A bill under consideration in New Jersey would require music licensors to provide businesses with song lists and schedules of fees to similar-sized businesses, would require company representatives to identify themselves upon entering a restaurant, and would set up an arbitration group to mediate disputes between restaurants and licensing organizations.

4. *Minimum wage.* In 1995, legislators in 21 states have proposed raising the minimum wage. There are currently laws in Alaska, Connecticut, Hawaii, Iowa, New Jersey, Oregon, Rhode Island, Vermont, Washington, and the District of Columbia that set the minimum wage above the federal floor of $4.25.

Source: "Taking the Battle from Capitol Hill to the State Capitols," *Restaurants USA*, vol. 15, no. 5, May 1995, pp. 8–9.

tive forms of competition, both domestic and foreign. In this area supermarkets and grocery stores have developed into an unlikely source of competition for foodservice operations. By upgrading their facilities to provide salad bars and various takeout meals, these stores represent an inexpensive alternative to people with little time to shop and cook.

While U.S. firms have increasingly been expanding overseas, foreign direct investment in the United States has been a recent victim of a slow economy worldwide. Between 1987 and 1989 foreign direct investment to acquire or establish U.S. businesses increased from $40 billion to $71 billion. However, in 1990 this figure declined to $64 billion, the majority (56 percent) coming from European countries, with an additional 32 percent coming from Japan.

Sources of Information

How can an operator be proactive by identifying changes *before* they occur rather than reactive and attempt to respond to changes *after* they happen? The key is to become a trend watcher. In its formal setting, trend watching involves reading or watching news media, keeping track of issues and events, noting the data, and using them to predict what might happen in the future.

A complete watch would involve keeping track of events as reported by the four major television networks: ABC, CBS, NBC, and Fox, the three national news magazines: *Newsweek, Time,* and *U.S. News & World Report*; and several influential newspapers, including the *Chicago Tribune, Los Angeles Times, New York Times, Wall Street Journal,* and *Washington Post*. For busy restaurateurs such a watch could become a full-time job. For the specialist trends can be evaluated by reading trade magazines, the front page of the *Wall Street Journal, USA Today,* and a technical precursor publication. Precursor publications are those that influence mainstream journalists by uncovering trends before they occur. The *Wall Street Journal* is not particularly good at forecasting what might happen in the future because by the time an item appears in the *Journal*, it is already fact. For general issues, magazines such as *Demography, Science News,* and *Utne Reader* have been found to be useful precursor publications.

COMMON DENOMINATORS

A useful way to explore the industry is to consider the factors that are common to all restaurants [6].

Utility versus Pleasure

Restaurants are built for utility or pleasure. Utility restaurants are "filling stations," seeing to the need we all have for periodic refueling during the day. Restaurants that are built for pleasure appeal to more than the need to refuel. The importance of good food and wine is shared with the desire to dine in comfortable surroundings. Some suggest that up to 75 percent of meals eaten away from home in the United States are for utilitarian purposes and the other 25 percent are for pleasure.

Imagine the following progression of foodservice operations:

- Vending machines
- Fast-food operations
- Cafeterias
- Coffee shops
- Family restaurants
- Dinner houses
- Luxury restaurants

As the utility of a concept decreases, the pleasure component increases. Going from high utility to high pleasure, we move from vending machines through luxury restaurants.

> *High utility/low pleasure*
>> Vending machines
>> Fast-food operations
>> Cafeterias
>> Coffee shops
>> Family restaurants
>> Dinner houses
>> Luxury restaurants
> *High pleasure/low utility*

Service and Menu Price

Restaurants can also be classified on the basis of the degree of service offered. The level of service offered can range from full service to self-service. In *full* or *table service* operation, servers take menu orders from customers and deliver those items to the table. This level or service requires more square feet of space per seat than that required by any other type of operation.

Counter service allows customers to sit at a counter facing the production area. A minimum of space is needed because the *production area*—where the food is prepared—and the *service area*— where the food is served—are one and the same. *Tray service* is used in such operations as airlines and hospitals. Food is delivered to the passenger or patient already plated on a tray. *Room service* is common in hotels. Orders are placed from the room by the guest and the meal is arranged on a tray or table and delivered to the room by service personnel.

In *self-service* operations customers serve themselves. This type of service is appropriate for serving large numbers of people in a relatively short period of time. Self-service operations may be found in cafeterias where customers pick up a tray and serve themselves from items displayed in a cafeteria line or in several areas in freestanding style. *Buffet service* is increasingly popular for breakfast at hotels, as it allows customers to get what they want for one price and to serve themselves as quickly as they wish. Some restaurants use buffet service for a particular meal, typically lunch or Sunday brunch.

Takeout service allows customers, for example, to pick up something on the way home from work and to enjoy it wherever they wish, whether in the privacy of their own homes or in their cars. *Vending machines* serve in-between meal snacks or simple meals that can be served cold or cooked by the customer in a microwave oven provided at the scene.

An increase in service typically comes with an increase in menu prices. The vending machine, relatively inexpensive, is totally self-service; a luxury restaurant may offer table-side carving. The progression from low prices and low levels of service to high prices and maximum service is the same as before.

> *Low service/low prices*
>> Vending machines
>> Fast-food operations
>> Cafeterias
>> Coffee shops
>> Family restaurants
>> Dinner houses
>> Luxury restaurants
> *High service/high prices*

Menu prices are also a function of when a meal is eaten, the cost of labor, the space per customer, and the cost of that space. Meals taken in the evening, when customers are more likely to stay longer, cost more than lunch meals, when customers stay for less time and the restaurateur can increase customer and seat turnover by "selling" the table again.

Since the restaurant business tends to be highly labor intensive, the cost of labor is a major determinant in the price of a meal—the more service, the greater the labor cost and the higher the price. There is also a relationship between the cost of space and menu prices. The cost of a facility is, in great part, determined by the size of the facility—the larger the operation, the more it costs to build. Part of the decision that must be made is how much of the facility should be revenue producing (where customers are served) compared to non-revenue producing (for example, kitchen, storage, and service areas). Less space given over to producing revenue means that more revenue per square foot must be generated from that space. In addition, the more square footage per customer (for example, greater space between the tables), the more it will cost the customer in menu prices.

Food Preparation Method

Restaurants have the option of preparing food from scratch or buying convenience items and finishing them in the operation. The decision as to which mix to operate under has many ramifications. Using convenience items will result in greater food cost but lower labor cost. The level of expertise needed by employees will be less if convenience items are used. The experience of the prevailing labor force may thus be a factor in the decision whether to make or buy. Different types of equipment may also be needed, depending on whether items are prepared from scratch or purchased as convenience items. Finally, the image of the operation may be a factor in this decision. A luxury restaurant, seeking an upscale image, may advertise preparation from scratch as part of its message. Most operations make some items while purchasing others in a convenience form.

Menu Development

All restaurants have menus. However, the format of the menu will vary greatly depending on a variety of factors.

Frequency of Change.   Menus can range from those that are completely fixed to those that change completely daily. The former is simpler to plan for than the latter. Menus that are completely fixed are used in fast-food and specialty operations. Changes are made only when individual menu items are dropped or added for reasons of popularity or profitability.

In some operations the menu is essentially fixed but changes are made depending on the season of the year or when daily specials are added. In the former case menus may change two or four times a year to accommodate seasonally popular items. Salads and lighter items may predominate in the summer, while stews and other hearty items provide the mainstay in the winter. Certain popular items may be kept year-round.

Daily specials help where there is repeat business. Customers who tire of the regular menu may find the specials appealing. The appeal to the customer also comes from the perception that if a dish is prepared that day, it is fresher or specially prepared. For the operator, daily specials can be a way of recycling leftovers. The baked chicken from one day becomes chicken à la king the next.

Daily changes can be cyclical or complete. Cyclical changes are used when the customer base is captive: that is, when they are tied to a particular operation such as in institutional feeding such as college dorms or prisons. In such an operation a menu is repeated on a cycle that can range from two to six weeks in length. A complete change would be appropriate for a captive audience in a resort setting where people stay for two weeks at a time. In this situation the entire menu is often changed daily.

Types of Offerings.   Menus tend to be *à la carte, table d'hôte,* or some combination of the two. On à la carte menus, items are priced individually. The appetizers, entrees or main course, potatoes, vegetables, and desserts are priced separately. A table d'hôte menu features a complete meal at a set price, with, for example, a choice of appetizer, main course, and dessert from several options. A combination menu might price appetizers and desserts separately while including salad, bread, potato, and vegetable in the price of the entree. An advantage of à la carte menus is their perception of being "classier." They certainly tend to be more expensive. By packaging a dessert in with the main course, the *average check*—total revenue divided by the number of customers—can be increased. People are "forced" to buy an item—the dessert—they might not purchase otherwise. If they feel the value is there, they will be satisfied and the restaurateur will have sold an item that would not have been purchased had it been priced separately.

Size of Menu.   Restaurants range from those that have a limited menu to those that offer an extensive menu. A limited menu offers fewer choices to the customers and relies on creating a large number of customers willing to purchase a small number of menu items. Care must be taken that the items offered are desired by a relatively large percentage of people.

A limited menu restricts the number of customers. If all the restaurant offers is salads and a party of four is eating out together, one person in the party who does not like salads can lose the restaurant four customers. For this reason fast-food operations tend to start out with a basic product and as the concept moves through the life cycle, add items to the menu to attract a larger base of people.

A limited menu allows people to make a very quick decision as to what to eat. This may appeal to customers who do not want to make extensive decisions at mealtimes. It also speeds customer turnover.

A limited menu also means less waste. For every item on the menu, there is a waste factor. It may occur as spoilage in storing; it may be that too much is made of a particular item and the remainder must be thrown out. Thus the more items on the menu, the more items will have to be ordered, stored, issued, prepared, and served. Inventory costs will be higher, as will waste costs.

The major advantage of an extensive menu is that there is a greater chance that one or more items on the menu will appeal to more people, thus increasing the menu range.

FINANCIAL OVERVIEW OF RESTAURANT CHAINS

The top 100 restaurant chains in the United States account for just under 60 percent of all restaurant sales [7]. Chains specializing in sandwiches dominate, with over 40 percent of total revenues. The 1994 top 10 were:

Rank	Chain	Concept	U.S. Sales (millions)
1	McDonald's	Sandwich	$15,800
2	Burger King	Sandwich	7,000
3	Pizza Hut	Pizza	5,189
4	Taco Bell	Sandwich	4,300
5	Wendy's	Sandwich	3,900
6	KFC	Chicken	3,800
7	Hardee's	Sandwich	3,550
8	ARA Services	Contract	2,990
9	Marriott Managment Services	Contract	2,890
10	Subway	Sandwich	2,600

Sandwich Chains

In an apparent reaction to the fact that customers have difficulty differentiating among the various sandwich operations, chains are focusing on their own brands rather than on those of the competition. The key word seems to be *value,* which, according to Piper Jaffray analyst Allan Hickok, "is no longer a point of differentiation. . . . Value itself is not price point; it is the whole experience." To do well, chains must return to identifying what differentiates them from the competition. In a segment where price-matching the competition is easy and commonplace, chains will have to concentrate on something else.

Pizza Chains

Pizza chains produced 10.3 percent of the revenue of the top 100 chains in 1994. After several years of discounting the pizza chains found that reduced prices and two-for-ones produced volume but did little for profits. Some chains are beginning to focus on core marketing and operational strategies at the expense of low-price promotions. The top chains in 1994 were:

Rank	Chain	U.S. Sales (millions)
1	Pizza Hut	$5189
2	Little Caesar's Pizza	2366
3	Domino's Pizza	2110
4	Sbarro, the Italian Eatery	385
5	Round Table Pizza	337

Dinner Houses

By some estimates, 75 percent of dinner houses are mom-and-pop operations. However, the top 10 chains account for 86 percent of total dinner house sales. Dinner houses made up 8.3 percent of top-100 chain revenue in 1994. In that year the top chains were:

Rank	Chain	U.S. Sales (millions)
1	Red Lobster	$1848
2	Olive Garden	1300
3	Chili's Grill & Bar	950
4	Applebee's Neighborhood Bar & Grill	848
5	TGI Friday's	722.8
6	Outback Steakhouses	531.6
7	Bennigan's	446.7
8	Ruby Tuesday's	433.2
9	Chi-Chi's	430.6
10	Ground Round	315

quick bite 1.4
The Restaurant Industry Dollar

	A	B	C	D
Sales				
Food sales	78.9	89.3	95.3	93.4
Beverage sales (alcoholic)	18.3	8.9	3.8	6.0
Other income	2.8	1.8	0.9	0.6
Total sales	100	100	100	100
Cost of sales				
Food cost	27.1	29.1	31.7	32.4
Beverage cost (alcoholic)	5.1	2.5	1.3	1.3
Controllable expenses				
Payroll	29.0	26.7	24.9	28.6
Employee benefits	4.9	3.7	2.8	4.0
Direct operating expenses	6.0	6.6	5.0	4.9
Music and entertainment	0.7	0.2	0.2	0.1
Marketing	2.4	3.8	3.9	4.3
Utilities	2.7	2.9	3.2	3.1
Administrative and general	4.3	2.6	3.1	4.9
Repairs and maintenance	2.0	2.0	1.8	1.8
Total controllable expenses	52.0	48.5	44.9	51.7
Occupancy costs				
Rent	4.3	6.2	5.8	5.5
Property taxes	0.5	0.9	0.5	0.3
Other taxes	0.5	0.5	0.5	0.6
Property insurance	0.6	0.7	0.5	0.4
Total occupancy costs	5.6	8.3	7.3	6.8
Interest	0.8	0.5	0.7	0.6
Depreciation	2.1	2.3	2.7	2.6
Other deductions	0.3	0.2	0.3	0.3
Corporate overhead	2.3	2.1	3.3	1.4
Net income before income taxes	4.4	6.5	7.8	2.9

Source: *Restaurant Industry Operations Report, 1994* (Washington, DC; National Restaurant Association, 1994). *Note*: 1. All figures are weighted averages and based on 1993 data. 2. All ratios are based as a percentage of total sales except food and beverage costs, which are based on their respective sales. A, full menu, table service; B, limited menu, table service; C, limited menu, no table service; D, Cafeteria.

According to Malcolm M. Knapp, president of Malcolm M. Knapp Inc., a New York consulting and research firm, "the No. 1 issue is intensity of competition." Despite (or, perhaps, because of) this, dinner houses were looking at an annual 15 percent increase in revenues.

Family Chains

In an attempt to maintain market share against competitors from other sectors of the industry, family chains are struggling to keep their 7.3 percent market share of the top 100 chains. Much remodeling and "reimaging" is going on. Denny's, for example, recently introduced a Baskin-Robbins ice cream module, a pie display case, Denny's clothing for sale, a new menu design, and new employee uniforms. The top chains are:

Rank	Chain	U.S. Sales (millions)
1	Denny's	$1555.2
2	Shoney's	1384
3	Big Boy	1024
4	Cracker Barrel Old Country Store	805.2
5	Friendly's Restaurants	645

Chicken Chains

The top five chicken chains in 1994 were:

Rank	Chain	U.S. Sales (millions)
1	KFC	$3800
2	Popeye's Famous Fried Chicken	624
3	Church's Chicken	460
4	Chick-fil-A	458
5	Boston Market	335

This segment of the industry has been characterized by the introduction of new products and concepts and development in nontraditional outlets. Typical of the new prototypes is the Chikita Grill, which features chicken fajitas, burritos, tacos, and other Tex-Mex items in a fast-food setting. Chick-fil-A has been expanding into such nontraditional outlets as hospitals and kiosklike carts at business and mall locations.

Common Concepts

Leaving quick-service restaurants aside, the major concepts in restaurants are:

1. *Steak houses.* Steak-house restaurants were hard hit in the 1980s as consumers reduced their red-meat intake. However, beef remains the most popular item on menus. George Rice, president of GDR/CREST, predicts that "the interest in red meat has come full circle . . . and we're going to see a resurgence of steak." Family-style businesses, relying on low prices, volume business, and high-traffic locations, have taken over from budget steak houses. The midscale market has added food buffet and salad bars.

2. *Seafood restaurants.* According to Carol Casper, contributing editor to *Restaurant Business* magazine: "Worldwide supply-and-demand pressures, volatile pricing, higher food costs than other entrees, and stepped-up safety concerns all contribute to making the seafood operations perhaps the hardest kind of restaurant to run." To a large extent, profit depends on successful purchasing decisions. Grilling, broiling, and baking have surpassed frying as the preferred cooking methods.

3. *Mexican restaurants.* Mexican restaurants are seen as family restaurants that are casual and moderately priced: two trends that will increase in importance in the 1990s. Two segments have developed: the midscale segment with fajitas, low prices, and a casual cantina atmosphere, and the upscale segment, specializing in regional cuisines such as southwestern and Tex-Mex.

4. *Italian restaurants.* While chains have moved wholesale in this concept, independents still maintain a measure of success, particularly in upscale operations. Despite some concerns that supply may be outrunning demand, movement into regional cuisines may be on the horizon.

5. *Asian restaurants.* Growing rapidly, Asian restaurants seem immune to chains and franchising. Industry analyst Ron Paul indicates: "Oriental food is sharply defined by the food and the staff. A chain doesn't really offer anything in a neighborhood that is fairly well saturated with independents, because the perception is that the Orientals do it better." Because Chinese food is labor intensive, success depends on having family members work in the restaurant while giving the customers what they want.

6. *Family-style restaurants.* This concept will grow in concert with changing demographics, which indicate growth of families and older people. Consumers are attracted by budget prices, good value, and professional service. The restaurants offer a step up from fast-food restaurants (with similar prices) while gaining customers from more expensive restaurants who trade down when the economy is in a downturn.

7. *Casual-dining restaurants.* Baby boomers have fueled the increased popularity of casual dining by demanding simple, fresh food of high quality with an

(continued)

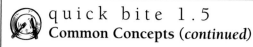
Steak Chains

Steak chains, which accounted for 3.1 percent of top-100 chain revenues, have lately been testing larger, updated stores. They are adding more variety to the menu while experimenting with bakeries and weekend brunch. The 1994 top steak chains were:

Rank	Chain	U.S. Sales (millions)
1	Ponderosa Steakhouse	$750.5
2	Sizzler	620.5
3	Golden Corral	575
4	Ryan's Family Steak House	498

WHY RESTAURANTS FAIL

By some estimates, one out of every three restaurants fails in the first year of operation. There are a variety of reasons for the high failure rate in this business [8]. Very simply put:

profit = sales − costs

Thus, to achieve profitability it is necessary to increase sales while reducing costs. Sales and costs tend to have an inverse relationship. By increasing costs through such things as bigger portion sizes or more service, a restaurant becomes more attractive to customers, thereby increasing sales. The reverse is also true. Costs can be trimmed by having fewer employees or cheaper cuts of meat, which might lead to the loss of customers, thereby reducing sales. We focus our discussion of the reasons that restaurants fail on the two sides of the profit equation: sales and costs.

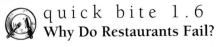
Failure to Increase Sales

Same Concept.   Many failures occur because management stays with the same concept for too long. Like other products and services, restaurants have a *life cycle*. In the early stages of a new operation, the restaurant goes through an introductory stage in which the concept is introduced into the marketplace. If all goes well, the operation experiences a period of growth, in which sales are increasing at an increasing rate. As the concept matures, sales continue to increase but at a decreasing rate. If no action is taken, a period of decline will set in, during which sales fall. Throughout the life-cycle curve, profits lead sales. That is, a downturn in profits will precede a downturn in sales. In this way it is possible to get advance warning about where the restaurant is in the cycle.

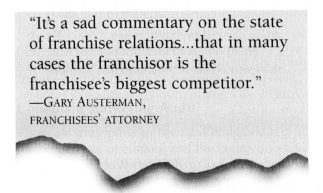

"It's a sad commentary on the state of franchise relations...that in many cases the franchisor is the franchisee's biggest competitor."
—GARY AUSTERMAN,
FRANCHISEES' ATTORNEY

Problems between franchisor and franchisee is one of the causes of restaurant failure. *Source: Nation's Restaurant News*, October 9, 1995, p. 118.

If advance notice is given and the operation changes, it is possible to go through a period of rejuvenation rather than decline. Fast-food restaurants attempted this a few years ago when they added breakfast items to their menus as a response to a slowdown in sales. One way to rejuvenate an operation is to sell a product or service at additional times: hence the breakfast menu. They made a similar decision when they expanded internationally. The domestic market was being saturated and future growth necessitated overseas expansion. This is another way to rejuvenate—sell to another market.

Lack of Creativity.   Lack of sales often comes from a lack of imagination and creativity in developing new ideas. We are conditioned to believe that "new is good." Increasingly, the public is looking for new ways to do things, new items on the menu, new experiences in general. Mangers cannot afford to rely on the status quo. Flexibility is the key—operators need to adopt an attitude that encourages them and their employees to seek constant improvement in their restaurants.

Falling sales may be due partially to the human tendency to react to new situations rather than to anticipate them. There are constant changes in the marketplace. Changing economic conditions may include a demand for less expensive menu items; increased concern over alcohol abuse leads to less consumption of alcohol. The reactive manager waits until trends work their way through society and manifest themselves in a different, reduced, or nonexistent customer base. The proactive manager reads newspapers and magazines, attends industry forums where trends are discussed, anticipates the likelihood of events happening, identifies their potential effects on the business, and changes the operation accordingly before the effects of the changes are felt. In other words, the proactive manager plans rather than simply operating the business.

Failure to Control Costs

Most restaurants operate on relatively small profit margins. Cost control is very important in ensuring a profitable margin. In foodservice operations, the principal areas of cost are labor, food, and beverages. Keeping a close watch on these three areas will help ensure profitability.

Productivity.   To a large extent, high employee costs are a result of poor productivity. Productivity is the ratio of outputs (sales, profits, etc.) to inputs (time, costs, etc.). Typically, this ratio is less for service industries than for manufacturing concerns. In fact, the National Restaurant Association has estimated that the restaurant industry is only half as productive as the manufacturing industries. To the extent that service is important to customers, it is difficult to achieve a sales increase by reducing staff. However, labor cost savings of 10 to 20 percent can be expected through improved employee scheduling alone, resulting in a savings of 3 to 6 percent of sales [9].

Cost Cutting.   Many operators fall into a cost-cutting mode that is counterproductive. When sales drop managers are often tempted to cut costs to compensate for reduced sales. Advertising may be reduced; employee uniforms are not laundered as frequently; less expensive cuts of meat replace menu staples. As

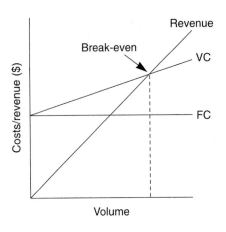
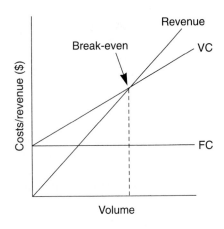

(a) High proportion of fixed costs
relative to variable costs

(b) High proportion of variable costs
relative to fixed costs

Figure 1.1   Break-even chart.

a result, the customers who remain become disenchanted with the operation and leave. The focus often is on cutting costs when it should be on increasing sales.

This comes about because of the cost structure of restaurants. So many of a restaurant's costs are fixed; they do not vary as sales volume varies. The mortgage or lease payment must still be made whether there is one customer or a thousand; the restaurant must be lit regardless of the number of patrons. As a consequence, only a limited amount of cost cutting can take place. In operations where a high proportion of costs are *fixed*, the *break-even point*—the point at which sales generated exactly equals costs incurred—is higher than for businesses in which a large proportion of the costs are *variable*. A variable cost is one that varies proportionately with sales volume (Figure 1.1).

However, once the break-even point has been passed, the only costs incurred are variable costs. In restaurants, the variable costs are relatively small compared to the fixed costs. As a result, once an operation has reached a sales volume above the break-even point, the profit potential from a relatively small increase in sales volume becomes great. Managers might therefore better focus their attention on increasing sales rather than on spending time seeking to minimize costs. This is not to negate the importance of cost control; it is, rather, to suggest that with a finite amount of management time available, profits might be increased more by focusing on the sales side of the profit equation than on the cost side.

SUCCESS FACTORS

The key to a successful operation is to develop the right concept, execute it skillfully, give timely service, and meet customer expectations [10].

Right Concept

For the immediate future the "right" concept will be one that gives off energy, meets customer needs for a convenient location and hassle-free experience, does not require that customers dress up, and offers an ethnic flair.

Execution

Employees are the key to execution of the concept. This involves finding the right kinds of people and training them to provide the level of service demanded by the customer. Table service operators identify "finding qualified labor" as either the number 1 or number 2 issue (depending on the average check of the operation) facing them today. A primary factor in this regard is the economic health of the country. When the economy is strong, fewer people are willing to enter the foodservice industry. The reverse is also true.

To ensure that employees have the skills to perform to a standard, employers should provide a full range of activities for employees. This begins with a handbook explaining company policies, written job descriptions, and an orientation program. Training manuals are an integral part of a training program, but films or videos are used increasingly in part to overcome language difficulties. A complete system includes regular job performance evaluations to ensure that standards are being maintained. In 1992, over 70 percent of operators reported that they had improved training, but only half indicated that training is accompanied by a handbook explaining company policies, written job descriptions, and an orientation program. Regular job evaluations are given by only six in 10 operators.

Service

As noted earlier, service is a major concern for both customers and operators. Indeed, service complaints dominate, far exceeding customer complaints about food or atmosphere. Five elements have been identified as important: providing timely service, answering customer questions, handling complaints, delivering accurately totaled guest checks, and recommending appropriate menu items. Customers seem most satisfied with the accuracy of the check and the server's ability to answer questions, although only 75 percent rated staff as "good" or "excellent" on these items. Almost two-thirds of respondents rated servers "good" or "excellent" in recommending appropriate menu items.

The two most common complaints in the categories above concern speed of service and inattentive staff. The former can involve service that is too slow or the feeling of being rushed. It is important to tailor the speed of service to the individual and the occasion. In the latter case, customers are upset by having to summon employees to give an order or by waiting for a check. For customers, the wait seems longest after the meal is over. Delays during a meal seem shorter than waits either before or after the meal. Customers are most dissatisfied with the way that complaints were handled. The subject of service is dealt with in more detail in Chapter 5.

Meeting Customer Expectations

Increasingly, customers have higher expectations, demanding more attention and friendlier service. Most customers seem satisfied with food quality, dining area cleanliness, comfort of the atmosphere, freshness of the ingredients, and portion size. Indeed, the only area where satisfaction is less than 50 percent relates to noise level. As the customer base ages this is expected to become of even greater concern. Rising expectations manifest themselves in a desire for a better price/value relationship.

MANAGEMENT SKILLS: BASIC FUNCTIONAL AREAS

The National Restaurant Association has identified the following nine functional areas as representative of a restaurant manager's job [11]. They are rank ordered based on mean importance ratings by restaurant managers.

---

 q u i c k   b i t e   1 . 8
What Makes Restaurant Managers Tick?

A survey of 200 general managers and assistant managers at six full-service and casual dining restaurant chains identified what managers look for when joining a company and what makes them stay.

Factors That Influence Managers' Motivation and Satisfaction
1. Opportunities for growth and development
2. Having fun on the job
3. Working a reasonable number of hours
4. Receiving a good salary
5. Getting vacation time
6. Having input into the company and its direction
7. Obtaining good bonuses
8. Getting a promotion
9. Overall quality of work life
10. Job security

Factors That Influence Managers' Decision to Stay
1. Overall quality of work life
2. Opportunities for growth and development
3. Receiving a good salary
4. Working a reasonable number of hours
5. Receiving positive feedback
6. Job security
7. Having a flexible schedule
8. Getting a promotion
9. Getting a benefit package
10. Obtaining good bonuses

Source: Janet Denefe, "What Makes Restaurant Managers Tick?" *F&B Magazine*, July–August 1993, p. 15.

Outback Steakhouse's management compensation plan gives managers ownership in their operation. *Source: Nation's Restaurant News,* March 27, 1995, p. 66.

1. *Cost control and financial management*: monitoring, controlling, and reporting the profitability indicators for the store.
2. *Supervision of shift operations*: running each shift efficiently, effectively, and in accordance with procedures.
3. *Organizing and planning shift operations*: making preparations for each shift so that operations will run smoothly and efficiently.
4. *Unit coordination and control*: communication and coordination among store managers and their supervisors and others in the organization.
5. *Customer relations*: improving customers' dining experiences.
6. *Motivating employee performance*: monitoring, enhancing, and controlling employee performance.
7. *Employment and development of crew members*: recruiting, selecting, developing, and retaining crew members.
8. *Communication with outside sources*: communicating with management, marketing, and community resources outside the store.
9. *Monitoring and maintenance of facility and equipment*: keeping all physical assets operational and in good repair.

An updated survey of a panel of experts identified the following three functional areas as most important [12].

Employment/Development of Crew

Managers will find that human resource issues will become a top priority. They will thus be spending more time training employees. One area in which this will be necessary is in the basics of service. Managers will need better skills in managing people and in teaching and training employees. They will also have to develop a higher commitment to their employees' career development.

Supervision of Shift Operations

The challenge for managers in this area will involve supervising a more culturally diverse staff. Through their employees, they will have to stress service as a

---

quick bite 1.9
Road to the Top: Scott Beck

Chairman and Chief Executive, Boston Market

It took Scott Beck (36 years old), chairman of the fast-growing Boston Market (originally, Boston Chicken), 13 years and two colleges to get his undergraduate degree, together with some detours along the way. In 1986, Scott and his father invested heavily in Blockbuster Video, then consisting of only one store. As the company grew, so did his investment. Three years later Beck was running 104 franchise units. At that time he sold all 240 units back to the parent company for $120 million in stock and became chairman and chief operating officer of the company.

Scott teamed up with now-partners Saad J. Nadhir and Jeffrey J. Shearer, who spent 14 years with Steak & Ale, while at Blockbuster. Nadhir is credited with discovering Boston Chicken when he noticed throngs of people in line at the then-unknown restaurant in 1991. The three partners bought the 33-unit company in 1992 by investing $22 million. Says Shearer: "Even though the stores were not that great to look at, the food was outstanding and the three of us asked ourselves what would happen if we applied just basic operating procedures here."

Beck attends church most Sundays and feels that "my primary purpose in life is to be a steward of what God has given me in talent, time and stamina, and I'm driven to do the best with those things."

According to Michael Mueller of Montgomery Securities: "He's [Beck] doing something I've never seen before. Usually when a restaurant company grows, the entrepreneurs refine the concept first and then push for market share. But Boston Chicken is doing that in reverse: market share first, concept refinement second."

The long-range goal is to have 1000 stores in the system by 1997.

Source: Milford Prewitt, "Scott Beck," *Nation's Restaurant News*, pp. 25, 27.

Courtesy Boston Market.

competitive point of difference. Higher levels of service will have to be provided in a more cost-effective manner. This will also be done in an environment that will place more stringent regulations on food handling and sanitation.

Motivating Employee Performance

Finding and motivating employees will become even more important than it is today. Managers will need excellent interpersonal skills as they empower employees to provide better service, becoming more like team leaders and coaches.

In Chapter 15 we look more closely at the skills necessary for restaurant managers as we approach the next century.

ENDNOTES

1. "'95 Forecast Predicts Sales Growth Slowdown," *Nation's Restaurant News*, September 19, 1994, pp. 1, 215.

2. Ibid., p. 215.

3. National Restaurant Association, *Tableservice Restaurant Trends, 1992* (Washington, DC: National Restaurant Association, 1992).

4. "National Restaurant Association 1993 Foodservice Industry Forecast," *Restaurants USA*, vol. 12, no. 11, December 1992.

5. "1992 Outlook for Foodservice," *1992 Outlook for Travel and Tourism: Proceedings of the 17th Annual Outlook Forum* (Washington, DC: U.S. Travel Data Center, 1992), pp. 135–140.

6. Donald E. Lundberg, *The Restaurant: From Concept to Operation* (New York: John Wiley & Sons, 1985), pp. 18–22.

7. "NRN Top 100," *Nation's Restaurant News*, August 1, 1994, pp. 83–159.

8. Lewis J. Minor and Ronald F. Cichy, *Foodservice Systems Management* (Westport, CT: AVI Publishing Company, 1984), pp. 18–23.

9. Robert Christie Mill, *Managing for Productivity in the Hospitality Industry* (New York: Van Nostrand Reinhold, 1989), p. 53.

10. "National Restaurant Association 1993 Foodservice Industry Forecast."

11. *Job Analysis Report for Unit Manager and Assistant Manager* (Washington, DC: Educational Foundation of the National Restaurant Association, 1988).

12. National Restaurant Association, *Foodservice Manager 2000*, Current Issues Report (Washington, DC: National Restaurant Association, 1992), p. 7.

chapter two

UNDERSTANDING THE CUSTOMER

learning objectives

By the end of this chapter you should be able to:

1. Describe the eating habits of various segments of the restaurant market.

2. Identify five major decision scenarios for the dinner market.

3. Identify major ongoing trends in customer behavior that will affect the restaurant industry.

INTRODUCTION

An understanding of the restaurant customer is useful as long as the limitations of such a study are appreciated. It is useful as a way of seeing the big picture: Why do people eat out, and what are the characteristics of this activity? However, any attempt to characterize the restaurant customer will result in a picture that while valid in the aggregate will probably not be accurate for any particular operation. Thus, although this chapter will be useful to managers overall, it will be necessary to develop a marketing plan (Chapter 3) to make the picture relevant to the individual operation.

MARKET CATEGORIES

One way to make market categories relevant is to think of the foodservice industry as being arranged in three general categories: the captive market, the mass market, and the status market (Figure 2.1).

Captive Market

The captive market—in institutions, industrial or school settings, and airplanes—is limited in the choice of what is available. These customers have little

---

q u i c k   b i t e   2 . 1
Hot Concepts: Cafe Express

Cafe Express was developed in 1984 by partners Robert and Mimi Del Grande and Lonnie and Candice Schiller. The concept is a combination of self-service and full service. The partners took the best elements of self-service, "convenience, informality, value, the freedom not to be tied down to a waiter," and then, according to Lonnie, "we wanted to provide some elements of a full-service restaurant: friendly staff, good food, and decor."

Annual sales range from $1.5 to $2 million, with a menu featuring salads, grilled chicken, pastas, and sandwiches. The $8 average check comes from the roasted chicken ($5.50), club sandwich ($4.50), BLT ($4.50), and one of the best-sellers, the grilled chicken sandwich at $6.25. Food costs are about 30 percent of food sales.

The newer facilities—there are presently five units, with planned expansion to 17 to 20 stores in the next two to three years—are 6000 square feet in size, consist of 240 seats, and cost about $1 million to build. The design is more urban than country and features such classic elements as Mexican volcanic stone floors, marble-topped tables, Holstein-print accents, and a condiment island with metal-sculpture palm trees. Plans are to expand in a prudent manner in concentric circles around Houston.

Source: Ron Ruggles, "Cafe Express," *Nation's Restaurant News*, May 22, 1995, pp. 96, 98.

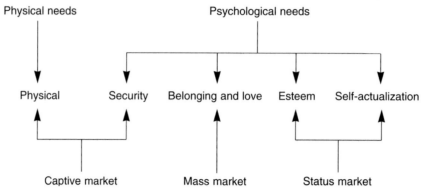

Figure 2.1 Needs and the food service industry. *Source:* "Food Merchandising: Gratifying Human Needs," *Cornell Hotel and Restaurant Administration Quarterly,* vol. 8, no. 3, November 1966, pp. 2–8, 19.

choice in what to eat, when and where to eat, and the price if a charge is made. The primary concern here is "how we eat."

When people are given little or no choice in the mechanics of the eating experience, there is a tendency to rebel. Having little or no choice in these matters is like being treated as a child. As a child, adults told us when to eat, what to eat, how to eat, and how much to eat. When people grow up, they want to make these decisions for themselves and resent being put back in the role of a child. Take, for example, eating on a plane. Passengers are locked into their seats, served when it is convenient for the cabin staff to do so, and remain trapped in place until the staff decides to collect the platters.

Research in British mental institutions has shown some rather sophisticated behavior on the part of patients regarding food. Hoarding of food, midnight snacks, and secret parties allowed the patients to exhibit some degree of control over their food intake—control that was not allowed in the way they were served their meals.

There is some indication that traditional complaints about institutional food have less to do with the food and more to do with the way the food is served and the lack of control the customers have in that process. Allowing some degree of choice in how, when, and where food is served may result in fewer complaints and more satisfied customers.

McDonald's is one company that combined cost and availability in their initial marketing thrust. The first national advertising campaign for McDonald's did not mention food or beverage. It said: "You deserve a break today; so get out and get away—to McDonald's." They were talking to the busy mother, trying to balance the needs of home, children, and often, a job outside the home. This person was hungry, the children were hungry, and the conflicting demands of the mother's life left her exhausted. The "solution" was a trip to McDonald's. Catering to physical needs, McDonald's offered a break from the work of preparing food by serving food at low cost to the customer.

Mass Market

The mass market looks for food in a social setting. This large segment of the market encompasses everyone from teenagers grabbing a burger in the company of friends and families eating out together to special dates and anniversary dinners. Whatever the occasion, the primary concern is the same: with whom we eat.

Status Market

The status market is more concerned with where we eat. To see and be seen is more important than what is on the menu. The choice of restaurant to which a business client is taken for lunch indicates what status the client "deserves." At the same time, the prices on the menu are, in part, a measure of the status accorded the host by his or her company. The person who selects the restaurant or suggests an item from the menu takes responsibility for that suggestion. If the experience is good, the recommendation is complimented and the recipient gets to bask in the admiration of others. The reverse is also true: More than an overcooked steak is on the line.

It should be emphasized that at different times of the week, the same person can be concerned with the satisfaction of different needs. An executive may grab a salad at Wendy's for lunch on Monday, dine with her husband at a romantic getaway on Tuesday, and treat a business client to lunch in an upscale club on Wednesday. In the first instance the concern is physical—to refuel; in the second it is belonging and love—to create the mood for romance; and in the third it is esteem—to impress the client. The key for the operator is to understand the underlying motivation for the dining experience and to organize all elements of the marketing mix to meet those needs and wants.

CUSTOMER SEGMENTS

The number and characteristics of potential customers have to be determined. The most important factors to consider are demographic: location, number, types, ages, sex, occupations, and spending habits.

From a customer-needs point of view, various market segments can be identified: children, adolescents, adults, senior citizens, students, shoppers, workers, travelers, and patients [1].

Children

According to the Bureau of the Census, in 1991 there were 32 million U.S. households with children under 18. This represented more than one-third of all households. However, because of the growth of singles and married couples without children, the share of households with children under 18 dropped from 38 percent of all households in 1980 to 34 percent in 1991. Per household, this group spends more than any other household type on food away from home. In 1990 married-couple households with children under 18 spent $2417 on food

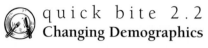

quick bite 2.2
Changing Demographics

Where is the Market Potential?

Population Projections by Age, 1995–2000

Age Group	Population (thousands)				Percent Distribution	
	1995	2000	2005	2010	2000	2010
18–24	24,281	25,231	26,918	27,155	9.4	9.6
25–34	40,962	37,149	35,997	37,572	13.8	13.3
35–44	42,336	43,911	40,951	37,202	16.4	13.2
45–54	31,297	37,223	41,619	43,207	13.9	15.3
55–64	21,325	24,158	29,762	35,430	9.0	12.5
65–74	18,930	18,243	18,410	21,039	6.85	7.4
75+	14,834	16,639	17,864	18,323	6.2	6.5

Source: Statistical Abstract of the United States, 1991 (Washington, DC: U.S. Government Printing Office, 1992).

away from home compared to $1811 for total households. However, on a per capita basis the average amount spent on food away from home was $696, compared to an average of $620 per person in married-couple households with children under 18. The older the children, the greater the per person spending.

Children are important because they influence where families eat out. Over half of adults surveyed by the National Restaurant Association [2] rate children of ages 6 to 12 as "influential" or "very influential" in the decision to dine at table service restaurants. Children are particularly susceptible to advertising and offers of special gifts. About one-half of all restaurants with an average dinner check of less than $8 and one-third of those with an average check between $8 and $15 use promotions aimed specifically at families with children.

Because the attention span of children is short, their behavior unpredictable and the income level of many young families limited, fast-food or quick-service restaurants tend to be favored by this group. According to the National Restaurant Association, operators of table service establishments with an average per person dinner check size of less than $8 are more likely to experience an increase in parties with preteen children (29 percent) than are operators with an average dinner check size of $25 or more (18 percent). About one in five operators of the former report that 30 percent or more of their restaurant parties include children under 13 years of age. In addition, households with children under 13 favor off-premises eating, evening meals, and weekend dining.

The way to attract this segment of the market is to offer the favorite foods of the children. According to the National Restaurant Association, this criterion is deemed "important" or "very important" to almost eight in ten parents.

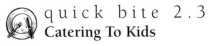

quick bite 2.3
Catering To Kids

It isn't enough to keep kids entertained these days; it is also important to provide kid-friendly food to attract families with children. Kid-friendly food includes items that are familiar to children, such as pizza, hot dogs, hamburgers, and chicken fingers, in addition to "fun" items such as dinosaur-shaped ravioli. Children are generally reluctant to eat strong or bitter flavors and spices because the flavors are unfamiliar to them.

At Tattaposto in Chicago kids eat free on Sunday from 4 to 7 P.M. Owner Tony Mantuano prepares dinosaur ravioli in a mold and stuffs it with a ricotta and chopped spinach filling. Other items include hot dog pizza, baked rigatoni and cheese, and grilled chicken breast. Mom and Dad, meanwhile, are eating the Mediterranean specialties: sesame crusted halibut with tahini dressing ($19) or roasted duck breast on grilled pizza with marinated cherry tomatoes and roasted poblano peppers.

Employees also act in a kid-friendly way by serving the children first and waiting a few minutes before serving the parents, to allow them to cut up the children's food. At the Daily Grill in Los Angeles, kids are given a small plate of banana, crackers, and cheese as soon as they sit down, to keep them occupied.

Cultural factors come into effect in developing taste. In Mexico, for example, children eat spicy sauces, in part, because it is considered macho to eat hot foods. Some studies indicate that the odor of pork seems stronger to children than to adults. In general, kids prefer things that don't require a lot of chewing because they are not physically equipped to chew.

In a survey by Holiday Inns, pizza was identified as the number 1 choice of kids. Over two-thirds choose chocolate chip cookies as the best dessert, while corn won out over carrot sticks as the premier vegetable.

Source: Pamela Parseghian, "Kid's Corner: Catering to Tots," *Nation's Restaurant News*, May 16, 1994, pp. 51, 57.

Children are likely to want items they do not get when eating at home. In 1991 the top choices of children under 18 were french fries, hamburgers, and pizza. Fried chicken, ice cream, and Mexican food were favored choices also. Additionally, more than six out of 10 adults rate speed of service, child-size portions at lower prices, and reduced-price promotions for children to be important criteria in selecting a restaurant.

The influence of children had long gone unnoticed by restaurants until, led by fast-food chains, certain segments of the industry added special menus, provided play areas, and targeted children in their advertising campaigns. About 80 percent of restaurants with an average per person dinner check of under $25 offer child-size portions at lower prices, while approximately 70 percent offer children's favorite food items. In fact, the number of children's entrees on table service menus has doubled over the past five years.

Adolescents

Adolescents are a particularly difficult segment of the market to please. Heavily influenced by the foods in fast-food chains, many institutions, in an attempt to satisfy this group, are putting such things as burgers, pizza, and chicken on their menus. The fact that many adolescents are health and weight conscious must be considered when developing a menu. Carbonated drinks and entertainment are important to this group.

Adults

Adults eat out for many reasons. It is useful to segment this portion of the market further based on marital status. Single people often eat out because of the hassle of cooking and cleaning up for one person. Fast-food restaurants offer speed of service and because of the informal atmosphere, less of a lonely feeling than do fine-dining establishments. Variety, ethnic foods (which are difficult to prepare at home), and takeout foods are attractive to this group.

Family income, time available, and family size are the major determinants in the eating-out habits of married couples. Childless married couples—defined as couples with no children under 18 living at home—totaled 27.8 million or 30 percent of all households in 1990, a segment of the market larger than the num-

---

 quick bite 2.4
Vive La Difference!

Men prefer:

1. Taste over nutrition
2. Bigger portions
3. Meat
4. Familiar food such as that experienced in childhood
5. Entrees rather than desserts

They are more likely than women to eat out.

Women prefer:

1. Foods of high nutritional value
2. To eat less
3. Fruit
4. More adventurous food choices

They are as likely as men to order desserts but less likely to eat out.

Source: Toni Lydecker, "Men and Women: Two Different Markets Sharing a Table," *Restaurants USA,* vol. 14, no. 7, August 1994, pp. 26–30.

Men prefer meat! *Source:* Monfort Foodservice advertisement.

ber of married couples with children younger than 18 at home. There are, in fact, three segments of this market: empty-nesters, defined as those 45 to 64 years old and representing almost half of all childless married couples; mature couples, those 65 or older, slightly less than one-third of the total; and childless young couples, those under 45 years old with no children.

Childless married couples eat out more often than do couples with children. At least once a week nearly 40 percent of all childless married couples eat out at a table service restaurant where the average adult check is under $10. Midpriced restaurants are favored for economic reasons. However, one in four childless young couples eat out at least once a week at restaurants where the average adult check is over $10. In determining good value in moderately priced table service restaurants, childless married couples consider a clean dining room, quality of food, fresh ingredients, friendly staff, and timely service. In evaluating fast-food places, importance is placed on an accurately placed order, a clean dining area, consistent quality of food, speedy service, and getting the correct change [3].

Because many couples have high incomes and dine out relatively more frequently than do other segments of the market, they spend more per capita on food away from home than do any other household type. According to the Bureau of Labor Statistics' 1990 Consumer Expenditure Survey, married childless couples spent an average of $1030 on food away from home. This represented 45 percent of their total food budget. By comparison, married couples with children spent $2417 per household ($620 per person), 40 percent of their total food budget, on food away from home. The addition of a child to the household reduces the per capita expenditure on food away from home by one-third.

Seniors

Senior citizens are a growing segment of the market. Their eating-out habits are influenced by a number of factors. For those who are widowed, the opportunity to eat out is important for social as well as physiological reasons. For many seniors, living on a limited income means that price is an important factor. "Early bird" specials, two-for-one deals, and happy-hour food buffets are attractive for this reason. Small to average-sized portions are desired, as are easily chewable, simply cooked foods. Liquid foods such as soups, stews, and casseroles are traditional favorites.

Seniors tend to have rather rigid food habits, although they are paying more attention to nutrition. In 1989, almost 60 percent of females age 55 or

---

quick bite 2.5
The Senior Segment

According to the American Association of Retired Persons: "Older people tend to dine with other people and not alone. So when seniors dine out that usually means larger parties." More than 55 percent of those age 50 or more eat out at least once a month. More than half of these meals are at midscale and upscale restaurants. To appeal to this group, many restaurants are offering higher price–value items, larger-print menus, and improved lighting.

At Sonny's Real Pit Bar-B-Q in Maitland, Florida, "Early Bird Specials" are priced at $3.99 for a chicken dinner plate and $4.99 for turkey, beef, or pork. Macayo's Mexican Restaurants give diners 60 years of age and older a discount card good for 20 percent off the check and available from 4 to 7 P.M. seven days a week. About 35 people volunteered suggestions to Tony Roma franchisees in Seattle to develop a "Senior Roma" menu aimed at those 55 and older. The result is an increase in business between 3 and 5 P.M. and a menu costed so that the gross profit is the same as on the standard menu.

Leverock's Seafood House has a two-step approach: offering a special "Sunset Menu" and hosting meal functions with local retirement facilities. The special menu offers 25 percent off the usual prices, runs from 3 to 6 P.M., and includes such things as onion-crusted salmon, beef stroganoff, grilled chicken pasta, and London grill. "Heart healthy" dishes are available and the operation customizes items to meet specific dietary needs. All-inclusive meals, good value, and early meals are important factors in appealing to this segment.

Source: Bill Carlino, "Operators Strike Gold with Seniors," *Nation's Restaurant News,* October 3, 1994.

---

older and 55 percent of males age 55 or older had restricted their diets in the preceding year to control cholesterol. More than 70 percent of this same group had restricted their intake of foods high in salt, sugar, and fat [4]. They prefer broiled foods to fried, breakfast foods, beef entrees, nonfried fish and poultry items, vegetables, soups, and desserts and shun hamburgers, french fries, pizza, and Mexican food.

Concerned about their relative lack of mobility, they prefer dining areas with bright lighting, easy accessibility, no waiting, and easy-to-read menus. Cafeterias allow them to choose a variety of food items and portion sizes.

Students

Convenience and cost are major factors that influence the eating-out habits of students. If they lack a car, they may be limited to facilities within walking distance of campus. Health and weight are concerns to many, so low-calorie and vegetarian foods are important. Breakfast is the meal they are most likely to skip.

It is difficult to cater to any group in an institutional setting, for no matter how good the food, the standardized recipes, surroundings, and mealtimes all contribute to complaints about "dorm food." Some colleges have added theme eating areas to provide choices in atmosphere in an attempt to provide variety.

Shoppers

For shoppers, dining is secondary to the shopping. A location convenient to the stores is thus an important factor. People are looking for fast service and an opportunity to rest.

Workers

At some times during the 8-hour workday there is a need to stop, to rest, and to refuel. Some companies see this as an opportunity to influence employee morale and motivation by providing discounted meals as a fringe benefit. Service has to be fast, meals have to be varied, and the atmosphere must allow for relaxation from the stress of the job. By providing facilities in the factory, employees can be kept on the premises while utilizing all of their free time for eating and socializing rather than commuting to an outside restaurant. Companies also use in-house facilities to entertain clients. Typically, these facilities are run by a contract caterer to specifications laid down by the client company.

Travelers

When traveling, people tend to be concerned primarily with the need for a break. Being away from home and unfamiliar with local facilities, franchise restaurants are popular because they offer quality standards in the areas of food and cleanliness.

The traveling market can be divided into domestic and international segments. The vast majority of leisure travelers are domestic travelers. Automobiles

quick bite 2.6
El Sabor De Mi Tierra Natal[*]

(The Taste of My Homeland)

When appealing to an ethnic market, translating the words is often not enough to attract customers. According to Guillermo Ceniceros of Casanova-Pendrill Publicidad, Inc., which handles the creative side of marketing for El Pollo Loco: "if you want to get to the Hispanic market, you have to hire someone who is in touch with the people in that market."

Sizzler, the casual steak-house chain, needed a different theme when translating its message to appeal to the Hispanic market. Peggy Goff, who works for Al Punto Publicad, the agency that created Sizzler's Spanish-language advertising, notes that "in the general market, Sizzler is seen as a blue-collar destination where friends get together for a good time. For Hispanics, however, Sizzler is seen as being more elegant. To dine out at a Sizzler is more of an occasion, a special event for families." In the advertisements aimed at the Hispanic market, the quality of the food is stressed before the affordable prices are mentioned. Large families are also shown having a good time. The English versions, in contrast, show friends out together.

The general slogan, "Sounds like Sizzler— sounds like fun," was replaced with "Comida sabrosa a precios que dan gusto" (Delicious food at prices you like).

One thing that companies are particularly careful about is the use of humor. Pollo Tropical, which operates in Florida in markets with large Cuban populations, has been advertising in Spanish since 1988. For their latest campaign, "The taste the whole world loves," they singled out Eskimos to convey the message to their Hispanic audience that "everyone loves Pollo Tropical." Says Debla Cabezas, director of marketing, "What's funny in Spanish might not be funny in English, and vice versa."

[*]Advertising theme of El Pollo Loco.

Source: Mark Hamstra, "Transcending Translation in Spanish-Language Ads," *Nation's Restaurant News,* May 1, 1995, pp. 12, 18.

are the most popular form of transportation used, accounting for 81 percent of the 2 trillion intercity miles covered in 1991.

In recent years there has been an increase in the number of foreign tourists visiting the United States. International travelers, particularly those from France, Germany, Japan, and the United Kingdom, identify dining out as one of their favorite vacation activities. Catering to international visitors can involve such things as providing multilingual menus and training employees in cross-cultural communication skills. Canada and Mexico bring the vast majority of international visitors to the United States. In 1992 there were over 27 million arrivals from these two countries. Japan and the United Kingdom, with 5.7 million arrivals in 1992, accounted for over half of all overseas visitors to the United States. However, continued strong growth is expected from Brazil and Italy, which together accounted for only 10 percent of all overseas traffic in 1992.

Patients

As mentioned earlier, people in institutional settings are difficult to please. This is particularly so in the case of patients, since in addition to being confined to a foodservice facility, they have physical and/or psychological ailments. Hospitals run on cyclical menus, with the meals specially tailored to the needs of the individual patient. Within dietary constraints, limited choices are offered. This gives the patient some feeling of control over the meals provided.

No matter which segments of the market are being sought, the key is to research the following topics:

- *Who they are*: families, shoppers, workers, etc.
- *When they eat*: lunchtime, dinner, snack, etc.
- *What they want*: low prices, variety, low-calorie items, etc.
- *Why they eat*: to refuel, to impress a date, to see and be seen, etc.
- *Where they come from*: nearby offices, within a 10-mile radius, etc.

THE BUYING PROCESS

Various internal and external factors combine to influence how customers choose where, when, how, and why to eat out. The vehicle used to explore this will be a national study prepared by the National Restaurant Association on the dinner market [5].

Decision Scenarios

This report divides all dinner decisions into five basic *decision scenarios*:

1. *"Fun time."* This relates to an upbeat mood and a sense of anticipation of fun; the decision tends to be made well in advance.
2. *"Nice meal out."* The desire is to enjoy the satisfaction or enjoyment of eating out, being served, and getting good food, lots of it, at a reasonable price.
3. *"Craving."* This refers to a desire for a particular type of food; seeing or smelling this type of food can set off the craving.
4. *"Making sure that everyone is getting something to eat."* This motivation comes from the hectic pace of everyday life, attempting to balance a variety of work and family schedules.
5. *"Easiest thing available."* This is an impulse decision by someone who is tired and pushed for time.

Fun Time.   When people go out to eat for fun it is because they feel they deserve a treat or reward. This segment of the market makes the decision anywhere from several hours to several days ahead of time. They anticipate the fun they will have and want a place that offers unique or original food. Atmosphere and variety are also important. People out for fun are evenly distributed across all life stages.

Nice Meal Out.   People in this group choose eating out as opposed to cooking. Often it is an impulse decision or one made only hours before the meal. The joys of good food and of being served are of prime importance, although all the basics are important: consistent food quality, variety, good portions, friendly and speedy service, no lines, and value for money. Older singles and older retired couples make up the bulk of this group.

Craving.   This impulse decision is made on the basis of a desire for a particular type of food. Interestingly, buying prepared food at a supermarket can trigger this desire. Young couples comprise most of these diners.

Making Sure That Everyone Is Getting Something to Eat.   This decision is made because of time constraints in fixing a home-prepared dinner for people who have conflicting schedules. This can involve such things as families with children who have to attend after-school activities and working parents who have to go out again in the evening after a day at work. There is a desire to indulge others, a desire to go along with another's suggestion and/or to please the children. Coupons are a significant factor in determining where to eat. Young and middle-aged parents are most prevalent in this group.

Easiest Thing Available.   When people are pressed for time and are tired, they choose the eating option that is most convenient. Speed of service and the convenience of the location are the most important benefits sought. As might be expected, young parents make up the largest category within this segment.

More than half of the decisions in these last three categories are made less than an hour before going out.

Sit-Down Restaurant More Than $10 per Person

The National Restaurant Association breaks "dining out" into seven categories: sit-down restaurant more than $10 per person; sit-down restaurant under $10 a person; fast-food restaurant; self-service cafeteria or buffet; carryout; delivery; and purchased freshly prepared carryout food.

Intrinsic Influences.   People looking for a "fun time" or "nice meal out" make up the bulk of this market. For both, food quality, a nice place, cleanliness, and nice people are important. The first segment is also concerned about fresh food and ingredients, while the second group is interested in value for money.

Extrinsic Influences.   People in the first category most often are between 40 and 60, single, male, and live in larger metropolitan areas. The favored time for eating out is Saturday between 6 and 9 P.M. Parties average 3.6 persons, stay almost an hour and a half, and spend (median) $40.30. Coupons are used 8 percent of the time.

The Buying Process.   This buying decision is usually made several days in advance of the meal. For the "fun time" segment a restaurant is selected where people can anticipate having a good time. They want a place where they will feel comfortable staying a long time; diners spend up to 90 minutes over the meal.

Both segments select steak and family/general menu restaurants, but the "fun time" group was also interested in places specializing in seafood and those offering an "American" menu.

Implications.   For the "fun time" group, anticipation of the meal is important, as is the desire to dine in a nice place. This impression can be given by means of either the exterior or the inside atmosphere of the restaurant, in addition to the friendliness of the service.

Customers looking for a "nice meal out" seek the pleasure of not having to cook. For this segment of the market, value for money is particularly important. Several specials and/or early bird specials—reduced priced meals offered during early evening hours—would be attractive to this group.

Sit Down Restaurant under $10 per Person

Intrinsic Influences.   As before, people seeking a "fun time"—the most common—and a "nice meal out" make up most of the parties in sit-down restaurants where the average check is under $10 a person. Such basics as food quality, friendly service, and cleanliness are important in addition to value and the convenience of the facility.

This type of restaurant also appeals to those interested in "making sure that everyone gets something to eat," "easiest thing available," and those for whom the meal out is a "craving." In the first two situations, convenience and the price range of the restaurant are important; in addition, speed of service is particularly important for those seeking the easiest thing available. Decisions are made impulsively. Customers seeking to satisfy a craving tend to choose seafood and steak places and consider food quality, freshness, convenience, price range, and value in making the decision.

Extrinsic Influences.   People who eat at moderately priced restaurants are most often widowed or divorced people 50 years of age and older from smaller metropolitan areas (between 500,000 and 2 million population). Customers are not as affluent as those in the first category noted above. Business is particularly brisk on Fridays between 4 and 8 P.M. The average party of 3.3 people stay just under an hour and spend (median) $16.24. Ten percent of this group uses coupons.

The Buying Process.   The buying decision is evenly split between those who make decisions less than an hour before the meal and those who decide longer in advance.

Implications.   Operators should note basic differences between the various segments of the market attracted to restaurants in this price range. Those looking for a nice meal out and a fun time want a slower, more leisurely experience where the basics are done right and the customer feels taken care of.

For the others, speed of service, convenience, and a number of moderately priced specials are important. Self-service soup and/or salad bars can give this impression by putting control of the speed of service in the hands of the customer.

The fact that different groups of people are looking for different things in terms of service puts a premium on the ability of the staff to "read" the customer and provide an appropriate dining experience.

Self-Service Cafeteria or Buffet

This dining-out experience is not as common as the two just described.

Intrinsic Influences.   The most relevant dining reason is for a "nice meal out." Particularly important are such things as cleanliness, value for money, variety, fresh food and ingredients, and food quality. A much smaller number of people in this category go out for a "fun time." In addition to the criteria already noted, this group wants to find a nice place to go to.

Extrinsic Influences.   Self-service cafeterias or buffets appeal most to those aged 60 and over, people who are widowed or divorced, and those either retired or not employed. The average party size is 3.2 people, who spend a median of $13.35. Coupons are used in one of 10 dining occasions. Sundays, particularly between 4 and 7 P.M., are especially busy times.

The Buying Process.   Forty percent of the decisions are made less than an hour before going to eat, while slightly less than one in four decisions are made a day or more in advance. Those looking for a "fun time" spend more time and make the decision earlier than those who want a "nice meal out."

Implications.   These older customers are looking for value. Much of the quality that they have come to expect derives from the importance of cleanliness to them. A clean, orderly dining room and an immaculate service area are very important.

Fast-Food Restaurant

Intrinsic Influences.   The reasons for eating out at fast-food restaurants fall into two categories. Those people seeking the "easiest thing available" look for places offering fast service, with the convenience of a good location, the right price range, cleanliness, and value for money. For people more interested in "making sure that everyone is getting something to eat," it is important that the restaurant appeal to children, offer coupons and other special deals, be convenient in terms of location and the hours they are open, and have items in an acceptable price range. For both segments food quality is not one of the top five criteria.

Extrinsic Influences.   Significant numbers of those who eat in a fast-food restaurant are under 40 years of age, young parents with a family income between $20,000 and $45,000, single males, and those from large metropolitan areas. Eating out occurs most frequently on Tuesdays, Wednesdays, and Thursdays between the hours of 4 and 7 P.M. The average party of 2.9 people spend 35 minutes in the restaurant, with a median bill of $8.17. Coupons are used 22 percent of the time.

The Buying Process.　The decision to eat out is spontaneous, being made less than an hour before going there in over two-thirds of cases.

Implications.　Convenience, speed of service, and cleanliness are crucial factors when catering to this market. Additionally, pleasing the children is vital for those to whom this represents the easiest thing available. The children are likely to have suggested this as the place to eat. This points to the importance of targeting the marketing message to the person who makes the decision. One of the success stories in this field continues to be that of McDonald's, which consistently targets its messages to children through such things as playgrounds and "Happy Meals."

Carry-Out

Carryout involves the purchase of food at either a table service or fast-food restaurant for consumption elsewhere.

Intrinsic Influences. Carryout appeals to three segments: those with a "craving", those seeking the "easiest thing available," and those concerned with "making sure that everyone is getting something to eat." In all three scenarios food quality, speed of service, convenience, and price range are important. Additionally, fresh food and ingredients are important for those with a craving; value for money for people seeking the "easiest thing available," and coupons or other deals and appeal to children for the segment interested in "making sure that everyone is getting something to eat."

Extrinsic Influences. People who buy carryout food tend to be under 30 and either single adults or households with children. For food purchased from a fast-food restaurant, two-thirds of the business comes from hamburger, chicken, and pizza restaurants. One-third of the purchases from table service restaurants were made from pizza places, 25 percent from Oriental restaurants, and 10 percent from Italian restaurants.

This occasion is spread evenly throughout the week but is low on Saturdays. In 80 percent of cases the food is eaten at home. Coupons tend to be used quite often. The average party of 3.1 people spend a median of $9.48 and use coupons almost one-third of the time.

The Buying Process. Most decisions are made less than an hour before going there.

Implications. Coupons seem to be important in attracting this market. Since the food is consumed off-premises, convenience means that customers do not have to travel far to eat it so that the food will not get cold. Geographic segmentation would be appropriate. Operators would identify a particular radius around their restaurant as the potential market for takeout and advertise accordingly.

Delivery

Intrinsic Influences. As above, delivered food appeals to those with a "craving," those concerned with "making sure that everyone is getting something to eat," and those seeking the "easiest thing available." Food quality and speed of service is important to all three groups, while price and consistency are important to the first two market segments. Additionally, fresh food and ingredients are sought by those with a "craving" and those concerned that "everyone is getting something to eat." The latter group is also concerned that the kids like it and that special deals and coupons are available. Value for the money was identified by those looking for the easiest thing available.

Extrinsic Influences. Pizza places dominate the food delivery business, accounting for 80 percent of the meals ordered. Italian and Oriental food makes up the remaining 20 percent. This segment is made up of singles, households with children under the age of 4, with incomes between $20,000 and $45,000.

Fridays after 6 P.M. is a particularly busy time. In over 90 percent of cases the food is eaten at home. The average party of 3.3 people spends a median of $11.89 and uses coupons 44 percent of the time.

The Buying Process.　Two-thirds of the decisions are made less than an hour before the meal.

Implications.　In most cases customers need a reason beyond convenience to place a delivery order. That reason appears to be either a desire to satisfy a "craving" or an attempt to ensure that "everyone is getting something to eat." In the latter case the needs and wants of children become particularly important. As might be expected, speed of service is relevant. Various operators have experimented with guaranteeing delivery within a certain period of time and/or offering price reductions or free meals if delivery is not made within the promised time.

Grocery Store or Deli

A relatively recent source of competition for traditional restaurants has been the emergence of grocery stores and delis where freshly prepared food can be purchased for consumption that same day.

Intrinsic Influences.　Customers are those with a "craving" and those seeking the "easiest thing available." Both segments are particularly interested in the same things: food quality, fresh food and ingredients, speed of service, convenience, and the range of prices.

Extrinsic Influences.　These operations appeal especially to those under 30, singles, and widowed or divorced people with a household income under $10,000. Business is strong on Mondays and Thursdays between 4 and 5 P.M. In 84 percent of cases the food is eaten at home. Coupons are rarely used by the average party of 2.8 persons, who spend a median $7.39 per party.

The Buying Process.　Over half of the decisions are made less than an hour before making the purchase and before people have thought about going out to eat.

Implications.　Because many of the purchase decisions are made impulsively, the presentation and aroma of the food takes on increased importance. Foods that evoke strong feeling—such as pizza, barbecue chicken and ribs, Oriental and Italian items—are likely to sell well. Similarly, the strong visual appeal of salad, appetizer, and salad bars tends to be popular.

For the restaurateur in competition with a deli, one key is to put the idea of dining out in the mind of the customer before she or he is exposed to the retail store. This might be done with flyers early in the day or billboards that will be seen before the person enters the store.

ONGOING TRENDS

There are a number of ongoing trends that will affect the foodservice industry in the coming years [6].

Children

Children are becoming increasingly important as a market segment for restaurateurs. Children influence the amount spent on food away from home as well as where families eat. The National Restaurant Association found that 35 percent of parents with one or more children younger than 6 years of age said that children were very influential in the decision to eat out. The proportion was similar for families with children aged 6 to 12.

Service

As the industry continues into the mature stage of the product life cycle, service becomes an effective way to differentiate one operation from another. It is expected that meeting customers' service expectations will increase in importance for foodservice operators.

There is a discrepancy between what operators think they are delivering and what customers believe they are receiving in terms of service. According to *Tableservice Restaurant Trends, 1991*, nine of 10 restaurateurs believe that customers are either satisfied or very satisfied with the service they receive at restaurants [7]. However, a 1992 customer survey found that less than 70 percent of adults surveyed reported that they were satisfied with the service received. It should be noted that this percentage is up from 60 percent satisfaction two years earlier. The discrepancy may be due to the fact that many dissatisfied customers do not complain (at least in the restaurant) or that operators are unable or unwilling to believe that their customers are not satisfied.

Takeout and Delivery

Picking up on the customers' need for convenience, more restaurants are offering takeout and delivery service. In 1990 almost half of adults under 55 indicated that they would be willing to buy ready-to-eat takeout meals if offered at table service restaurants. In that same year 90 percent of operators with a check size of less than $15 offered ready-to-eat takeout meals.

Nutrition and Health

The desire for better health continues, although there is some question as to whether that desire translates into appropriate action on the part of the customer. The national priorities are to cut back on foods high in saturated fat and cholesterol while increasing the intake of complex carbohydrates and fiber.

In response, more and more operations are using all-vegetable oil and/or shortening for frying, while adding such things as decaffeinated coffee, entree salads and/or salad bars, poultry without skin, reduced- or low-calorie salad dressings, low-fat milk, fruit juices, and margarine. Additionally, the National Restaurant Association reports that over 90 percent of operators with a check average over $25 offer vegetarian entrees, as do 70 percent of operations with an average check below $25.

quick bite 2.8
Road to the Top: Samuel E. Beall III

President and Chief Executive, Morrison Restaurants Inc.

In his freshman year at the University of Tennessee, Samuel E. Beall III was managing Pizza Hut units on campus; in 1992 the 44-year-old became chief executive of Morrison Inc., then a cafeteria, contract catering, and casual dining company. While at the university, he was introduced to several mentors, who in addition to teaching him to surround himself with the best people he could find, gave him part of the seed money for the eventual founding of Ruby Tuesday, a company he started when he was 21 years of age. He also learned from his father, who put himself through college by dint of hard work and discipline.

By 1982, Ruby Tuesday had expanded to seven units. At this time, Morrison, then a regional cafeteria chain, purchased the company for $11 million and hired the 32-year-old as vice president of the Specialty Restaurants Division. According to fellow board member Donald Ratajczak: "Sandy has the three key disciplines of a top manager. He's a strategist who sees the future; he's a numbers man who worries about today; and he's a leader who cares about people."

Morrison is now made up of two distinct parts: the Ruby Tuesday Group, containing the 250 units of Ruby Tuesday and a 40-unit specialty division made up of Mozzarella's and Snapp's, all casual restaurants, and the Morrison Group, a division of 170 cafeterias and 300 hospital dining operations.

Source: Jack Hayes, "Samuel E. Beall III," *Nation's Restaurant News*, January 1995, pp. 19, 22.

ENDNOTES

1. Mahmood A. Khan, *Concepts of Foodservice Operations and Management,* 2nd ed. (New York: Van Nostrand Reinhold, 1991), pp.18–26.

2. "Restaurant Parties with Children," *Restaurants USA*, vol. 12, no. 5, June–July 1992, pp. 39–41.

3. "Focus on Childless Married Couples," *Restaurants USA,"* vol. 12, no. 2, February 1992, pp. 41–43.

4. Ibid; p.43.

5. *National Restaurant Association, Dinner Decision Making: A Consumer Attitude Survey,* vol. 1 (Washington, DC: National Restaurant Association, 1989).

6. "1992 Outlook for Foodservice," *1992 Outlook for Travel and Tourism: Proceedings of the 17th Annual Outlook Forum* (Washington, DC: U.S. Travel Data Center, 1992), pp. 135–140.

7. National Restaurant Association, *Tableservice Restaurant Trends, 1991* (Washington, DC: National Restaurant Association, 1991).

chapter three

DEVELOPING
A MARKETING PLAN

learning objectives

By the end of this chapter you should be able to:

1. List the steps involved in producing a marketing plan.

2. Describe how to conduct a customer, property, and competitor analysis.

3. Compare and contrast the various ways by which a market can be segmented.

4. Identify the elements of the marketing mix for restaurant operations.

5. Describe how to monitor each step of a marketing plan to ensure its effectiveness.

MARKETING DEFINED

The American Marketing Association defines marketing as the "process of planning and executing the conception, pricing, promotion, and distribution of ideas, goods, and services to create exchanges that satisfy individual and organizational objectives" [1]. This definition indicates that marketing is much more than advertising, much more than sales promotion. Marketing encompasses everything from the development of the concept, product, and/or service to how it should be priced, promoted, and made available to people. It works only if an exchange is made between buyer (the individual) and seller (the organization) that benefits both. The seller receives something of value and the organization receives revenue.

Reid developed a definition that brings together the financial concerns of management and the need to satisfy consumer needs. His definition encompasses three items [2]:

---

q u i c k   b i t e   3 . 1
Hot Concepts: Cafe Tu Tu Tango

This three-unit company began in Miami in 1991. It specializes in *tapas*, the Spanish word for "appetizers". However, founder Bradley A. Weiser insists that the word *tapas* never be used—he prefers *grazing*. Customers share appetizer-sized entrees in an operation set up like an artist's loft.

From a building that costs between $1.3 and $1.5 million to develop Tu Tu Tango has average revenues of $3.5 million. The 5500- to 7000-square feet operation provides seating for between 180 and 250 customers and has a staff of between 60 and 70 employees. Their 45-item menu features Asian, Mediterranean, and regional American dishes priced below $8. The menu features items such as rosemary flat bread, baked goat cheese and marinara, alligator bites, and shrimp orzo paella. The most popular item is Barcelona stir fry: shrimp, calamari, chicken, andouille sausage, mushrooms, red and green peppers, and garlic sauteed in olive oil for $7.95. With this as a base, the per person check is $10 at lunch and $14 at dinner.

Weiser defines the theme as "imitating the loft as a wealthy patron in Barcelona whose house is always the scene of partying by his many artist friends." Local artists use the restaurant to both work in and exhibit their work. This helps create a relaxed atmosphere that is further encouraged by a cutlery setup featuring a paintbrush and a batch of forks, to stimulate sharing. In 1993, Planet Hollywood founder Robert Earl bought a 50 percent interest in the company, fueling speculation that he would bring his expertise in themed entertainment to the operation.

Each unit has an arts and entertainment manager who arranges "appearances" from within the local community.

Source: Jack Hayes, "Cafe Tu Tu Tango," *Nation's Restaurant News*, May 22, 1995, pp. 100, 102.

---

1. Determining the needs and wants of consumers
2. Creating the mix of products and services that will satisfy these needs and wants
3. Promoting and selling the product–service mix to generate a level of income satisfactory to the management and stockholders of the organization

J. C. Penney is thought to have put it this way: "If you satisfy the customers but fail to get the profit, you'll soon be out of business; if you get the profit but fail to satisfy the customers, you'll soon be out of customers." The idea is to generate profits by producing satisfied customers.

Inherent in these definitions are several ideas. First, there is the focus on the customer. Marketing is a way of thinking about the business that makes the satisfaction of customer needs paramount. Second, there is the practical implication that businesses cannot be all things to all people—cannot satisfy all the needs and wants of all the people. Some choice must be made as to which segments of the market are to be targeted. Third, there is an appreciation of research to determine customer needs and wants. The idea of sequential steps—that products and services are developed only after customer needs and wants have been identified—is a fourth idea. Customer satisfaction is the fifth idea. It is not enough to promote and sell the service. Customer satisfaction implies that the operation must not only bring customers in, it must bring them back. Finally, the idea of exchange means that the satisfaction of customers' needs must bring economic benefit to the organization.

DEVELOPING A MARKETING PLAN

There are six steps involved in the development of a marketing plan [3]:

1. Conduct a marketing audit.
2. Select target markets.
3. Position the property.
4. Determine marketing objectives.
5. Develop and implement action plans.
6. Monitor and evaluate the marketing plan.

Conduct a Marketing Audit

There are three parts to the marketing audit; it is an analysis of the customers, the property or operation, and the competition. Given the foregoing definitions of marketing, it is appropriate to look first at customers.

Customers. The purpose of the customer, property, and competitive analysis is to develop a profile of the customers and to evaluate, in an unbiased way, how the operation stacks up relative to the competition in providing what they want.

Information about the customers breaks down as follows:

- Who are they?
- Where do they come from?
- When do they visit, and when is the decision made?
- How do they reach us?
- Why do they come and how satisfied are they?

This information can come from sales histories, employees and management staff, the customers themselves, and outside research sources. Sales histories should be kept for six distinct dining segments [4].

1. Weekday breakfast: Monday–Friday
2. Weekday lunch: Monday–Friday
3. Weekday dinner: Monday–Thursday
4. Weekend breakfast: Saturday and Sunday

5. Weekend lunch: Saturday and Sunday
6. Weekend dinner: Friday–Sunday

Note that while weekday breakfast and lunch run from Monday through Friday, weekday dinner runs from Monday through Thursday. The breakdown is in terms of the characteristics of the meal. Friday dinner is regarded by customers as part of the weekend.

For each day it would be appropriate to collect data on:

- Number of customers
- Total sales in dollars
- Number of meals sold
- Number of beverages sold
- Number of appetizers sold
- Number of side items sold
- Number of desserts sold
- Number of breakfast customers
- Breakfast sales in dollars
- Number of lunch customers
- Lunch sales in dollars
- Number of dinner customers
- Dinner sales in dollars
- Average entree in dollars
- Average check in dollars
- Number of beverages, appetizers, side items, and desserts per customer
- Average breakfast, lunch, and dinner check
- Daily sales as a percentage of the week
- Breakfast, lunch, and dinner sales as a percentage of day's sales
- Weekend and weekday sales as a percentage of week's sales

The information collected basically breaks down into how many people we serve, how much they spend, what they order, and how our business is spread throughout the week. From this analysis we can see when business is strong and, more important, when it is weak. In addition, specific objectives can be set to improve sales of specific items or numbers of customers.

A core store panel provides the head office with information from the field through the collection of data from a representative sample of stores. The sample chosen should be representative of the company's geographic distribution and sales volume. Data should be collected on [5]:

- Sales by day and week
- Transaction count
- Product sales mix

- Advertising activities
- Promotional activities
- Competing activities
- Weather

On an informal basis, management and staff can provide information about the customers because they are constantly in contact with them. While such data are not scientific, they can give a picture of the items that are selling and why, what customers like and do not like, and what types of people visit at different times during the week. In addition to providing useful information, asking the opinion of employees makes them feel important and can serve as a motivational tool.

More formal questionnaires can be used to collect information on the customer base. The key in developing a questionnaire is to develop the research objectives first, decide on the questions that will provide answers to the information being sought, select an appropriate research methodology, and conduct the research.

A simple category of data that can easily be collected and is very useful is customer zip codes. Most restaurants attract customers from a relatively small area. Some consultants estimate that 80 percent of a restaurant's business comes from within a 3-mile radius. Having servers and/or cashiers ask for customers' home and work zip codes, management can readily identify where customers come from.

The best way to find out what a restaurant is doing well and poorly is to ask customers. The key to increasing sales and customer count is to identify the characteristics of existing customers and to use that profile as a basis for attracting more customers who fit that profile.

One way to get this information is from a focus group. A focus group consists of six to 10 former or existing customers, led by a discussion leader, who express their feelings about various aspects of the operation. Questions go from the general to the specific and concentrate on motivations, feelings, and gut-level issues. Although not statistically reliable, such sessions can indicate a great deal about what motivates customers.

Customer comment cards are a favorite way of collecting information. There is probably a positive bias built into any research conducted in the restaurant. Most customers will not complain in the restaurant unless there is something really wrong. An average or mildly unpleasant experience may not result in negative comments from the customer until they leave the operation.

Property.　The property analysis is an unbiased evaluation of the strengths and weaknesses of the operation. A "typical" checklist would evaluate the property and the competition as to the following factors [6]:

- Menu variety
- Menu appeal
- Food/beverage quality

- Food/beverage taste
- Food/beverage consistency
- Portion size
- Pricing
- Service speed
- Service quality
- Service friendliness

- Cleanliness
- Promotional activity
- Visibility
- Image
- Atmosphere
- Facility
- Sales level
- Point of sale
- Happy-hour offerings

The problem is that such a list does not indicate how important these things are to the customer. A better starting point is to look at the operation from the viewpoint of the customer. By identifying the factors important to customers and using these items as a checklist to evaluate both the operation and the competition, a focus on the customer is assured. For example, if a restaurant features an excellent salad bar but that factor is unimportant to the customers, is the salad bar a strength, a weakness, or a neutral factor?

It will be recalled from Chapter 2 that the National Restaurant Association identifies the "fun time" segment of the dinner market as seeking out places that excel in five things:

1. Food quality
2. Nice place
3. Cleanliness
4. Friendly people
5. Fresh food and ingredients

If the operation appeals to this segment of the market, they could identify from them just what is meant by each of these five factors and use the resulting list as the basis for evaluating the property and the competition.

Some restaurants use mystery shoppers to evaluate the operation. These people should always remain anonymous and conduct random evaluations. There are typically three or four visits the first month, followed by monthly visits thereafter. Management receives a report on the exterior, interior, and signage of the facility in addition to comments on the appearance, performance, and service provided by the employees.

Competition. A competing facility is any operation that seeks to attract the business being sought by the restaurant under consideration.

A competitive analysis compares competing facilities with the operation under study. The purpose of such an analysis is to discover [7]:

1. Profitable market segments being served by competitors that are not being served at the operation under study
2. Some competitive benefit or advantage the property has that cannot be matched by the competition

3. Weaknesses in the marketing strategy of the competition that can be capitalized on

A competitive analysis involves getting as much relevant information as possible and includes eating at the facility and evaluating the advertising.

Select Target Markets

The idea behind the selection of market segments is that people are different in what they want from a dining experience and that it is not possible to be all things to all people. Market segmentation involves dividing a heterogeneous market into smaller homogeneous segments. While the members of a segment have characteristics similar to each other, they differ from people in another market segment. In this way operators can more effectively target marketing efforts to those people who are most likely to patronize the restaurant.

Segmentation Variables. Marketers segment the market on the basis of one or more variables. The major variables used are geographic, demographic, psychographic, usage or behavioral, and benefits sought. Geographic segmentation involves identifying the geographic limits of the trading area and appealing to people within the boundaries of that area. The National Restaurant Association estimates that people will travel an average of 15 to 18 minutes for special-occasion meals. A radius of 18 minutes' driving time from the operation would be a geographic segmentation of the market.

Demographic segmentation involves dividing the market on the basis of such things as age, income, gender, annual income, family size, stage in the family life cycle, educational level, occupation, ethnicity, religion, nationality, and social class. In earlier chapters we discussed the eating-out patterns of various market segments. The National Restaurant Association notes that for dinner in a sit-down restaurant where the average check is over $10, the most likely customer is male, between the ages of 50 and 59, single, with an income of $45,000 or more. Conversely, a fast-food customer is more likely to be either male or female, under 39 years old, just as likely to be single, married, widowed or divorced, with an income between $20,000 and $44,999 [8].

Psychographic segmentation divides people based on their attitudes, interests, and opinions. In the foodservice business this might involve separating out groups based on how they spend their time and the importance to them of eating out. For example, while 45 percent of adults say they would eat out more often if they had the cash available, the rates vary depending on age. Fifty-two percent of 35- to 44-year-olds agree, whereas only 29 percent of 55- to 64-year-olds do [9]. Obviously, eating out is more important to some people than to others.

Segmenting on the basis of use or behavior is based on the oft-quoted 80–20 rule. This rule states that 80 percent of the business comes from 20 percent of the customers. If the operator can identify the frequent customers who make up a substantial part of the business, he or she can do a more effective job of marketing.

The Simmons Market Research Bureau, Inc. breaks restaurant use into five segments: nonprospects (those who are never likely to become users), prospects (those who might become users), light users (1 to 5 times per month), medium users (6 to 13 times per month), and heavy users (over 14 times per month). Heavy users account for 44.8 percent of total restaurant revenue in a typical month, medium users account for 40.8 percent, and light users bring in the remaining 14.8 percent of revenue. Giving the light user an index of 100, the heavy user has an index of 522. For every $1 spent by a light user, a heavy user spends $5.22 [10].

Benefit segmentation separates people out on the basis of the benefits sought from the meal experience. As identified in Chapter 2, there are five different decision scenarios for people dining out. These are:

1. Fun time
2. Nice meal out
3. Craving
4. Making sure that everyone is getting something to eat
5. Easiest thing available

Those eating out for a "fun time" believe that they deserve a treat or reward and feel like having fun. They have the time to plan the event, and price is not very important to them. On the other hand, the "easiest thing available" group eat out when they are tired and pressed for time. They choose options with the least number of hassles. For them, speed of service and a convenient location are important benefits they look for.

Market segments should be selected on the basis of size, likelihood of growth, competitive position, the cost of reaching the segment, and how compatible the segment is with the company's objectives and resources.

Revenue Grid. For an existing business a revenue grid and an analysis of activity can be helpful in selecting workable market segments. A revenue grid identifies how much revenue is brought in from the various segments of the market presently being served. A useful rule of thumb in marketing is: "Attract customers similar to those already being attracted." For some reason the restaurant attracts a certain kind of clientele. An examination of the existing customer base broken down by how much sales each segment brings in is an excellent start to identifying future potential. In other words, find out who the customers are and seek to find more people with similar characteristics.

An analysis of business activity will tell when business is good and, more important, when it is bad. This can suggest areas of importance for increasing sales. The marketplace can then be searched for prospective market segments consisting of people who eat out when the operation needs the business. The segments are then evaluated relative to the criteria noted above to determine their suitability.

Position the Property

Positioning Statement. The image that customers have of an operation is its position in the marketplace. A good positioning statement will accomplish several things. First, it will create an image in the minds of the customers as to what it stands for. In the foodservice business, as in any other, image is reality. People make decisions based on their perceptions rather than on the reality of the situation. If the image is positive—that the restaurant offers good value—the decision may be made to eat out there. Image alone will not induce the customer to buy. That willingness comes from a variety of promotional means described later.

The actual meal experience offers a reality check to the guest. The actual experience may be less than expected. The result is a disappointed customer. The image portrayed by the operation must be positive enough to encourage people to visit the operation. The actual meal experience must be equal to or greater than the image for the guest to leave satisfied.

Second, the positioning statement will describe the benefits the restaurant offers to the guests. Restaurants offer features but people buy benefits. Customers, in fact, "buy" a bundle of benefits. When going out for a meal, different people look for different things. For some, a large variety of menu choices is important. For others, price is a major concern. Still others emphasize privacy. Since people buy benefits, the operation must communicate what benefits it offers to its potential customers.

Third, it differentiates the property from the competition. Everyone offers "good food", "atmosphere", and "value". But just what is it that makes one restaurant different from the other? Why should I come to your place rather than the restaurant across the street?

The key is to find a difference, an advantage, that is difficult for the competition to replicate. Every business seeks a unique selling point or a competitive differential advantage, something that makes it different from the competition that can be used to advantage. The nature of business means that unique selling points are subject to the principle of *perishable distinctiveness*. If one restaurant develops an advantage that makes it more attractive to customers, the competition becomes aware of that advantage and seeks to copy it, thus neutralizing the previously unique selling point. That which made the restaurant distinctive is gone; it is perishable. "What can separate me from my competition that is difficult, if not impossible, for them to copy?" This is the third element that must be answered from a positioning statement.

It should readily be seen that a positioning statement can come only after an analysis has been made of the market, the property, and the competition.

The key is to identify what the target market wants (the benefits) from a dining-out experience and how one operation is perceived (in the minds of the customers) as providing these benefits compared to the competition.

Perceptual Maps. Perceptual maps can be useful tools in developing a positioning statement. A perceptual map is a visual representation of two elements: the relative importance of various benefits to guests and their perception of how well a facility does in providing these benefits. In essence, customers from the market segment being sought are asked two questions: "What things are important to you when dining out?" and "How well do you think restaurant X does in providing these things?" The benefits considered important to customers can be identified from informal discussions with guests or from a focus group session. The focus group can identify what the members like and dislike about the company and the competition. The results are qualitative rather than quantitative. They will not disclose percentages, but they will indicate "gut issues." From such a group a list of benefits sought when dining out can be obtained. For example, it may be that customers decide that the benefits they are looking for when dining out are:

A	Prices in their range
B	Nice place
C	Cleanliness
D	Friendly people and service
E	Cleanliness
F	Speed of service
G	Food quality
H	Value for money
I	Kids like it
J	Hours open
K	Consistency
L	Special deals and coupons
M	Variety
N	No lines and no waiting
O	Size of the portions
P	Food presentation
Q	Convenience of location
R	Comfortable seating
S	Fresh food and ingredients
T	Unique or original food

This list can then be used to construct a questionnaire to be presented to a sample of present and prospective customers who are asked to rate the importance of these items to them on a scale of 1 (very important) to 5 (not important). Those customers are then asked how well the restaurant under study does

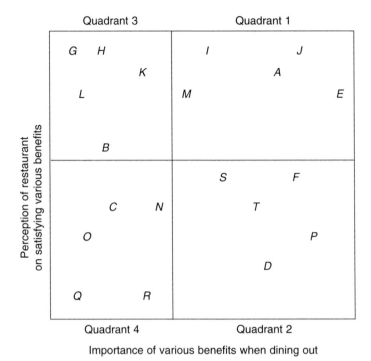

Figure 3.1 Perceptual map.

in providing these things, again on a scale of 1 (totally) to 5 (not at all). The resulting scores can be placed on a matrix as in Figure 3.1.

Crosshairs are drawn on the graph such that half of the 20 items are above the horizontal line and half below, and half of the 20 items are to the left of the vertical line and half to the right. The result is four quadrants. In the upper right section, quadrant 1, are items that are not important to the customers and which they think the restaurant does not satisfy. In this example guests say that the following factors are not important to them and, furthermore, the restaurant does not, in their mind, provide these things:

- Prices in their range
- Cleanliness
- Kids like it
- Hours open
- Variety

In quadrant 2 there are factors that, again, are not important to the guests. However, in this case they do think that the restaurant provides these:

- Friendly people and service
- Speed of service

- Food presentation
- Fresh food and ingredients
- Unique or original food

Quadrants 3 and 4 are made up of factors that customers consider important. In quadrant 1 are factors that they perceive the restaurant does not do a good job of providing. In quadrant 4 there are factors the customers think the operation does do well on.

The factors in quadrant 3 are:

- Nice place
- Food quality
- Value for money
- Consistency
- Special deals and coupons

The remaining factors, in quadrant 4, are:

- Cleanliness
- No lines and no waiting
- Size of the portions
- Convenience of location
- Comfortable seating

From these findings the restaurant can identify where it stands in the minds of its customers and determine appropriate actions. The factors in quadrants 1 and 2 should be ignored. Customers tell us that these items are not important to them. If they are not important to the customers, they are not important to the foodservice operation. There will be a tendency for restaurants to want to play to their strengths. The customers perceive that the restaurant offers friendly service that is fast and includes original dishes made with fresh ingredients and presented well. However, these factors just are not very important to them. The facility that markets to guests on factors not important to them will not attract those people.

The important items are in quadrants 3 and 4. These factors are important to guests. But they do not believe that the restaurant is a nice place that offers consistent, good-quality food, special deals, and delivers value for money. They do believe that it is clean, offers correctly sized portions, comfortable seating, and a convenient location with no lines.

At this point it is necessary to do a reality check. How accurate are the customers' perceptions? The answer will determine the appropriate action. Where the image is negative but the actual situation is positive, we need to improve the image. For example, it may be that special deals are offered but customers are unaware of them. Where the image is negative and the actual situation is negative, or when the situation is positive but the actual situation is negative, the product or service must be changed. For example, if people believe that consistency is a problem and it really is a problem, the food served must be improved so that it is consistent. Similarly, if the perception is that the seats are comfortable, but in reality they are not, that also must be changed. If customers are drawn to a restaurant expecting comfortable seats, the visit will show that they are not and the customer will be dissatisfied. Finally, where the image is positive and the actual situation is positive, we have the basis for a positioning statement.

Similar perceptual maps can be drawn for the competition to determine just where, in the minds of the customer, we are perceived as doing a better job of providing benefits important to them. The resulting positioning statement will be based on research that has identified the benefits the customer is looking for, what is provided to satisfy these desired benefits, and how the restaurant differs from the competition in providing these desired benefits. In essence, the positioning statement says: "For _____ seeking _____, we provide _____ ."

The first blank should be filled with the segment of the market being considered, the second blank identifies the benefits being sought, and the third space says what will be provided to satisfy customers.

Determine Marketing Objectives

Criteria. The very act of setting objectives increases the likelihood that they will be achieved. The reason is that management now has something to work toward. Developing objectives gives managers a way to determine the extent to which they are moving forward and to allow them to change strategies if positive movement is not being made. It allows for a way of keeping score. This in itself is a motivational tool as well as a method of assigning responsibility and rewarding the achievement of results.

To be useful, objectives should be set for each segment of the market to which the restaurant is appealing . Each market segment is different in terms of dining and spending patterns and the extent to which the operation is presently successful in its marketing effort. For seniors it may be appropriate to increase the number of such customers, whereas for businesspeople it may be more appropriate to have existing customers patronize the operation more frequently.

Second, objectives should be results oriented. This usually means specifying an improvement in volume, revenues, or market share. It is only by identifying the desired results that management can set targets and, later, measure to see whether the effort has been successful.

Objectives should also be set in quantitative rather than qualitative terms. The problem with qualitative objectives (for example, "to improve service") is that the measurement of such objectives is open to subjective judgment.

There should be a time element to each objective. It is not enough to say that the foodservice operation wants to increase its customer count by 100 customers a week. A time limit must be set as to when this objective should be achieved.

Life-cycle Curve. Objectives have to be set consistent with where the operation is in the product life-cycle curve. The concept of a product life cycle is that a business goes through various stages during its lifetime. A business is introduced into the marketplace and will grow, mature, and decline. Different marketing objectives are appropriate at the various stages of the life cycle. In the introductory stage, the key is to create awareness and trial on the part of customers; in the growth stage, sales are increasing at an increasing rate and market share should be maximized; in the maturity stage, sales are increasing but at a decreasing rate and profits should be maximized while market share is defended; and finally, in the mature stage of the life cycle, sales are decreasing and expenditures are reduced and as much is extracted from the business as possible.

Buying Process. It is also important to set objectives that are consistent with where customers are in their buying process. The concept of a buying process is that potential customers go through a series of stages in their own minds before making a purchase. They must first be made aware of the existence of the operation. Then they need to have information outlining the operation's benefits to them. At this point, if the campaign is successful, customers form a positive attitude about the restaurant, develop a preference for it, are convinced they should go there, actually visit the restaurant, and if satisfied, return. The objectives set will vary depending on where the market is in this process.

At the awareness stage, the objective is to expose people to the operation. How successful we are can be measured by identifying the number of people exposed to the message: number of readers, viewers, and so on.

At the knowledge or comprehension stage, when customers are trying to identify what the restaurant can offer them, the objective is to transmit information. How well this has been accomplished can be determined by measuring the percentage of readers or viewers who remember essential parts of the message.

The objective in the attitude stage is to changes people's attitudes about the operation. The success of a program can be determined by measuring consumer attitudes before and after the campaign to determine whether or not a change has occurred. Similarly, during the preference stage— where the objective is to create a preference in the mind of the customer—preference surveys before and after the campaign can be done. It may be, for example, that prior to the campaign one restaurant places sixth out of 10 on a list of preferred operations. If the restaurant places third, after the program, the campaign can be called a success.

The conviction stage seeks to have customers *do* something. The number of actions taken—phone reservations made, for example—can be measured. Purchase is measured by the number of people who come in the door or who order the item being promoted. Finally, adoption—where the objective is repeat purchase—can be measured by the percentage of customers who are repeats.

Develop and Implement Action Plans

The implementation of an action plan actually involves the development and execution of a specific marketing mix for each segment of the market being sought. It involves developing the means to carry out the job, developing a budget to accomplish the plan, and assigning responsibility for the plan.

The marketing mix has been variously defined by different authors. Originally comprised of product planning, pricing, distribution, promotion, servicing, and market research, it has been standardized into the "four P's" of product, price, promotion, and place. Other elements have been suggested to make the four P's suitable for the hospitality industry. It is suggested that the marketing mix for foodservice operations consists of four elements: product–service mix, price, promotion communication, and place distribution mix [11]. The mix chosen will vary depending on the industry, the position of the operation in the marketplace, and how it fares presently relative to the competition.

Product–Service Mix. The product–service mix consists of the various products and services offered by the operation in an attempt to satisfy customer needs. It covers such things as the options on the menu, quality, reputation, image, the furnishings and decor, the exterior structure and interior layout, and the various service features of the operation. It includes elements that the customer pays for either directly or indirectly. The price charged for the steak on the plate covers not only the meat itself but also the plate it is served on, the napkins used, background entertainment, and even the view from the table, the "price" of which is reflected in the cost of buying the facility and is passed on to the customer in the prices charged. Even the status of visiting a particular restaurant is something that is paid for in increased prices.

According to Lewis and Chambers [12], the following factors are associated with successful new products and services:

- The ability to identify customer needs.
- Use of existing company know-how and resources.
- Developing new products in the company's core markets.
- Measurement of performance during the development stage: screening and testing ideas before spending money on development.
- Coordination between research and development and marketing.
- An organizational environment that encourages entrepreneurship and risk taking.
- Linking new product development to corporate goals.

Price. Several points regarding price bear mentioning. First, the importance of price comes from the fact that it is one-half of the price–value relationship that customers seek. If, in the minds of the guest, the value received is less than the price paid, the experience will be viewed negatively. Second, in the foodservice business much of the pricing that goes on is product-driven pricing. That is, restaurants often have a particular facility that has various fixed costs and items on the menu that can increase in their cost to the restaurateur. The operator has to meet these costs by finding a segment of the market willing to pay the price for the product. However, it should always be remembered that the customer is the final arbiter of whether the price charged is acceptable. The latter concept, consumer-driven pricing, has often been ignored in the restaurant industry [13]. In the 1970s, restaurants responded to price increases of various food items by raising prices—in effect, passing their price increases on to the customer. After awhile customers decided that the prices charged were more than the value received. As a result, many customers traded down. Fast-food restaurants gained business from table service restaurants, and convenience stores benefited from customers who saw fast-food prices increase. Many customers decided to stay home and eat, satisfying their desire for quality by eating better at home. The smarter operators recognized this customer resistance and

Jay Solomon suggests using coupons for bringing in business on slow nights.

adjusted concepts and prices accordingly. The point is that the customer, not the product cost, will determine whether an item will sell.

Promotion-Communication Mix. The promotion-communication mix consists of all of the communications between the company and the customer and consists of media advertising, word of mouth, merchandising, promotion, public relations, publicity, and personal selling. These items are covered in greater detail in Chapter 4.

Place-Distribution Mix. The channels that connect the company and its various customers are referred to as the distribution mix. Channels can either be direct or indirect. A direct channel of distribution means that the restaurant communicates directly with its customers. In indirect distribution there are one or more intermediaries between the restaurant and its customers. For example, a restaurant may decide to be listed in a discount book sold by high school students as a fundraising device. A restaurant may decide to become part of a package tour being promoted by a tour operator. The decision to accept credit cards also brings an intermediary—the credit card company—between the restaurant and the customer.

There are several factors to consider before deciding the form of distribution. If there is an existing or a proposed distribution network, it may be in the interests of the operator to use it. If the seniors in the local high school propose

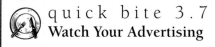

quick bite 3.7
Watch Your Advertising

Here are the major elements of Outback Steakhouse's marketing program:

1. Sports-programming commercials are themed to the program in which it will be shown. For example, "Ultimate Goal" depicts a game that is a combination of rugby, football, and boomerang throwing in a desert setting. There are no rules other than meeting the "ultimate goal", which means, for Outback, serving the perfect steak.
2. TV advertising is selected based on the watching habits of the core customer. While the demographics of Outback's customers suggest they should be cable TV watchers, cable is too fragmented to make a regional impact.
3. By sponsoring the Outback Bowl the company is able to get name recognition into geographic areas in which it intends to operate.
4. Radio commercials are based on two of the chain's strengths, music and humor. Radio is used to promote special occasions and in the off-months, while television is used to generate increased general awareness.
5. On a selective basis Outback works with local charities. Grand opening charity events are selected, in part, based on how active the board is in a given community. An active board will work hard to ensure that people come to the opening charity fundraiser.
6. Print advertising, including direct mail, is a low priority for the company because the primary purpose of the marketing effort is to communicate image. The company feels that print advertising is more suitable for communicating price than for communicating image.

Source: "Outback Advertising Campaigns: Throwing Out All the Rules," *Nation's Restaurant News,* March 27, 1995, pp. 12, 96.

to sell discount books as a fundraiser, it is probably easier to tap into that effort rather than to duplicate it by distributing fliers on the restaurant directly to the parents and friends of the students.

Several years ago the Scottish Tourist Board began a program called *A Taste of Scotland*. Restaurants were asked to provide a special menu using locally produced items and to price it within a certain range. In return, the Scottish Tourist Board listed them in a booklet distributed to tourists which informed them of the operations participating in the scheme. Again, the network provided by the board was not available to the individual operation.

People in the indirect channel of distribution between the restaurant and the customer make their money by helping generate sales. They do not get paid

Courtesy Outback Steakhouse, Inc.

unless a sale is made. Thus the selling cost for the restaurant is a variable one. This compares to the selling cost for direct distribution, which is a fixed cost. The promotion is directed by the operator directly to the customer and must be paid for in full whether it attracts one customer or a thousand. On the other hand it must be remembered that everyone between the restaurant and the customer must get a cut of the selling price charged by the operation. If a menu item regularly sells for $18 and the restaurant sells that item directly to the customer, it receives $18. However, if a credit card is used, a percentage of the sale is paid to the credit card company and the bank handling the collection. The bus operator willing to bring in two busloads of tourists three times a week during the season will pay less than the $18 because he or she is buying in bulk and expects to pay less by buying wholesale. Every restaurant manager would prefer to sell every meal for the retail price. At times during the day, or the week, or the year, however, the business is not there to pay the full asking price. This is when, and only when, discounts paid to intermediaries can be justified.

The key for the operation is to know when *it* wants the business and to know the cost structure sufficiently well to realize how low it can price the product and still make money. As a minimum, it is important to know what the break-even point is. As discussed in Chapter 1, the break-even point for a food-service facility is that point at which the operation exactly breaks even. No profits are made; no costs are incurred. At the break-even point, total revenues taken in exactly equal total costs incurred. The important distinction here is that after the break-even point, the only costs incurred by the operation are variable costs. If break-even can thus be assured, the product can be priced to cover variable costs. Anything over the variable cost is profit.

A third factor to consider is the image of the intermediary. The image of the people or organizations distributing the product represent, for the customer, the image of the restaurant being sold. Operators would want to ensure that this image is consistent with the one they want to portray.

When sales are made directly, they are made through the employees of the restaurant. Those employees are employed by the operation and should therefore be more motivated to ensure the success of the restaurant than others in the channel who are not employees. The operator needs to determine the needs and wants of those in the channel to ensure a match with her or his own needs.

A final factor to consider is who has the power in the channel. To the extent that a restaurant relies on a tour operator to bring in a significant amount of business, that operator has increased power to demand better prices and services at the risk of taking the business to another restaurant. Recently, a number of restaurants in the northeast were successful in their attempts to reduce the percentages paid to American Express. The individual operation must balance the various forms of direct and indirect distribution in such a way that it feels in charge of its own destiny rather than being at the mercy of others in the channel.

Budget.   A crucial part of the action plan is the budget that is developed to carry it out. Various means have been used to develop a budget. A common way of developing a budget is to base it on a percentage of sales. Restaurants typically spend from 0.4 to 6.8 percent of sales on marketing depending on whether it is a full- or limited-service, limited-menu with no table service facility, or a cafeteria. This option can work with businesses with a high percentage of repeat business. However, if sales go down in a particular year, the following year's marketing budget will be cut when it should probably be increased.

Another option is to spend in line with what the competition is spending. This effectively puts one's fate in the hands of the competition, who may not know what it is doing.

A third option is to spend what the business can afford. This approach is a reactive way of deciding action plans.

The fourth approach is the best but also the most difficult. Action plans are developed that will be successful and an amount budgeted to ensure their completion. At this point the desired budget may have to be modified in light of the amount of money available. However, the point is first, to determine how much is needed to do the job, then determine if the business can afford it, rather than vice versa.

Monitor and Evaluate the Marketing Plan

It is easy to see when a marketing plan is successful—there are more customers coming in more often and paying a higher average check. Equally, it is easy to determine when a plan has not worked—fewer customers coming in as often and spending less. What is difficult, however, is to determine why the plan failed. The exciting part of putting a marketing plan in place is the operation of the plan. But the most important and most overlooked part is determining whether or not it was successful and how and where it succeeded or went wrong. Even when the plan is evaluated, it is often done after the event as a kind of postmortem. This may be useful in helping to ensure the success of the next marketing effort. It does nothing for the existing campaign.

The marketing plan must be monitored at each step of the way to ensure that it is on track, and corrective action must be taken at each step of the way if

quick bite 3.8
Road to the Top: Norman Brinker

Chairman, Brinker International

Norman Brinker has been described as the midwife at the birth of the casual-dining segment of the restaurant industry. His Steak & Ale concept, which he opened in 1966 in Dallas, Texas, set the standards for casual dining and influenced many who came after him. Born in Denver, Colorado, and raised as an only child, Brinker was delivering papers, raising rabbits, and breeding cocker spaniels as businesses before he could drive.

His values came from parents. His father said: "if you say you are going to do something, you do it. Never, never take a shortcut and never, never tell anything but the truth." From his mother he was taught to do things for the community and the church.

Graduating with honors from San Diego State University, he joined Jack in the Box founder Robert Peterson in 1957 and stayed with him until 1965, by which time he owned 20 percent of the chain. Then, at the age of 32, he branched out on his own, starting with a coffee shop in Dallas before opening the first Steak & Ale in 1966.

According to one of Brinker's "graduates", Richard Rivera, the key to Norman's success is "his absolute integrity, quality-mindedness and yet being really tough-minded about results." Steak & Ale went public in 1971 and was merged with Pillsbury five years later. Brinker became executive vice president of Pillsbury, supervising the restaurant group.

In 1983 he invested in and became chairman of Chili's Inc., taking it public and directing its growth to Brinker International, with more than 400 restaurants and annual sales of more than $1 billion.

A polo accident in 1993 left him paralyzed on his left side. He approached this accident as he deals with business—setting a goal that two months later, he would be home. He arrived home one day before the goal, without the aid of canes or crutches. Says Brinker: "I teach philosophy. When I first came into this business people were called operators. . . . Then, about twenty years ago, I said we need to talk about managers and management. . . . Now, we've got to be leaders. . . . It means you must have vision, you're ahead of the game, you inspire people."

Source: Ron Ruggles, "Norman Brinker," *Nation's Restaurant News*, January 1995, pp. 33, 36.

it is off track. The first point at which a plan can falter is in the selection of the correct market segment. No matter how good an advertising campaign, if it is directed at the wrong people, it will not work. For control purposes, the restaurateur needs to ask:

- Do I know what my customers want?

- Do I know what people in the marketplace, who are not yet my customers, want?
- Do I know the characteristics of the target market I want to attract?

Assuming that the answer to all the questions above is "yes," the next step is to evaluate the objectives that have been set. The objectives should be:

- Specific
- Measurable
- Achievable
- Realistic
- Time-based
- Consistent with the operation's place in the product life-cycle curve
- Consistent with the customer's place in the buying process

In monitoring the theme of the program, research is essential to determine the extent to which it is desirable and believable in the eyes of the target market. Additionally, it must be action oriented. In other words, will it produce action on the part of potential customers?

In selecting the appropriate promotional mix, the key concern is whether or not the message is being placed where it will be seen, heard, and/or read by the target market. Media planning involves making decisions on the timing, frequency, size, and position of promotional messages. At this stage messages should be tracked to see whether they meet the objectives set earlier. Were customers exposed to the message? Did the message convey to them the necessary information about the operation? Were their attitudes about the facility changed as a result of the message? Did they develop a preference for the operation because of the message? Were they driven to action by the message? Will they come back again? Finally, the budget must be examined along two lines: (1) is it sufficient to meet the objectives set, and (2) is it an amount that the business can afford?

ENDNOTES

1. "AMA Board Approves New Marketing Definition," *Marketing News*, March 1, 1985, p. 1.

2. Robert D. Reid, *Hospitality Marketing Management*, 2nd ed. (New York: Van Nostrand Reinhold, 1989), p. 8.

3. James R. Abbey, *Hospitality Sales and Advertising* (East Lansing, MI: Educational Institute of the American Hotel and Motel Association, 1989), p. 34.

4. Tom Feltenstein, *Foodservice Marketing for the '90s* (New York: John Wiley & Sons, 1992), pp. 51–54.

5. Ibid., p. 29.

6. Ibid., p. 23.

7. Abbey, *Hospitality Sales and Advertising*, p. 37.

8. National Restaurant Association, *Dinner Decision Making: A Consumer Attitude Survey* (Washington, DC: National Restaurant Association, 1989), pp. 8–9.

9. National Restaurant Association, *Tableservice Restaurant Trends, 1992* (Washington, DC: National Restaurant Association, 1992), p. 104.

10. Eric N. Berkowitz, Roger A. Kerin, Steven W. Hartley and William Rudelius, *Marketing,* 3rd ed. (Homewood, IL: Richard D. Irwin, 1992), p. 204.

11. Abbey, *Hospitality Sales and Advertising,* p. 20.

12. Robert C. Lewis and Richard E. Chambers, *Marketing Leadership in Hospitality: Foundations and Practices* (New York: Van Nostrand Reinhold, 1989), p. 327.

13. Ibid., p. 354.

chapter four

PROMOTING THE OPERATION

learning objectives

By the end of this chapter you should be able to:

1. Describe the various stages in the promotional process.

2. Compare and contrast the various methods of establishing a promotional budget.

3. Describe the functions of advertising.

4. Identify the criteria used in selecting which media should be used.

5. Compare and contrast the effectiveness of various media.

6. Identify the key parts of a successful sales promotion: merchandising effort and public relations campaign.

THE PROMOTIONAL PROCESS

Objectives of Promotion

Modern marketing calls for more than developing a good product, pricing it attractively, and making it available to target customers. Restaurants must also communicate with their customers.

Management communicates with customers—both existing and potential—through what is known as the promotional mix. The end goal of promotion is behavior modification: We want to initiate or change the behavior of customers such that they will dine with us.

Specifically, promotion seeks to inform, persuade, and remind. For new or remodeled restaurants the task is to inform the public about the operation; for existing operations the job is to persuade customers to visit; to existing customers it is necessary to keep them consciously aware of the operation so that when they think about eating out, one restaurant immediately springs to mind.

Steps in the Process

The communications process is illustrated in Figure 4.1. A target market is identified, objectives set, the content and form of the message established, the promotional mix determined, appropriate media selected, and a budget established. It is important to set up controls at each step of the way to determine whether the campaign is on track.

Target market. The various segments of the market have been covered in earlier chapters. To determine whether the correct market has been chosen, the operator must answer the following questions:

- Do I know what my customers want?
- Do I know what the marketplace wants?
- Do I know the characteristics of the target market I want to attract?

Objectives. To determine the objectives of the campaign it is important to determine where the operation is in the life-cycle curve and where the customers are in the buying process. The concept of a life-cycle curve involves the notion that a business goes through various stages. The length of time in each stage will vary from business to business. At each stage, different operational strategies are important. Typically, a business will be *introduced* into the marketplace, then go through stages of *growth, maturity,* and *decline* or *rejuvenation.* In the first stage the new or remodeled concept is introduced into the marketplace. At this point potential customers are unaware of the operation. The objective is to inform customers of the restaurant's existence.

If all goes well the restaurant goes through a period of growth. One characteristic of the operation is that sales or customers are increasing at an increasing rate. Perhaps there was a 5 percent increase in sales last year, a 7 percent increase this year, and a projected 8 percent increase next year. At this point customers are obviously aware of the operation and the objective is to persuade.

quick bite 4.1
Hot Concepts: Cheesecake Factory

David Overton, chairman and chief executive of Cheesecake Factory, believes the chain is successful because it broke the rule of conventional wisdom. Consider conventional wisdom and Cheesecake Factory's response:

1. "Don't develop if real estate is too high." Development costs are among the highest in the industry, at $300 a square foot. Restaurants range from 5000 to 24,000 square feet at the 650-seat location in Redondo Beach, California. Overton is able to counter high development costs with landlord participation by convincing them to contribute to development costs by promising high volumes and traffic. Although the menu is casual dining, the atmosphere is upscale.
2. "Maintain a limited menu to reduce waste and staffing costs." Overton's menu is 18 pages long and consists of over 200 items. Menus have been expanded to accommodate regional preferences and menu trends and is updated twice a year. The best-selling dishes include spicy items, pastas, Chinese chicken salad, and jambalaya.
3. "You must have restaurant experience." David's parents started the company as a wholesale bakery. When the family had trouble convincing other restaurateurs to carry their line of cheesecakes (they said the prices were too high), the family decided to open their own restaurant as a showcase for the desserts. Says David: "We did not know anything about running restaurants. We just knew that people valued fresh foods. In some ways our naivete helped us because we didn't know what you are not supposed to do."
4. "People don't eat desserts." Cheesecake Factory features 50 different kinds of cheesecake.
5. "Sales must continue to grow." Because stores are full most of the time with customers willing to wait for up to two hours for a table, sales volume is flat at an average of $8.5 million per store. This is the highest average volume of all publicly held restaurant chains.

Outside of southern California and the Washington, DC area the company keeps a one-unit-per-city policy. Says Overton: "What we like in a site is one that gives us 250,000 people in a five-mile radius, medium-to-high incomes, and we like opening near apartment dwellers rather than around homeowners. Apartment dwellers go out more frequently." He reckons the company has another five years before it will have trouble finding the kind of sites it prefers. In preparation for that, they are experimenting with a 4500-square foot type of operation.

Source: Milford Prewitt, "Cheescake Factory," *Nation's Restaurant News,* May 22, 1995, pp. 106–107.

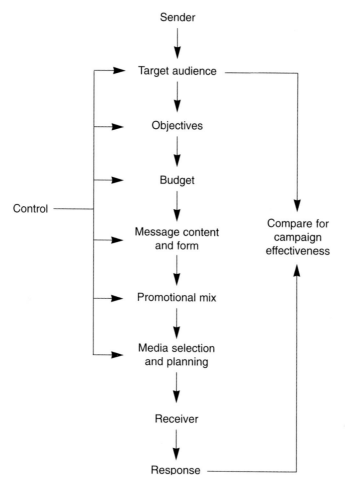

Figure 4.1 The promotional process. *Source:* Adapted from Robert Christie Mill and Alastair M. Morrison, *The Tourism System: An Introductory Text,* 2nd ed. (Upper Saddle River, NJ: Prentice Hall, 1992), p. 448.

In the mature stage of the life cycle, sales and/or customers are increasing but at a decreasing rate—last year's growth of 6 percent is replaced this year by a growth of 5 percent and a projected growth next year of 3 percent. Profits begin to peak before sales decline. The promotional objective is to differentiate the operation from the competition.

If no remedial action is taken, the business will go into the decline stage of the cycle. Sales and/or customers are going down. At this point it is important to take the appropriate steps to get out of that particular business segment.

Remedial action can be taken to rejuvenate the business to produce another spurt of growth. This might involve getting existing customers to come in

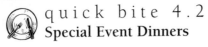

quick bite 4.2
Special Event Dinners

Here are 10 ideas for special events dinners:

1. Tobacco–liquor combinations, such as cigars and bourbon, pipes and port
2. Winemaker dinners featuring vineyard proprietors
3. Single-malt scotch dinners
4. Single-barrel bourbon dinners
5. Coffee brunches
6. Italian foods with Italian wines
7. Champagne and chocolate tastings
8. Tequila tastings with Tex-Mex foods
9. Microbrewery-beer tastings
10. Cookbook-author dinners

How would *you* go about developing a process for implementing these ideas?

Source: Leah Smith Spangler, "Successful Event Dinners," *Restaurants USA*, vol. 14, no. 7, August 1994, pp. 31–33.

more often and/or at different times of the day, going after another segment of the market, or introducing new items on the menu (or a change of theme altogether). A number of the fast-food chains noticed a slowdown in sales as the industry entered the mature stage of the life cycle and introduced breakfast menus as a way of rejuvenating sales. In addition, many expanded overseas to reach an entirely new market.

For control purposes objectives should be SMART—that is, they should be specific, measurable, achievable, realistic, and time-bound. To make the objective specific, it is necessary to quantify it. It is not enough to "increase awareness"; it is necessary to "reach 1000 prospects." The sheer fact that a specific target has been set increases the chances of reaching it.

Similarly, objectives must be measurable. There is no way that an objective of "increasing awareness" can be measured; it is just too vague. It is possible, however, to determine whether or not 1000 people have been exposed to a promotional message. Newspapers count circulation, radio stations count listeners, and direct mailings can be tabulated.

If objectives are not achievable, setting them becomes a meaningless exercise. They must also be realistic in the eyes of the people whose job it is to meet the objectives. If objectives are set at an unrealistically high level—"we want to sell an additional 200 bottles of wine next week"—the servers who are charged with the task of selling the wine will not even try, realizing that it is impossible.

Finally, objectives must be time-bound. There must be a time frame within which the objective is to be achieved. If there is no time frame, it becomes impossible to determine whether the objective has been reached.

Message Content and Form. A variety of themes can be developed as part of a promotional campaign. A restaurant may stress reputation, food taste or type, quality, or service. The "proper" message is one that is desirable, believable, exclusive, and action oriented. It must make the customer want what is being offered; it has to be believed; it should "belong" to one operation and no one else; and it should induce action on the part of the customer.

Promotional Mix. The major elements of the promotional mix are [1]:

- *Advertising*: any paid form of nonpersonal presentation and promotion of ideas, goods, or services by an identified sponsor.
- *Personal selling*: oral conversations, either by telephone or face to face, between salespersons and prospective customers.
- *Sales promotion*: short-term incentives to encourage purchase or sales of a product or service.

---

quick bite 4.3
Let's Get Serious

For 47 years Luby's Cafeterias Inc. relied on word of mouth to get customers in the door—not any more. Their first-ever advertising campaigns— built around the slogan "What you'd cook at home if you had the time"—aim to build repeat business while seeking to get rid of the image that only seniors go to cafeterias.

Says Joyce E. Rothenberg, vice president of marketing: "Luby's has never really marketed. Less than half a percent of sales was spent on marketing. When you're playing in the world of people spending 4, 5 or 6 percent on marketing, you've really got no voice." Luby budgeted 1.5 percent of its 1994 $368 million sales volume for marketing purposes.

The first campaign was run in cooperation with Sea World of Texas and had the joint objectives of promoting a "Monster Marsh" Sea World exhibit while increasing weeknight family business at Luby's. A "Kids Night Out" program allowed kids 12 and under to enter a sweepstakes with a grand prize for four to Sea World if they visited Luby's after 4 P.M. Sunday through Thursday. Complementing the advertising was a point-of-purchase dinosaur display in the restaurant, cards for a free ticket to Sea World after two Luby's visits, and children's dinosaur books given free at each visit to the restaurant.

By the end of the campaign 43 families were sent to Sea World and Luby's gave out 8000 Sea World tickets to repeat customers.

Source: Robin Lee Allen, "Luby's Eyes Updated Image with Two New Campaigns," *Nation's Restaurant News,* June 6, 1994, pp. 12, 81.

- *Merchandising*: materials used in-house to stimulate sales, including brochures on display, signs, posters, tent cards, and other point-of-purchase promotional items.
- *Public relations and publicity*: the nonpaid communication activities involved in maintaining or improving relationships with other organizations and individuals.

The principles and practices involved in the proper selection of the various parts of the promotional mix will make up much of the remainder of this chapter.

Media Selection and Planning.   Various elements of the promotional mix involve the use of paid or unpaid media. While the selection of appropriate media will be covered in more detail later, the key control question is this: "Is my message in a place where it will be seen, read, and/or heard by my customers?"

Budget.   The place of budgeting in the promotional process will depend on the approach to promotion taken by the operation. In a bottom-up approach, objectives will be set, the methods of reaching the objectives determined, and a budget agreed upon that will do the job. All too often, however, a top-down approach is used whereby the budget is determined first and objectives set relative to the amount of money available. Budgets can either be set according to industry standards, to what the competition is spending, to what amount of money is available, or to meet the agreed-upon objectives.

The restaurant industry spends an average of 2.2 to 4.2 percent of sales on marketing expenses [2]. Full-menu table service restaurants average 2.2 percent of sales, while the corresponding percentage for limited-menu table service, limited-menu no table service, and cafeterias is 3.2, 4.2, and 2.7, respectively. The problem with an average is just that—it is an average. This figure represents a number for newly opened operations (which probably need to promote more) and established facilities, which may not need to promote as much. This figure should only be used as a very rough starting point.

Often a manager, noticing that the competition has taken out an advertisement in the local paper, responds with an ad of her own. Although it can be important to match the competition, this policy has two major drawbacks: It means that the manager's actions are being "controlled" by the competition and assumes that the competition knows what it is doing!

For many managers promotion is seen as a cost of doing business rather than as an investment. Too often the refrain is, "I can't afford to advertise" to which the answer is, "You can't afford not to." Promotional expenses must be planned for in advance as a part of doing business rather than being relegated to the category of an "extra" for which money may or may not be available after all other bills have been paid.

The best and most difficult method of establishing a budget is to identify the objectives and set a budget sufficient to meet the objectives. At the same time, it must be an amount that the business can afford. Promotion is more art than science. There is no scientific way to determine how many advertisements it will take to produce x number of customers. For this reason alone, there is a common tendency to view budgeting as a top-down effort.

Response. If promotion is communication, it does not work unless communication occurs, unless the object of the communication receives it and responds. If each step of the process has been controlled, there is a greater chance that the campaign will be a success and that customers will respond to an advertisement, buy the bottle of wine from the server, or order the appetizer noted on the tent card.

This final part of the control process is vital. Did the promotion do what it was intended to do? Can we trace the impact on sales to a particular effort? Only through such tracking can a cost-benefit analysis be done in an effort to measure the effectiveness of the various parts of the promotional effort.

Industry Use of Advertising and Promotion

According to the National Restaurant Association [3], newspapers are the most popular form of advertising for table service restaurants, being used by approximately 80 percent of all operations. More than half of all establishments used team and community sponsorships, radio advertising, and restaurant guide advertising. Operators with check averages below $15 (1991 figures) are more inclined to utilize billboard advertising and team sponsorships than are businesses with an average check greater than $15 per person. The latter, however, are more likely to advertise in restaurant guides, magazines, and to use media press releases and direct mail than are operators of lower-check-size restaurants.

Most restaurants use promotions as a means of building traffic. About nine of 10 operations use gift certificates and daily specials, and about 70 percent utilize sea-

---

 q u i c k   b i t e   4 . 4
Why Advertise?

According to Greg Kaplan, vice president of marketing for the 609-unit Captain D's, a series of "seafood experts" commercials was an attempt to "reposition the chain as a notch above Long John's but not a Red Lobster Jr." The seafood expert theme began in 1991 with Gregory Holder, a man with a deep Caribbean voice and an imposing physical presence. Some customers noted that they were unable to understand the actor because of his thick accent.

Since the concept was on target, the company sought out other "experts." Actors, including Sandra Dee, appear in a Captain D's talking about their favorite dishes. As the advertisements unfold they are shown in the roles that made them famous.

The words *special price* are used rather than *value meals*, as the company does not want to get into a battle over price. Says Kaplan: "In seafood, when you get to too low a price point, [customers] start questioning the quality."

Source: Theresa Howard, "Captain D's Lentan 'Experts' Campaign Hooks Patrons," *Nation's Restaurant News*, February 28, 1994, p. 12.

---

sonal specials. Those businesses with average per person checks below $15 are more likely to use senior citizen discounts than are operators of higher-average-check restaurants. The latter, however, have a greater tendency to offer pre-theater specials and frequent-diner programs, this option being offered by about three in 10 of the higher-check facilities. Operators feel that the most successful promotions for them are daily specials, word of mouth, general reputation, and holiday specials.

ADVERTISING AGENCIES

When to Use an Agency

A foodservice company can handle its own promotional campaign or it can hire an advertising agency. Some owners, managers, and key personnel are clever with words and ideas. They may actually be better than some professionals at creating ads and promos. They may need only occasional outside services and suppliers to help them promote their businesses. Other operators may not be so fortunate or creative, and may wish to contract with outside companies for publicity services and suppliers to help them promote their businesses. Another option could be to create an in-house advertising agency—that is, an agency within the firm.

Operators of many small or beginning businesses have little choice. Their advertising budget is not big enough to justify hiring an independent agency, much less setting up a house agency. These operators must look after their own promotion, calling on representatives of local media for expertise. Fortunately, many local broadcast or print media prepare advertising quite competently. The restaurateur has only to coordinate the themes and timing of the various efforts—and be sure that he or she is buying what is needed. It is always worth remembering—advertising salespeople are paid for selling advertising, and believing in their service, they will sell as much as they can.

Agencies are paid in a variety of ways [4]. Often, they receive commissions from the media in which the message is placed. The usual commission is 15 percent of the cost of the advertisement. If an advertisement cost $400, for example, the client would pay the agency the $400. The agency would subtract 15 percent ($60) and pay the media $380.

Agencies also charge the client for production and creative services involved in creating the advertisement. Typically, these fees consist of monthly retainers in addition to hourly charges for creative work, photography, and typesetting. Finally, agencies charge for advertisements on which commissions are not paid, such as direct mail and local newspaper advertising.

How to Select an Agency

When an agency wants a restaurant's business, or a restaurateur wants to hire an agency, it is customary to arrange an agency presentation. The larger the account and billing, the more attractive the company will be to agencies.

An agency presentation can be accomplished over a simple lunch or may take the form of a full-blown display of what the agency can do. A presentation will include a description of the personnel of the agency and some representative work they have performed successfully for others. A list of past and present clients will usually be offered for reference checks. The pitch can be conducted in the client's offices or at the agency. Most agencies prefer to use their facilities to avoid interruptions and to put on a proper show.

Presenting agencies will try to sell an entire marketing plan rather than just a media plan. Even if they do not know the idiosyncrasies of the business, they may be able to lay out a plan of attack to help a restaurateur get more mileage out of an ad budget.

If the restaurateur's budget is large enough to interest them, it is wise to listen to more than one agency's presentation. It is not wise to make a hasty decision. References of past and present clients of the agencies that are being considered should be checked before committing to an outside agency.

Most agencies will not represent more than one client in a given business or industry. If an agency already has a restaurant or hospitality account, it will probably be prepared to quit or lose it before taking another.

Before making a decision, the agency offices should be toured and meetings held with the personnel. The person who will be working with the account representing the client should be identified. Agency personnel who do not own a piece of the action in their agencies tend to move about in their industry just as restaurant people change jobs in theirs. It may become an important issue if an account executive leaves the agency. An account may be bound by an employment agreement that forbids taking clients along to a new agency.

Studying how an advertising agency works will help improve cooperation with the agency's efforts. An outside agency representative can instruct a client in how they operate, purchase media, perform research, order graphic artwork and photography, handle copyrighting, and conduct publicity. In the process a restaurateur will sign all insertion orders and okay all copy. It is important for clients to receive copies of all work done on their behalf.

The agency relationship should begin with a complete understanding of how all items, services, and media are to be purchased. Both parties must exert every possible effort to be open to what the other is doing for their mutual good. Both client and agency must anticipate problems and discuss them beforehand to establish the best possible relations and to achieve the best results.

Most client–agency relationship and agreements, either oral or written, can terminate almost immediately. Agencies know that they cannot work where they are not wanted. There should be one item that should be understood when a split occurs—all bills and invoices should be paid by the client to the agency or be guaranteed to all other suppliers and media. When this is fully done, the agency should relinquish all the materials and support information that belong to the client.

ADVERTISING

As noted above, advertising can be defined as any paid form of nonpersonal presentation and promotion of ideas, goods, or services by an identified sponsor.

Functions of Advertising

Advertising seeks to inform, persuade, and remind. It can accomplish a number of things [5]: It presents information to the customer about the operation, it encourages first-time visits, it enhances the image of a particular company or operation, and it reinforces the behavior of customers who have eaten there in the past.

Types of Campaigns

National/Local. Advertising campaigns can be either national or local. National advertising uses network media—television, radio, and magazines—to reach a national audience. The effort is essentially directed toward promoting the general name or image of the company rather than toward any one establishment. At the local level promotions are tailored to the local market in an attempt to promote specific restaurants.

Cooperative Agreements. To maximize use of the promotional dollar, individual restaurants can enter into cooperative agreements whereby a number of individual operations pool their resources to produce an advertisement promoting eating out in general or restaurants in a geographic area. This allows an individual facility to advertise in media that it could not afford on its own. Individual managers must determine whether or not the benefits of inclusion outweigh the costs.

Another example of cooperative advertising is when restaurants who are members of chains cooperate with the corporate office in producing a promotion. A national chain would pay the "national rate" for a series of advertisements in print, television, or radio. This rate is higher than the "local rate," that paid by a local business. By splitting the cost of the campaign 50–50 and having the local business book the advertisement, the company gets a lower rate while the individual business effectively doubles its advertising budget.

Media Selection Criteria

A variety of criteria are used to determine which media should be used. The most important criteria are the cost per contact, total cost, market selectivity, geographic selectivity, source credibility, visual quality, noise level, life span, pass-along rate, and timing flexibility.

The cost per contact, usually expressed as cost per thousand (CPM), refers to the cost of reaching 1000 people. The total cost is the actual cost of the message. Market selectivity refers to the extent to which an advertiser can reach a specific market segment. In recent years magazines aimed at a general readership has given way to a variety of magazines targeted toward specific groups of people. This makes it easier to reach particular segments of the market.

Similarly, geographic selectivity refers to the ability to reach a particular part of the country, state, or town. Many magazines run regional editions while small townships put out local papers. Source credibility considers how believable the medium is viewed to be by the reader or listener. Certain media offer better quality visuals than others. Generally speaking, the quality of visuals in newspapers is poor.

When an advertisement competes with other activities for a person's attention, the noise level is said to be high. If the tendency is to give total attention to the message, the noise level is said to be low.

Life span and pass-along rate are closely related. A newspaper has a life span of one day. One person reads it and usually discards it. A magazine, on the other hand, is kept around longer and may be read by someone other than the person who purchased it. A radio advertisement has an even shorter life span than that of a newspaper, as the message cannot be referred to again. Among other things, this means that radio advertisements have to be repeated a number of times to have any kind of impact.

Finally, timing flexibility refers to the lead time needed to run or change an advertisement.

Newspapers

Effectiveness. Newspapers, as noted above, are the primary advertising medium for table service restaurants. They generally offer the most cost-effective means of reaching potential consumers, both in terms of total cost and cost per contact. Market selectivity is low, and geographic selectivity is average. It is possible, for example, to zero-in on specific towns. The trust factor appears to be low and the visual quality less than average. To counteract a high noise level, low life span, and pass-along rate, newspapers offer a great deal of flexibility in the timing of advertisements.

Copy/Layout. When using a newspaper advertisement copy, layout and photographs/sketches must be considered. The copy consists of the headline and body. The headline of the ad must catch the reader's attention while the body includes the details. A good advertisement starts with a headline that is enticing, provocative, and attention grabbing. A clever, punch headline with few words is preferable to one that attempts to tell the entire story.

Size/Shape. Choosing a different size and shape is one way to make an ad stand out. If most other ads are 1/4-page vertical, a 1/4-page horizontal space may attract more attention.

Suppress the urge to crowd as much information as possible into an ad. The most successful ads tell a simple story in clear, concise language. Ads jammed with too many facts and figures are least likely to be read. All ads create certain types of impressions. A simple test can determine what stands out most in an ad. The ad is turned upside down to see what is most noticeable. People are used to reading left to right, top to bottom. Once a page is turned upside down, the viewer's mind's eye becomes disoriented and he or she cannot read according to learned methods. At first, an ad may look like a big blur, but later the viewer will be able to detect the most outstanding element in the ad, the one that will have the most impact on readers. If that element is not the one intended, the ad needs to redesigned. If the big blur remains and viewer finds it difficult to determine any outstanding elements, the ad needs to be redesigned. A catchy headline, a strong graphic, a bold price, or any other single element should be prominent.

Radio

Radio is an immediate medium for quick news and information. Advertising time can readily be bought and commercials produced quickly for relatively low cost. It is selective for broad market segments and has a high geographic selectivity. Credibility is low and noise level high, while timing flexibility is better than average.

Station Formats.   In seeking a share of the market, radio stations have created many individual formats that reach different target audiences efficiently. Radio station formats include talk, Spanish, middle-of-the-road, top 40, black,

---

 q u i c k   b i t e   4 . 5
Radio Advertising

Here, from one professional, is how to get the most out of radio advertising:

1. Use your own voice. Nobody knows your product as well as you; people trust "real" voices and often tune out professional voices; speak a little deeper than you usually do; don't yell.
2. Build name recognition. Say the name of your restaurant a minimum of four times during each ad.
3. Be specific. Advertise one item, one promotion; come up with one reason to visit the restaurant.
4. Let the music play—softly. Use upbeat music; never use music with words in it; tie music into the theme of your restaurant.
5. Promote the event. Give the particulars of an event at least twice during the ad.
6. Think tasty and visual. Use taste-tempting words such as like "hot melted butter; oozing with cheese; melt in your mouth."
7. Never assume that they know you. Always include the name and location of your property—exactly where you are.
8. Choose a radio station intelligently. Choose radio stations on the basis of what your customers like, not what you like.
9. Run your radio ads at the correct time. For lunch, run your ads between 6 A.M. and 1 P.M. because that's when the decision is made. Dinner is more of an occasion, so select a variety of times.
10. Advertise long enough to have an impact. Try out a new station for at least three months. Pick one day a week and dominate that day. Thursday is a good day.

Source: A. Dyal Bailey, "Radio Advertising Works for Me," *Restaurants USA*, vol. 13, no. 8, September 1993, pp. 32–34.

---

classical, contemporary, religious, adult contemporary, nostalgia/big band, news/talk, oldies, disco, educational, jazz, progressive rock, beautiful music, blues/soft, and gospel music. Individual stations claim that their listeners are loyal and selective because of their strong preferences for a station's format and their personal identification with the particular interests reflected by the station.

Effectiveness. Radio uses words and sounds to describe products and services and special occasions. Radio plays on the imagination of the listeners and attempts to sell the sizzle rather than the steak.

Many radio stations in a market result in fragmented audiences. Radio advertising can therefore be costly and inefficient when many stations are needed to reach a broad cross section of target audiences. Radio cannot show or demonstrate products or services. The advertising message usually must remind people of things they know. New, unique, or complicated ideas may be difficult to express. Radio is a transient medium. Messages cannot be kept for later reference. Listeners, for example, must remember addresses and telephone numbers. Coupon offers are out.

The Federal Trade Commission (FTC) regulates the percentage of total air time that can be devoted to commercials. Many listeners, however, believe that some radio stations are over commercialized, particularly at peak periods. Advertising messages therefore need strong creative treatment to be noticed and remembered.

Commercial formats. Commercials generally come in two formats: 30 and 60 seconds. The half-minute spots do not cost 50 percent of the cost of full-minute spots. The expense is so close that many advertisers use 60-second commercial spots for the greatest cost efficiency. Also, 30-second commercials are very brief. A 30-second spot involves 65 to 70 words of copy, while a 60-second commercial generally accommodates 125 to 135 words of copy.

Television

Unquestionably, television is the powerhouse medium. It combines most of the advantages of sight, sound, immediacy, dramatization, and emotional involvement of the viewers in a way that no other medium can match. It is also expensive. It can make customers aware of what there is to offer, at a price that requires considerable planning and budgeting.

Effectiveness. Television is the dominant medium. It reaches people of every type and is of average market selectivity while covering large areas of geography quite efficiently. However, television is inefficient when advertisers need to reach a highly selected group of people. It cannot isolate distinctively differing groups of people as does radio with its highly categorized formats.

Television can also show how a product or service works and it provides strong name identification. It builds awareness rapidly and, by its intensity, increases audience perception of commercial message. As a medium it is not credible, the noise level is high, and the timing flexibility is low.

Television ads cannot be saved for later reference or couponing. In addition, commercial time is generally short and, like radio spots, television messages must have an immediate impact on viewers. Television cannot be used for long, complicated explanations.

Magazines

Effectiveness. There are almost as many different kinds of magazines as there are different kinds of restaurants. Therefore, a magazine will pinpoint the market by the type of publication chosen. However, any bona fide publication seeking advertisers should provide information concerning its readership, circulation, and advertising costs to permit a restaurateur to determine where it should fit into the advertising program.

Some magazines devote special sections to restaurant advertising. Frequently, the readership of such columns is high and comparable to an editorial feature of the same length. Most magazines are read by the same people, issue after issue. An eating establishment whose advertisement is noted regularly becomes a part of the readers' subconscious mind. An acceptance is established because of the familiarity of name or message.

Yellow Pages

Effectiveness. Yellow Pages advertisements are important in every promotional campaign. They provide good value for the investment. It is important to have the advertisement draw in the reader. However, to compete with all the listings in the Yellow Pages, many restaurants find it advantageous to palace an ad close to their listing or to have their business name set in bold type.

In Yellow Pages advertising the name, address, and phone number of the restaurant are highlighted for people who have sought out the restaurant section for a specific interest. If a person is scanning the pages to decide on a place to dine, an advertisement has an opportunity to direct him or her to the establishment.

Layout. Advertising space in the Yellow Pages is sold in standard-size units. The sizes are usually; one-fourth of a page, one-eighth of a page, and one-sixteenth of a page. The rates vary according to the number of phone books printed. Based on a cost per thousand impressions, it is not an expensive medium. The total bill, a combination of rate and production costs, can be paid in advance or prorated to coincide with the restaurant's regular service billing.

Signs and Billboards

Signs and billboards can be found on location, on highways or on buildings. The message should be brief, yet eye catching. Gigantic signs are now being constructed that swing and shimmer at the slightest touch of wind. Changeable copy panels make it possible to advertise daily menu changes and even provide public service messages from time to time. Generally, a contract for painted display advertising runs for one, two, or three years. The contract specifies the number of times that copy will be renewed or changed during the contract period. It is a rule of thumb in the outdoor advertising business that the message should be renewed or changed every four months. Many advertisers consider outdoor reminder advertising to be supportive rather than primary in nature. Outdoor posters must be brief with just a few bold, easy-to-read words to tell a story or theme.

Direct Mail

Direct mail marketers send mailings that include letters, glossy advertisement, samples, and foldouts to prospects on their mailing list.

Advantages.   Direct mail offers a number of advantages to the restaurateur. This form of advertising has a high degree of control as the manager decides to whom the message is to be sent. The number of pieces mailed can be tailored to the size of the budget available. It is highly audience selective in that the mailing lists are developed from customer lists or from lists obtained from mailing-list houses, which can provide lists of names broken down into a variety of specific segments. Direct mail is increasing in popularity because it permits high target-market selectivity.

It is also highly flexible, in that the message can be personalized to different market segments. There is some question as to whether or not it is cluttered. Certainly, people are unlikely to be doing anything else when they read their mail. On the other hand, so much mail is now regarded as "junk mail" that any and all nonpersonal mail stands a good chance of being thrown out unopened unless the piece is carefully designed. The ability to assess responses from a mailing by enclosing a coupon or a phone number allows easy measurement of the results of a campaign.

Disadvantages.   Direct mailings tend to have a high discard rate, high total cost, and long lead time. A rule of thumb is that a direct mailing gets a 1 to 3 percent response rate. This means that for every 100 letters sent out, the operator will receive only an average 2 percent response rate to a mailing. To get 100 customers with a response rate of 2 percent would require a mailing of 5000 pieces. The response rate can be improved by having a high-quality list and a mailing that is targeted to the needs of the potential customers being sought.

It is estimated that between 15 and 30 percent of mailing lists change each year. The cost of updating lists, in addition to the low response rate, can result in a relatively high cost to conduct a campaign. Implementing direct mail through a list house can furnish a lengthy list. If you were to send a mailing to each name, it could develop into a high-priced expenditure.

Mailing Lists.   A properly conducted campaign requires the preparation of up-to-date mailing lists, designing of the piece, processing of the bulk mailing, and responding to inquiries. This can involve a long lead time, ultimately resulting in higher costs.

Commercial lists can be purchased or rented from companies specializing in the development of such items. They can also be obtained from general lists through business directories or membership rosters of associations, or from house lists developed by the restaurant itself. The best source for a mailing list is the property's own customers. The major problem is that such a list takes time to develop. To "prime the pump" a general list tied to the zip codes within a 3- to 5-mile radius of the operation is probably the second-best alternative.

Types of Mailings.   The most appropriate options for restaurants are letters, newsletters, and menus. Letters are very simple to prepare and can be used for such things as announcements, invitations, and so on. Newsletters to regular customers can be sent monthly, bimonthly, or quarterly, to keep the property in the customer's conscious awareness. As with all direct mail, newsletters should be filled with information that is interesting and important to customers. Seasonal messages and recipes and informative tips regarding food and wine are some of the items to consider. Many people select a restaurant based on the type of menu. For them, mailing the menu itself may induce people to try the operation, particularly a new facility.

Mailing can be either first class, suitable for letters and postcards; third-class single piece, best for booklets and brochures; and third-class bulk, for newsletters or other items mailed in bulk. The latter is the least expensive, but takes longer than first class to be delivered. There are a variety of restrictions and regulations that must be met for the use of third-class mailing.

Success Factors.   To be successful a mailing piece should follow the five P's [6]. First, it should form a *picture* in the mind of the customer. We think in terms of pictures, not letters or words. Second, it must offer a *promise* and show how the promise will be fulfilled. The promise should be something that is important to the customer.

Next, the message must *prove* to the reader that what is being promised is true. "Proof" might come in the form of testimonials, success stories, or statistics. Fourth, the message should *push* the customer to action—ask for the sale. This might involve making a reservation, sending in a coupon, or showing up for dinner.

Finally, there should be a *postscript*. In reading a direct mail piece, most people first read the letterhead, then check to look at the signature and to see if there is a P.S. Interest can be generated by means of a clever postscript.

The effectiveness of a direct mail campaign is measured by the number of responses generated. As noted earlier, one of the advantages of direct mail is that the results are readily measurable against the costs involved.

PERSONAL SELLING

Personal selling consists of oral conversations, either by telephone or face to face, between salespersons and prospective customers. In a restaurant situation, personal selling occurs outside the operation as staff attempt to book business and inside as employees try to "sell up", get customers to increase the amount spent. The latter topic is dealt with in Chapter 6.

SALES PROMOTION

Incentives

Sales promotion consists of short-term incentives to encourage the purchase of a product or service. Consumer promotions may include coupons, premiums, patronage rewards, contests, sweepstakes, and games.

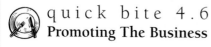

quick bite 4.6
Promoting The Business

Percentage of Table Service Operators Who Intend to Use Promotions in 1994

	Average Check Size			
	Less Than $8	$8 to $14.99	$15 to $24.99	$25+
Gift certificates	86	93	98	91
Daily specials	86	92	89	75
Seasonal specials	70	70	77	76
Free samples	49	43	42	22
Pre-event specials	25	39	32	27
Regional food fair	20	29	44	38

Source: National Restaurant Association, *Tableservice Restaurant Trends, 1994*, reported by Stephen Chapdelaine, "Nondiscount Promotions Lure Value-Hungry Customers," *Restaurants USA*, vol. 14, no. 5, May 1994, pp. 46–47.

Promotions may be open or contingent. Open offers do not require the customer to do anything other than buy the product. Special meals and discounts are examples of open offers. The advantage to the restaurant is that the promotion will have broad customer appeal since no effort to redeem a coupon, for example, is required. On the other hand, the restaurateur has no idea how many people will take advantage of the promotion. More people may show up than was anticipated, creating bad will if items being promoted are not available or high costs if they are.

A contingent offer requires the customer to do something: clip a coupon, eat out three times within a month, or make a specific purchase. The redemption rate is more easily controlled, although fewer customers will be attracted. The latter method is preferred for cost-control reasons.

Because of their short-term nature—good promotions have an expiration date—they can have the benefit of stimulating sales during the period of the promotion. Promotions cannot be used as the sole or even most important part of the marketing effort. If the business makes too much use of promotions there is a danger that customers will wait for the next promotion before they buy. This, in essence, is what has happened in the pizza business. Many, if not most, households will simply not buy pizza unless they have a coupon for a discount or two-for-one.

Coupons. Coupons are certificates that give the customer a savings when they purchase a product, as in a two-for-one meal purchase. This is the most widely used special offer, surpassing such things as restaurant specials, combination offers, or senior discounts. A 15 to 20 percent discount is needed to induce customers to buy.

Coupons offering free products are used to generate customer trial. Thus the measure of success is whether or not the customer count increased. A successful trial promotion would attempt to get customers to buy something they would not ordinarily order. For this reason, a free beverage with a sandwich is not a good idea, as most people will order a beverage anyway. It might be better in this situation to offer free onion rings.

Premiums. Premiums consist of items given away free or at reduced cost. The best and most successful premium has been glasses. The reasons? Glasses break, so households continually need them and it is easy to tie them into popular movies or sports teams. Premiums should be structured to sell higher-priced items—a larger drink, for example, and to encourage repeat visits—collecting all six glasses in the set.

Patronage Rewards. Patronage rewards are cash or other awards for regular use. Restaurants might start a VIP club and establish an awards system based on how many times customers come in or how much they spend. Punching a customer card means that the card is carried around in the customer's purse or wallet, thereby acting as an advertising reminder.

Contests, Sweepstakes, Games. Contests, sweepstakes, and games give customers the chance to win something. A contest calls for the customer to submit an entry, a jingle, a guess, or a suggestion—to be judged by a panel that will select the best entries. A sweepstake calls for names to be entered into a drawing. A game presents customers with something every time they buy that may or may not help win them a prize.

Key Steps

In setting up a promotion the objective needs to be determined, the target market selected, a strategy for implementing the promotion outlined, ways to promote the promotion identified, and evaluation methods set up.

Objective. The purpose or objective of the promotion needs to be determined up front. The objective can be thought of as the problem to be solved. Typically, promotions are used to attract new customers, keep existing customers happy, speed up slow periods, or to spotlight specials. The implementation of the promotion will differ depending on what the objective is.

Target Market. As part of the objective it is necessary to identify the market segment to whom the promotion is to be directed. As stated above, the promotion will be to either existing or potential customers. Existing customers have already tried the restaurant and know what to expect. They will require less information on the facility than will new customers, who will have to be sold on trying out the facility.

The promotions used must be compatible with the set of objectives. Slow periods can be offset by coupons, contests, packages, gift certificates, or discounts. Low check averages are best dealt with through coupons, product samples, contests, or premiums. Contests and product samples can help if existing customers are bored and want something new and different. The point is that the promotion selected will depend on the objective or problem to be solved.

Strategy. The success of a promotion will depend on how it is promoted. The concept of vertical integration is important here. Vertical integration means that the same message is given to the target market through a variety of interconnected means. For example, a Halloween-theme evening could be promoted through radio spots announcing the promotion, newspaper ads with cut-out coupons for specials, local promotions inviting kids to wear costumes, and in-house activities with posters in the restaurant and an employee costume contest. The important point is that all methods are coordinated to complement each other in promoting the event.

Promotion. Restaurants may split the cost of a promotion by hooking up with a supplier interested in moving his or her product. Similarly, cross-promotions can occur with a noncompeting business. A restaurant close to a theater may offer a discount to theater patrons upon presentation of the theater ticket.

Disclaimers and disclosures are often overlooked in putting together a promotion. The following guidelines are important [7]:

- *Product size and specifications*. Clearly identify the menu item and size being promoted.
- *Price/discount*. Highlight the price savings by stating the regular price and the promotional price.
- *Where to find the offer*. In smaller markets, identify your location; in larger markets, stating that the offer is good at participating restaurants will suffice.
- *Expiration date*. Make this date clear and easily readable.
- *What to do*. Let the customers know precisely what is expected of them: whether they must bring in the coupon, or buy two meals within a certain period of time.
- *Avoid double hits*. State that the offer is not good with any other promotional offer.
- *Limitation*. If the offer is limited to a number, state the number. It may be one per customer or one per household, for example.
- *Time and day restrictions*. Since one of the purposes of a promotion is to stimulate sales during slow periods, it may be necessary to note the times when the promotion is in effect.

Evaluation. It is important to determine whether the promotion has been effective. The true measure of a promotion is whether or not there was an increase in sales activity. This requires a comparison of sales activity—number of customers, sales in dollars, average check, and so on—before and after the promotion. If a promotion were being targeted for the month of August, the July sales figures would serve as the base. This year's August figure would have to be adjusted in light of sales trends to give an accurate picture. Suppose, for example, that sales revenue in July of this year were up 6 percent over those of the preceding year. It would be reasonable to expect that even without a promotion, sales figures for this August would be up 6 percent over sales in the preceding year. Any increase above 6 percent in this August's sales figures would then be attributed to the promotion.

A target for increased sales that will be necessary to cover the cost of a promotion can be determined if the restaurateur knows the promotional costs and his or her cost structure. As identified in preceding chapters, costs can be either fixed or variable. The variable costs—food or beverage, labor, discounts, and supplies—should be determined as a percentage of sales and totaled. This total is subtracted from 100 and the resulting percentage figure divided into the promotional cost in dollars to determine the sales necessary to cover the promotional costs.

For example, if a sandwich that normally sells for $9 costs $3.50, the food cost percentage is 39 percent. If it is being discounted by 15 percent, and extra employee costs and extra supplies are estimated at 5 and 1 percent of sales, respectively, total variable expenses for the promotion are 39 plus 15 plus 5 plus 1, or 60 percent. Subtracting this from 100 leaves 40. If the cost of the promotion is estimated at $350, the sales necessary to break even on the promotion are $350 divided by 40 percent, or $875.

Working backward, $875 in increased sales will result in $525 of extra costs ($875 multiplied by 60 percent). The remaining $350 ($875 minus $525) represents the cost of the promotion. Anything more than an increase in sales of $875 will result in increased profit; anything less will result in a loss. For example, sales of $1200 will result in $720 in costs (60 percent of $1200). When the cost of the promotion—$350—is subtracted, the resulting profit is $370.

MERCHANDISING

Merchandising consists of materials used in-house to stimulate sales. The difference between merchandising and promotions is that promotions are used to get customers in the door, whereas merchandising occurs once the customer is inside the restaurant. Merchandising includes brochures on display, signs, posters, tent cards, and other point-of-purchase promotional items.

Purpose

The purpose of merchandising is twofold: to retain a store's loyal customer base, and to increase the percentage of total business generated by these loyal customers. In the former case, this means developing ways to prevent core customers from becoming bored with the restaurant. In the latter situation it involves ways to increase the visitation and/or average check of existing customers.

Effectiveness

One of the primary merchandising tools available is the menu itself. By changing the menu periodically, or through the development of daily or holiday specials, a restaurant can continually offer something new and different to its customers.

Effective merchandising can also come from displays and samples of food. It is said that we eat with our eyes rather than our mouths. Nowhere is this as true as in the way in which desserts are sold. The presence of a dessert tray can be very effective in increasing sales. Similar displays for wine, entrees, and salads as well as table-side preparation can be equally effective.

Care must be taken that the number of tent cards and promotional materials not overwhelm the customer. The intent is to prevent boredom, not create confusion because of all the choices available.

Many operators with limited advertising/promotional budgets will learn to develop ongoing and ever-changing activities for their guests and personnel to enjoy. The element of surprise and fun can be one of a restaurant's major strong points.

New themes, catchy ideas, and fresh gimmicks require careful planning and follow-through. Meals will, as always, be the star attraction, but the presentation may need serious rehearsal and trial runs. Customers enjoy being invited to dress rehearsals. The wrinkles can be ironed out for unveiling in such a way that competition will pale in comparison.

Merchandising of Beverages

Beverages can be merchandised in a variety of ways. Easy access can be made by having portable bars in the lobby while customers are waiting for a table. Once

---

q u i c k   b i t e   4 . 7
Promoting Profits by the Glass

In recent years there has been tremendous growth in the sale of premium wines by the glass. Stephen Hade, director of purchasing for Cattlemens, a California-based steak-house chain, was doubtful of the strength of this trend until recently.

"I've been surprised at what has happened in our restaurants over the past five to six years," he says. "Our customers have shifted away from bulk wine to varietal wine. Sales of bulk wine have dropped more than 50 percent, while our varietal wines shot up from more than just a few percentage points to more than 50 percent of total sales." The market share of generic wines for this company has gone down from 75 percent of total wine sales throughout the 1980s to 43 percent in 1993 and 21 percent in the first quarter of 1994.

As part of this trend, Cattlemens is selling more Chardonnay, White Zinfandel, Cabernet Sauvignon, and Merlot for $3 to $4 a glass instead of the $1.50 glasses of Chablis and Burgundy. The result is a 5 percent increase in sales that has resulted in an increase in profits of several percentage points.

Hade serves 6-ounce glasses of wines that were purchased at $48 to $80 a case, giving him a wine cost of 35 to 40 percent. He negotiates prices based on volume, getting 25 to 30 percent discounts on his purchases of anywhere from 112 to 896 cases of wine at a time.

The result? Better quality—more sales—more profit.

Source: Nation's Restaurant News, August 1, 1994, p. 79.

Serving wine in a variety of glasses. *Source:* Cardinal International catalog, Wayne, New Jersey.

seated, the drink order should be taken and delivered right away. Some restaurants promote a happy hour with free hors d'oeuvres to attract cocktail business. The price and quality of hors d'oeuvres must be kept in mind. The price of the hors d'oeuvres must be absorbed by the price of the drink, and the quality must be indicative of the facility.

Another area to expand into is wine sales. Wine merchandising must be realistic and uncomplicated for the consumer. Many people find wine intimidating and will not order for fear of the unknown or fear of looking foolish. An awareness can be generated through wine displays, lists, and verbal reminders from wait staff. The ability of employees to sell is a major merchandising tool.

PUBLIC RELATIONS AND PUBLICITY

Public relations includes everything that a restaurant does to maintain or improve its relationship with other organizations. Publicity is the use of nonpaid communications such as press releases and press conferences [8].

Businesses have a number of different "publics": individuals and organizations with whom and with which it interacts. These range from employees and their families, unions, and owners to customers, competitors, government, hospitality schools, and the media. It is the job of public relations to represent the operation favorably to these publics.

Word of Mouth

The value of public relations is that although the organization gives up total control of the message, the resulting message is very persuasive because it is perceived as being more objective than a commercial advertisement. Word-of-mouth publicity is by far the most desirable form of advertising. It means that someone was sufficiently impressed with your establishment to discuss it with others. An endorsement by a friend is usually enough to cause a person to try a place. Potential customers are bombarded with every sort of advertising every day. Advertisers are always proclaiming how great their places, foods, quality, service, and prices are. Customers can get tired of all the exaggerated promises, especially when a few places do not measure up to what was promised. Understandably, people tend to be skeptical and often discount an advertiser's claims. In short, there is a gap between what advertisers say and what customers believe. There is, however, little or no gap when a friend recommends an eating place to another friend. The friend has no motive for profit or gain; therefore, the suggestion is appreciated and believed.

While the power of word of mouth has been demonstrated time after time, it takes too long to develop positive word of mouth into sufficient numbers of customers to ensure the financial success of the establishment. It has been argued that the role of advertising is primarily to expose people to the fact that the facility is out there but that it will take word of mouth to induce actual patronage. This is probably true of more expensive purchases such as weddings or anniversary parties but is less true for an individual or family decision to eat out.

Similarly, editorial and commentary reviews in the media are not suspect. Readers, listeners, and viewers have more trust in these reviews than in advertising messages. The idea, then, is to get the media to write or talk about a business without the suggestion that they are in it for personal profit. Newsworthy events, for example, are not considered by masses as being commercial. If it is news, it is fact.

Implementation

Implementing a program of public relations requires care. Objectives need to be set that tie into the overall market plan. Public relations activities can be continuous, preplanned short-term activities, or unpredictable, short-term activities [9].

Continuous activities. Continuous activities can include such things as:

- Being involved in the local community by donating food for local charity events
- Being involved in industry organizations, serving as an officer, and/or giving seminars
- Communicating to various publics through newsletters
- Engaging in a variety of employee relations programs, such as employee-of-the-month awards, sending birthday cards, or employee incentive programs

- Keeping in regular touch with the media by offering yourself as an industry spokesperson
- Continually updating media kits and photographs to meet editorial deadlines
- Preparing annual or periodic reports to owners
- Acting as guest lecturer at hospitality and/or local schools
- Becoming involved with government agencies in a proactive rather than a reactive way
- Develop a format for keeping in touch with customers through newsletters or other means

Preplanned Short-Term Activities. Preplanned short-term activities revolve around something of interest such as an opening, a prestigious award, or a special employee. This type of information is typically communicated through a press release—an announcement or short article written in an attempt to attract the attention of the media. If something is to be printed or viewed, it must, in the opinion of the editor or director, be of interest to readers or viewers. For press releases, this should be kept in mind. An item of "major" importance to a restaurateur may be of little or no interest to the average reader or viewer.

Press Release. A good press release should answer the questions "who, what, when, where, why, and how." Ideally, this information will be summarized in the opening paragraph. In addition to being newsworthy, the press release should be dated, list a contact person and phone number, indicate when the information can be released (usually, the indication is that the information is "for immediate release"), be typed double spaced, have an eye-catching headline, be printed on specially designated paper, be no more than two pages in length, and be factual.

As a restaurateur with many things going on, there is the opportunity to make news with virtually everything. Consider these new possibilities even before the restaurant doors are opened:

- Releases to the press on the signing of a lease or the construction of a building to house a restaurant
- Advance announcement of the number of local people who will be employed
- Notices of the grand opening
- Arrangements with public figures to appear at a fundraising opening

Press conferences can be held when there is something really important to announce to the media. The press should be given a summary in writing of the news story in addition to being given the opportunity to ask questions.

Ceremonies and openings offer yet another opportunity for a planned event. Remember, the event will probably be more important to the company than to the media. The task is to make it equally important to readers or viewers.

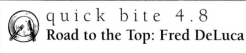
Unpredictable Events.   The third type of activity involves events that are unpredictable. These usually involve some type of activity wherein the purpose for the restaurant is to avoid negative publicity. It may be that patrons became ill after eating at the restaurant or that an employee is a suspect in a crime. The rules of thumb are:

- Tell the truth.
- Do not cover things up.
- Collect the facts and communicate these to the media.
- Take action to correct the situation.

The best measure of a public relations plan is: Did it meet its objective? When people are asked if they have frequented a particular business and reply "No, but it has a good name," the goal of public relations has been reached.

ENDNOTES

1. T.F. Chiffriller, *Successful Restaurant Operation* (Boston: CBI Publishing Company, 1982), p. 278.

2. Ronald A. Nykiel, *Marketing in the Hospitality Industry* (Boston: CBI Publishing Company, 1983), p. 240.

3. National Restaurant Association, *Tableservice Restaurant Trends, 1992* (Washington, DC: National Restaurant Association, 1992), pp. 72–86.

4. Robert D. Reid, *Hospitality Marketing Management*, 2nd ed. (New York: Van Nostrand Reinhold, 1989), pp. 284–286.

5. Ibid., p. 233.

6. James R. Abbey, *Hospitality Sales and Advertising* (East Lansing, MI: Educational Institute of the American Hotel and Motel Association, 1989), pp. 336–337.

7. Tom Feltenstein, *Foodservice Marketing for the '90s* (New York: John Wiley & Sons, 1992), pp. 101–102.

8. Alastair M. Morrison, *Hospitality and Travel Marketing* (Albany, NY: Delmar Publishers, 1989), p. 420.

9. Ibid., pp. 429–440.

chapter five

PRICING AND DESIGNING THE MENU

learning objectives

By the end of this chapter you should be able to:

1. Identify the functions of the menu.

2. Compare the three different philosophies of pricing the menu.

3. Illustrate by means of examples the various methods of menu pricing.

4. Describe the different methods of listing prices on a menu.

5. Compare and contrast the different methods for measuring the strength of a menu.

6. Give specific guidelines on the design, layout, and pricing of a menu to increase the average check while boosting the sales of specialty items.

IMPORTANCE OF THE MENU

A menu lists the various product offerings of a restaurant. However, it does much more than that. First, it is a contract with the customer, an indication that what is described on the menu is what will be delivered to the customer. At a minimum the menu should identify the name of each dish, the major ingredients, and how the dish is prepared. Second, it is an essential part of the marketing effort. As a merchandising tool the menu seeks to do certain things. Properly priced, designed, and presented, the menu can increase the average check, boosting sales of specialty items while complementing the overall atmosphere of the facility.

---

quick bite 5.1
Hot Concepts: Cozymel's

Cozymel's restaurants position themselves as "destination opportunities where the customers say, 'We don't want just a meal tonight, but we want to escape. We want to take a mini-vacation'," according to John Miller, senior vice president for Brinker International.

Music, lights, a glassed-in patio, and a festive atmosphere throughout set the mood. The waiting area features a courtyard retail area selling T-shirts, jewelry, and imported items from Mexico and Central and South America. The idea, says Phil Romano, who developed the concept for Brinker's, was to "set the theme of it as if a couple of guys came up from Mexico and they wanted to put up a restaurant and they put it together without much money. Nothing fancy. Concrete floors. Old, used lumber. The ceilings are covered with burlap and papered with billboard paper." The retail area sells everything from $1 trinkets to $200 pieces of furniture and gives customers something to do while they wait for their table.

The theme is carried out throughout the operation by using galvanized steel, which has the same properties as stainless steel but is not quite as slick looking. Background music consists of familiar pop songs from the 1960s, 1970's and 1980's that have been remixed in Spanish.

The check average is $12 and the menu features authentic country Mexican dishes, such as roast pork ($8.95), snapper grilled in a chile-ancho crust ($10.95), shrimp Aztec (served with sour cream for $10.95), and a lamb shank that is roasted for 4 hours ($11.95).

As with other Mexican-theme operations, alcohol sales are higher than at other dinner restaurants. Nine margarita machines serve different flavored drinks that are themed to the location. For example, in Arkansas the restaurant serves a Hogarita and Razorita in honor of the University of Arkansas Razorbacks.

Source: Ron Ruggles, "Cozymel's," *Nation's Restaurant News*, May 22, 1995, pp. 110, 114.

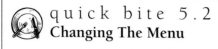

quick bite 5.2
Changing The Menu

Amid attacks on Mexican food from the Center for Science in the Public Interest (CSPI), Taco Bell introduced a new "Border Lights" menu featuring items with one-fifth fewer calories and less than half the fat of its regular menu. Michael Jacobson, executive director of CSPI, predicted that the new menu would set "a new standard for healthier fast food that should have a ripple effect throughout the industry for years to come."

The menu was also in response to Taco Bell's own research on the increasing importance of health to customers, as evidenced by the following data:

Consumers' Priorities as a Percentage of Age Group

	Age Group			
	18–24	25–34	35–44	45+
Health	17	28	32	41
Cost	18	11	8	6
Convenience	22	18	15	13
Taste	43	43	45	40

Source: Taco Bell Corp.

Source: Richard Martin, "Taco Bell's 'Lights' Menu Seeks Fix for Setbacks," *Nation's Restaurant News*, February 20, 1995, pp. 1, 65.

MENU PRICING

The pricing of items on the menu requires a knowledge of both marketing and accounting. From the marketing side, this means setting a price that will appeal to the market while being competitive; from the accounting side it involves establishing a price that will contribute to the profitability of the operation.

Pricing Philosophies

Before setting the prices of individual menu items, management should have determined what the pricing philosophy is to be. As noted above, three common approaches to pricing involve [1]:

1. Demand-oriented/perceived-value pricing
2. Competitive pricing
3. Cost-oriented pricing

Demand-Oriented/Perceived-Value Pricing

Demand-oriented or perceived-value pricing looks at the menu from the viewpoint of the customer and prices relative to what the item is worth to the customer—its perceived value. It is important to realize that it is the customer's reaction that is being sought rather than the manager's or employee's. Although an employee may consider the price charged exorbitant, a customer may perceive that the value gained is greater than the price charged.

The items being served are only part of the experience of the meal. The attention gained from having a special dessert flambéed table side may be worth much to the customer in terms of prestige, and the value thus gained can offset the price charged. This approach prices menu items on the basis of what the customer will pay.

The perceived value in the mind of the customer has to do with more things than the items on the plate. Certainly, customers might be willing to pay extra for menu items advertised as prepared daily from scratch. People expect to pay more for dinner than for lunch; for more service than for self-service; for an inviting atmosphere rather than an austere environment. A brand-name fast-food chain may be perceived as delivering more value than an independently owned operation, whereas the reverse may be true of a fine-dining establishment. A number of things can be done to increase the perceived value of the meal experience (see Chapter 4), while, as we will see later, prices can be set in such a way that they appear less than they are.

Two common approaches in demand-oriented pricing are market skimming and market penetration [2]. Conventional economics indicates that as prices rise, demand for the product falls. Total revenue is a combination of price charged and number of items purchased.

Market Skimming. In the market skimming approach to pricing operators use a relatively high price to attract or skim a small segment of the market. This philosophy works best when there is a small percentage of a large potential market who can and will pay the higher prices; where the competition is unlikely to undercut the prices set for similar product offerings, and where customers perceive that the value given in the form of the restaurant experience is greater than the prices charged.

Market Penetration. Market penetration, on the other hand, involves setting prices as low as possible while still making a contribution to profits. This approach sets out to attract as large a market as possible. Ideally, lower prices will create a loyal following, which will translate into greater sales volume and long-term profitability. This philosophy works best when demand is *price elastic*: that is, when changes in price result in a greater change in demand, and when lower prices will deter competition from invading the market.

Care must be taken when reducing prices in an attempt to increase sales revenue. An item priced at $12 and selling 120 portions produces $1440 in revenue. A reduction in price of 10 percent will bring the selling price down to $10.80. This will require that 134 portions be sold to produce a revenue of $1447.20. This is an 11.7 percent increase in the number of portions sold.In other words, a reduction in price will require a greater percentage increase in portions sold just to maintain total revenue.

Competitive Pricing

Competitive pricing establishes prices according to those set by the competition. Prices set are typically slightly below or above those of the competition. The major drawback to this pricing method is that it allows the competition to "control" the pricing of the operation. The competition may have a cost structure that is different and can afford to advertise lower prices.

It is not advisable to compete principally on the basis of price because price is a factor that can readily be met by a strong competitor. In such a situation the customer gains in the short run from the lower prices until the weaker operation, unable to sustain profits based on the prices charges, goes out of business.

However, the prices set must take the competition into account. It is unwise to offer essentially the same product as the competition but at a higher price. An increasingly value-conscious and educated consuming public will buy from the competition.

Cost-Oriented Pricing

Cost-oriented pricing is the oldest, and still the most commonly used, method of pricing in the industry. Prices are set on the basis of the costs incurred by the operation.

PRICING METHODS

A variety of quantitative or rational pricing methods are available to the restaurateur.

Factor, Cost-Multiplier, or Markup System

The factor, cost-multiplier, or markup system is very popular, due to its simplicity. In it the raw food cost is multiplied by a pricing factor or divided by the desired food cost percentage to arrive at a selling price:

$$\text{selling price} = \text{raw food cost} \times \text{factor}$$

where

$$\text{factor} = \frac{100}{\text{desired food cost}}$$

or

$$\text{selling price} = \frac{\text{raw food cost}}{\text{desired food cost percentage}}$$

The raw food cost is obtained easily enough. This is the cost to the restaurant for the items in the dish. Standardized recipes and recipe cost sheets are essential to determine the actual food cost of every item served.

The factor is obtained by dividing the desired food cost into 100. For example, if a 30 percent food cost is desired (industry averages range from 28 to 34 percent of sales), the factor to be used will be

$$\frac{100}{30} = 3.33$$

The raw food cost is then multiplied by this factor to obtain the selling price. If the raw food cost on an item is $5.25, the selling price will be

$$\$5.25 \times 3.33 = \$17.50$$

The selling price can also be obtained by dividing the raw food cost by the desired food cost *percentage*. With a raw food cost of $5.25 and a desired food cost percentage of 30 percent, the selling price is

$$\frac{\$5.25}{30\%} = \$17.50$$

This method is simple to use. However, it should be noted that it is inexact because no costs other than food costs are used. When a combination of items prepared from scratch and convenience foods are being used, a high convenience food cost may be offset by a low labor cost to produce the item. Conversely, a low food cost for an item prepared from scratch may require costly amounts of time to prepare. Consider, for example, stew as a convenience product compared to stew prepared from scratch:

	Raw Cost	Labor Cost	Total Cost	Factor	Selling Price
Convenience	$2.25	$0.75	$3.00	3.333	$7.50
Scratch	1.10	1.90	3.00	3.333	3.67

While the total cost of preparing the dish is the same ($3), the higher food cost for the convenience item means that it would be priced higher than the stew made from scratch. Additionally, it disregards the fact that customers may be willing to pay extra for the perceived value of the item.

Prime Cost

The prime cost of a menu item is defined as its raw food cost plus the labor cost involved in preparing the item. The raw food cost of a dish is added to its labor cost.

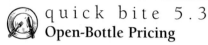

quick bite 5.3
Open-Bottle Pricing

At Romano's, a 30-unit chain owned by Brinker's International, customers serve themselves and pay based on what *they* say they've drunk. According to one manager, customers "are 80 percent truthful; 10 percent report using more wine than they actually consumed, and 10 percent want to beat the house." The house wine, a jug chianti, white or blush, is priced at $2.85 for a 10-ounce glass.

At Frontiere, a bistro in New York, the owner, Andrew Nathan, introduced an honor system in an attempt to re-create the warm European tradition of drinking the *vin du patron*. Customers find a partially open bottle on the table when they sit down. The wine sells for $17 a bottle or $4 a glass. As above, customers pay for what they drink.

Source: Mort Hochstein, "Building Sales with an Open-Bottle System," *Nation's Restaurant News*, February 21, 1994, p. 27.

The desired prime cost percentage is then divided into 100 (as above) to determine the factor. The prime cost is then multiplied by this factor to determine the desired selling price. For example, the prime cost of the beef stews above is $3. Assuming a prime cost percentage of 50 percent, the factor is

$$\frac{100}{50} = 2$$

and the selling price is

$$\$3 \times 2 = \$6$$

The cost of producing the item can be determined by means of a time-and-motion study. The actual time involved in preparing 100 portions of beef stew can be multiplied by the hourly rate of the person preparing the dish and divided by 100 to get a preparation cost per serving.

A variation breaks labor cost into unskilled, semiskilled, and skilled and assigns a dollar cost for each. A beef stew, 30 portions, might take 15 minutes of skilled time, 30 minutes of semiskilled time, and 20 minutes of unskilled time to prepare. If the pay rates for skilled, semiskilled, and unskilled labor were $12, $8, and $5, respectively, the labor cost to prepare the stew would be

$$\frac{\$12}{4} + \frac{\$8}{2} + \frac{\$5}{3} = \$8.67$$

The labor cost per portion would be 28.9 cents ($8.67 divided by 30 portions).

A second method assigns an average labor cost to each item produced by dividing the number of meals prepared by the actual production labor cost. The drawback here is that the method assumes that all items take the same amount of time to prepare. Labor-intensive items will be underpriced, and vice versa.

Third, menu items can be designated as involving low, medium, and high labor costs and a dollar value assigned to each. It might be that low-cost items are defined as those requiring less than 10 minutes to prepare, medium-cost items those taking from 11 to 20 minutes, and high-cost dishes those requiring more than 20 minutes of labor time. A unit production cost can be determined by dividing labor cost by the number of low-, medium-, and high-cost meals produced. For example, assume that during a given period when production costs were $3145, 2000 meals were produced, of which 700 were low-cost meals, 800 were medium-cost meals, and 500 were high-cost meals. If we further assume that the medium-cost meal takes twice as long and the high-cost meal takes three times as long to prepare as the low-cost meal, the unit labor cost is

$$
\begin{aligned}
700(x) + 2(800x) + 3(500x) &= \$3145 \\
700x + 1600x + 1500x &= \$3145 \\
3800x &= \$3145 \\
x &= 0.83
\end{aligned}
$$

The cost of preparing a low-cost meal would be 83 cents; for a medium-cost meal, $1.66; and for a high-cost meal, $2.49.

The major drawbacks to this pricing method are that it ignores the other costs of preparing and serving the item in addition to the profit desired by management. The assumption is that desired profits will ensue as long as the prime cost percentage is not exceeded.

Actual Pricing or All Costs Plus Profit

The actual pricing or all-costs-plus-profit method takes into account all the costs involved in running the business. In addition, the percentage of profit desired from each menu item is added before establishing a selling price.

Previously, we established a methodology for determining both raw food cost and preparation cost. Service and other costs can be divided by the number of covers served to get a cost per cover. This cost would then be added to the raw food and production costs to obtain the total costs for the dish. The desired profit percentage is subtracted from 100 and divided into the total costs to obtain the selling price.

If total costs are $9.50 and management wants a 15 percent profit,

$$
\text{selling price} = \frac{9.5}{(100 - 15)\%}
$$

$$
= \$11.18
$$

In this method all costs are accounted for, then profit is planned for and built into the price. The price of higher-cost entrees is reduced when compared to using other methods of pricing. In previous methods the factor used had to take into account both high- and low-cost items. The factor used is higher than reality for high-cost items and lower than reality for low-cost items. Thus high-cost items tend to be priced higher than they should be while low-cost items tend to be priced lower than they should be. Reducing the price of higher-cost entrees should lead to increased sales (and profits).

This method is more complicated than either of the first two, tends to increase the prices of lower-cost items (for the reverse of the reason cited above), and the determination of average cost may not be totally accurate. In addition, the desired profit percentage tends to be determined arbitrarily.

Gross Markup or Gross Profit

The gross markup or gross profit pricing method assumes that every customer should pay a specific amount to cover nonfood costs and profit. It can be used in situations where there is to be a narrow range of prices on the menu. The gross markup is determined by subtracting the cost of food sold from projected sales and dividing the result by the projected number of meals or covers.

For example, if $800,000 in annual sales is projected with a food cost of 30 percent, or $240,000, and an anticipated customer count of 120,000:

$$\text{gross markup} = \frac{\text{gross sales} - \text{cost of food sold}}{\text{forecasted customer count}}$$

$$= \frac{\$800,000 - 240,000}{120,000}$$

$$= \$4.67$$

This markup is then added to the raw food cost of each item to determine the selling price. This method is easy to use and, like the previous method, tends to reduce the price of higher-cost items. It is best used in operations that are not susceptible to changes and that have enough history to be able to accurately forecast sales, costs, and customers. Any change in any of these items makes this method inaccurate.

Base Price

The base price method identifies the desired selling price and works backward from that to determine how much can be spent for the raw food cost. Analysis of guest checks can identify the price range preferred by customers. It is necessary to know what the labor and other costs are in addition to the desired profit percentage. If the operator wants 15 percent profit and has a labor cost of 30 percent and a fixed cost per item of 20 percent, total costs will be 65 percent (15 + 30 + 20). This leaves 35 percent (100 − 65) for the raw food cost. If the customer is willing to pay $12 for a menu item, the amount that can be spent on the raw food cost for that item is $4.20 ($12 × 35 percent).

Alternatively, the selling price of the item can be multiplied by the desired food cost to identify the maximum amount that can be spent on the item. If, in the example above, a food cost of 33 percent is desired, the maximum that can be spent on food cost would be $3.96 ($12 × 33 percent). Some way would have to be found to produce the menu item for that amount. This method has the advantage of taking the customer's willingness to pay into account.

Texas Restaurant Association

The Texas Restaurant Association pricing method identifies actual costs incurred over a period of time and the sales associated with these costs, and adds the desired profit percentage to get the ideal or optimal food cost. If, over the course of a year, a restaurant has sales of $600,000, labor costs of 180,000 (30 percent of sales), other costs (excluding food costs) of $150,000 (25 percent of sales), and the owners want a 15 percent profit, the ideal food cost percentage is

$$100 − (30 + 25 + 15)\% = 30\%$$

This ideal food cost is divided into 100 to obtain a multiplier or factor, in this case 3.33. The raw food cost of the menu item is then multiplied by this factor to obtain the recommended selling price.

Recommended profit percentages will vary depending on the item. The common ranges are [3]:

Menu Category	Profit Markup Range (%)
Appetizers	20–50
Salads	10–40
Soups	100–500
Entrees	10–25
Vegetables	25–50
Beverages	10–20
Breads	10–20
á la carte	10–40
Desserts	15–35

Marginal Pricing

An operation's costs are either fixed or variable. Fixed costs do not vary as volume varies; variable costs vary proportionately with volume. After a restaurant has reached its break-even point, the fixed costs have been covered. At this

Marginal versus Average Contribution Margins

Menu engineering compares the average contribution margin to individual contribution margins and, on this basis, divides menu items into high- and low-contribution classifications. However, by using an average as the separation point, some items will always be above the mean and some below. A menu item that has either tremendously high or tremendously low sales will skew items closer to the average. Using an average means that it is impossible to have a menu where all items are performing as "stars."

Thus, it is argued, it is better to consider marginal contribution, the contribution gained from selling one more item. A menu can be evaluated based on actual total sales and total contribution margin by developing a graph where the horizontal axis is the total contribution by item and the vertical axis is the total sales by item. By drawing lines from the position of each item on the graph to the zero coordinate, slope lines can be developed. The more horizontal the slope line, the more contribution per item is being produced compared to items with a greater vertical slope. Thus, in the accompanying graph, item A is a better producer than item B. In this analysis minimum levels of acceptance are developed by management for both contribution margin and sales and items compared to these levels to determine whether or not to leave them on the menu.

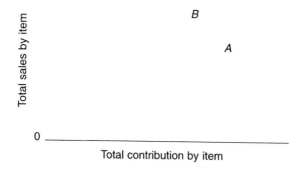

Source: Bradley Beran, "Menu Sales Mix Analysis Revisited: An Economic Approach," *Hospitality Research Journal*, vol. 18, no. 3/ vol. 19, no. 1, 1995, pp. 125–141.

point the only costs incurred by the restaurant are the variable or marginal costs, those extra costs incurred in serving another customer. Marginal pricing covers the marginal costs. Any revenue beyond this is profit. In this way, a facility, if it is sure that break-even will be reached, can offer special prices on slow nights.

Marginal pricing can be successful if it brings in business at the reduced price that would not come in at the full price. However, the operation must, at some point, account for covering fixed costs in pricing menu offerings.

Daily Pricing

When the cost of items varies from day to day (for example, fresh seafood) a menu offering may be listed as having a *market price*. This indicates that the price varies depending on the cost that day.

In Table 5.1 a comparison of menu prices using different methods, but assuming the same cost structure and desired profit level, is shown. Note that different selling prices and profit margins are obtained depending on the method used. Selection of an appropriate method should take costs, competition, and the desires of the customers into account.

Handling Price Increases

There is both a practical and a psychological side to handling an increase in prices. From the practical side, as costs increase, profits decline. Cost increase can come from such things as an increase in the minimum wage, in the cost of borrowing money, or higher wholesale prices charged for food and beverage items. Typically, an increase in costs is passed on to the customer in the form of higher prices. The key is to increase prices while maintaining customer counts such that sales volume is maintained.

Several strategies can be effective. Generally speaking, for minimum negative impact, price increases should be limited to 2 to 5 percent. Prices should also be kept stable during four to six customer visits. If an increase in the wholesale price of food is announced, the time to increase menu prices is when the announcement is made public rather than when the increase in prices is passed on to the operator. The reason for this is psychological—the public is aware of increased prices and, as such, is more likely to accept it at that time rather than later, when the memory of the price increase has vanished from their minds.

Another approach, used by the fast-food chains, is to price the items á la carte, that is, individually. The price of the hamburger seems very economical to

Table 5.1   Comparison of Menu Prices Using Various Methods

	Roast Rib of Beef Dinner		Stuffed Flounder Dinner	
	Menu Price	Profit Margin	Menu Price	Profit Margin
Factor method	$10.04	$6.53	$6.95	$4.52
Prime cost method	10.67	7.16	8.79	6.36
All-cost-plus-profit method	8.28	4.77	7.96	5.53
Gross markup method	8.16	4.65	7.08	4.65
Texas Restaurant Association method	9.86	6.35	6.83	4.40

Source: Robert D. Reid, *Foodservice and Restaurant Marketing* (Boston: CBI Publishing Company, 1983), p. 229.

the customer. Most people will add french fries and a drink. This increases the average check, but in the mind of the customer, the meal price is acceptable because the price of the main item in the meal seems reasonable.

The key in keeping sales volume up is to ensure that the perceived value received by the customer is equal to or greater than the price charged. When prices are increased, one answer is to increase the value. Perhaps additional accompaniment can be added to the entree at the time of the price increase to increase the value to the customer.

Listing Prices

Menu prices can be listed in a variety of ways [4]. The way the prices are presented should be part of the overall marketing plan for the operation. In the *one-price* or *prix fixe* method, a fixed price is set for all meals. Pricing is simplified. However, since the gross profit varies depending on the item chosen, the total gross profit may be reduced if too many higher-cost entrees are chosen. This can be avoided by having items on the menu that cost approximately the same to produce. Low-price operations offering few choices often choose this method of listing prices.

The á la carte menu was mentioned earlier. It is associated with upscale restaurants. The initial perception is that prices are low. "Sticker shock" may set

---

 quick bite 5.5
The $1 Menu

Forget about fancy ways to price the menu. Frannie Ward operates Frannie's lunchroom in Yates Center, Kansas, where full-plate meals (as of September 1993) cost $1. The average check (with pie) is $2.12. How does she do it?

1. Everything is bought in bulk and on sale. She plans the menu around what is on sale in the store.
2. No waste. If 17 of 18 hot dog buns are used on Monday, the eighteenth one is kept for dressing on Thursday.
3. Do-it-yourself labor. Her two full-time employees (both paid above minimum wage) cook, serve, and clean up. Orders are spoken rather than written and customers make their own change from the open cash register.
4. No phone. The cost of a phone would be $80 for the installation and $37.50 a month. Says Frannie: "if you want to know, then come and see."
5. No debt. The only money she ever borrowed was $5 from her granddaughter to make change on the first day. All profits go back into the business to finance improvements.

Source: Pat DiDomenico, "The Whole Shebang for a Buck," *Restaurants USA*, vol. 13, no. 8, September 1993, pp. 12–13.

---

in when the final bill is presented unless the perceived value is greater than the amount of the check. This approach appeals to customers who like to individualize their meal. It does complicate the pricing of checks for the employees. A version of the á la carte menu prices the entrees separately but includes potatoes and vegetables in the entree price.

A table d'hôte meal consists of a set number of courses at a set price. The price of the meal is determined by the price of the entree. It is assumed that all other courses cost about the same. Additional charges may be made for a special appetizer and/or dessert.

Finally, customers can be offered the choice of a platter or a complete dinner. Platters may appeal to those who wish to have a smaller meal. A modification involves serving a smaller portion of the entree at a lower price.

In selecting a method for listing menu prices, management should consider the overall impression they are seeking to give while attempting to produce satisfied customers and maximum revenue.

MEASURING MENU STRENGTH

A variety of ways exist to quantify the strength of the overall menu or of one item relative to another.

Average Check

Operators will have determined that a specific average check—total sales divided by the number of customers—is necessary to ensure a particular level of profitability. The simplest method of evaluating menu prices is to compare the average check desired with the actual average check.

This method assumes that there will be a normal distribution of customers around the average, something that rarely occurs. For this reason, the average check method is not very useful.

Range

A better method is to establish menu ranges based on price—for example, $6 to $8; $8 to $10; $10 to $12—and track the number of actual sales in each of the ranges. The result is a frequency distribution graph. This will show the range of prices that customers are willing to pay. In addition, the graph can spotlight potential problem or opportunity areas. If the graph is skewed around the low-price end of the menu, it indicates that the items offered are outside the prices that customers are able or willing to pay. On the other hand, clustering toward the high end of the menu indicates that patrons are willing to spend more.

Menu Scoring

Menu scoring combines the profitability and popularity of menu items to arrive at a consensus score. The higher the score, the better the menu. An existing menu can be scored, then compared with a proposed new menu, after sales for the new menu have been estimated. Table 5.2 illustrates a menu scoring comparison for several items on a menu. After the initial menu score of 4.42 is developed, one or two items could be substituted for items on the list and another score developed. By comparing the two scores, a determination can be made as to which menu listing is better.

Menu Engineering

Menu engineering combines the concepts of menu mix percentage and dollar contribution margin to determine the relative strength of menu items. An item with a relatively low contribution margin percentage may still deliver a healthy dollar margin.

Table 5.3 and Figure 5.1 illustrate an analysis of a menu using menu engineering. The contribution margin of each menu item is determined and compared with the contribution margin for the menu as a whole. Similarly, the popularity of each item on the menu is compared with the average popularity of the items assuming an even distribution of purchases. Various authors have said that sales are acceptable if an item achieves anywhere from 70 to 90 percent of the average item sales per entree. If, for example, there were 10 items on a menu and sales were distributed evenly, each item would account for 10 percent of sales. Thus a sales percentage of 7 to 9 percent would be acceptable. This example uses 80 percent of sales as the acceptable figure.

Table 5.2 Menu Scoring

(1)	(2)	(3)	(4)	(5) Total Sales (2) × (3)	(6) Total Food Cost (4) × (5)
Menu Item	Number Sold	Item Sales Price	Food Cost Percentages		
Chicken	65	$9.95	35	$646.75	$226.36
Beef	75	11.95	38	896.25	340.58
Turkey	90	10.25	31	922.50	285.98
Filet	55	12.95	45	712.25	320.51
Total	285			$3177.75	$1173.43

(7) Meal check average: (5) ÷ (2)   = $11.15

(8) Gross profit: (5) − (6)   = $2004.32

(9) Gross profit percentage: (8) ÷ (5)   =   63%

(10) Gross profit average per meal: (7) × (9)   = $7.02

(11) Total meals served: =   450

(12) Popularity of meals analyzed: (2) ÷ (11)   =   63%

(13) Menu score: (10) × (12) =   4.42

Source: Adapted from James Keiser, *Controlling and Analyzing Costs in Foodservice Operations,* 2nd ed. (New York: Macmillan Publishing Company, 1989), pp. 61–62.

Table 5.3 Menu Engineering

(1) Menu Item	(2) Number Sold	(3) Item Sales Price	(4) Food Cost Percentages	(5) Total Sales (2) × (3)	(6) Total Food Cost (4) × (5)
Chicken	65	$9.95	35	$646.75	$226.36
Beef	75	11.95	38	896.25	340.58
Turkey	90	10.25	31	922.50	285.98
Filet	55	12.95	45	712.25	320.51
Total	285			$3177.75	$1173.43

(7) Food cost percentage: (6) ÷ (5) =   36.93%

(8) Total contribution margin: (5) − (6) = $2004.32

(9) Average contribution margin/customer: (8) ÷ (2) = $7.03

(10) Contribution margin per menu item: $\dfrac{(5) - (6)}{(2)}$

Chicken: $\dfrac{\$646.75 - 226.36}{65}$ = $6.47

Beef: $\dfrac{\$896.25 - 340.58}{75}$ = $7.41

Turkey: $\dfrac{\$922.50 - 285.98}{90}$ = $7.07

Filet: $\dfrac{\$712.75 - 320.51}{55}$ = $7.12

(11) Average popularity:
80 percent of the average item sales per entree: 100 ÷ 4 × 80% = 20%

(12) Popularity of each menu item:
number of portions sold divided by total number of meals sold

Chicken: 65 ÷ 285 = 22.8%

Beef: 75 ÷ 285 = 26.3%

Turkey: 90 ÷ 285 = 31.6%

Filet: 55 ÷ 285 = 19.3%

Source: Adapted from James Keiser, *Controlling and Analyzing Costs in Foodservice Operations,* 2nd ed. (New York: Macmillan Publishing Company, 1989), pp. 61–62.

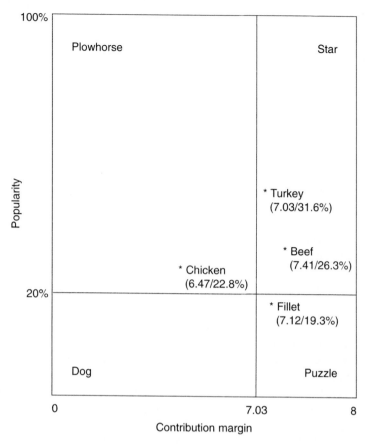

Figure 5.1 Menu engineering analysis.

The scores on both dimensions are combined and placed on a graph (Figure 5.1). Plowhorses are items that are relatively popular but have a high contribution margin. Items falling into this category can have their menu prices increased or the portion size cut in an attempt to increase the contribution margin. If the market does not resist the price increase, this action will move a plowhorse into the star category. If the market is price resistant, the items can be buried in an inconspicuous place on the menu in the knowledge that people will find these relative bargains anyway. Stars have both high popularity and high contribution margins. It may be possible to increase menu price and/or cut portion size to increase profits while maintaining volume. Puzzles have relatively low popularity and high margins. They need to be promoted more to stimulate sales. Dogs are low in popularity and contribution margin. They are prime candidates to be dropped from the menu. In the example used, chicken would be dropped from the menu, while the filet would be promoted more heavily. The prices on the beef and the turkey might be raised a little and these items featured visibly on the menu.

MENU DESIGN

The menu, to a large extent, determines what customers will order and how much they will spend [5]. A properly designed menu helps achieve the objectives of increasing the average check and promoting the sale of specialty items. This is done by presenting the product offerings of the restaurant in an attractive manner, describing them in a way that paints an attractive picture, and pricing them to give the impression of value.

Cover

The menu cover should be designed to complement the overall theme of the restaurant. Line graphics or photographs are often used to present an attractive first impression. Black-and-white photographs are easy to reproduce and less expensive than color.

The name of the restaurant is the only copy required on the cover. Additional information regarding the address, phone number, acceptance of credit cards, and so on, is best left to the inside or the back cover.

Size

The size of the menu will vary depending on the number of items being featured and the amount of copy used to describe them. Traditionally, one menu listed appetizers, soups, salads, side dishes, entrees, desserts, and beverages. A separate menu was common for breakfast, lunch, and dinner. Today, many of the rules have been broken. Separate menus can be created for children, wine, desserts, cocktails, and so on. The key is to design the menu in such a way that it is effective in communicating with the customers. For example, many think that a separate dessert menu is more effective than listing them on the entree menu. They argue that this helps create the feeling that this is another separate occasion. Customers, in selecting an entree, may notice the price of desserts, add it to the price of the entree, and decide at that point not to order dessert because of the combined cost of entree and dessert. A separate dessert menu means that the decision to order dessert is more likely to be made on the basis of desire than of cost.

When presented with the entree menu for a dessert selection, diners may cast their eyes back to an item not ordered and wish that they had taken the chicken rather than the sole. A dessert menu says "forget the entree; this is different; this is separate; let's have dessert." As has been pointed out previously, a person can still have an appetite for dessert even though the taste for the entree has been satisfied. Presenting a separate menu reinforces that thought. According to the National Restaurant Association [6], separate dessert menus are used by between 23 and 37 percent of table service restaurants to promote desserts. The favored method of promoting desserts is to have the wait staff describe the desserts to customers. More than 90 percent of operators in the $15-and-over category use employees in this way. About half of all operators have a dessert display.

Materials

The weight and quality of the paper on which the menu is printed adds to the impact. Heavier paper gives a feeling of quality. It also adds to the life of the menu. This has to be weighed against the menu price change cycle. When price changes are listed by stickers covering the previous price, the impression is not a good one. Similarly, menus that are torn or dirty give a very poor impression of the operation.

The life of the menu can be increased through the use of water-resistant paper or lamination. The latter is more appropriate for lower-priced operations. A compromise might be to have an expensive cover, which would not change, with a less expensive insert.

Placement

Menu Sequence.   There are two schools of thought regarding the placement of items on a menu. Some believe that the sequence of dishes on the menu should follow the progression of a meal. Just as a meal moves from appetizers and soups through entrees to desserts, with side orders, salads, sandwiches, and beverages interspersed, so should the layout of the menu.

Focal Points.   Others believe that use should be made of the various focal points on a menu. Customers' eyes are naturally drawn to specific points—focal points—when presented with a menu. The restaurateur should place menu items that he or she wants to push in the focal points of a menu.

The focal point varies with the type of menu. On a single-sheet menu, the eye initially focuses on the area just above the centerline. With a twofold menu the upper right part of the menu is the focal point.

On a threefold menu, the eye moves from the center to the upper right-hand corner, then to the upper left-hand corner, bottom left-hand corner, through the center to the upper right-hand corner, bottom right-hand corner, and back to the center. In all, the center is crossed three times. It makes sense to place in the center items that the restaurant wishes to push. In this regard it is not necessary to use the focal point to highlight items for which the restaurant is famous. Customers will search the menu for these items. Focal points are to be used to highlight items that the restaurateur wants to sell and that customers would not ordinarily search for.

A typical threefold menu lists appetizers in the left-hand column, entrees in the middle column, and desserts at the bottom of the right-hand column. However, the items that increase the average check are appetizers and desserts. One enterprising restaurant in Scotland features its appetizers in the center of the menu. Customers will not necessarily order an appetizer. However, they do see a listing of items that they might not generally search for.

Specials

There are various ways to draw attention to particular menu items. Specials can be listed in larger and bolder type than that used on the rest of the menu. They can also be given a longer description. The concept of closure indicates that peoples' eyes are drawn to whatever is enclosed by a box. By drawing a box around a menu description, attention is drawn to what is inside the box. In addition, color, illustration, and/or pictures can be used to draw attention to the restaurant's signature items.

Menu Descriptions

The objective in describing menu items is to present them in a way that will give customers an accurate picture of the dish, while increasing the likelihood of their sale.

Accuracy. Municipalities are becoming more vigilant about prosecuting restaurants for false statements on the menu. Typical errors deal with the grade, point of origin, size, weight, prepared form, preparation method, picture, price, or dietary or nutritional content of the product.

Government grades can and should be used accurately to describe fish. A USDA Choice piece of meat should be just that. Listing where the item came from can help sales. However, Lake Superior whitefish has to have come from Lake Superior. The precooked weight of menu offerings should be listed, as shrinkage during cooking can reduce the size and/or weight of an item. A great deal of controversy has arisen over the use of *fresh* or *frozen* on a menu. Fish that is frozen on the boat minutes after it is caught may actually taste fresher than "fresh" fish consumed two days after being caught. However, customers still seem to believe that fresh is better than frozen. The word *fresh* cannot be used to describe fish that has been frozen. A number of operations use pictures on the menu to help sell items. The dish being served should look like the one in the picture.

Many operations automatically include a 15 percent service charge on parties of six or more. If this is the case, it should be stated prominently on the menu. Additionally, it should be clear to the reader what is, and is not, included in the price of a meal. Finally, there is a great deal of confusion about the dietary and/or nutritional claims of certain dishes. A term such as *low-calorie* is too vague and should not be used. What does it mean? Low-calorie compared to what? Increased concern for health on the part of consumers is causing a number of operations to list nutritional information on the menu or, as in the case of the major fast-food chains, in prominent positions in stores. Organizations such as Healthmark certify certain menu items as being healthy choices.

Menu items can be described in such a way that customers can see them in their minds. This is important because we think in pictures, not in words.

Typeface

The typeface used must be large enough and legible enough to allow customers to read the descriptions. Type sizes are listed by point size, with 72 points to the inch. A type size of 12 or larger is recommended for menus.

The main styles used on menus are Roman, modern, and script. Most books and magazines are set in some version of a Roman typeface. Modern typefaces are newer, clean looking, and do not have the serifs or flourishes of

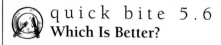

quick bite 5.6
Which Is Better?

Here are two ways of listing prices on a menu:

Auberge du Soleil (Rutherford, California) Menu Sampler

Hedgehog mushroom and asparagus soup
with marjoram cream $7

Thyme-roasted pheasant ravioli
with woodland mushrooms, lemon-maple glaze $12

Potato-crusted Chilean seabass
with caraway-Savoy cabbage, truffled beet relish $14.50

Hickory-smoked duck
with red lentil confit salad, bourbon-giblet gravy $25.50

Ginger-grilled New York strip steak
with sambal whipped potatoes,
mango-lemon grass sauce $30

Pear-walnut tart
with Maytag blue cheese cream,
Port reduction $7.50

Le Bernardin (New York) Menu Sampler
(Prix Fixe at $68)

First Course
Fish soup "Bernardin"

Lightly smoked salmon gravlax
with horseradish vinaigrette

Fricassee of mussels, clams, and oysters
in their broth, with sweet garlic
and tomato butter

Main Courses
Roast tournedoes of monkfish,
wild mushrooms, and a "jus de viande"

Crusted codfish on a bed of haricots vert,
fingerling potatoes, and diced tomato
with basil oil vinaigrette

Crispy Chinese spiced snapper with cepes,
aged port, and Jerez sherry vinegar reduction

Source: Alan Liddle, "Auberge du Soleil," and Milford Prewitt, "Le Bernardin," *Nation's Restaurant News*, Section Two, May 22, 1995.

the Roman typeface. Script imitates handwriting and should be used primarily for headings and subheadings, as it is difficult to read. Some upscale restaurants, however, use script for the entire menu, to give a handwritten look.

Typefaces can be set in uppercase or lowercase, regular or italics. It is easier to read letters that are set in regular lowercase. Italics and uppercase letters are tiring on the eyes and should be used sparingly for maximum impact.

Many feel that operators should stay away from unusual type styles, as they clutter a menu. This is an individual decision based on the image that is being portrayed.

Leading refers to the space between the lines of type. Three points of leading between lines is regarded as a minimum for a menu to ensure easier reading.

Type that is black and printed on white or light-tinted paper, such as tan, cream, ivory, or gray, is easy to read. Where colored inks are used, it is important that the shade be dark, to make it readable. Reverse type—white type on a black background—is very difficult to read and should be avoided.

Verbal Pictures

The words used to describe items on the menu should be chosen carefully to add to the sales appeal of the dish. The following questions can be used as a guide to writing compelling copy [7]:

1. What is it?
2. How is it prepared?
3. How is it served?
4. Does it have unusual taste and quality properties?
5. Where do the ingredients come from?

Menu descriptions should aim to excite the senses. People think in pictures. Consider the image given by the following:

new   moist   crisp   succulent

Certain words have been overused and have lost their effectiveness. These words do not excite the senses:

excellent   classic   special   the best

Consider the following:

BEEF TENDERLOIN

or

GOURMET SLICES OF BEEF TENDERLOIN

Generous slices of tenderloin, sauteed in butter and served with a sauce made with a delicate Madeira wine, shallots, and mushrooms.

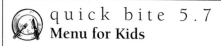

quick bite 5.7
Menu for Kids

Here are some ideas on how to design menus to appeal to children:

1. *Let kids design the menu.* At the Italian Oven, kids illustrate the menu. Inspired by *Jurassic Park*, the dinosaur concept was drawn by the 9-year-old son of the owners. The restaurant also features make-your-own pizza, pasta necklaces, and drawing on tabletops.
2. *Don't think of it as one market.* According to Banger Smith, vice president of Menu Workshops in Seattle, there are three markets: tykes (ages 1 to 7), 'tweens (ages 8 to 13), and teens (over 13).
3. *Treat them with respect.* Jim Gardner, president of Restaurant Concepts, which owns Bazooka Joe's Rock 'n' Roll Diner in Kearney, Nebraska, believes that letting kids order off their own menu says: "You kids are important to us."
4. *Give them something to do.* ZuZu Handmade Mexican Food revamped its children's menu to give the kids something to play with as well as to order from. It gives the kids something to do and helps take some pressure off the parents.
5. *Give them familiar food.* Kids like things they are familiar with. ZuZu is experimenting with a peanut-butter-and-jelly quesadilla. They found that kids don't like spicy foods. At the French Room the chef prepared macaroni and cheese by covering elbow macaroni with a creamy cheddar cheese sauce and a sprinkling of parsley. Parents loved it—kids said: "Where's the Kraft macaroni and cheese? Get that green stuff off of there."
6. *Let the kids judge.* At the Wyndham Anatole Hotel a panel of 8- to 12-year-olds decided what items should go on the menu.

Source: Melanie A. Crosby, "Menus That Speak (and Sell) to Kids," *Restaurants USA*, vol. 15, no. 5, May 1995, pp. 19–23.

The key is to praise the virtues of the dish while avoiding hyperbole; say it in words that are understandable to and that will move the customer while avoiding cutesy topical references that have a short shelf life.

Menu Pricing

In a previous section we considered menu pricing in terms of profitability. In this section we deal with pricing as a marketing tool.

Odd-Cents Pricing. The vast majority of menu prices end in either a "5" or a "9." There is psychology involved here. The real difference between $12.99 and $13.00 is one penny. However, psychologically, the former seems less expensive than the latter. The customer perceives that she or he is getting a "discount" from the higher price. This method of odd-cents pricing was actually instituted as a control method by R.H. Macy. By pricing items at $2.99, when a customer paid with three $1 bills, cashiers had to ring the item up on the cash register to give the penny change. This guaranteed that the sale was recorded.

First-Figure Dominance. A price change from 25 cents to 29 cents seems less than one from 29 cents to 33 cents. The reason is that, in the first case, the dominant first figure remains at 2, whereas in the second situation, it increased from 2 to 3.

Length of the Price. The length of the price is also important. A price increase from $9.95 to $10.25 is perceived as being more than an increase from $9.25 to $9.55. In the former case the length of the price has increased from three to four digits.

Price Rounding. Price rounding also goes on in the mind of the customer. Within certain price bands, price increases have little negative impact on customers.

Price spreads. The price spread of a menu refers to the difference in price between the least expensive and most expensive item on a menu within a specific category. Excessive price spreads encourage the sale of lower-priced menu items. In general, the highest-priced item on the menu should be no more than twice the price of the lowest-priced menu item.

People tend to buy in the middle price range of a menu. By pricing new items slightly higher than the average guest check while lowering the price of the most expensive items and raising the prices of the lower-priced items, it may be possible to increase the size of the average check.

Placement. Many customers read a menu from right to left. They look at the price first before considering the description of the dish. Consider the following:

Baked Chicken $8.99
Lemon Sole $11.99
Lamb Steak $12.99
Swordfish Steak $14.99

By using the same typeface for the prices as the menu items and listing them to the right in a straight line, attention is drawn to the price rather than to the dish. Compare that method with:

BAKED CHICKEN
Tender pieces of boneless breast of chicken served with stuffing $8.99

LEMON SOLE
Fresh filets of sole sauteed in a sweet lemon caper sauce $11.99

LAMB STEAK
Center cut of lamb steak served on a bed of rice with mint sauce $12.99

SWORDFISH STEAK
Charcoal grilled and served with a beurre blanc sauce $14.99

Packaging

One way to increase the sale of items not usually ordered is to include them with the entree and charge more for the package. If it is found that customers are not ordering appetizers, the inclusion of an appetizer with the meal can increase the average check size. Similar strategies have been adopted by restaurants to sell soup-and-sandwich combinations.

Wine Menus

There has been a turnaround in the consumption of wine in table service restaurants. After a decline in wine consumption of 8 percent between 1980 and 1987, consumption increased 17 percent between 1987 and 1991. In large part this growth has been due to increased consumption by females, especially those between 30 and 49 years of age [8].

A 1987 study by the National Restaurant Association found that for just under 60 percent of consumers, the decision to order wine with a meal is spontaneous. Over three-fourths of consumers surveyed said they like it when servers suggest a wine.

Wines can be described in a variety of formats. Some operations list suggested wines next to the entrees. If this approach is taken, two suggestions should be given for each entree: one in the low-to-moderate price range, the other in the moderate-to-high range. This gives customers a choice without the feeling that higher-priced wines are being pushed exclusively.

The most common thing for table service restaurants, however, is to have a separate wine list. A list of the more popular wines can be given to customers with a note that a more extensive list is available to the "connoisseur." This approach appeals to customer seeking to impress a companion, be it a date or a business client. A short description is appropriate, indicating the relative sweetness or dryness of the wine and the types of dishes it will complement.

It is common for restaurants to offer a house wine by the glass, half liter, or liter. This offers good value, especially to the wine novice who might be intimidated by the thought of ordering a bottle of wine.

To appeal to the discriminating diner, an increasing number of restaurants are offering better-quality wines by the glass. Improvements in storage techniques allow them to keep opened bottles of wine fresher longer. Few half bottles of wine are found on menus. It may well be that customers could be enticed to "trade up" from having a glass by effective merchandising of half bottles of wine. Adults who drink alcoholic beverages away from home are more likely to order wine by the glass over wine by the carafe.

Wine should always have a bin number listed on the menu. This prevents the guest from the embarrassment of mispronouncing the name. In the survey noted above, two-thirds of consumers indicated that they feel comfortable ordering from a wine list, although a lower 46 percent reported feeling well informed about wines. Wine glasses on the table are a subtle reminder that wine is appropriate.

A sommelier or wine steward can offer specialized knowledge to the customer while adding to the ambiance of the occasion. Care should be taken not

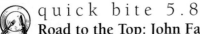

quick bite 5.8
Road to the Top: John Farquharson

Chairman, ARA Global Food Services

As Chairman of ARA Global Food Services John Farquharson is on the look-out for new contract accounts anywhere in the world. Graduating from the University of Denver in 1960, he immediately went to work as assistant food-service manager at North Central College in Napervile, Illinois. Continuing in contract catering with Slater Foodservices, he became area president for 13 midwestern states in 1971. He was next promoted to an executive position in parent company Aramark in 1978, becoming president the following year. He continued in that post until 1993, during which time he was named president of the National Restaurant Association.

John grew up in the hospitality industry, working numerous jobs at the Maine resort owned by his parents. According to colleague Harris H. "Bud" Ruzitsky: "I think what's most likable about him is his sincerity. He's humble and he cares."

Farquharson sees a number of growth fields for contract catering. He believes that the campus dining market is only 60 percent penetrated by con-tract caterers. He also predicts growth in leisure services, including expansion in ballparks, sports stadiums, and convention centers. He is less optimistic about health care and feeding in the public schools. The former is made diffi-cult because of insurance regulations and insurance, while the latter requires years of cultivation until the right mix of school board members is elected. Finally, he is bullish on the nonconventional area of supermarkets that are moving into preparing food. He says: "Some of these companies are going to need us to provide chefs and manage that service for them."

Source: Jack Hayes, "John Farquharson," *Nation's Restaurant News,* January 1995, pp. 61, 64.

to intimidate the customer with the mystique of wine: choosing the wine, feel-ing the cork, and tasting. The purpose is to sell the wine, not to impress the guest with one's wine knowledge. Whatever format is used, the wines offered should be those that appeal to the segments of the market being served.

Menu Alternatives

Restaurants can present their product offerings in a variety of ways. In keeping with the theme of the operation, some use chalkboards to announce the dishes. Items and prices can be changed with the swipe of an eraser. Menu cards placed strategically throughout is another alternative.

A hand-held menu is not practical for some segments of the industry, such as fast-food operations and institutional feeding. One such innovation won first place in 1991 in the Institutional Category of the National Restaurant

Association's Great Menu Contest. Because the menu changes four times a day at the High Plains Inn facility at Malmstrom Air Force Base in Great Falls, Montana, employees had to take out the plastic strips listing the menu items and replace them with the new choices. This turned out to be labor intensive and resulted in the strips being torn. The operation changed to an electronic menu that in addition to listing the menu items, could display graphics, messages, and digitalized photographs.

As mentioned earlier, wait staff are used when selling desserts. The use of the menu as a primary merchandising tool has eclipsed the traditional role of the employee in performing this function. It is a way for management to standardize the merchandising message—to have the menu "say" what management wants in a way that is not dependent on the ability of the server. It also means that servers do not have to have the knowledge previously expected of someone expected to recite the choices, methods of preparation, and ingredients of everything on the menu. A few operations do not present the customer with a menu but rely totally on employees to describe the items for sale. This can only be used when attempting to present an upscale image and where relatively few items are offered. Many table service restaurants use employees to describe the daily specials.

ENDNOTES

1. Robert D. Reid, *Foodservice and Restaurant Marketing* (Boston: CBI Publishing Company, 1983), pp. 207–209.

2. Ibid., pp. 204–206.

3. James Keiser, *Controlling and Analyzing Costs in Foodservice Operations*, 2nd ed. (New York: Macmillan Publishing Company, 1989), p. 56; Reid, *Foodservice and Restaurant Marketing*, p. 228.

4. Keiser, pp. 49–50.

5. Albin G. Seaberg, *Menu Design: Merchandising and Marketing*, 4th ed. (New York: Van Nostrand Reinhold, 1991), p. vii.

6. "Popularity of Desserts Remains Healthy," *Restaurants USA*, vol. 12, no. 8, September 1992, pp. 36–38.

7. Seaberg, *Menu Design*, p. 207.

8. "Wine Consumption in Tableservice Restaurants Advanced in 1991," *Restaurants USA*, vol. 12, no.6, June–July 1992, pp. 42–43.

chapter six

DELIVERING
HIGH-QUALITY SERVICE

learning objectives

By the end of this chapter you should be able to:

1. Identify the various features that make the service encounter unique.

2. Identify ways to determine service problems.

3. Specify the gaps that explain customer dissatisfaction with service and suggest ways to close these gaps.

4. Identify the various procedural and convivial dimensions of service.

5. Describe the principles of waiting.

6. Describe the duties and responsibilities of captain, server, and busperson in providing quality service.

THE SERVICE ENCOUNTER

During restaurant service there is an encounter between customers and employees. It should not simply "occur." Management is responsible for ensuring that the encounter is planned, organized, and to the extent that it can be, controlled to ensure customer satisfaction.

Enduring Insights

Hollander has noted that a review of the historical literature on service uncovers certain features of the service encounter that persist [1]. Service encounters and purchases are considered important to the customer and routine to the service provider.

---

quick bite 6.1
Hot Concepts: Maggiano's Little Italy

Lettuce Entertain You Enterprises has traditionally grown by developing totally new concept restaurants. However, in an attempt to grow faster, they have chosen to expand a few concepts. The leading candidate for national expansion is Maggiano's Little Italy.

The restaurant is designed as a mom-and-pop Italian restaurant specializing in huge portions of familiar dishes served family-style on large platters in a warm atmosphere. Says Gerard Centioli, division president: "It's the type of food that you would eat at home in my mother's kitchen."

The restaurant is entered through a European-style bakery because people like to see and smell bread baking. The seating varies from 190 seats in the original operation in Chicago to 400 seats in Oak Brook. Turnover is high, with tables on Saturdays turning an average of 3.5 times in Oak Brook and five times in the original facility. Weekday turns are slightly smaller. Banquet rooms capable of handling from 300 to 600 customers help push annual sales to between $8 and $10 million per unit. The high food and labor cost is offset by the volume of business done. The high volume can mean customer waits of two hours or more. The company only takes reservations for large parties, because, according to Richard Melman, chairman of Lettuce Entertain You Enterprises: "When you run strictly on reservations, it takes more people to run the restaurant, and you will never serve as many people. Somewhere along the line you will end up raising prices."

In selecting new sites the company is looking for places with characteristics similar to those of Chicago. According to Centioli: "Intuition is all we have ever used for site selection, but now we're also doing research on out existing restaurants to determine demographics and psychographics of our customers." The goal is to open three to four new restaurants a year.

Source: Carolyn Walkup, "Maggiano's Little Italy," *Nation's Restaurant News*, May 22, 1995, pp. 124, 126.

Courtesy Maggiano's Little Italy.

Employees serve scores of customers a day. For the customer that meal out may be a once-a-week occurrence. It is difficult for the employee to generate the same level of enthusiasm for every customer that each customer has for the occasion.

Second, many service employees resent some or all of their customers. This may be due to one of a number of factors. For some employees there is the feeling that customers do not appreciate all the work that is necessary to provide good service. Others feel lower in status because they are serving the customer and may resent their job because of it. In some cases the difficult or rude behavior of customers generates negative feelings on the part of the employee.

Third, many customers want special treatment in a service situation. Perhaps they feel the need to throw their weight around or they feel that by demanding special treatment, they are accorded more status. This places the employee in a difficult situation. They probably resent the fact that everyone pays for equally good service, while some expect to receive more what everyone else is getting.

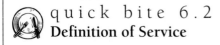

quick bite 6.2
Definition of Service

According to Bill Fisher, executive vice president of the National Restaurant Association, *service* means:

- Spirit of the employees who perform it
- Empathy in placing oneself in the shoes of the customer
- Responsiveness in taking timely and appropriate action to meet the needs of the customer
- Visibility to let customers know they are being served
- Inventiveness to do a little extra
- Competency on the part of service performers
- Enthusiasm to maximize the exchange value with the customer

Source: William P. Fisher, "S.E.R.V.I.C.E.," *Nation's Restaurant News*, vol. 15, no. 3, March 1995, p. 39.

Fourth, customers have differing needs and wants regarding service. Some prefer an unobtrusive manner of service, while others revel in a fawning, attentive style. It is up to the employee to match the level of service expected to the service delivered.

Related to customer expectations is evidence that factors such as the age, gender, and dress of the employee affect customer perceptions of whether or not the service to be provided will be satisfactory. A customer in a first-class restaurant may feel that "proper" service in such a setting would come from an older, male waiter. A younger, female waitress—no matter how skilled—may well set up negative initial reactions from the customer.

Finally, Hollander notes that many service encounters appear successful—or at least tolerable—because customers bring lowered expectations to the service encounter and employees develop coping strategies to deal with potential problems arising from the points made above.

Service Problems

What kinds of things can go wrong? A study by the National Restaurant Association indicated that in the restaurant industry, complaints about service far exceed complaints about food or atmosphere. The five items noted as being most important were providing timely service, answering customer questions, handling complaints, delivering accurately totaled checks, and recommending appropriate menu items.

A study of airline, hotel, and restaurant interactions between customers and employees by Nyquist et al. [2] indicated two major problem areas. Difficult interactions were caused when customer expectations were greater than could

Common Customer Complaints

Here are some common customer complaints cited by Pat DiDomenico, as well as suggestions on how to avoid them.

1. "Where did our waiter go?" Many servers disappear after serving the entree. Servers can avoid this mistake by checking their entire section visually every time they enter the dining room area.

2. "We've been waiting for an hour!" Some tips: Give an honest estimate of the wait time; offer video games, television sets, contests; give restaurant pagers that allow customers to leave and be paged when their table is ready; offer free wine (at night) or coffee (in the morning).

3. "Our waiter was a little *too* friendly." Limit conversations to topics dealing with the food and the restaurant; act according to the type of service the customer wants.

4. "Is this a no-smoking section?" Avoid complaints by rotating the smoking section to avoid regulars getting stuck in the same seats; use natural barriers to help control smoke; install a good ventilation system; make both sections equally appealing.

5. "Our waiter had an attitude." Says Nick Nickolas, owner of Nick's Fish Market in Chicago: "A good waiter can save a bad meal, but a good meal can't bail out a bad waiter." Attitude cannot be trained—it has to be hired. Treat your employee the way you want them to treat the customers.

6. "Tell me the specials, not the whole menu." Tell people the price of each of the specials mentioned—they may be too embarrassed to ask. Limit the specials to three. If they are so special, why aren't they on the menu?

7. "Take my plate. No, don't take my plate." In more casual restaurants servers tend to remove a plate as soon as a person is finished; in more upscale operations, servers tend to wait until everyone at the table is done. According to Judith Martin, Miss Manners, the latter is preferable.

8. "I can't even hear myself think." Reduce the noise by installing windows to let the noise out, adding plants, tablecloths, tapestries, carpeting, acoustical ceiling tiles, and a separate bar area.

9. "Where's my waiter with the check?" According to Gen LaGreca, owner of Hospitality Industry Training in Lakewood, Colorado, at breakfast, bring the check with the meal; for lunch, deliver it with the coffee and dessert; at dinner present it as the coffee and dessert is being finished. Make sure, however, that customers do not feel that they are being rushed.

Source: Pat DiDomenico, "Customer Complaints . . . and How to Avoid Them," *Restaurants USA,* vol. 13, no. 10, November 1993, pp. 20–25.

be delivered by the service system or when the performance of company or employee did not match up to the potential of the system.

In their study, difficulties regarding the former accounted for three out of every four problem encounters. Difficulties occurred for a variety of reasons:

- Demands by the customer that the industry typically does not or cannot offer
- Demands against company policies that are difficult or impossible to fulfill
- Unacceptable treatment of employees by customers
- Drunkenness of customers
- Breaking of societal norms by customers
- Customers with special needs

When performance did not match the capacity of the system, problems arose when services or products were unavailable, performance was slow, or where the service or product was unacceptable.

Assessing Customer Satisfaction

There are a number of ways in which restaurateurs can determine the extent to which customers are satisfied with the level of service they are being provided [3]. Probably the most commonly used method for collecting this information is through the use of comment cards. A card may be available on the table or it can be brought by the server at the conclusion of the meal. In either case, customers are asked to evaluate various aspects of the meal experience. The concern with comment cards is that they tend to be filled out either by people who have had a wonderful time or by those who have major complaints about the meal and/or the service. In either case those who respond are not typical of most customers. As such, this is a biased sample on which to make decisions about changing the service.

A similar comment can be made about customers who verbally complain or compliment the operation. Most people, if they have a mild complaint, will say nothing within the restaurant but will not return. Management does not hear from them and has no idea about what caused the problem. Neither will management hear about experiences that were just "OK." The meal may have been adequate, but who wants to be "adequate"? In both situations management is unaware of potential problems.

One indirect measure of customer satisfaction is the percentage of repeat customers. If it is correct to assume that customers will not return to a place they are not satisfied with, this is an indication of potential problems with the operation.

Similarly, increasing sales are an indication of satisfied customers, while decreasing sales are a sign of problems. Care must be taken to measure sales changes in real terms, discounting sales increases by any change in menu prices. In addition to looking at sales trends, management can consider changes in market share. If the size of a market decreases but a restaurant's share of that

quick bite 6.4
How to Measure Customer Satisfaction

The *service attribute matrix* compares the importance of various items to customers with their satisfaction regarding how a restaurant performs in delivering on these items. Operators can use the results in developing a marketing strategy.

Customers are given a list of attributes and asked to identify how important each is to them. Using the same list, they are asked how satisfied they are with how the restaurant delivered on these attributes. A generic list of attributes can be taken from this list of the most frequent complaints and compliments in restaurants.

Complaints
1. Availability of parking
2. Traffic congestion in establishment
3. Quality of service
4. Price of drinks, meals, and other services
5. Noise level
6. Helpful attitude of employees
7. Food quality and method of preparation
8. Spaciousness of establishment
9. Hours of operation
10. Quantity of service

Compliments
1. Quality of service
2. Food quality and method of preparation
3. Helpful attitude of employees
4. Cleanliness of establishment
5. Neatness of establishment
6. Size of portions
7. Employee appearance
8. Quantity of service
9. Responsiveness to complaints
10. Price of drinks, meals, and other services

(continued)

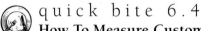
How To Measure Customer Satisfaction (*continued*)

Scores are then plotted on the service attribute matrix and fall into one of four categories:

High

Competitive vulnerability	Competitive strength

Importance

Gray zone

Relative indifference	Irrelevant superiority

Low ———————————————— High

Satisfaction

Items in the competitive vulnerability zone are those that customers consider important but where performance is not up to par. Performance on these items has to be improved. Attributes in the relative indifference area are not considered important by the customer. Neither is the performance of the restaurant. These should be ignored with a caution: If the importance of these items to the customer increases and the competition provides better quality in these areas, customers could be lost to the competition.

Items in the irrelevant superiority box are not important to the customer but the level of satisfaction is high. Unless the customer's need for these items can be increased, it is a waste of resources to provide them. Finally, attributes in the competitive strength area are those that customers consider important where the satisfaction is high. These are the items that should be marketed to potential customers.

Source: Barbara A. Almanza, William Jaffee, and Lingchun Lin, "Use of the Service Attribute Matrix to Measure Consumer Satisfaction," *Hospitality Research Journal*, vol. 15, no. 2, 1992, pp. 63–75.

market increases, sales overall may be down but the operation is more than holding its own. It is much more difficult to get a handle on the size of a particular market segment than on individual sales.

Finally, many companies use "mystery shoppers" to evaluate an operation anonymously. Since employees are unaware of the identity of the shopper, the report is a true indication of the physical and service aspects of the meal. Properly trained evaluators, oriented toward the unique aspects of a particular operation, can give very valuable feedback on potential problems.

SERVICE GAPS

Customers develop certain expectations about the service they are to receive based on such things as their own past experience, word of mouth from friends who have tried the restaurant, the advertisements of the restaurant itself, and their own needs and wants. During the restaurant visit they compare what they expected to get with what they *perceive* they got. The key word is perceive. The portion on the plate may be large. However, if the customer perceives the portion to be skimpy, it *is* skimpy. Perception, for the customer, is reality. The problem for the restaurant may to change the image or perception of the customer rather than to increase portion size. However, a problem does exist.

If the perception of the service received is less than expected, the customer is dissatisfied; if the service received is perceived to be equal to or more than expected, the customer is satisfied. One Denver restaurant— now out of business—would advertise "Warm Beer, Lousy Food." By producing low expectations that are easily met, one would think that customers would be satisfied. However, expectations have to be raised to a level high enough that customers will want to eat out. The problem then becomes how to produce service good enough that their (raised) expectations are met.

Service problems occur because [4]:

- Management does not know what is important to customers.
- Management knows what is important to customers but does not translate that knowledge into service standards.
- Service standards are in place but employees do not practice them.
- Customers are promised a level of service that is not delivered.

Lack of Knowledge

The first gap in delivering service occurs when management's perceptions about what customers expect are different from the customer's expectations. Management may not be aware of what is really important to the customer for one or more of several reasons.

Marketing Research Orientation. The best way to find out what is important to customers is to ask the customer! As obvious as this seems, many people think that they know best when it comes to satisfying customers. Research should be conducted on an ongoing basis, both formally and informally, to understand the needs, motives, and expectations of existing and potential customers.

Upward Communication. Too often, communication is primarily downward from management to employee. Managers may think that they

As the industry continues into the mature stage of the product life cycle, service becomes an effective way to differentiate one operation from another. It is expected that meeting customers' service expectations will increase in importance for foodservice operators. There is a discrepancy between what operators think they are delivering and what customers believe they are receiving in terms of service. According to *Tableservice Trends: 1991*, nine out of 10 restaurateurs believe that customers are either satisfied or very satisfied with the service they receive at restaurants. However, a 1992 customer survey found that less than 70 percent of adults surveyed reported they were satisfied with the service received. It should be noted that this percentage is up from 60 percent satisfaction two years earlier. The discrepancy may be due to the fact that many dissatisfied customers do not complain (at least in the restaurant) or that operators are unable or unwilling to believe that their customers are not satisfied.

In a survey of a chain restaurant in South Carolina it was found that customers ranked quality factors as follows:

1. Assurance
2. Reliability
3. Assurance
4. Responsiveness from servers
5. Access to servers

The difference between perceptions and expectations reflect the service gap. The largest gaps were in reliability and responsiveness; the smallest in knowing the customer.

Source: David C. Bojanic and L. Drew Rosen, "Measuring Service Quality in a Restaurant: An Application of the SERVQUAL Instrument," *Hospitality Research Journal*, vol. 18, no. 1, pp. 3–14.

should know the answers to operational problems without having to ask employees. For others it is beneath them to seek guidance from their subordinates. Yet front-of-the-house employees have much more contact with customers than does management. They are in the best position to identify which features of the operation and menu are pleasing to customers and which are turning them off. To put such a system in place requires overt action on the part of the manager. Suggestions have to be encouraged from customer-contact employees. A system put in place to reward *any* idea about improving service will produce more ideas than a system to reward only good (in the eyes of management) ideas. Good ideas have to be rewarded and implemented if management wants the flow of ideas to continue.

The success of such a system will depend, to a large extent, on how management handles bad news—feedback about service problems. If the orientation is to find out who messed up and to punish the offender, employees will be reluctant to report bad news to management. On the other hand, if the emphasis is on finding out why the mistake happened and improving procedures to ensure that it does not happen again, employees will be more willing to share with management.

Levels of Management. The further that decision makers are from the customer, the greater is the likelihood that they will be out of touch with what is important to the customer. Many companies are flattening their organizational structure, getting rid of middle management, in a dual attempt to cut costs and get closer to the customer.

Lack of Standards

Appropriate service standards may not be set if management does not believe service quality to be a strategic goal, if management thinks that customer expectations cannot be met, if service cannot be standardized, or if standards are set based on management, rather than customer, expectations.

Management commitment. As noted earlier, J. C. Penney has been credited with saying: "If you satisfy the customers but fail to get the profit, you'll soon be out of business; if you get the profit but fail to satisfy the customers, you'll soon be out of customers." The question is: Which comes first—profits or customers? Restaurants are in business to make money. Will the provision of quality service result in profitability? In *In Search of Excellence*, Peters and Waterman [5], compared the bottom-line profitability of companies that stressed financial goals—return on investment, net profit, and so on—with those that stressed nonfinancial goals—cleanliness, quality, and service, for example. They found that the companies that stressed nonfinancial goals actually produced better bottom-line results than companies that stressed financial goals. A major reason, they argued, was that employees could relate more to such things as quality and service than to return on investment and were more likely to support a program to improve these things than to get behind an effort to improve profit.

First, then, management has to set quality service as an important strategic goal. According to Zeithaml et al., there are five dimensions of service [6]:

1. *Tangibles:* appearance of physical facilities, equipment, personnel, and communication materials
2. *Reliability:* ability to perform the promised service dependably and accurately
3. *Responsiveness:* willingness to help customers and provide prompt service
4. *Assurance:* knowledge and courtesy of employees and their ability to convey trust and confidence
5. *Empathy:* caring, individualized attention provided customers

Tangibles in a restaurant setting might refer to the cleanliness of the rest rooms, the personal hygiene of employees, and the ease with which the bill can be understood. Reliability covers such things as a table being available at the time the customer was told it would be available, a steak being cooked as ordered, and the bill being free of errors. When employees correct problems immediately or when they show a willingness to answer customer questions about the menu, the company is demonstrating its responsiveness to the customer. Assurance comes from such things as employees demonstrating their knowledge and competence, being polite and friendly, and offering guarantees of satisfaction. Empathy is shown by how approachable employees are, talking to customers in language they can understand, and making an effort to understand the needs of the customer.

Surveys of customers of various service companies (which did not include the restaurant industry) indicated that of the five factors mentioned above, reliability was the most important factor, followed by responsiveness; tangibles was regarded as the least important of the five factors, although all five are regarded by customers as being critical.

Setting Service Standards

Martin suggests that service standards need to be developed in two areas: procedural and convivial [7].

Procedural Aspects. The procedural part of service consists of what is involved in getting the products and services to the customer and consists of:

- Incremental flow of service
- Timeliness
- Accommodation
- Anticipation
- Communication
- Customer feedback
- Supervision

Incremental Flow of Service. This first aspect of the procedural dimension of service is concerned with ensuring that there are no bottlenecks in any part of the restaurant. A slowdown in service can occur because one part of the service system is overloaded. An inexperienced bartender may result in drink orders arriving long after the food has been served; overloading one server with too many tables in too short a time may mean slow service for his or her customers while other servers are underworked; it might also mean that in one station, all the tables are ready for their entrees at the same time. The result of any or all of these is poor service.

Standards can be set to help ensure that a breakdown in service does not occur. Customers can be seated in alternate sections, thereby ensuring an even spread of people throughout the restaurant. Within a particular section this will help ensure that each party is at a different stage of the meal: some being seated, others having appetizers, others enjoying entrees, with some relaxing over coffee.

Timeliness. Timeliness means giving customers the service they want when they are ready for it. This involves setting standards as relative to how long a customer should wait before being greeted, before being seated, and before a food and a beverage order is taken and delivered. Notations of the time made on the order pad can serve as a way of measuring whether or not standards are being met.

Accommodation. Accommodation implies that procedures are designed around the customer rather than around the restaurant or its employees. Often a customer will have a drink in the bar before dinner. The customer is then told that the bar charge cannot be transferred onto the dinner bill. It would be easier for the customer to pay one bill at the end of the night. The reason typically given is that the bar's computer system is different from that of the dining room.

---

 quick bite 6.6
To Team or Not to Team, That Is the Question

Many people feel that server teams can improve customer satisfaction by speeding up service. Under the team concept no one server is responsible for a customer—individual servers do what has to be done, irrespective of station. Here are some arguments both for and against the concept:

Pro:

1. Teams provide constant attention to customers: "Whoever gets to the guest first handles the request."
2. Service is more consistent: "All the tables around me will receive the same level of service."
3. There is more staff enthusiasm because teams are given more authority to deal with problems.
4. Absenteeism is less disruptive to service since everyone does everything.

Con:

1. More training is needed.
2. The team concept may confuse customers.
3. Tips have to be distributed differently. The most common approach is to collect and distribute tips from only one station, even if servers move outside their individual stations.
4. Teams can lead to too much service because no one server knows what has or has not been done.

Source: Robert Liparulo, "Server Teams," *Restaurants USA*, vol. 13, no. 2, February 1993, pp. 28–31.

The obvious response from the customer's viewpoint might be: "Buy a system that is compatible and that makes it easy for the guest."

In many cases the real reason for this policy is to ensure that the bar server receives the tip for providing service in the bar. Here we have an example of a policy that is designed to accommodate the property and/or the employees rather than to serve the guest.

Another example is that of menu substitutions. Substitutions may either not be allowed or be actively discouraged because they make things more confusing for the server and cooks. The question needs to be asked: Who is most important—the customer or the employee?

An accommodating policy standard would be one that allows bar tabs to be transferred to the dining room, that allows menu substitutions, and that makes every effort to meet the needs of the customer.

Anticipation. Anticipation ensures that customers never have to ask for something—that service is provided before customers request it. Whenever customers have to ask for something, service is less than perfect. When customers arrive with little children, booster chairs should appear automatically. Servers should come by with something to keep the child occupied while the meal is being prepared. Customers should be asked about water and/or wine refills before a request is made, typically when the glass is one-fourth full. When a customer has to ask for something, the server has failed to anticipate the needs of the guest.

Communication. The provision of topnotch service requires effort on the parts of many people: servers, bussers, chefs, and management. Accurate, complete, and timely information is required between all parties to ensure customer satisfaction. Standards must be set to ensure, among other things, that servers are understood by customers, cooks can read the written orders of servers, and that customers receive exactly what they ordered.

Customer Feedback. To determine whether or not customers are satisfied with the level of service provided, it is necessary to get a reaction from them. At some point in the meal, every customer should be asked how it is and management should be made aware of any and every complaint. Often this is done in a perfunctory way. The first mouthful of food has barely been chewed when someone arrives to inquire about the food. A typical customer response is "fine" or "OK" and the employee leaves. This, is not enough if the true intent of the question is to get customer feedback.

The natural tendency when there is a minor problem is to mumble "fine," continue with the meal, and never return. Don Smith of Washington State University suggests that employees should ask "Is everything FANTASTIC?" This question would probably elicit fewer noncommittal responses. A more subtle method would be for the employee to take note of the tone of voice and body language used by the customer in responding. A person given minimal training in nonverbal communication can tell whether or not an honest response is being given.

The truth is, however, that many employees do not want to hear about problems. If something is wrong, the employee will be expected to take care of it. This will slow down service for the other tables. Worse still, the manager may find out about the problem and blame the employee. This point is explored in more detail later.

Supervision. The six elements of service noted above will not happen smoothly unless the efforts of the staff are coordinated and monitored. This is the task of the dining room supervisor.

While an increasing number of companies are "empowering" their employees to handle any problems that arise, customers appreciate seeing and hearing from a "manager type" in the dining room. It is a mark of status to have a manager rather than an employee available. Where this is important to the level of service being provided or the type of customer being catered to, it may be desirable to have a supervisor check with each table at least once during the service.

As with all of the convivial elements of service, quantifiable standards are more difficult to develop than are procedural dimensions. The key is to identify, preferably with the help of employees and customers, the visible, measurable behaviors that are examples of the various factors.

Convivial Aspects. The convivial dimension of service is made up of:

- Attitude
- Body language
- Tone of voice
- Tact
- Naming names
- Attentiveness
- Guidance
- Suggestive selling
- Problem solving

Attitude. Attitude, the first element of the convivial dimension of service, refers to the way people act, think, and/or feel and is expressed through the way they act and the things they say. A smile is a visible manifestation of a positive attitude. Thus a standard could be set that in all interactions with customers, employees should exhibit a smile before talking.

Body Language. People communicate much more through nonverbal communication than through the words that are used. Entire books have been written on the subject of body language. One point that is usually made is the desirability to maintain eye contact with the person being spoken to. This can be yet another standard of quality service.

Tone of Voice. The second most important way in which people communicate is through the inflections used in speaking. Although difficult to measure, standards can be set to ensure that servers communicate in an enthusiastic, friendly, and/or upbeat way, depending on the type of atmosphere desired by management.

Tact. Tact involves saying the correct thing at the right time. Standards can be set regarding proper etiquette for various situations. This will include the

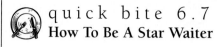

quick bite 6.7
How To Be A Star Waiter

Here are some tips on how to survive and prosper as a server:

1. Enjoy your work. Don't act subservient to a customer, but don't be a snob either.
2. Say something good about each table. Don't say "Is this all right for you?" Instead, say, "This is our best table for people-watching."
3. Be alert; be aware. Learn to "read" your customers to determine their mood.
4. Know the menu. People want suggestions—but they may be inquiring about the ingredients because they have food allergies.
5. Remember who ordered what by writing orders in sequence, left to right. Organize the tray in the kitchen the same way and double check each plate.
6. Avoid dropping items by organizing your tray. Stemware goes in the center; put plates on the tray such that the edges lie over the base of the glasses so they won't spill. Point the spout of the teapot inward.
7. Watch how fast or how slow customers eat and adjust your pace of service accordingly.
8. Check every table in your station every time you enter the dining room. Don't go back to the kitchen for just one item—check all the tables and make just one trip to get all the needed items.
9. Don't intrude. Some people don't want to be bothered.

Source: Tim Dewey, "Secrets of a Five-Star Waiter," *Restaurants USA,* vol. 12, no. 2, February 1992, pp. 33–34.

terms used to address people, how to respond to complaints and special orders, the avoidance of restaurant slang in front of customers, how to handle unruly customers, and so on.

Naming Names. We all like to think of ourselves as individuals. One way that service people can communicate individuality to customers is to call them by name. Standards can be set such that an individual is called by name when being seated by the host or hostess as well as when a credit card or check is being used to pay for the meal.

Attentiveness. Attentiveness implies that people are treated as individuals, not just numbers. It goes beyond calling people by name but means that service is adjusted to the special needs of the individual patron. Servers can be told to inquire, at the beginning of the meal, whether there are any particular restrictions on the party, such as requiring quick service to make the opening curtain of a play, or whether this is a special occasion. The latter situation is often self-evident, as when a large family group enters the restaurant with presents for the guest of honor. Management would want the server to follow up on the inquiry to make whatever adjustments were necessary to provide individualized treatment. In the former case, service would be speeded up; in the latter situation, a birthday treat might be provided on the house.

Guidance. When customers are perplexed about what to do or to order, the convivial server offers appropriate suggestions. To offer guidance, service personnel would have to be familiar with all the dishes on the menu, including the ingredients and the method of preparation and suggest items appropriate to the various perceived needs of the customers. This effort is hindered by management that refuses to allow servers to taste-test items—both food and wine—on the menu. The server, when asked what is good, is left to respond rather weakly: "Everything is" or (more truthfully) "I don't know; I haven't tasted anything."

Suggestive Selling. Some people think of selling as pushing unwanted choices on someone. The servers' job is, in part, to expose customers to items that might enhance the experience of the meal. Effective suggestive selling will result in a higher check. What should be set as a standard, however, is that servers ask all customers if they would like appetizers, drinks, desserts, and other specialty items. Further, servers should describe the benefits of these choices in ways that paint a verbal picture of them. Not everyone who is asked will buy dessert. But no one will buy if they are not invited to.

Problem solving. Finally, service providers are there to solve any problems that might arise. Rather than taking the attitude "I don't want to hear about any problems you are having with the meal," employees have an obligation to identify any problems that customers are having. This provides them with the opportunity to solve these problems and ensure a satisfied customer.

Problems will occur in any setting. The measure of excellent service is what happens after the problem is noted. Earlier we noted the desirability of identifying problems. At this point attention turns to the resolution of these problems. Standards can be set such that within the boundaries of reason and the law, every problem brought to the attention of an employee and/or management is dealt with to the satisfaction of the customer. Will this result in some customers taking advantage of the situation to get a discount or a free meal? Undoubtedly, yes. However, the cost involved will be small compared to the goodwill gained from attending to the real concerns of the restaurant patrons.

Feasibility. One reason that goals are not set is management's perception that customer expectations cannot be met. While customer expectations are seen as limitless, the resources of the company are not. Certainly, businesses have to make money. They do so by satisfying the customer. Too many managers use the idea of unlimited customer expectations as an excuse to maintain the status quo. If, in fact, satisfaction equals perception minus expectations [8], satisfaction is increased if expectations are lowered or perceptions are heightened.

The problem of attracting customers if expectations are lowered was noted earlier. It may, however, be possible to change the *perception* of the customers to increase satisfaction. Take as an example the problem of waiting. Given the fact that in a restaurant, supply is fixed in the short run and demand is variable, there will be times when there are more customers than tables available and a wait ensues. Management may take the view that nothing can be done to alleviate the situation.

Yet there are various principles of waiting that management can utilize to improve customer perceptions of service. Maister has identified eight such principles [9]. First, unoccupied time feels longer than occupied time. To reduce the *perception* of the wait, various strategies can be used. Menus can be handed out while customers are waiting for a table; the waiting area can be the bar, typically a scene of activity; and/or entertainment can be provided to occupy the time of the waiting patrons. The activity provided, according to Maister, should offer intrinsic benefit as well as being somehow related to the meal experience.

Second, the same amount of time after service has ended seems longer than that before service has begun, which, in turn, seems longer than that endured during service. In other words, a 5-minute wait after the meal has ended and customers are waiting for the bill seems longer than a 5-minute wait for a table which seems longer than a 5-minute wait between courses.

Handing out menus as soon as people arrive gives the impression that the meal service has begun. Consequently, the wait appears shorter than it really is. Even when customers are seated, it is wise to bring water, menus, or, at least, acknowledge the customers' presence to let them know that they have not been forgotten.

Air travelers flying to an international destination are typically instructed to report to the airport two to three hours before takeoff. A series of activities helps to convince them that the "flight experience" has begun. Baggage is checked; they go through passport control; they are told to report to the international departure lounge; they go to shop duty free; they report to the gate. Each activity piece divides up a large block of time while attempting to give the impression that the "flight" has begun.

Third, anxiety makes the wait seem longer. Customers worry about such things as whether or not they have been forgotten, whether others are being seated out of turn before them, or whether they will still be able to eat and make the opening curtain of a play they intend to see after the meal. The idea is to be aware of the fact that customers have worries that are both rational and irrational, to identify them, and to seek to reassure the customer. Checking with people by name and giving them progress reports on the wait indicates that they have not been forgotten; asking if they have a deadline and indicating that they will have plenty of time to make it (if, in fact, that is the case) can also alleviate tension.

Fourth, uncertain waits are longer than known waits. When a customer makes a reservation for 7:30 P.M. there is an expectation that a table will be ready at that time. The customer may arrive 30 minutes early, wait contentedly for the 30 minutes, but get very agitated at having to wait 10 minutes beyond the deadline. Yet restaurants may have parties who linger over a meal. They cannot be eased out. Some operations choose to handle this situation by refusing to take reservations. On the surface this seems fair. Yet the absence of a reservation system will be a turnoff for many, particularly if they travel a significant distance to the restaurant.

Another problem occurs when people who have made reservations do not show up but the table is kept for them even as others wait. In taking reservations, a small number of operations, ask for a credit card number and charge $10 per person against the card. The amount charged is credited to the bill for the meal. If the party does not show up, the $10 per person goes on their bill.

One thing that can be done is to let the customer know *specifically* how long the delay will be. "Your table will be ready in 10 minutes" is better than "your table will be ready in a few minutes."

Closely related to the principle noted above is the idea that unexplained waits are longer than explained waits. Not knowing why there is a delay creates a feeling of powerlessness. Customers are angry because employees do not share the reason for the delay. Respect the customer by sharing this information.

Sixth, unfair waits seem longer than equitable waits. In a restaurant situation there are two typical problem areas. The first occurs because restaurants have a limited number of tables for two, four, or more people. Customers are seated by matching the number in the party to the size of the table. From an operational viewpoint it does not make sense to seat a party of two at a table for six. Thus, even if the larger party came in later than the party of two, they would be seated before them. This seems unfair to the smaller group.

The second situation arises when a host or hostess is responsible for answering the phone in addition to seating people. Who has priority when the phone rings just as a table is about to be seated? The people who are there may resent the fact that a potential customer on the other end of the phone is receiving a higher priority than they—the actual customers—are receiving.

The point is that customers have a sense of equity that may be different from that of management. This has to be recognized and managed. In general this means matching the policy to the customer's feeling of equity or persuading the customer that the rules are fitting. In the examples given above the policy regarding seating can be explained to the customer. In the latter case the customer who is present should be given preference. This might involve having another employee who is nearby seat the customer while the host or hostess responds to the call or by putting the person phoning on hold or transferring the call while the party is seated.

The seventh principle indicates that the more valuable the service, the longer people will wait. Airlines segregate lines based on those with simple transactions—seat selection—and those who have more complex arrangements to make—ticket purchase. Supermarkets also have express checkout lines for people buying a limited number of items. In a restaurant situation a bar area may be set aside for snacks and light meals. Those wishing to spend a little can be seated immediately in the bar, while those desiring a larger meal will be willing to wait for a seat in the dining area.

Last, solo waits are longer than group waits. Although there is little that an operation can do in this regard, it is wise to note that people waiting alone will experience the wait to be longer than will those in groups, so more attention should be paid to alleviating their concerns.

Standardization.   Some argue that because service is intangible and delivered individually, it cannot be standardized. Standards can be developed for a recipe, but how, it is argued, can a smile or a tone of voice be standardized?

Service standardization can occur with the use of hard or soft technology or with a combination [10]. Pizza Hut uses hard technology to improve its service. Instead of having order taking, baking, and delivery in all its stores, order taking is centralized and computerized in a customer-service center. With a data base that shows what has been ordered in the past, an operator can take an order and verify directions to the house of the customer in an average of 17 seconds. The order is then delivered electronically to the store nearest the customer's house, from where it is baked and delivered usually in less than a half hour from the order being phoned in.

Self-service salad bars exemplify the use of soft technology. By passing some of the service tasks to the customer, management diverts some of the responsibility for service from the operation and its employees to the customer.

Customer Requirements.   The concept of a perceptual map was developed in Chapter 3. A perceptual map is drawn indicating what customers consider important when dining out and how they perceive the job the restaurant does in meeting these expectations. This approach ensures a focus on what the customers think is important rather than on what management thinks is important.

Goals should be set that are [11]:

- Designed to meet customer expectations
- Specific
- Accepted by employees
- Designed to cover the important dimensions of the job
- Measured and reviewed with appropriate feedback to the employee
- Challenging but realistic

Who should set the goals? In a customer-oriented operation, customers would be asked what they consider to be the main features of excellent service. They can then give examples of specific behaviors that employees would exhibit when giving excellent service. These behaviors can serve as the basis for setting standards for employee service.

Employee acceptance can come from involving them in setting quality service standards. Employees can also be asked to give examples of specific behaviors that would indicate, for example, that employees were displaying a positive service attitude toward customers. These behaviors, as identified by the employees themselves, become the standards by which quality service is provided.

Lack of Performance

Even when service standards have been determined, they may not be carried out by the employees whose task it is to deliver them. In fine dining establishments, service work is handled by one of four people: captain, front server, back server, or busser [12]. The positions of front and back servers are commonly combined into one job. Various operations will, in addition, combine the functions of their employees such that, for example, servers also bus tables or act as their own captains. This designation is useful, as it focuses attention on what has to be done in providing the highest level of service. Management can then tailor these functions to the level of service provided in their operations.

Busser. The busser is responsible for [13]:

- Setup of the station
- Water, coffee, and tea service
- Bread and butter service
- Clearing of soiled dishes, glassware, and flatware from tables
- Resetting of tables

Server. A server is responsible for three things [14]:

- Representing the operation to the customer
- Selling the dining experience, including food and beverage items, to the customer
- Delivering on that promise

Captain. In an upscale restaurant the captain is in charge of a serving team consisting of several servers and bussers and a specific station consisting of a number of tables. The captain is responsible for ensuring that customers receive the level of service that is proper for the establishment. Captains coordinate the efforts of servers and bussers in providing the desired service.

The captain will:

- Take the order for food and beverages
- Use suggestive selling to increase the average check
- Perform any tableside cooking necessary
- Stagger seating within the section to ensure that no server is overloaded

There are a number of potential reasons why employees will not produce the service expected by management [15]. Employees may lack the information and/or training to do the job; they may feel they cannot possibly satisfy all the demands placed on them by the variety of people they must please; the skills of the employee may be wrong for the job that he or she is in; employees may not have the tools to perform up to the standards set; the supervisory control system may reward actions inconsistent with the provision of excellent service; employees may feel that they have insufficient control over their ability to deliver service; and employees and management may not be pulling, as a team, in the same direction.

Information and Training. When employees do not know what management expects from them or how to go about satisfying management's expectations, they experience *role ambiguity*. Ambiguity is a result of the employees being given insufficient information and/or training to perform their jobs.

Employees need to know what they are supposed to do, what parts of the job to focus on, how and for what they will be rewarded, and how well or how poorly they are performing. If skills are lacking, it is management's responsibility to train employees so that they can provide the level of service expected by management.

In the restaurant business there is a heavy reliance on on-the-job training. Many think this means following an experienced server around for a few days to observe what they do. Yet on-the-job training requires as much care in the planning as do more formal training methods. The design and implementation of an on-the-job training program are described in Chapter 13.

Satisfying Demands. The job of customer-contact employees is made more difficult by the fact that they have, at minimum, two bosses: the manager, who hired and can fire them; and the customer, who they are expected to please and who probably accounts for most of the employee's pay through tips.

When employees feel they cannot satisfy all the demands placed on them by the people—management and customers—they are responsible to, they experience *role conflict*. The expectations of management and customers may be very different (but they should not be!). Customers want service; management wants a higher average check. Customers want leisurely service; management wants turnover. Customers want more service; management, in an attempt to save money, has increased server station size to a point where personal attention is reduced.

Customers themselves are very different in their needs and wants. The term *contact overload* has been coined to refer to the emotional "work" that comes from having to deal with too many customers over a prolonged period of time. The result can be emotional burnout, resulting in emotionless emotions. The problem is compounded by the fact that servers have to rely on other employees to provide excellent service. When items are held up in the kitchen or are cooked improperly, the result is a less than satisfactory experience for the customer through no fault of the employee.

Role conflict can be reduced by setting employee standards and behavior based on the expectations of customers rather than those of management. If employees know that given a conflict between what management wants and what customers want, the customer prevails, they can go about their work with less confusion. Take, for example, the customer who complains that a steak is not cooked to their satisfaction. If employees know that the customer is always right, neither server nor cook will attempt to argue with the customer. Servers will know that they can go back to the kitchen without getting an argument from the cook. Similarly, if in this situation, the server decides to make an adjustment in the customer's bill, they will know that they will be backed up by management rather than chided for "giving away something" and, thus increasing costs.

By actually involving employees in the setting of service standards, some believe that standards will be set that are higher than would have been set by management alone. In addition, employees are more committed to achieving these standards because they were involved in their setting. This point is made in Chapter 14 in a discussion of management by objectives (MBO). The basic premise behind MBO is that employees will work toward meeting objectives to which they are committed. The way to get that commitment is to involve employees in the setting of objectives.

Employee–Job Fit. The basic skills used in any restaurant service are [16]:

- Loading and carrying a tray with food and/or beverages
- Loading and carrying a bus box or tray with soiled wares
- Handling serviceware
- Clearing a table during service

In more upscale settings, restaurant personnel will also be called upon to perform Russian or French service and to reset a table during service. Russian service, as noted previously, consists of using a spoon and fork to serve from a platter, while in French service, a serving spoon and fork are used to serve a plate from a gueridon. Resetting a table during service includes changing the tablecloth with minimum disturbance.

In addition to the technical skills of service, dealing with the public requires certain skills not needed for employees in back-of-the-house positions [17]. Successful service providers possess interpersonal skills, demonstrate behavioral flexibility and adaptability, and show empathy.

Education in college programs and training on the job tend to focus more on providing technical skills than interpersonal skills. Yet successful service depends more on the latter than the former. Such skills can either be "bought" by hiring people who possess these skills or developed through training.

Servers who are successful are able to adapt their behavior to that of the guest and respond accordingly. So-called "flexible-focus" employees can be found through their scores on the Central Life Interest Measure [18]. Adaptable people would be low in dogmatism, high in tolerance for ambiguity, and/or high on self-monitoring. Simulations, assessment center techniques, and situational interviews are ways to determine the existence of all of these.

Finally, employees should demonstrate empathy—a temporary merging—with customers. Employees can demonstrate empathy through such techniques as repeating back to customers what they have heard and giving feedback that indicates an understanding of customer concerns.

Minor and Cichy suggest a number of open-ended questions suitable for identifying servers with service potential [19].

Question	Intent
How do you feel about working here?	How does the applicant feel about the company?
What is the most important responsibility of a server? Why?	What is the person's attitude about the job?
Who has more responsibility: a server or a cook?	Does the applicant appreciate the cook's job?

Question	Intent
What are the most important qualifications of a server?	Does the applicant understand the responsibilities of the job?
Are servers usually fair to each other?	Can the applicant get along with people?
What would you do if a guest made insulting remarks to you?	Is the applicant easily upset?
Suppose the manager insists that you do a job a certain way when you know there is a better way to do it: What would you do?	What is the applicant's attitude toward authority? Toward supervisors? Is this person stubborn?
What do you think about servers who change jobs often?	Is this person a job hopper?
What is more important: courteous service or prompt service?	What is the applicant's attitude toward both?
What would you do if your tips were falling off?	Can you admit mistakes?

Personal hygiene for service people is also critical. This involves the following [20]:

- A daily bath or shower
- Daily use of an effective deodorant or antiperspirant
- Clean hair restrained above the shoulders
- Clear or natural nailpolish
- Clean fingernails
- One ring per hand
- Avoiding ornate jewelry and excessive cologne or perfume
- No gum chewing
- Moderate use of natural-looking makeup
- Clean uniform and well-polished shoes

Jobs that require customer contact tend to be rather low paying. This severely limits management in attracting highly skilled employees. Companies argue that because of low margins, they are unable to pay wages high enough to attract high-caliber employees. The result is that companies have to compromise in their hiring. For the customer that often means less than desirable service.

Companies are beginning to learn that they get, in employees, what they pay for. There is anecdotal evidence that paying premium wages will result in employees with better skills and lower turnover and absenteeism. Whether or not the bottom line improves is a matter open to debate.

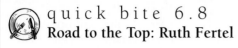

quick bite 6.8
Road to the Top: Ruth Fertel

Chairman, Ruth's Chris Steak House, Inc.

In 1965, Ruth Fertel mortgaged her home to help raise the $18,000 needed to buy a restaurant. At the time she was a divorced mother of two teenagers and looking for an investment that would return more than her lab technician wages. Ignoring the advice of both family and her lawyer, she bought Chris Matulich's steak house in New Orleans. She admits, "The first years were long hours, especially the first few months when I was learning everything, even the butchering, which I did for five years."

The 45-unit company now has annual sales of $130 million on average checks of just over $40. Nineteen of the units are franchised, although there are no plans to allow any new franchises into the company.

Ruth's motivation came from her parents. She says: "We came from a very conservative family. My dad was an overachiever, an insurance salesman . . . I guess I got my honesty from both my mother and dad; they were the most honest people I've ever known. They instilled that in me." Being a single mother and running a business was difficult. "A lot of women say they can handle both career and family; well, I think they are full of baloney. Something has to give. . . . But you have to do what you have to do and I had to make a living." Ruth also gives back to the community. According to Ralph Giardina, vice chairman of the board, "she's done an awful lot to help those in need in a quiet fashion, without a lot of publicity."

Source: Ron Ruggles, "Ruth Fertel," *Nation's Restaurant News,* January 1995, pp. 69, 72.

Technology–Job Fit.   Similarly, employees need the tools necessary to perform their jobs. Advances in technology have enabled servers to send customer orders to the kitchen by means of hand-held computers. As a result, servers are able to stay on the floor attending to customer needs and make fewer trips to the kitchen.

Supervisory Control.   If companies wish to improve service, they need to set up a supervisory system that rewards employees who exhibit behaviors that are regarded as providing quality service. Employees are expected to engage in suggestive selling, describing a dish in such as way that the likelihood of the customer ordering that dish increases. An employee may engage in suggestive selling, painting a verbal picture of that dish while accurately describing its contents.

Suppose the customer is full and does not order the dish. Should the employee be rewarded? In many operations employees are rewarded solely on the basis of results, such as the number of desserts sold. Yet this employee has engaged in high-quality service behaviors. The employee who sells the dessert may have used tactics to get the order that leave the customer unhappy.

To be successful, employee recognition programs must set challenging standards, be accepted by employees, have the right number of rewards, and be

Courtesy Ruth's Chris Steak House.

long-lasting [21]. British Airways has identified for its middle managers 60 statements of behavior necessary for providing good-quality service. Their bonuses—worth 20 percent of their base pay—are determined half by their achievements and half by the behaviors used to get results.

Employee Control.   Employees experience less stress in their jobs when they feel that they have control over situations that occur in their work. Customer satisfaction with the service depends on the efforts of several people: the host or hostess who receives the reservation and has a table ready at the appointed time, the busser who has set the table in the proper manner, the cook who prepares the order, and the server who delivers it. Yet if there is a problem, it is the server who is the recipient of the complaint. Giving the server—or, for that matter, any employee—the authority to resolve the complaint is an example of *employee empowerment*. Employee empowerment entails pushing authority down to the lowest level possible. Instead of getting a manager to hear a complaint and to make a decision on how it should be resolved, the employee who gets the complaint owns that complaint and is responsible for solving it to the satisfaction of the customer. The result is a faster response to complaints and motivated employees who feel that *they* can control the delivery of high-quality service.

Teamwork.   In the restaurant business there are a number of traditional rivalries: management and employees; kitchen staff and wait staff as a whole; dishwasher and busser as a specific. Quality service requires that everyone work together for the goal of good-quality service. Cooks may feel that their job is done when they cook the food even if the timing means that it is ready either before or after the customer is ready for it. Problems of timing? That is the concern of the server. Or consider the dining room that never seems to have enough silverware. Servers take to stashing a supply to take care of their individual stations.

The result of such practices is that employees feel they are working against one another instead of being united in a common goal. Management's task is to provide the climate for this unity to happen. Tom Peters has said that if employees are not serving the customer, they had better be serving someone who is. This type of attitude ensures that everyone realizes the importance of working together to serve the customer.

Promising Too Much

It was noted earlier that customer expectations have to be raised to a level high enough to motivate people to leave home for the restaurant. It is more difficult to sell a meal than a part for a car because if the part does not work, it can be returned and replaced. This is not true of a restaurant meal, which is consumed before the customer can determine whether or not it is all right.

This means that expectations have to be raised even higher for an intangible product such as food plus service than for a tangible good. This can lead to a tendency to promise too much in an attempt to get customers in the door. When customers come in with unrealistic expectations, employees may not be able to deliver, no matter how well they perform.

A second problem arises because of a lack of communication between those who sell the experience and those who are expected to deliver it. Employees who cook and serve the food must be involved in marketing decisions to provide a reality check on those who plan the advertising.

By the same token, employees should see what customers are being told in advertisements for the restaurant in order that they know what customers are being promised—promises they will be expected to deliver on.

Planned Attack

Where is the manager to begin? Closing all four gaps may require time, money, and effort. If all four gaps exist, management would be wise to begin with the fourth gap noted above, the tendency to promise too much.

It may not be possible to improve service immediately. In such a situation, the one thing that management can influence is customer expectations. It may, initially, be necessary to lower customer expectations to a level closer to the service provided. Care must be taken to ensure that the lowered expectations are high enough to induce patronage.

The other three gaps must be closed in order. Customer expectations have to be identified before standards can be set; appropriate standards must be set before they can be implemented.

ENDNOTES

1. Stanley C. Hollander, "A Historical Perspective on the Service Encounter," in John A. Czepiel, Michael R. Solomon, and Carol F. Surprenant (Eds.), *The Service Encounter: Managing Employee/Customer Interaction in Service Businesses* (Lexington, MA: DC Heath and Company, 1985), pp. 48–53.

2. Jody D. Nyquist, Mary J. Bitner, and Bernard H. Booms, "Identifying Communication Difficulties in the Service Encounter: A Critical Incident Approach," in Czepiel et al., *The Service Encounter*, pp. 113–123.

3. Robert Reid, *Foodservice and Restaurant Marketing* (Boston: CBI Publishing Company, 1983), pp. 129–130.

4. Valarie A. Zeithaml, A. Parasuraman, and Leonard L. Berry, *Delivering Quality Service: Balancing Customer Perceptions and Expectations* (New York: Free Press, 1990), pp. 36–45.

5. Peters and Waterman, *In Search of Excellence*.

6. Zeithaml et al., *Delivering Quality Service*, pp. 21–22, 26.

7. William B. Martin, *Quality Service: The Restaurant Manager's Bible* (Ithaca, NY: Cornell University Press, 1986), pp. 79–81.

8. David H. Maister, "The Psychology of Waiting Lines," in Czepiel et al., *The Service Encounter*, p. 114.

9. Ibid., pp. 113–123.

10. Zeithaml et al., *Delivering Quality Service*, pp. 80–82.

11. Ibid., pp. 84–86.

12. Bruce H. Axler and Carol A. Litrides, *Food and Beverage Service* (New York: John Wiley & Sons, 1990), p. xiii.

13. Ibid., p. 1.

14. Ibid., p. 59.

15. David H. Maister, "The Psychology of Waiting Lines," in Czepiel et al., *The Service Encounter*, pp. 89–113.

16. Axler and Litrides, *Food and Beverage Service*, p. xv.

17. David E. Bowen and Benjamin Schneider, "Boundary-Spanning-Role Employees and the Service Encounter: Some Guidelines for Management and Research," in Czepiel et al., *The Service Encounter*, pp. 137–139.

18. Ibid., pp. 144–147.

19. Lewis J. Minor and Ronald Cichy, *Foodservice Systems Management* (Westport, CT: AVI Publishing Company, 1984), p. 148.

20. Ibid., p. 150.

21. Zeithaml et al., *Delivering Quality Service*, p. 103.

chapter seven

THE PHYSICAL FACILITY

By the end of this chapter you should be able to:

1. Identify the various elements of the immediate package and the external environment.

2. Show how elements of the immediate package can affect the psychological needs and behavior of customers.

3. Give examples of the ways that the size and shape of the room, seating arrangements, light, and color combine to influence customers.

4. Suggest procedures to improve existing layouts.

5. Develop more productive procedures for completing individual jobs.

FRONT OF THE HOUSE: LAYOUT

The size of an operation will vary depending on the type of service to be provided and the extent of menu offerings: The more extensive the menu, the larger the operation tends to be. In the estimates given below, the higher-range figures refer to facilities with more extensive menus and that allow for more room. It is estimated that the total facility size for various types of foodservice facilities is as follows [1]:

Type of Operation	Total Area per Seat (square feet)	Dining Space per Seat[a] (square feet)
Table service	24–32	12–18
Counter service	18–24	16–20
Booth service	20–28	12–16
Cafeteria service	22–30	12–16
Banquet service		10–12

[a]*Includes space for tables, chairs, aisles, and service stations but excludes waiting areas and rest rooms.*

The amount of space required for the dining area depends on the number of people to seated at any one time and the square feet of space per seat. The former is, in turn, a function of the total number of people to be served within a given period of time and the turnover. Turnover is a measure of how many times a seat will be occupied during a given meal period and is usually expressed on a per hour basis. It is, in essence, the average time a seat will be occupied during a particular time or meal period. If, for example, people stay an average of 30 minutes during lunch, the turnover is two times per hour. Turnover rates will vary depending on the time of day and the type of meal service. A dinner crowd will stay longer than a group of lunch people on a schedule. While turnover for the former might range from 1/2 to 1 (indicating an average stay of between 2 and 1 hours), regular table service tends to have an average turnover of 1 to 2-1/2. Cafeterias average higher turnover, anywhere from 1-1/2 to 2-1/2 for commercial cafeterias to 2 to 3 for industrial or school cafeterias.

Where a high turnover is desired, the concept can be built into the design by [2]:

- Using items that do not take long to prepare
- Using preprocessed items
- Using a high level of lighting and light colors in the serving area
- Arranging the tables close to each other
- Designing chairs that become uncomfortable after a short period of time
- Having enough employees to provide prompt service

The square feet per table is a function of the type of seating to be provided—the relative proportion of tables to booths to counters to banquettes—the

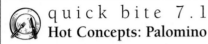

quick bite 7.1
Hot Concepts: Palomino

The first Palomino bistro opened in 1989 in Seattle as a result of developers willing to forward "up to $2 million in cash." The concept differentiates itself by using wood-fired cooking. Despite the difficulties involved—timing is crucial and can lead to undercooked or dried-out food and shortages during busy times—the company is wedded to the concept. Says Don Adams, Palomino director of food and beverage, "There's a lot of romance to cooking with wood."

The parent company, Restaurants Unlimited, plans one to two new units a year. Because of higher-than-average ventilation costs (needed because of the wood fires), construction costs range from $2.5 to $3.5 million for a 10,000-square foot restaurant that seats 300 people. Imported wood, marble, and arty light fixtures also contribute to the cost.

Regular mailings to 1200 preferred customers and an additional 2800 repeat users help bring core customers back an average of 10 times a year. Annual sales volume is about $5.4 million per unit. The average check ranges from $12 to $14 at lunch and $26 at dinner. Diners feast on such items as small pasta corkscrews with seared tuna, spit-roasted salmon stuffed with herbed polenta, and wood-oven roasted mussels served with a rosemary-lemon sauce.

Beverage sales are about 30 percent of total sales and are driven by moderately priced wines and microbrews. Food costs are in the high 20s, with labor close to 30 percent, both as a percentage of sales.

Source: Alan Liddle, "Palomino," *Nation's Restaurant News,* May 22, 1995, pp. 128, 130.

table sizes and shapes that are preferred, how the table will be arranged, the aisle space desired, and the number of serving stations required.

FRONT OF THE HOUSE: ATMOSPHERE

Atmosphere is the general mood or tone set by the restaurant. While excellent food and beverage items are crucial to the success of any operation, the surrounding atmosphere can significantly add to or detract from the diner's enjoyment of the experience of the meal. Research studies have consistently identified the top four reasons influencing a decision to return to a restaurant as:

- Quality of food
- Service
- Price
- Atmosphere

While food and beverage items are the basic product of a restaurant, they are "surrounded" by an immediate package that includes the table arrangements,

Courtesy Palomino Euro Bistro.

furniture, and the provision of entertainment. This, in turn, is presented within an environment made up of the space, seating arrangements, lighting level, and the colors used. All elements have to come together to form a complete picture.

There is a difference between eating and dining. When customers go out to eat, their principal concern is the food and beverage items served, and their principal need is physiological. On the other hand, when people go out to dine, they want a complete meal experience and their needs are both physical and psychological. It is up to the atmosphere to cater to the psychological needs of the customer. This can be done in a variety of ways, by appealing to the guest through sight, touch, hearing, smell, temperature, and movement [3]. How people perceive and are affected by these elements make up, in their minds, the atmosphere of the restaurant.

It is also important that the elements that make up the atmosphere be designed in accordance with each other and bearing in mind that there will be customers present. The story is told of the modern Dutch painter, Mondrian, who was asked to design a stage set. Upon the completion of his work, he is reported to have said, "The actors must read their lines from the wings: other-

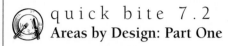

Front-of-the-house restaurant interiors are divided into four areas: the entry area, the dining area, the beverage area, and the rest rooms. The function of the entryway is to invite people in and to protect those inside from the elements outside. In a fast-food operation customers are divided into queues in the entry area. One way this can be done is by a single line where one person takes the order and handles the cash while another assembles it. This system can save time because of the specialization of tasks and responsibilities. Additionally, less counter space and cash registers are needed than in the other system of queuing, where a number of separate lines lead to separate cash registers. The advantage of the latter system is that customers entering the operation see lines that are smaller and think that they will get served faster.

In table service restaurants the entry area serves as a small area that pass people through to the dining area. A coatroom may be provided in addition to a host and cashier station. More expensive restaurants have a maître d' station where patrons check in before entering the dining area. In this type of operation the entry area is more important, setting the tone for the dining experience. Typically, these stations do not handle the cashiering function.

In table-side restaurants highlighting the bar, where the accent is on an evening's entertainment rather than the food, the entry area merges with the bar and dining areas to create what Baraban and Durocher call a "see-and-be-seen atmosphere."

Source: Regina S. Baraban and Joseph F. Durocher, *Successful Restaurant Design* (New York: Van Nostrand Reinhold, 1989).

wise, they will spoil the set." An appropriately designed interior must be include the presence of the customer as part of the final package.

Several elements of the immediate package are explored here: table arrangements, furniture, and entertainment.

Table Arrangements

The table top has been described as the center of the selling action—the silent sales promoter. The first impression for customers is visual and the first thing they see is the table setting. It is important to coordinate table settings to the mood of the restaurant: formal or informal; expensive or economical. The table arrangement should be an attractive blend of dinnerware, glassware, flatware, linens, and accessories.

Dinnerware. Many operators stick with simpler dinnerware patterns in order that they not detract from the food. There are four basic shapes for china: rolled edge, narrow rim, coupe, and scalloped edge. It is difficult to set specific rules for choosing china because of the variety of available colors and patterns.

However, it is important that the china chosen fit the mood of the restaurant. For example, the narrow rim or coupe is preferable for a contemporary setting. Similarly, a formal atmosphere deserves softer, more delicate shades and a lighter weight than a family-style restaurant. On the other hand, heavier plates give customers the impression that they are getting a lot of food. This is the same rationale that bars have when they serve beer in heavy-bottomed beer mugs.

The average piece of restaurant china is used approximately 7000 times and lasts about three years if handled properly. Operators should expect to replace 25 percent of their china every year due to breakage. In this regard, stock patterns of commercially made designs can be least expensive.

It is important to consider the total effect of the food item and the plate. Overfilled plates look cluttered and are messy; sparsely filled plates give an impression of poor value. Perceptually, the size of the item compared to the size of the plate can make the item appear to be a better or worse value. Consider

 quick bite 7.3
Areas by Design: Part Two

In table-side restaurants, beverage areas tend to be screened from the dining area. They can be places for drinking, a service bar for the dining room, or a spot for patrons to wait for their table. Operations may choose to serve appetizers or full meals in the bar. Of particular interest to the single diner, this option means that a table for four in the dining area may be freed up for a larger party instead of being occupied by one or two people.

The beverage area can be used to introduce people to the menu, thereby speeding up turnover in the dining area, or as a way of merchandising specialties of the house through displays of food in the area. In gathering places the bar tends to dominate the scene and is integrated into the dining area.

In most rest rooms the concern of the customer is for efficiency and cleanliness and for the operator, ease of maintenance. Although traditionally given little attention compared to other front-of-the-house elements, rest rooms are important. Dirty rest rooms can equate to a dirty kitchen in the mind of the customer. Design elements in the dining area can be carried over to the rest rooms through the use of color and background music. In too many places the effect of soft lighting and background music is ruined through the use of harsh fluorescent lighting in the rest rooms.

According to the National Restaurant Association, women spend an average of 8 to 10 minutes on a trip to the rest room, compared to an average of 4 minutes for men. While men use bathrooms for utilitarian reasons, women see it as a place for sprucing up their appearance and talking with others. In gathering places, this is particularly true. More room, a makeup table or cosmetics shelf, and a full-length mirror are needed.

Source: Regina S. Baraban and Joseph F. Durocher, *Successful Restaurant Design* (New York: Van Nostrand Reinhold, 1989).

Figure 7.1. In reality, both inner circles are of the same size. However, the inner circle on the right *appears* to be larger because it is surrounded by a smaller setting. Similarly, the same food item placed on a smaller plate will appear to be larger. A strip steak placed on an oval-shaped plate with mashed potatoes piped the length of the steak will tend to accentuate the length of the steak.

Specialty dishes for specialty items add value to the item. For example, soups can be served in small crockpots, fish on a fish-shaped platter, and desserts in a variety of differently shaped glasses.

Restaurants that cater to families with small children—for example, fast-food operations—will clear the table of most items, preferring to achieve the desired atmosphere through other means.

Glassware.   Glassware is typically lime, or plain glass, and lead, or crystal glass. In selecting glassware two things should be considered: design and color. Design encompasses such things as heavy or light, simple or ornate, stemmed or unstemmed. Rustic or family operations might call for a heavier weight or heavy-bottomed glass; fine dining establishments would select a finer, lightweight stemmed glass. Unusually shaped glasses are ways to add interest to the table. However, the more different types of glasses are used, the greater will be the storage space needed.

Wine glasses can suggest that this is the type of facility where wine with the meal is appropriate. Favorite colors for glass in restaurants are red, green, gold, and smoke blue. They can help give a totally coordinated look to the table.

Flatware.   In selecting flatware—knives, forks and spoons—the basic decision comes down to a choice of silver plate or stainless steel. The latter is less expensive, although fine-dining establishments may feel that silver plate is more in keeping with the atmosphere provided. In this case, consideration will have to be given to periodic burnishing or polishing. This can be done by machine, in a soaking bin, or by hand, but it must be planned for in the warewashing area.

Today's stainless pieces can be delicately embossed and carved to give the look and feel of silverplate. The important consideration is to select the best-quality flatware consistent with the type of restaurant. Some experts suggest that a stainless steel mix with 18 percent chrome and 8 percent nickel give excellent resistance to corrosion while giving off maximum luster.

Linen.   Linens add to the feeling of quality within an operation. They come in a variety of colors that can be chosen to blend with the mood of the operation. Special attention should be given to flame retardancy, resistance to stains, color-fastness, and texture. Linen, polyester, cotton, or cotton–polyester blended nap-

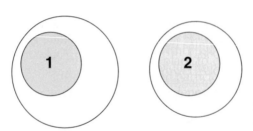

Figure 7.1   Effects of food on different-size plates.

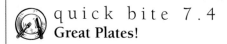

quick bite 7.4
Great Plates!

Here is how to promote healthy dishes:

1. *Keep it simple.* Use high-quality ingredients, cook the dish properly, and keep it simple. The less you mess with the food, the better. Chef Lynne Aronson of Lola in New York likes seared red snapper and scallops layered with braised leeks, topped with a roasted-red-pepper rouille and tomato-horseradish broth.
2. *Select the right foods.* Use foods that are usually eaten together—a peanut and celery pasta salad. Imagine what a dish would taste like if everything on the plate were eaten in one bite. Use seasonal items.
3. *Consider shape.* Don't have everything on the plate the same size.
4. *Consider color.* Select vegetables based, in part, on the effect on the eye.
5. *Consider texture.* Put crunchy vegetables together with smooth purees. Whip vinaigrettes to give a creamy consistency.
6. *Consider height.* Put the highest item in the center of the plate and build around it.
7. *Fill up the plate.* Fill small-portion plates with low-fat vegetables, beans, and grains.
8. *Keep healthy foods hot.* Since slicing meat causes it to dry out faster, slice the meat at an angle and fan it out. But cut only a few slices, leaving the customer to cut the rest. Put the denser item—usually the starch—in the center, as it does a better job of retaining heat. Bunch items close together for the same reason.
9. *Use only edible garnishes.* Garnish with the herb used in the cooking.

Source: Diane Welland, "Making a Healthy Plate Look Great," *Restaurants USA*, vol. 13, no. 7, August 1993, pp. 20–23.

kins all feel different. Operators have to determine what feels right for their facility. Resistance to stains is important because of the constant wear and tear inflicted on napkins. Linked to this is the colorfastness of the napery. If linens start out deep red and, after a few washings, the color fades, the combination of deep-red new napkins and faded-red older napkins will create a negative impression.

The cost of laundering can be greatly reduced by having a full table covering that remains during the meal period and a smaller piece overlaying this that can be changed after each party on an as needed basis. Inexpensive or family restaurants prefer no table covering, utilizing placemats for a touch of color.

The use of warm and inviting colors for place settings in institutions can take the edge off the sterile dining environment. A cloth or doily lining on a tray can also create a warm feeling.

In cafeteria dining it is possible to use Formica tops, such as imitation marble patterns, which tend not to show stains.

Accessories. Many restaurants insist on covering the table with a variety of table tents advertising special menu items. Operators need to consider carefully whether or not these items produce increased sales or a cluttered image in the minds of the guest. Most texts advise against having too many table decorations. According to them, a flower vase, a candle or lamp, and an ashtray (if the table is in a smoking section) are the only "decorations" that should be on the table. On the other hand, a small bowl of nuts on the table can be a useful way of getting people to order drinks before a meal.

In addition, small touches to the table can add to the mood of the meal. Bringing a hot loaf of bread on a cutting board to the table accomplishes several things: It allows guests to participate in the meal; it keeps them busy during waits before the meal or between courses; and by allowing them to cut slices as thin or as thick as they wish, it gives some degree of freedom over part of the meal. At the same time, the smell of hot bread can act as a stimulant to the appetite.

Furniture

The selection and placement of chairs, tables, and banquettes has a physical and a psychological dimension. The physical dimension involves having enough room to be comfortable; the psychological dimension involves the feeling the furniture gives the customer.

Chairs. Chair or banquette seats of breathable vinyl are practical, durable, and allow for easy maintenance. Placing fabric on the inside and outside back where there is less wear adds an attractive touch. Fabrics can be treated with either vinyl or acrylic coatings to make them more soil resistant and to last longer.

Particular attention should be paid to firm construction in the legs and backs of chairs, as these factors influence how comfortable it feels to customers. Some restaurants specialize in the "15-minute chair"—so named because after 15 minutes it becomes uncomfortable and the customer is "reminded" that it is time to go. The idea for this chair came from Henning Larsen, who built it after consultation with Copenhagen cafe owners distressed that their customers loitered too long over their coffee. Conrad Hilton noticed that in the lobby of the Waldorf-Astoria, the comfortable divans were utilized every day by the same people. Although well-dressed and well-mannered, they were not spending money in the hotel. His solution was to move the comfortable divans into the nearest food and drink area of the hotel.

Chairs with arms make it easier to rise from the table. People can get up from a sitting position by pushing upward and outward until the body's center of gravity is moved forward to a position over the feet. This takes the strain off the leg muscles.

Traditional seating will appeal to a discerning clientele. Business travelers, who may walk on hard floors or pavements all day, will appreciate big plush chairs; hard plastic chairs and Formica tables will move people in and out very quickly.

Chairs should be selected in combination with the tables chosen. It is important, for example, that, if armchairs are purchased, the arms fit under the tabletop. Although more comfortable, armchairs take up more space.

Tables. The most important characteristic of a table is that it should be sturdy. Tops should be a minimum of 1 inch thick. Most tables are made of flakeboard with a topping of a material such as Formica. While durable and practical, it tends to look "cheap" if left uncovered. If linens are not to be used, the only alternative is a solid wood top.

The shape of the table is also important. Round tables, because they offer more opportunity for eye contact with others around the table, promote more communication. This tends to slow down turnover but increases the check average. Rectangular tables do the opposite.

Many people prefer booths as seating. A booth will offer a feeling of privacy, something that may be important for sensitive business meetings or romantic meals. By extending the back of each booth to come behind the customer's head, the guest, when seated, cannot see into the other booths. A feeling of privacy is created.

Entertainment

Provision of the right kind of entertainment can influence customer enjoyment and customer behavior. In a dining situation the entertainment should complement the overall atmosphere in the operation. In some types of facilities the entertainment may be a major reason why people come in.

Cost. The cost of providing entertainment must be justifiable from a profit standpoint. The objective behind the provision of entertainment is that the cost involved will result in greater profits for the operation. This can come about in one of four ways. Customers who would not come in except for the entertainment can be drawn into the lounge and/or the restaurant; customers stay longer; they eat and/or drink more; or they come back again.

The cost of entertainment must produce a revenue increase greater than that cost. Consider the following example:

Before entertainment:

150 customers buy, on average, three drinks at $1.75 each.

Revenue produced each night =	$ 787.50
	× 6 nights
	4725.00
Subtract cost of goods sold (assume 25%)	1181.25
	3543.75
Subtract payroll and related expenses	350.00
Gross operating profit	$3193.75

After entertainment:

182 customers buy, on average, three drinks at $1.75 each.

Revenue produced each night =	$ 955.50
	× 6 nights
	5733.00
Subtract cost of goods sold (assume 25%)	1433.25
	4299.75
Subtract payroll and related expenses	350.00
Subtract cost of entertainment	750.00
Gross operating profit	$3199.75

Note that approximately $1000 in additional revenue must be generated in order to pay for the $750 in entertainment costs. This can be done by attracting more customers (as above), charging higher drink prices during the entertainment, charging a cover charge to offset the entertainment cost, realizing an increase in beverage revenue because people stay longer and/or drink more, or having an increase in restaurant food sales because of increased business in the lounge.

Programmed Music. In lounge settings offering dancing, proper programming of the entertainment can encourage and control alcohol consumption by alternately encouraging patrons to the dance floor and sending them back to their seats for a thirst-quenching drink.

Programmed music with a disk jockey can cost 50 to 60 percent of the cost of providing live music and, depending on the skill of the disk jockey, can be easier to program relative to the needs of customers. This involves playing a type of music in the first set that will appeal to a majority of the crowd. The second set would have music appropriate to the next largest audience, followed by a set of music that would have limited appeal. This may satisfy a small number of customers, while sending the majority back to their seats for rest and refreshment. A fourth set of slow music provides a contrast to the faster earlier sets. The format should be adjusted to changing demographics as the programmer notices what music keeps people on the floor and what sends them back to the bar. In nightclubs, where customers are more homogeneous, the same kind of music tends to be played most of the night.

Effect on behavior. The provision of background music has been shown to affect customer behavior in restaurants. In one experiment [4] the effects of slow-tempo background music (72 or fewer beats per minute) were contrasted with fast-tempo background music (92 or more beats per minute). It was found that:

- Customers eating with slow-tempo background music took longer to finish their meals than did customers eating with fast-tempo background music—56 compared with 45 minutes.
- When fast-tempo music was being played, the waiting time per group was reduced from the 47 minutes usual when slow-tempo music was played to 34 minutes as a result of the diners eating faster.
- The tempo of the music had no impact on the decision to wait for a table.
- The tempo of the background music did not significantly affect the speed with which customers and orders were handled by employees. (The increased time came from the time it took the customers to eat rather than the time it took them to be served.)
- While the tempo of the background music had no impact on food sales, it did affect bar sales. Slow-tempo music increased bar sales. (This has been verified in studies that show increased drinking in bars featuring slow country music.) Because the gross margin (the difference between selling price and food or beverage cost) is greater for drinks than for food, this had the effect of significantly increasing gross margins for the restaurant.

Space

Early concepts of layout have given way to a field of study known as environmental psychology which looks at the influence of the physical environment on people's behavior. Four concepts are of particular importance: privacy, personal space, territoriality, and overcrowding [5].

Privacy. The more people are afforded privacy, the more control they feel over their behavior. Little is known of the effects of privacy on such things as turnover, conversation levels, and so on.

Personal Space. There are four zones within the concept of personal space. Intimate distance extends 18 inches around a person. If others enter this space, people back off to establish a more comfortable distance between themselves and others. Personal distance goes from 18 inches to about 4 feet and allows an exchange of conversation. Social distance extends from 4 to 12 feet, while public space involves anything beyond that. The amount of personal space and personal distance that people feel comfortable with varies by culture. The British have a larger comfort zone than that of Americans, who in turn, feel more comfortable farther apart than the space preferred by Latin Americans.

Forcing people together, as in a nightclub, induces conversation between them. On the other hand, a wide table introduces a more formal space between parties and indicates more formal behavior is appropriate.

Territoriality. Territoriality refers to the need to control a defined space. When space is restricted, people move objects to define boundaries. In British restaurants it is common for two parties of two to be seated at a four-top (a table set for four people). This would not be tolerated in American restaurants, where "having one's own territory" means not sharing a table with others. More work needs to be done to identify how much space people need compared to how much is provided.

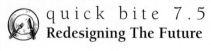

quick bite 7.5
Redesigning The Future

In an attempt to increase both customers and sales, family restaurants are updating their appearances. The goal, according to Perkins' Donna Guido, is to "make sure our restaurants remain comfortable enough at breakfast but are upscale enough to provide a nice dinner experience." Here's what they are doing:

1. At Denny's, gabled entrances and new signage outside lead to new interiors—"southwestern: bleached oak with blue and red highlights; contemporary: oak with splashes of blue, green, and mesa red; or traditional: mahogany wood grain with green and brick colors."
2. Perkins' dining area features four separate dining rooms clustered around a central kitchen. The design is more efficient and allows flexibility in decisions about expanding. Display bakery cases have been added to all stores.
3. International House of Pancakes (IHOP) is able more easily to seat different-sized groups since replacing booths with tables.
4. Country Kitchen has designed a pub module to allow the option of selling alcohol in an attempt to look more like a dinner house while taking "away veto power from the public in deciding not to go there."

Source: Carolyn Walkup, "Redesigning the Road to Success," *Nation's Restaurant News,* September 12, 1994, pp. 65, 68.

Crowding.   Crowding refers to the feeling of being one of a large number of people in a small space. The perception of crowds, whether real or not, may influence a person's decision to leave one restaurant for another.

The space allocated to diners may range from 8 square feet in a cocktail lounge or bistro to 18 square feet in an upscale establishment.

Lighting

The cost of lighting ranges from a low of 10 percent of total energy consumption for a fine dining restaurant to 25 percent of the total for a fast-food operation.

Lighting serves four basic purposes. It helps set the mood of a restaurant; it should make both the food and the customers look good; it has to be bright enough to allow employees to complete their work; and in places, it helps provide for the safety and security for the guests.

Five factors must be considered in selecting the type of lighting in a restaurant: time, size, contrast, brightness, and sound [6].

Time.   The lighting level should be selected in accordance with the amount of time a customer has to enjoy a meal. Low lighting levels mean that customers have to take longer to read the menu. It also encourages them to

Courtesy Vicorp Restaurants, Inc.

linger over the meal. High levels of lighting help provide an atmosphere that encourages people to leave. Low lighting permits greater intimacy between couples, thereby increasing seating capacity.

Size. As with colors, careful selection of lighting systems can affect people's perceptions of the physical facility. A low ceiling, brightly lit, will appear higher; high ceilings, dimly lit, will look lower; a narrow room will appear narrower if the long walls are lit. Bright lights will give an impression of speed, thereby increasing turnover. Similarly, trash cans in white or bright colors will appear lighter weight than those in dark colors.

Contrast. Contrast is the perceived difference between the detail of an object and its background. Use can be made of direct, indirect, or spotlighting. Direct lighting is stronger, indirect lighting is softer, and spotlighting can be used to focus attention on particular features or objects.

An important consideration is the reflective difference level of the task at hand and the surrounding area. Strange as it may sound, a brightly lit area against dimly lit surroundings make the former more difficult to see. For example, a cash register keyboard can be made easier for the cashier to read by increasing the lighting of the immediate surrounding area to a point where there is only a 10 percent difference between the reflective level of the cash register—reflecting back 50 to 60 percent of the light—and the immediate surrounding area—reflecting back 40 to 50 percent of the light. In short, the correct levels of lighting can improve employee productivity and reduce errors.

Brightness. Of the two types of lighting systems—incandescent lights and mercury vapor lights—mercury vapor or fluorescent lights produce up to

4-1/2 times the light and have 9 to 10 times the life of standard incandescent lamps but have lower aesthetic appeal. Incandescent lights, on the other hand, enhance reds and are easier to control; they can be turned down with a dimmer.

Because fluorescent lights pick up most of the color spectrum, blues and greens dominate reds and oranges, causing skin to look pasty and food to look gray. In addition, food looks best and more natural under this system of lighting. Green fluorescent light makes roast beef appear greenish gray, a red pear becomes purple, shrimp cocktail is grayish pink, and coffee becomes muddy green.

Candlelight, with its reddish flame, gives off a light that is flattering to both food and people. Additionally, it gives a romantic feeling of intimacy.

To be as kind to the customer as possible, lights should be placed at or slightly below eye level. Having high-angle lighting produces glare while enhancing shadows and wrinkles on the face. This effect can be reduced by having light-colored tablecloths which reflect light onto the unlighted portion of people's faces.

In bars there seems to be a connection between lighting, noise level, and duration of stay. As the lighting level increases, so does the noise level, and both reduce the amount of time customers stay. The lighting levels in bars should be 20 to 30 percent brighter than in the dining area.

In discotheques, lighting and sound are combined to give a total effect. In the early days of discotheque clubs—the 1960s—the sound budget was often 90 percent of the budget. Because people are more visually oriented, today's budgets tend to be closer to 80 to 90 percent on lighting and 10 to 20 percent on sound. The dance floor will take up 50 to 60 percent of the total lighting budget, depending on how important it is in attracting customers.

In selecting the appropriate type of lighting there is an order that should be maintained: The light must be selected before the bulb and the bulb must be chosen before the fixture. One way to prolong the life of the bulb is to stipulate higher-wattage lamps than required for the space, and keep them dimmed by using lower-wattage bulbs. For example, operators might request 150-watt lamps from the designer for a particular location, but use only 75-watt bulbs. The bulbs will last much longer. This is particularly important if the location of the lamp makes it difficult to replace the bulb. The ease with which bulbs can be replaced is yet another factor that must be considered.

Color

Colors are classified as either primary, secondary, or intermediary. The primary colors—so called because other colors are obtained from them—are red, yellow, and blue.

Secondary colors are made by mixing two of the primary colors. Green is made by mixing blue and yellow; orange from red and yellow; violet from blue and red. Intermediary colors are a combination of a primary and a secondary color—such as red-violet and yellow-orange. The color wheel is shown in Figure 7.2.

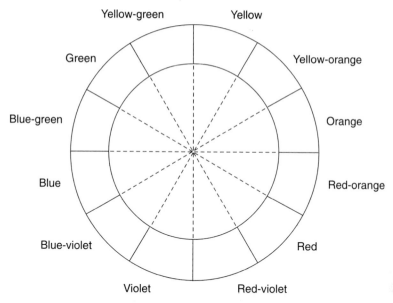

Figure 7.2   Color wheel.

Colors are referred to as either warm or cool. The warm colors, so-called because they give off a feeling of warmth, are red, yellow, and orange. The cool colors, which are relaxing and cooling, are blue, green, and violet.

Harmony.   Colors should be selected that are harmonious together. Five harmonic principles are useful in the selection of colors: monochromatic, analogous, complementary, spilt complementary, and triad.

Monochromatic harmony involves the use of a single color as either the pure color itself, as a tint (that is, mixed with white) of the pure color, as a shade (mixed with black) of the pure color, or as a tone (mixed with both black and white) of the pure color.

Analogous harmony comes from the use of any three or four consecutive colors on the color wheel. Blue-violet, blue, and blue-green would be an example of analogous harmony.

Complementary harmony is obtained by using any two colors directly opposite each other on the color wheel. Blue-violet and yellow-orange or red-violet and yellow-green are examples of this.

Split or near complementarity comes from the use of three colors. One of the two complementary colors is used in combination with the two colors adjacent to the other complementary color. For example, blue and orange are complementary colors. A split complementary would be blue, yellow-orange, and red-orange; or orange, blue-green, and blue-violet.

Triad complementarity involves the use of three colors. Every fourth color on the color wheel is selected.

Once the colors are selected, a decision must be made as to the tint, shade, or tone to be used. As noted above, a color is tinted when white is added to it; a shade comes from the addition of black; and a tone comes from adding both white and black to the color.

Contrast.   One of the most important elements in dealing with color is the idea of contrast. One color cannot operate alone. The guidelines for dealing with contrast are [7]:

- Use a light form (pink) with a darker form (red) of the same color.
- Use a weak version (pale blue) with a stronger version (royal blue) of the same color.
- Use a warm color (red) with a cool color (blue).
- Use complementary colors, such as peach and gray-blue.

Contrasts in colors can have a safety effect by making obstructions and exits stand out.

Effects.   We can now turn to the overall effect of color on the room, the food, and the customers. Colors should be selected under the type of lighting in which they will be used, as they will look different under fluorescent lighting then under incandescent lighting. Care should be taken in selecting a color from a small sample, as it will appear brighter in a larger area than on the small sample.

Colors can give a feeling of spaciousness or of intimacy. Light colors make a small room look larger, while dark colors make high ceilings appear lower. In general, dark colors will make objects appear smaller; light colors make them appear larger. Similarly, the use of dark colors to emphasize horizontal lines will make the ceiling appear lower, while using dark colors to emphasize vertical lines will make the ceiling appear higher. The ceiling can also be "lowered" by carrying a wall color over to the ceiling.

Long, narrow rooms can be made to feel squarer by using colors on the end walls that are warmer or deeper than those on the other walls.

Another factor to consider is the location of the restaurant. It has been found, for example, that, in the northern states, people will stay longer if warm colors—reds, oranges, yellows—are used, while in the warmer south, greens and blues encourage longer stays.

The location of different rooms in the facility must also be taken into account. Rooms with a northern or eastern exposure will tend to be cool in the afternoon. Muted warm colors will offer a counterbalance. Rooms with a southern exposure will already be pleasantly warm and can benefit from the coolness of green, blue, and turquoise. The natural light in rooms with a western exposure will be tinted by the sun and, in the evening, the sunset. Earth tones—brown, tan, yellow, burnt orange, and copper—will complement the natural light.

Food looks better under warm colors such as red, brown, yellow, gold, and orange. People like food in the red-yellow spectrum: roast beef, brown rolls, french fries, red apples, strawberries, cherries, oranges, and so on. Yellow-greens, apart from the green of salads, peas, broccoli, and spinach, are not highly regarded. Blue, purple, and pink have much less appetite appeal.

Another important consideration is not only how the food looks but how the customers look. Greens and grays tend to make people look pale and is most unflattering. The combined effect of color and light is important. Green lights tend to show up wrinkles, while pink lighting pales lipstick colors, and amber lights wash out colors.

Some researchers argue that colors affect a person's mood, while others feel that the intensity is the key. Red is perceived as exciting, intense, and stimulating; orange is jovial, exhilarating, and energetic; yellow is cheerful, inspiring, and boosts morale; green is quieting, refreshing, and peaceful; blue is subduing and melancholic; purple is gracious, elegant, and dignified; brown relaxes; white is pure and clean; black is depressing and ominous.

There is some research to indicate that older people have more trouble distinguishing between blues and greens than among the warmer reds and oranges. In general, they prefer brighter primary, secondary, or tertiary colors to pale pastels.

High turnover can be encouraged by having bold colors and high intensity lighting. The closer to the primary colors of yellow, blue and green, the bolder the effect. Fast food operations, in their early development, utilized bright yellows and reds for this reason.

BACK OF THE HOUSE: SPACE REQUIREMENTS

The following rules of thumb regarding the amount of production space for various foodservice facilities should be taken as general guides only. These recommendations should be adapted to the special needs of particular projects.

The amount of production or back-of-the-house space required will vary depending on the type of service. Table service restaurants will require 8 to 12 square feet per seat; counter service, 4 to 6 square feet; booth service, 6 to 10 square feet; and cafeteria service, 8 to 12 square feet [8].

Once the amount of space required has been determined, the amount for each of the functional areas must be calculated. The top-down method allocates certain percentages of the total space to each of the functional areas. One suggestion is as follows [9]:

Functional Area	Space Allocation (percent)
Receiving	5
Food storage	20
Preparation	14
Cooking	8
Baking	10
Warewashing	5
Traffic aisles	16
Trash storage	5
Employee facilities	15
Miscellaneous	2

Making the Most of Space Available

Here are some tips on how to make the most of available kitchen space:

1. Design the kitchen according to the menu. The Top O' The Cove restaurant, a 95-seat dining room and 90-seat cafe in La Jolla, California, has a menu that features sauteed items. To make the most of the 925 square feet available, designers got rid of the "traditional" stock pots and back burners found in most kitchens. Says owner Ron Zappardino, "You can't saute on a back burner." When Rhys Lewis, executive chef at the American Club in Kohler, Wisconsin, changed the menu at Cucina to serve lesser-priced pastas and gourmet pizzas, he realized that "pasta makes the kitchen a little faster. There is less time between courses." He concentrated on selecting equipment that saved time and labor. A dough cutter was purchased to reduce the preparation time of the pizzas, while the pizza oven is also used to prepare the sandwiches on the lunch menu. The $15,000 cost of redoing the kitchen was saved in the first four months through increased sales and lower labor costs.

2. Design the kitchen according to the shape of the kitchen. The Riveranda is a cruise ship equipped with a 700-square foot kitchen used to serve four-course dinners to 275 passengers. Two of the bulkhead walls taper in toward each other. Designer Tony Mazurkiewicz built shelves into the bulkhead, thereby freeing up floor space. Refrigerators were custom built to the shape of the ship's hull. Tony believes the kitchen uses 95 percent of the usable space available.

3. Involve the designer early in the project. Many operators take an available space, squeeze the maximum number of seats into the space, and what is left over is the kitchen. Mazurkiewicz suggests showing a kitchen consultant several locations and getting designer input on what would work best. He charges from $5000 to $15,000 to design a kitchen.

4. Watch storage space. Storage needs can be reduced by using ingredients in more than one menu item and by buying dishes prepared elsewhere. Centro Ristorante serves 500 to 600 dinners a night in a kitchen that is 8 by 10 feet. Instead of spending 40 minutes cooking whole chickens, they feature boneless breasts that are sauteed in minutes. Design storage shelves to be just 14-1/2 inches tall, the space needed for a size 10 can. Clear plastic containers allow cooks to see what is inside without leaving the can open.

5. Design for the most frequent motions. Says Sam Abrahms, "The standard cook's aisle is 42 inches because designers are thinking about the people passing by . . . but people cross over only a few times a day. The cook has to turn around in that space much more often." The narrower aisle lets cooks reach without moving their feet.

Source: Cheryl Ursin, "Making the Most of a Cramped Kitchen," *Restaurants USA*, vol. 13, no. 6, June–July 1993, pp. 18–21.

BACK OF THE HOUSE: WORKPLACE DESIGN

A bottom-up approach to determining space requirements involves designing individual workplaces and assembling them into functional areas.

The workplace is where people perform their jobs. The amount of space made available at each workstation and the way it is laid out can aid or hinder employee productivity.

Systematic Approach

A systematic approach to workplace design begins with an analysis of the menu. Each item on the menu should be identified, together with the portion size, the estimated total number of portions per meal period, the materials, utensils, or hand tools and process required to prepare the item, together with the type of work surface needed [10]. A similar process will determine the area needed for other nonfood functions.

Work Aisle Space. Work aisle space is the term used for the floor space needed by an employee to perform a task. Traffic aisles, on the other hand, refer to areas where there is foot traffic. Work aisles and traffic aisles should be kept separate wherever possible to avoid hindrances to employees as they work. A single-person work aisle requires a space of between 24 and 36 inches, depending on the tasks to be done. To allow for employee bending or oven door opening, the larger space is needed. For two employees working back to back a minimum of 42 inches is required; more—6 to 12 inches more—if equipment projects into the work space.

Traffic Aisles. Traffic aisles are used to move people and materials. They should be kept separate from work aisles. Traffic aisles are not productive space and should be kept to a minimum while allowing easy movement. It may be possible to have one aisle serve two or more functional areas. They should not be placed along perimeters, as this allows access to only one working area. An aisle width of 30 inches will permit one person to walk without a problem. When carts are being pushed or containers carried down an aisle, 24 inches plus the width of the equipment is necessary to allow two people to pass. If a work aisle is combined with a traffic aisle, a minimum of 42 inches is required to allow one person to pass someone who is working. Where two people are working back to back, 48 inches is needed to allow someone else to pass between them. The less movement within the operation, the less aisle space is required.

Work Surface Space. The space required for work surfaces depends on the materials to be used and the hand and arm movements required to perform the task. Normal and maximum hand and arm movements can be identified for the "typical" employee and the work area built to allow employees to perform their jobs within these areas. The normal work area for a work surface is defined as "the space enclosed within the arc scribed by pivoting the forearm in a horizontal plane at the elbow" [11]. For most people this is 14 to 16 inches. Cutting, slicing, mixing, and assembling are best done within this area.

To determine the maximum work area, the entire arm is pivoted at the shoulder. When a task has to be performed outside this area, the employee must bend his or her body. The result will be a less productive worker. Most food facility jobs can be performed within an area 2 feet deep by 4 feet wide.

Workstation Height. The height of a workstation depends on the task to be performed there. Lightweight tasks can be done at a surface height 2 inches below the employee's elbow. The larger or heavier the materials used, the lower the work surface should be. For light tasks the preferred height should be 37 to 41 inches; heavy jobs should be 34 to 36 inches off the ground, depending on the height of the employee.

Storage. Tools and utensils should be close to where they will be used and readily accessible to employees.

Equipment. Equipment is either mounted or freestanding. The feeding and working height should be appropriate to the employees who will use them. Freestanding equipment can be moved from one location to another. This makes it easier to clean under and behind the equipment. In addition, changes in layout can be made to accommodate more efficient layout when changes occur in the menu.

Workplace Environment. Productivity is affected by the physical conditions under which employees must work. A temperature between 65 and 70° F in winter or between 69 and 73° F in summer with a relative humidity between 40 and 60 percent is comfortable for most people. The heat and moisture generated in a kitchen can be contained by purchasing equipment that is well insulated.

Despite some research which indicates that kitchen workers are up to 25 percent more productive in the summer if kitchens are air conditioned, most people consider it economically unfeasible to air condition this part of the operation. There are some measures, however, that can be taken to reduce kitchen temperatures [12].

- Steam and water pipes and equipment that emits heat can be heavily insulted, as can the entire building.
- Hot-water heaters, refrigerator compressors, and condensers can be placed away from the kitchen.
- Equipment can be preheated for the minimum amount of time necessary.
- Sun-reflecting windows can be used to reduce sun heating.
- Whenever feasible, heat-emitting equipment can be covered during preheating and after use.
- Lower temperatures can be used to cook food.
- Gas flames should be adjusted so that they do not come up around the sides of pots.
- The building can be aired out at night.

The amount of lighting required depends on the job to be done. Lighting levels in a kitchen range from 15 to 20 footcandles in nonwork areas to 30 to 40 footcandles for most kitchen tasks. General white fluorescent lights tend to distort food color and are not recommended. Incandescent or color-improved fluorescent lighting should be used for work areas. The latter is more expensive to install but cheaper to operate.

There are two other considerations related to lighting: the brightness ratio and glare. The brightness ratio—the relative brightness between a lit and nonlit area—should not exceed 3:1 where the work area is the brighter area. Direct glare occurs when light sources are placed near the line of sight. Both direct and reflected glare tires employees and is an annoyance. The latter tends to come from the large number of stainless steel tables and amount of equipment used in kitchens.

Three aspects of color are important in the workplace: contrast, actual color used, and color coding. Objects are easier to see and the eye is less tired when there is a color contrast between two areas. This can be achieved in one of several ways [13]. A light color can be used with a darker version of the same color; a warm color can be combined with a cool color; a color can be used with its complementary color (for example, pale and gray blue). The level of contrast in the workplace should be at a moderate level, as too much contrast can be just as bad for the eyes. Warm colors—reds and oranges—tire the eyes easily. Blues and greens are much more restful. In a similar fashion, pure colors, as distinct from tones, strain the eyes after a short period. Pure white is usually not recommended for a work area because it reflects light too much, again tiring the eyes. Colors can be used to color-code various pieces of equipment. Green tends to be used for first-aid equipment; red signifies danger; steps coded with yellow can serve as a signal to be careful.

Exposure to noise levels above 50 decibels for a prolonged period can lead to contentious employees. Silencing enclosures can be placed around equipment, acoustical materials can be utilized on ceilings, walls, and floors, and sound-absorbing materials can be used to construct work surfaces.

Music has been shown to boost employee morale. It is particularly useful for workers performing physical tasks. Most workers are productive for the first 2 to 2-1/2 hours after they begin work. Their work performance then declines and holds steady at the lower level until shortly before a meal break, when it improves. Upbeat music during the lull in performance can help a worker perform more productively.

Because of the type of work performed in the kitchen, ventilation is important to remove odors, moisture and the smell of grease, but air conditioning creates special problems in the kitchen. When food is cooked, the work area becomes hot. Air conditioning aims to cool the work area down. The control system used is very important to ensure that the working conditions are comfortable for the employees without causing the cooked food to cool before it is taken into the dining room.

Safety in the Workplace. Unsafe workplaces increase costs for the employer by increasing insurance coverage and reducing productivity. Accidents in the kitchen can occur for a number of reasons [14]. Falling results from slippery floors, floors that are highly polished, and stairways that are too steep. Nonskid flooring or carpeting can help with floors that are wet and/or greasy. Accidents from cuts happen because moving edges are not sufficiently guarded or employees are not using hand tools properly. These can be reduced by guarding cutting edges and ensuring that workers are trained in the safe and proper use of their tools.

Burns can be caused by hot grease, steam, hot water or hot pipes. Steam and hot-water lines should be insulated and/or placed out of the way of employees, who should be trained in the proper use of equipment.

Electrical shocks in the kitchen are the result of frayed wires, poor insulation on wires, or improper grounding of equipment or machines. Built-in ground wires with three-pronged plugs can be used with portable equipment and grounding outlets provided. Heavy-duty waterproof wiring is recommended.

When hands are sweaty or greasy or when fingers are stiff due to exposure to the cold, there is a tendency to drop things. Keeping hands dry and using gloves when picking up hot or cold items over a long period of time will reduce such accidents.

Layout of Functional Areas

By identifying the functions within the kitchen and the order in which they are undertaken, management gets a feel for the flow of activities within the operation. Boxes of canned goods are received, the boxes are unpacked, the cans are checked for quantity and quality, the boxes are discarded and the cans are placed on shelves. The order in which activities occur is referred to as flow. The idea is to minimize the amount of movement of both people and goods.

Layout Principles. The layout process consists of two steps [15]: arranging individual pieces of equipment into a functional area (for example, salad preparation) and arranging the functional areas into the entire operation. Both steps tend to occur at somewhat the same time in the designer's mind.

Industrial engineers have developed various principles of layout that serve as a guide to this process. The more important of these tend to stress such things as designing the layout to make the production process as easy and as flexible to change as possible; allowing for ease of access for such things as maintenance and the taking of inventory, protecting the equipment from damage, providing a safe and productive environment for employees, and minimizing movement of both materials and employees.

Principles of Flow. A flow diagram showing the flow of employees, customers, and primary materials helps determine where areas should be, relative to one another. For example, after being received, items are separated into either dry or refrigerated storage, from where they go to either baking, meat, or vegetable preparation. From vegetable preparation items go to salad preparation; items from meat preparation go to final cooking and then either to salad preparation or to serving, then to the dining room, and finally, to dish washing. Silverware and flatware from the dishwashing area go back into the serving area. The pot wash area receives items from both baking and cooking.

In a station manned by one employee, a flow diagram is best accomplished by surveying the employee's movements between various pieces of equipment and placing pieces involving most movement between them next to each other.

Where employees are engaged in tasks that do not require them to move much, as in dishwashing, where employees scrape dirty dishes prior to loading them into the dishwasher, the most important consideration would be the flow of materials rather then the analysis of employee movements.

Generally speaking, when material flow is minimized, employee movement is minimized. Whichever criterion is used, the following principles are important [16]:

- Flow should be along straight-line paths as much as possible. This principle is particularly important, as it results in minimum movements. Various layouts can be charted and the one giving the best straight-line pattern selected.

- Cross-traffic results in bottlenecks and congestion. The amount of cross-flow or cross-traffic should be minimized. This can be done by locating aisles, passageways, and doors such that traffic flows do not cross.

- When people move back to where a particular activity occurred, they are guilty of backtracking. This should be minimized.

- Bypassing should also be minimized. This occurs when material or people pass one or more pieces of equipment to get to the next part of the process.

Configurations.   Five basic layout patterns are common (see Figure 7.3). The single straight-line arrangement consists of pieces of equipment laid out next to each other in a straight line. They may be laid out along a wall or in an island. It is simple but the layout options are very limited.

An ell-shaped arrangement places equipment on two legs that are perpendicular to each other. It is a useful arrangement where linear space is restricted. Different types of equipment can be separated by using one leg for each type.

U-shaped arrangements are particularly useful for confined areas where only one employee is working. A problem is that this layout does not allow for straight-line movement through the area.

Parallel, back-to-back arrangements consists of two parallel lines of equipment placed next to each other back-to-back. In this way the utility line for each line can be centralized between them.

Parallel, face-to-face arrangements utilize two lines of equipment with a work aisle between them. Very commonly used, this arrangement requires separate utility lines for each line of equipment.

Arranging Functional Areas

As noted above, the layout process consists of arranging individual pieces of equipment into a functional area and arranging the functional areas into the entire operation. A relationship chart is useful for this second step. A relationship chart shows the desired physical relationship between various functional areas. Such a chart is shown in Figure 7.4. Departments involving a great deal of movement between them are located in relative closeness to each other.

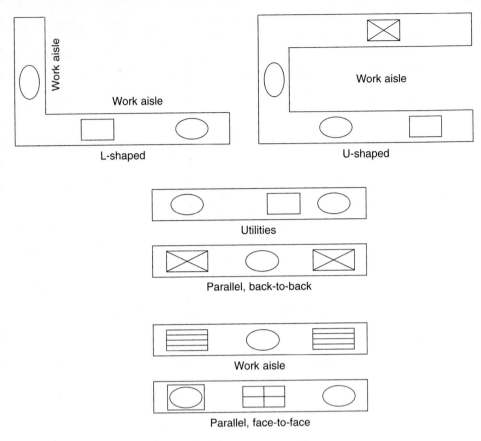

Figure 7.3   Equipment layout patterns.

IMPROVING EXISTING LAYOUTS

The layout of existing operations is improved if the flow between various workplaces can be reduced. Travel charts can be used to evaluate the flow involved in a kitchen layout.

Two methods are used. The first looks at the movement of individuals between workplaces; the second considers the flow of materials between workplaces. Whichever method is used, the objective is the same, to minimize movement of both people and materials.

Individual Movements

When the weight or volume of materials involved in a process is not great, analyzing the movements of individuals is the best method of evaluating equipment layout.

When using individual movements, the most common form of travel charting involves analyzing workplaces that are in a straight line and where

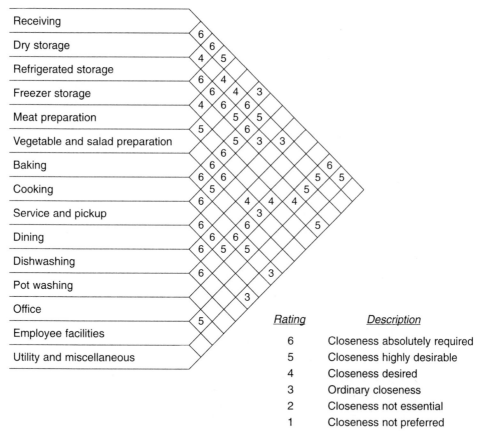

Receiving	
Dry storage	
Refrigerated storage	
Freezer storage	
Meat preparation	
Vegetable and salad preparation	
Baking	
Cooking	
Service and pickup	
Dining	
Dishwashing	
Pot washing	
Office	
Employee facilities	
Utility and miscellaneous	

Rating	Description
6	Closeness absolutely required
5	Closeness highly desirable
4	Closeness desired
3	Ordinary closeness
2	Closeness not essential
1	Closeness not preferred

Figure 7.4 Relationship chart with closeness ratings for a typical foodservice facility. *Source:* Edward A. Kazarian, *Foodservice Facilities Planning,* 3rd ed. (New York: Van Nostrand Reinhold, 1989), p. 283.

workplaces next to each other are equal or can be assumed to be equal. A workplace may be a sink, piece of equipment, worktable, or counter. Watching employees as they work, the sequence and frequency of movements between workplaces can be determined.

A chart can then be constructed showing the number of times an employee moves from workplace to workplace. A travel chart is shown in Figure 7.5. The numbers in each cell represent the number of movements from one workplace to another. For example, the employee moves from *C* to *B* twice, while there are four movements from *B* to *C*. The cells below the diagonal show forward movements; those above show backward movements. The farther the cells are from the diagonal, the greater will be the number of workplaces that have been bypassed. For example, there are four movements from *D* to *A*. This represents backward movement that bypasses three workplaces.

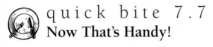

quick bite 7.7
Now That's Handy!

Servers can improve the way they do their jobs by using hand-held terminals. Orders are entered at the table and sent immediately to the kitchen or bar, allowing servers to spend more time with their customers. Using runners to bring the food from the kitchen service is faster and customer–server interaction is improved. Because of the initial investment involved, they work best in fast-paced, high-volume operations.

According to Kevin and Brain Blonder, owners of Buddy's Crabs and Ribs in Annapolis, Maryland, "We can use it for inventory control, to keep average check count, to keep average dollar per guest or per table. We can set up automatic happy-hour prices . . . We can do separate checks . . . The hand-helds will notify the server if we're out of something or how many of a certain item we have in stock."

At Joe Robbie Stadium in Miami, the food and beverage "captains" punch in orders from the club seats. The kitchen receives the order together with seat, row, and section number. Runners deliver the orders to the customer an average of 4 minutes after the order is taken.

In addition to giving servers more time to sell, the hand-helds act as a control device. Says Blonder, "You don't have the servers saying to the kitchen staff, 'Hey, put another crab cake on the plate; it's for my buddy'."

Source: Jennifer Batty, "Service in the Palm of Your Hand," *Restaurants USA,* vol. 14, no. 4, April 1994, pp. 35–38.

Those movements next to the diagonal—for example, from *A* to *B*—indicate that no bypassing takes place.

If it is assumed that the distance between workplaces is equal, the total distance covered can be determined by adding both forward and backward movements and multiplying the totals by a factor of 1 plus the number of workplaces bypassed.

Referring to Figure 7.5, we find the following values:

		From:				
		A	*B*	*C*	*D*	*E*
To:	*A*		5	2	3	6
	B	3		4	0	2
	C	3	4		1	4
	D	1	2	4		3
	E	2	4	3	5	

Figure 7.5 Travel chart for five workstations showing frequency of employee movements. *Source:* Idea adapted from Edward A. Kazarian, *Foodservice Facilities Planning,* 3rd ed. (New York: Van Nostrand Reinhold, 1989), p. 298.

	Total Movements		Bypass Factor		
No bypassing:					
3 + 4 + 4 + 5 + 3 + 1 + 4 + 5	=	29	× 1	=	29
Bypassing one workplace:					
3 + 2 + 3 + 4 + 0 + 2	=	14	× 2	=	28
Bypassing two workplaces:					
1 + 4 + 2 + 3	=	10	× 3	=	30
Bypassing three workplaces:					
2 + 6	=	8	× 4	=	32
					119

This index of 119 provides a base against which other arrangements can be compared. One way of improving the index is to get the larger numbers as close to the diagonal as possible while getting the smaller numbers as far from the diagonal as possible.

Another possibility is to reduce backward movements. The objective would be to get more numbers above the diagonal and fewer numbers below it. The percentage distance moved forward is the index for forward distances divided by the total distance moved. In our example the calculations would be:

	Forward Movements	Bypass Factor		Backward Movements	Bypass Factor	
No bypassing	16 × 1	=	16:13	1 = 13		
Bypassing one workplace	8 × 2	=	16: 6	2 = 12		
Bypassing two workplaces	5 × 3	=	15: 5	3 = 15		
Bypassing three workplaces	2 × 4	=	8: 6	4 = 24		
			55	64		

So the percentage distance moved forward is

$$\frac{55}{55 + 64} = 46 \text{ percent}$$

When the distances between various workplaces vary, a simple adjustment can be made to construct a travel chart. In such a case the number of movements from one workplace to another is multiplied by the distance from the midpoint of one to the midpoint of another to give the total distance traveled. For example, if A is 6 feet wide and is placed next to B, which is 2 feet wide, the distance from A to B is 4 feet (6 + 2 ÷ 2). If there are three movements from A to B, the total distance traveled is 12 feet. In this way a travel chart can be constructed using the same methodology as suggested above and different configurations tried to reduce the distance that employees move.

Product Flow

Where large quantities of heavy material are moved, it is better to construct a travel chart based on product movement. The methodology is similar to that described above except that the amount of weight multiplied by the distance covered is used instead of the number of feet traveled by an employee.

A travel chart is constructed by multiplying the distance traveled between two workplaces by the amount of material moved. If, for example, A and C are 4 feet apart and 300 pounds of material travels from A to C, the travel chart would indicate the index from A to C to be 1200. The amount of product flow for a given arrangement of workplaces is found by totaling the sums of each column. Various workplace arrangements can then be tried to find the one that minimizes product movement. Product movement can be minimized by locating workplaces involving large quantities of material close together.

TASK PLANNING

Task planning involves the "analysis of specific actions involved in carrying out a job, in order to establish a more productive procedure for completing that job" [17].

The task to be analyzed is chosen and the various factors affecting it determined. The accessibility and storage of the raw materials used in performing the job is one such factor. Since handling materials does not add to their value, such handling should be kept to a minimum. How far an employee has to walk to get the raw food items prior to preparation will affect the amount of time and effort taken to complete the job.

Figure 7.6 illustrates what can be achieved. Prior to analysis a cook had to walk 235 steps to prepare a batch of macaroni. The process involved:

- Ten steps to the pot-and-pan rack to get the pan
- Thirty steps to the sink to add the water
- Fifteen steps to the range carrying the pan and the water
- Fifty steps to the storeroom while the water is heating, to get the macaroni
- Fifty steps back to the range
- Ten steps to the drawer in the salad table for a spoon
- Ten steps back to the range
- Fifteen steps to the cabinet for salt
- Fifteen steps back to the range
- Fifteen steps to the sink for a little more water
- Fifteen steps back to the range

Storing the macaroni in the lower cabinet, using the steam-jacketed kettle instead of the range, locating the spoon on a rack above the table, having a hot-

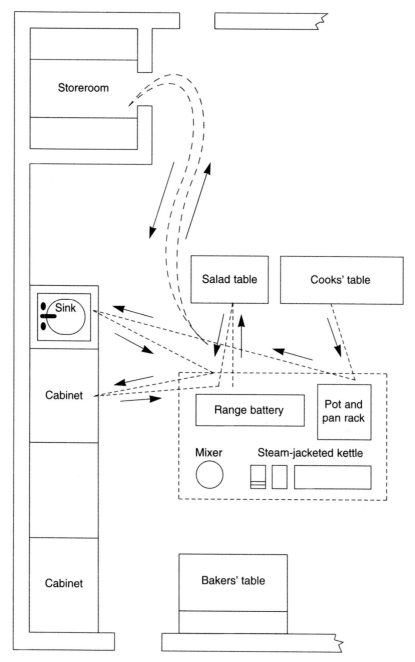

Figure 7.6a Steps involved in preparing macaroni.

water faucet above the kettle, and remembering to get the salt and the macaroni at the same time reduces the procedure to 50 steps. The cook begins at the baker's table, walks 10 steps to the steam-jacketed table, turns on the hot-water

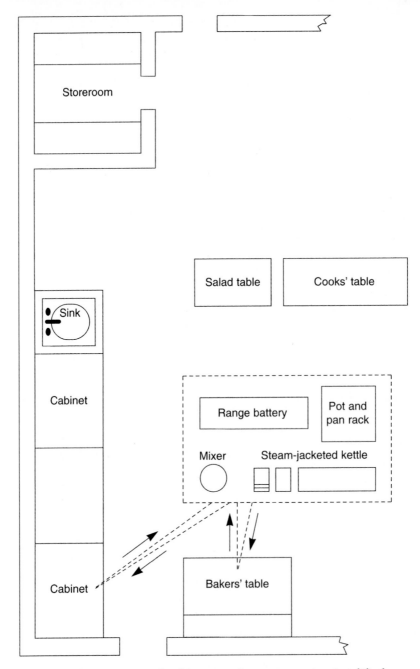

Figure 7.6b Steps involved in preparing macaroni—simplified.

faucet located above it, fills the kettle, and turns on the heat, walks 20 steps to the cabinet for the macaroni and salt, walks back to the kettle, and adds the macaroni and salt with a spoon that is located on a rack over the kettle.

Next, the process used in completing the task is identified. In the kitchen this means identifying every item on the menu and its proposed preparation method. The desired quality level and the quantity to be produced must also be determined, as both will have an impact on the process to be used. For example, hamburger patties can be prepared in different ways depending on the quantity to be produced. Large quantities can be readied by spreading the meat evenly in a rectangular baking pan, covering the pan with waxed paper, flattening with a rolling pin, and cutting into squares prior to cooking. This method presupposes that a square burger is acceptable to the customer. Small quantities can be shaped by hand.

The task itself is also affected by the amount of space employees have to work in, the availability of the right kind of equipment, the number and type of employee, how long it takes to perform the task, and when it has to be done relative to the completion of other tasks. Certain menu items require that several tasks be done at the same time. Of necessity, more than one employee will have to be involved. On the other hand, in certain situations, some activities can be completed ahead of service and finished at the last moment.

Procedures can now be established to get the job done as effectively and efficiently as possible. Several questions help in this process.

- *Can it be eliminated?* The purchase of a potato-peeling machine eliminates the need to peel potatoes by hand.

- *Can it be combined?* Can one employee perform several different jobs? Can employees work with both hands at the same time?

- *Are there unnecessary delays?* Are insufficient supplies causing slowdowns in service? One bar the author worked with was experiencing service delays because management, in an attempt to save on inventory costs, stocked only 12 highball glasses behind the bar. When the bar got busy, servers would have to clear the tables of glasses and have them washed and dried before drinks could be served to additional customers.

- *Is there misdirected effort?* Can a conveyor belt be used to move food, supplies, and/or dishes? Can wheels be put on equipment to roll rather than carry it?

- *Are employees doing too many unrelated tasks?* Have a $5-an-hour employee perform a $5-an-hour task.

- *Is work spread evenly?* At one hotel, 500 room service breakfasts were served between 7:00 and 11:00 A.M. In the dining room, service was busiest between 8:30 and 9:00 A.M. Although most of the soiled dishes did not reach the dishwashing area until 10:00 A.M., the entire dishwashing crew was on duty from 7:00 A.M. Upon analysis of the situation, they were brought in at 9:00 A.M.

quick bite 7.8
Road to the Top: John D. Folse

President, American Culinary Federation
Proprietor, Lafite's Landing

His first foodservice job was in the late 1960s as an assistant manager at the Howard Johnson operation in Baton Rouge; now John Folse and his wife, Laulie, preside over a company that has gross revenues of $16.5 million: $4 million from the restaurant, $3 million from catering, $6.5 million from food manufacturing, and $3 million from video production and cookbook publishing.

Raised by his father after his mother died in childbirth, John tried a variety of jobs, all the while believing in what his father had taught him—work hard and believe in the impossible. At HoJo's, "I couldn't learn it fast enough. That's my style—to get consumed, take it all in." Within six months he was promoted to general manager. Finding that food was of more interest to him than management, he took a position as sous chef at the Prince Murat Inn in Baton Rouge. His mentor, Fritz Blumberg, taught him the importance of learning the classical techniques as a basis before branching out into other areas.

Two years later, with a $110,000 loan, he took over a dying restaurant before, in 1978, moving into Lafite's Landing. This was about the time that Cajun cooking was hitting mainstream America. Although bankers approved a $30,000 loan, there were problems. The restaurant was located 70 miles from New Orleans and 40 miles from Baton Rouge. Realizing that a plan was needed, John put together a package—John Folse's Taste of Louisiana—and within two years had every tour operator stopping at Lafite's.

After Cybill Shepherd dined at the restaurant during the filming of a movie, she invited John to Hollywood. From there John took his "act" on the road, opening units in Hong Kong, Japan, and the then-USSR.

John branched into cookbooks and television—his "Taste of Louisiana" is in its sixth season—while his line of products sells at national chain stores. His goal as president of the American Culinary Federation is to ensure that a cook or chef working anywhere in the United States can join the organization. Says Folse, "It goes back to my first embarrassment about being a cook. It's about pride in my profession."

Source: Jack Hayes, "John D. Folse," *Nation's Restaurant News,* January 1995, pp. 93–94.

ENDNOTES

1. Edward A. Kazarian, *Foodservice Facilities Planning,* 3rd ed. (New York: Van Nostrand Reinhold, 1989), pp. 239,242.

2. Ibid., p. 240.

3. Ibid., pp. 116–119.

4. Ronald E. Millman, "The Hidden Influence," *N.R.A. News,* vol. 6, no. 5, May 1986, pp. 28–29.

5. Carolyn U. Lambert, "Environmental Design," *Cornell Hotel and Restaurant Administration Quarterly*, May 1981, pp. 62–68.

6. Richard E. Hopkins, "Light," *The Consultant*, vol. XVI, no. 4, Fall 1983, pp. 34–37.

7. Marilynn Motto "Profit by Design," *Cornell Hotel and Restaurant Administration Quarterly*, May 1970, pp. 113–116.

8. Kazarian, *Foodservice Facilities Planning*, 3rd ed. p. 401.

9. Ibid., pp. 246–247.

10. Ibid., pp. 393–398.

11. Arthur C. Avery, *A Modern Guide to Foodservice Equipment* (Boston: CBI Publishing Company, 1980), pp. 18–19.

12. Ibid., p. 142.

13. Ibid., p. 150.

14. Ibid., pp. 159–161.

15. Kazarian, *Foodservice Facilities Planning*, p. 272.

16. Ibid., p. 275.

17. Robert Christie Mill, *Managing for Productivity in the Hospitality Industry* (New York: Van Nostrand Reinhold, 1989), p. 65.

chapter eight

FOOD AND BEVERAGE: FROM SUPPLIER TO CUSTOMER

learning objectives

By the end of this chapter you should be able to:

1. Develop procedures for the effective purchasing, receiving, storing, and issuing of items used in the operation.

2. Compare and contrast the various production and service systems.

3. Illustrate the importance and use of purchase specifications, yield, standardized recipes, and portion control in implementing a system of cost control.

STEPS IN THE PROCESS

The process by which food and beverage items find their way to the customer consists of several steps:

- *Purchasing.* Items are ordered from vendors.
- *Receiving.* Items are delivered by vendors and accepted at the restaurant.
- *Storage.* Items are kept in a secured area until needed by the kitchen staff.
- *Issuing.* Items are released from storage to the kitchen staff.
- *Preparation.* Items are prepared for cooking.
- *Cooking.* Items are prepared for customers.
- *Service.* Items are served to the customer.

After service there is a need to wash dirty dishes, pots, and pans and dispose of waste. At each stage there are specific procedures to be put into place to ensure that costs are controlled while quality is maintained.

---

quick bite 8.1
Hot Concepts: Pasqua

Pasqua, which opened in 1983, is a specialty coffee bar with a food menu of sandwiches, salads, and baked goods. Principals Mark Zuckerman and Martin Kupferman have, at the time of writing, 46 units grossing $25 million in California and New York. Plans are to expand into areas such as Dallas and Las Vegas.

Their market niche is business centers. They look for "5000 to 7000 office workers or 1 million to 2 million square feet of occupied space in a business district." Stores range from 35 to 2300 square feet. They believe they are successful in keeping their costs under control. Says Kupferman: "You can't have rents that are 15 percent of your gross sales." Pasqua manages to keep its rent at 8 percent of gross sales, with depreciation adding another 3 percent.

Speed of service is important to the customers they go after. A brewed coffee and food item takes 22 seconds, while specialty coffees are served in 45 seconds. There is a 50–50 food-to-beverage ratio with baked goods accounting for 20 percent of food sales. Items are "Italian-Californian" and include panini sandwiches, such as roast turkey with salsa cream cheese and sun-dried tomatoes ($5.50) and sharp white cheddar with sun-dried cherries and curry sauce ($4.95). Running an average check of $3, food and beverage costs run in the mid-to-high 30 percent range.

Their "bread and butter"—the coffee—is roasted at their own facility in San Francisco, while all products are prepared at commissaries in San Francisco and Los Angeles. Plans include the development of a commissary in New York.

Source: Suzanne Kapner, "Pasqua," *Nation's Restaurant News*, May 22, 1995, pp. 132, 134.

PURCHASING

Importance

According to Khan, "The primary function of any type of foodservice operation is to convert raw food into cooked products" [1]. Profits come from converting and serving the food as efficiently as possible. High-quality dishes come from high-quality ingredients—thus the importance of purchasing. The objective is "to obtain the *right quality* and quantity at the *right* time and price and from the *right* source [2].

Process

Forecast. Once the menu is set, the number of servings of each item needed for each meal period must be forecast. This serves as the basis for the quantities of each item to be ordered. The easiest forecasting method is to use the average number of dishes ordered in the past. Poor forecasting will result in too many or too few items ordered. If too many items are ordered, there will be increased waste; too few items will mean that the restaurant will run out of specific items and customers will be dissatisfied.

---

 quick bite 8.2
Supplier Relations

A survey of the chief purchasing officer of all firms listed in the *Restaurants and Institutions "400" Executive Directory* found that:

- About 40 percent of the companies used 100 or fewer vendors annually.
- The number of new vendors used increased. This might indicate poor performance on the part of existing vendors and/or an increase in product diversity.
- There is an increased use of international vendors. This may be due to greater demand for products not available or in short demand in the United States.
- A surprisingly small 12 percent make annual visits to most of their vendors.
- The major criteria used to select suppliers are accuracy in delivery and on-time delivery. Training in product use and providing recipe ideas were not seen as valuable. To ensure on-time delivery, organizations begin by relying on good supplier relations. If that fails, they use economic clout.

Source: R. Dan Reid and Carl D. Riegel, "Supplier Relations and Selection in the Foodservice Industry," *Hospitality Research Journal*, vol. 13, no. 2, 1989, pp. 51–62.

Quantities Needed. A standard procedure for identifying how much needs to be purchased involves five steps [3]:

1. Determine, from the recipe, the factor to be used to determine the number of servings. If the recipe is for 50 and the number of servings needed is 150, the factor will be 150 divided by 50, or 3.
2. Multiply all the ingredients in the recipe by the factor. This will give the edible portion (EP) weight of each item. The "as purchased" (AP) amount of each item is found by dividing the EP by the percent yield (see above).
3. Select the wholesale purchase unit (case, box, carton, etc.) nearest to the AP weight.
4. Complete the calculations for every item on the menu for that day.
5. Calculate the amounts needed for the delivery. The amount ordered will depend on such things as how much inventory is on hand, the storage space available, seasonal availability, and the time between deliveries. The latter will vary by operation depending on the kind of service given by the suppliers. It is better for an operation to have the supplier maintain inventory rather than having the restaurant keep too many supplies on hand. An order form can then be filled out and the order processed.

Buying Methods

Informal. Purchasing may be done formally or informally. Informal buying usually occurs over the telephone. Several vendors may be called for a price quotation and the order placed with the lowest bidder. This method is ideal for a small operation, as there is little paperwork and the buying can be done quickly. It may be possible to take advantage of lower costs in the marketplace. However, because prices have not been agreed upon ahead of time, price increases will result in higher costs.

Buying can be done on a cash basis at markets or after getting quotations from various vendors. A quotation-and-order sheet would be made out, listing specifications for the various items needed. Several vendors would then be called and asked to quote prices for these items. Space would be available on the form to write down the various prices. The cost of items purchased should be lower because prices are being compared. However, more time is needed to compare the quotes of the vendors.

Under the blank-check method, certain vendors are given authority to deliver various items and bill the restaurant without quoting prices beforehand. This would be done on a very limited basis with vendors who have shown they can be trusted and for items that are in short supply. It is advisable to set a range of prices beyond which the vendor must communicate with the restaurateur.

For items whose price varies erratically, the cost-plus or fixed-markup method ensures that the supplier will have a guaranteed profit, negotiated ahead of time and typically 10 to 30 percent over cost.

Formal. There are also a variety of formal buying methods. The most common formal method of buying is the competitive-bid method under which vendors submit written quotes based on specifications sent out by the restaurateur. Bidding is competitive, so a good and fair price can be negotiated. Because everything is done in writing, the process takes longer but provides written safeguards should disputes arise.

In another form, prices may be negotiated with vendors before the formal written bid. Prices are usually set for a relatively long period. Under the standing-order method, vendors send items at predetermined intervals. Milk and bakery items are usually purchased in this way. Once the vendor has been chosen and the quantities set, time savings result because the decision does not have to be revisited every time an order is needed. The quantities ordered should be checked periodically to ensure that the amounts bought are appropriate to the needs of the business.

Prices, but not quantities, are determined under a future-contract method. For a specified amount of time, prices of specific items are guaranteed.

Finally, under the buy-and-hold method, the restaurateur buys large quantities of an item at a good price and the vendor is responsible for storing the item until it is needed by the operation. In this way the restaurateur can take advantage of cost savings even if he or she does not have large storage space.

Standards

The following items indicate specific guidelines for purchasing food items.

Fresh Fruits and Vegetables

1. Specific standards can be obtained from the United States Department of Agriculture (USDA).
2. Because these items are perishable, specify the grade desired at the time of delivery rather than the time of shipping.
3. Look for "bright, attractive colors, good shape and appearance, good proportion of weight and size, and absence of any mechanical damage or signs of decay" [4].
4. Specify size, especially for fruit. Smaller sizes tend to have more flavor, while larger sizes are important for display.

Processed Fruits and Vegetables

1. As specified by the USDA, processed fruits and vegetables come in the following grades:

Fruits	Vegetables
U.S. Grade A or U.S. Fancy	U.S. Grade A or U.S. Fancy
U.S. Grade B or U.S. Choice	U.S. Grade B or U.S. Extra-Standard
U.S. Grade C or U.S. Standard	U.S. Grade C or U.S. Standard

U.S. Grade A items are "practically perfect" and score between 85 and 100 points; U.S. Grade B items are "reasonably perfect" and score between 75 and 89 points; U.S. Grade C items are "fairly perfect" and score between 60 and 74 points. For items where there are only two grades, A and B, the specifications for A are as above, while for B they must be "fairly perfect" and score between 70 and 84 points.

2. Specify minimum drained weight needed, as this is a better indicator of yield.
3. Syrup density is important because the heavier the syrup, the less chance the product will break up. Also, for dietetic menus, the sugar content of the syrup is important.

Frozen Vegetables.   As above, with the following notes:

1. They may be packed in sugar or syrup.
2. They may be treated with an antioxidant to prevent browning.
3. Salt may have been added as a preservative.

Meats and Meat Products

1. Meats are graded on the basis of quality and yield.
2. The various grades are U.S. Prime (highest grade), U.S. Choice, U.S. Good (lacks juiciness, relatively tender), U.S. Standard (tender); U.S. Commercial (lacks tenderness, more waste), U.S. Utility, U.S. Cutter, and U.S. Canner (for processed meat products).

Poultry and Eggs

1. Available grades are U.S. Grade A, U.S. Grade B, U.S. Grade C, U.S. Procurement Grade I, and U.S. Procurement Grade II.
2. Order poultry as follows: breasts, breasts with ribs, wishbones, legs, wings, drumsticks, thighs, halves, quarters, and backs.
3. Eggs are graded by size and most are packed in 30-dozen cases. The grades most often used in restaurants are large and medium. Medium eggs are a better buy if they are 12 percent or more cheaper than large eggs, while small eggs are a better buy if they are 24 percent or more cheaper than large eggs [5].

Size	Weight (oz) per Dozen	Weight (lb) per 30-Dozen Case
Jumbo	30	56
Extra large	27	50.5
Large	24	45
Medium	21	39.5
Small	18	34
Peewee	15	28

Milk and Milk Products

1. Specify the type of product, grade, milk fat content, and type of packaging.
2. Pasteurization is done to destroy bacteria; homogenization is done to prevent the formation of cream and results in an enhanced flavor.

Fish and Shellfish

1. Items are available as U.S. Grade A (top quality), U.S. Grade B (good quality), and U.S. Grade C (fairly good quality).
2. Specify whether or not the skin should be left on and whether the item should be fresh, chilled, or frozen.
3. Fish may be whole (just as they came from the water); drawn (entrails removed), dressed (cleaned with head on), chunks, steaks, or fillets.

Control

Within the purchase function two important aspects of control are the need for purchase specifications and an understanding of yield.

Purchase Specifications. Specifications are "the description of a particular commodity in terms of its size, quality, or condition" [6]. Using specifications lets the vendors know exactly what is required. Specifications ("specs") should be detailed, in writing, and cover the following [7]:

1. Common, trade, or brand name of the product
2. Amount to be purchased in the most commonly used units
3. Recognized trade, federal, or local grade
4. Name and size of the basic container
5. Count and size of the items or units within the basic container
6. Ranges in weight, thickness, or size
7. Minimum and maximum trims, or fat content percentages
8. Degree of maturity or stage of ripening
9. Type of processing required (for example, freeze-dried)
10. Type of packaging desired

Yields. The yield percentage must be known before ordering. The yield percentage indicates how much usable food will be obtained from a particular purchased item. Standardized recipes will indicate the number of portions from a specific item. The number should take waste and shrinkage into account. If this has not been done, the yield can be calculated as follows [8]:

$$\text{percentage of yield} = \frac{\text{weight after cooking}}{\text{weight before cooking}} \times 100$$

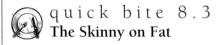

The yield percentage will vary depending on such things as the cooking temperature and type of oven and percentage of fat in the item. Cooking at lower temperatures, for example, will result in less shrinkage or waste.

Food can be purchased in one of two ways. Food as purchased (AP) refers to items bought without prepreparation. Edible portion (EP) indicates that the item has been processed and is ready for cooking. The EP to be ordered is calculated as follows [9]:

$$EP = AP - \text{shrinkage (or preparation losses)}$$

$$\text{percentage shrinkage or preparation losses} = \frac{\text{losses due to shrinkage or preparation (wt)}}{\text{AP (wt)}} \times 100$$

$$= \frac{\text{AP (wt)} - \text{EP (wt)}}{\text{AP (wt)}}$$

RECEIVING

The objective in the receiving function is to ensure that the items delivered are exactly what was ordered. Ideally, for quantity and quality verification, the person who ordered the item should receive it. In large operations this is not feasible.

Methods

There are three methods that can be set up for receiving goods: invoice, blind, and partially blind [10]. Under the invoice method, the delivery is accompanied by an invoice prepared by the supplier and listing the quantities, prices, and specifications for the order. The order is compared against the invoice by someone at the restaurant. This method is simple and fast. It works only if the person receiving the delivery takes the time to thoroughly compare the physical order to the invoice.

Under a blind receiving method the invoice accompanying the order is blank or, at most, lists only the items being delivered. The receiving clerk is forced to physically count the number of items being delivered and judge their quality to complete the invoice. A separate and fully completed invoice is sent directly from the supplier to the person in charge of purchasing. This supplier-supplied invoice is compared to the one filled out by the receiving clerk and any discrepancies reported to the vendor. While this method is very accurate, it is also very time consuming.

The partially blind receiving method attempts to combine the primary advantages of the previous methods. The delivery comes with an invoice that contains all relevant information about the order except the quantities delivered. The receiving clerk is forced to physically count the number of items received and input those data on the invoice that comes with the order. This invoice is then compared with the order and a later invoice sent by the vendor.

Space Requirements

The following tasks are involved in receiving [11]: examining, moving, receiving, unpacking, and verifying. The amount of space required for receiving depends on the number, type, and size of deliveries. If deliveries are accepted only between certain restricted hours, for example, the receiving area will be larger than if deliveries are spread out over a longer period.

Large deliveries might require specialized equipment for handling the goods as they come in. This might range from a cart to a moving conveyor belt system.

Getting the distributor to make smaller, more frequent deliveries will mean that the restaurant will requires less moving equipment and storage space for both perishable and nonperishable items. If moving equipment is required, some provision will have to be made for its storage. In addition, space must be available to verify the order and dispose of packing materials.

Practices

Good receiving practices involve several steps [12]:

1. An invoice or delivery sheet should be used to verify each delivery.
2. All deliveries should be checked in the following ways:

- Each container should be inspected for signs of external damage.
- Each item should be weighed and/or counted, checked, and noted on the receiving invoice.
- When appropriate (as for eggs), convert the weight of the item into the relevant quantity. Conversion tables should be readily available.
- Remove all packing before weighing items.
- Tag all wholesale cuts of meat. Meat tags consist of two parts; one stays on the meat while the other goes to accounting. The tag identifies the supplier, cut, weight, and unit price and is used for control purposes as well as to ensure the first in, first out (FIFO) system of inventory control.

3. Verify the quality of the items delivered. This can be done by random inspection using the specification guidelines developed by the restaurant and/or standard USDA criteria. Date all items in order that the operation use a FIFO inventory method. Expiration dates should be identified on cans and packages and cans specifically checked for bulging and leakage. Inspection stamps should be verified on meat items.

4. Checking temperatures is particularly important for frozen or refrigerated items. Recommended standards are [13]:
- Frozen foods, 0 to 20°F
- Dairy products, 38 to 46°F
- Meat and poultry, 33 to 38°F
- Fish and shellfish, 23 to 30°F

5. Any shortages or other discrepancies should be noted and the invoice signed, dated and stamped. One copy is kept at receiving, another sent to management, and a third given to the delivery person.

6. All items should be sent immediately to the appropriate storage area.

7. Invoices would then be filed.

STORAGE

Storage will be needed for dry, refrigerated, and frozen goods in addition to beverages and nonfood supplies. The objective is to have enough items on hand so that the restaurant does not run out while minimizing loss due to spoilage and/or theft. Spoilage comes from holding items for too long. Excessive amounts of various food and beverage items tie up money and space.

In storage the following tasks are common [14]: inspecting, inventorying, issuing, rotating, and storing.

Space Requirements

The number of days of storage to be provided determines how large this area must be. An isolated resort community that gets deliveries once a week will require more storage space than a restaurant that can demand daily deliveries. Since buying in bulk will costs less, it is desirable to analyze the reduced costs of buying in bulk against the cost of providing additional space.

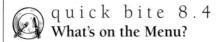

quick bite 8.4
What's on the Menu?

The National Restaurant Association reports the following menu trends from an analysis of the menus submitted for the NRA's Great Menu Contest:

1. Ethnic dishes grew, with African–Moroccan, German, Middle Eastern, and soul cuisines making their first appearance in the sample studied. In fusion cuisines the most significant change was in the combination of three or more cuisines such as Italian–Vietnamese–Thai and Japanese–French-Cajun. More foreign ingredient listings were available.

2. Seasonings continue to be popular, basil being the most widely used. Use of cilantro increased, as did items such as mustard and ginger, reflecting more use of spicy foods. Garlic was the most-mentioned herb on appetizer menus, while more entree sauces and salad dressings are utilizing seasonings.

3. The median number of appetizers listed remains at eight. The increase in cheese, poultry, and vegetable dishes was offset by a decline in beef listings. Shellfish remains the most popular appetizer. More ethnic and ethnic-fusion items were listed, notably Mexican and Mexican–Italian.

4. The median number of soups listed remained at two and moved away from the traditional staples.

5. The median number of entrees listed remained at 17. There were increases in pasta and meatless dishes; more combinations such as beef with seafood and veal and prawns; fewer veal and pork entrees (although beef was the number 1 entree item listed). There was a significant increase in grilled items as well as more seared and barbecued entrees.

6. More main-dish salads are available, the median number being five. Increases in chicken breast, Caesar, and Greek main-dish salads were offset by declines in chef, taco, and spinach salads.

7. The presence of sandwiches increased from a median of 15 to 18 over a five-year period. Creative variations of traditional favorites—avocado burger, Mexican chili burger—are increasingly available, as are grilled chicken breast sandwiches. Bacon, beef, and sausage sandwiches declined in number.

Source: Heather Papadopoulos, "Menu Analysis 1994—Variety Spices Up Menu," *Restaurants USA*, vol. 15, no. 2, February 1995, pp. 42–45.

Note: The report is *Ethnic Cuisines: A Profile* and can be ordered from the National Restaurant Association at (800) 424-5156, ext. 5375.

The following rules of thumb can be used to estimate the storage space required [15]:

WOLLENSKY'S GRILL

Soup	4.50
Mixed Green Salad	5.50
Shrimp Cocktail	12.50
Fried Zucchini & Onion Rings	6.75
Fresh Lump Crabmeat	12.50

Our Cruvinet Has 7 Vintage Cabernets By the Glass

The Grill Sirloin	25.75
English Cut Prime Rib	22.50
Roast Beef Hash	16.50
Wollensky's Burger	9.75
Memphis Ribs	18.50
Lamb Chops	19.75
Grilled Chicken Club	15.75
Filet Mignon	24.50
Veal Chop	22.50
Filet Tips	18.50

Lemon Pepper Chicken	18.75

Chef's Salad	16.75
Cobb Salad	17.75
Stone Crabs	- -
Sea Scallops	17.75
Capt. Kissane's Catch of the Day	18.75
Wollensky's Steamed Lobster	19.50

Smith & Wollensky's Menu Available

Cheesecake	5.50
Chocolate Cake	6.50
Melon or Ice Cream	4.50
Apple Betty	5.50
Chocolate Basket	7.50
Fresh Fruit	6.75
Pecan Pie	6.50
Napoleon	6.50
Apple Strudel	6.50

We are open every day from 11:30 A.M. to 2 A.M.

Our classic Smith & Wollensky steak knife is available for purchase.
49th Street Off of 3rd Ave., N.Y. 10017, Telephone: 753-0444

Wollensky's Grill—a classic!
Courtesy Wollensky's Grill,
New York City.

- Two to four weeks' supply for dry storage goods
- A weight per meal of 1/4 to 1/2 pound
- An average density of 45 pounds per cubic foot

If an operation plans on serving 400 meals a day and wishes a two-week supply of dry goods, the space requirements can be estimated as follows:

Required storage will be for 400 meals × 14 days	= 5600 meals
Total weight (1/2 pound per meal)	= 2800 pounds
Total volume (45 pounds per cubic foot)	= 62.2 cubic feet
Shelving required (at a height of 1.5 feet) (62.2 ÷ 1.5 feet)	= 41.5 square feet

Length of shelving required if shelving is 9 inches wide   = 53.3 feet
   (41.5 ÷ 0.75 foot)

Convenience and accessibility are the principles upon which storage areas are laid out. They should be designed such that heavy and/or bulky materials are moved as little and as easily as possible. Many operations will find that a central storage area combined with smaller storage spaces scattered throughout the facility will cut down on the movement of people and goods. For example, a hotel with several restaurants will benefit from one major store serving all restaurants, each of which has space for storing small amounts of frequently used products. A combination of one walk-in and several reach-in refrigerators spread throughout the operation can reduce the walking employees would have to do to get required items. A restaurant serving over 300 to 400 meals a day should have a walk-in refrigerator.

It should be noted, however, that more storage areas will lead to increased inventory and greater control challenges. Combination walk-in and reach-in storage facilities greatly assist in increasing access to and within storage areas. Cleaning of walk-in storage areas is made easier by having items stored at least 8 inches off the floor. Mobile bins and containers also achieve this objective. All chemical items and cleaning supplies should be stored separately from foods because of the contamination risk.

Dry Storage.   Dry storage for food items requires a temperature between 50 and 70°F and a relative humidity of 50 percent. As such, heat-generating equipment should not be located in these areas. Similarly, pipes carrying hot water should be insulated to prevent temperatures from rising beyond the highs noted above.

Refrigeration.   Fresh meats, vegetables, and fruits, dairy products, beverages, and leftover items require refrigeration at temperatures between 32 and 37°F. Items should not be in direct contact with the floor, walls, and/or ceiling. In addition, air circulation is needed to help eliminate odors and remove moisture.

Calculations similar to those above can be made for refrigerator and freezer storage. The weight per meal of refrigerator and freezer items will vary from 0.75 to 1 pound. The average density of refrigerator and freezer items is approximately 30 and 40 pounds per cubic foot, respectively. With refrigerated areas, temperature control is vital. Periodic checks should be made of the temperature at various points in the storage area. As with dry storage areas, items should not be in direct contact with floors, ceilings, and/or walls. Refrigerated areas can also be used to store cooked food items. It is imperative that cooked and raw items not come into contact with each other. Additionally, hot, cooked items should not be placed in the refrigerator as, in cooling down, they will increase the temperature of the surrounding area.

Frozen Foods.   If frozen foods are used, thawing facilities, sufficient for one day's production, will have to be provided. Frozen foods should be stored at −10 to −15°F. It is possible, and highly desirable, to have a layout wherein walk-in freezers open into walk-in refrigerators [16]. Thawed food items should never be refrozen. As above, raw food items should never come into contact with items that have been cooked and then frozen.

ISSUING

For control purposes it is advisable that as few people as possible have access to the storage and issuing areas. Some type of requisition form, signed by someone in authority, is needed before food and beverage items can be released from storage. Such forms aid in inventory control and analyzing menu costs. The objective is to ensure that only authorized personnel are allowed to requisition food and beverage items.

Control

A system of inventory management helps ensure cost control. The inventory refers to the items available in storage. Commonly, two types of inventory are kept: physical and perpetual [17]. A physical inventory refers to the actual number of each item on hand. It is typically taken on the last day of each month.

Perpetual inventories are continuous records of what is bought and issued. While time consuming, especially if manual records are kept, the perpetual inventory will alert management to what must be reordered when, as well as to items that are overstocked.

Food and beverage costs are calculated on the basis of the value of the inventory as follows: cost of food (beverage) for a specific period = value of opening inventory + food (beverage) purchases after opening inventory − value of closing inventory.

PREPARATION

Function

In the production area, functions tend to be divided into meat/fish/poultry preparation, vegetable preparation, salad preparation, and sandwich preparation. In smaller operations the salad and sandwich and/or the vegetable and salad functions are often combined. The objective is to prepare items to predetermined quality levels in sufficient quantities to meet customer demands while minimizing waste.

The preparation area is where items are made ready for final cooking. Operations that purchase preportioned items—a growing trend—will have minimal need of such facilities for the preparation of meat, poultry, and fish. Similarly, the use of preprocessed and/or frozen vegetables has reduced the need for space to perform the traditional functions of washing, cutting, and chopping.

Space Requirements

Equipment layout in this area can be arranged in a straight line because the tasks involved in preparing food occur in a logical sequence. Vegetables are trimmed, washed, and reduced in size, in that order. A worktable for trimming can be placed next to a sink for washing and draining, which, in turn, can be placed next to the area where vegetables are cut, diced, or chopped.

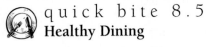

quick bite 8.5
Healthy Dining

More and more people want healthy meal options. Here is how to deliver:

1. Use egg substitutes, flavored with herbs. The Inn at Twin Linden in Churchtown, Pennsylvania, makes a light eggs benedict with grilled portobello mushroom instead of bacon, and a tomato confit instead of hollandaise.
2. Go lean with the protein—use poultry sausage, marinated chicken breasts, and fish. The Shelburne Inn in Seaview, Washington, has a smoked seafood hash with smoked oysters, salmon, sturgeon, and onions.
3. Use whole-grain and multigrain items. IHOP turns out a harvest-grain pancake made with whole grains.
4. Offer hot cereals—try oatmeal with raisins, cinnamon, low-fat or nonfat milk, honey, and yogurt. The Greenbrier serves oatmeal with sour cherries.
5. Serve fruit—baked apples, grapefruit soaked in Grand Marnier.
6. Serve bagels, muffins, and breads. The bread at the Firehook Bakery and Coffee House in Alexandria, Virginia, is naturally leavened, made with organic flour and baked in a wood-burning stove.
7. Offer breakfast shakes with powdered milk, yogurt, and fruit.
8. Offer sugar-free condiments.
9. Serve juices—pear and pineapple, carrot, and apple.

Source: Sylvia Somerville, "Getting Diners Off to a Healthy Start," *Restaurants USA*, vol. 15, no. 1, January 1995, pp. 32–36.

Since vegetables come from the storage area and go on to the main cooking or salad preparation area, the trimming table is located close to the storage area and vegetables are chopped near the cooking and salad preparation areas.

Vegetables will have to be stored temporarily prior to processing and a waste disposal area will also have to be included. Similar considerations are necessary for a salad preparation area.

COOKING

Service Systems

Minor and Cichy have identified four major foodservice systems based on the extent to which processed foods are used [18]. Many operations use a combination of systems. The four systems are:

- Convenience systems (maximum use of processed foods)
- Conventional systems
- Ready-food systems
- Commissary systems (minimum use of processed foods)

In convenience or assembly–serve systems, foods are purchased completely prepared and assembly, consisting of heating and/or minor preparation, is done in the operation. Although food cost is high and selections limited, only unskilled, low-cost labor is needed at the service point. Less preparation equipment and energy are required, but more storage space, particularly frozen storage, is needed.

There is some concern over product quality and customer acceptance of various convenience items. Foods are available in bulk, preportioned, and pre-plated form. Bulk convenience foods are portioned either before or after heating; preportioned items require only assembly and heating, while preplated foods need only be heated before serving.

A conventional system is one in which dishes are prepared from raw ingredients in the restaurant itself. Yet compromises, due to increased labor costs, are being made. Few operations have their own bakery or butcher shop on premises. More employees, equipment, energy, and space are needed in a conventional systems compared to one relying on convenience items.

In a ready-food system the food is prepared on-premises, then chilled (cook–chill) or frozen (cook–freeze) for service later. Chilled items are usually held for 1 to 3 days; frozen foods for 30 to 60 days. This system is more complex than the previous two because of the need to package, distribute, and store the food. Management has more control over the handling, quality, and cost of the food because the items are prepared ahead of time. Consequently, there is less of a pressure atmosphere then when cooking items to order. These systems are best suited for large operations such as hospitals, airlines, banquets, and schools.

In a commissary or satellite system, food is prepared in large quantities at a central source and distributed to various service outlets. Economies of scale are possible in purchasing and production, and quality assurance is made easier. Distributing the food to the various satellite units is a major part of the system. Care must be taken to ensure that food safety is assured as the items are moved from the central facility to the outlying units.

Space Requirements

The design of the cooking area is dependent on the type and amount of items to be prepared. A market analysis should determine what items will go on the menu; a market forecast will predict the amounts to be cooked at any time. From this estimate the type and size of equipment needed and the relationship of one piece to another can be determined.

The amount of space required for baking will depend on whether or not the restaurant prepares its baked goods from scratch. Most operations use either basic mixes or prepared unbaked goods requiring thawing and baking rather than the full line of baking functions.

Goods come into the cooking area from storage and preparation areas; utensils and cooking containers come from the pot-and-pan-washing locations. Food goes out to the service, salad, and sandwich preparation areas.

Equipment that produces heat and/or moisture must either be located under ventilating hoods or have their own ventilating systems. Equipment that uses steam to cook the food must be installed carefully using curbs or in depressed areas of the floor.

Vents and grill openings that are required for equipment that needs air for ventilation or cooling must not be blocked. The location of the air conditioning for the main kitchen is extremely important in order that the air be kept reasonable cool while the food and cooking equipment remains reasonably hot.

If a great deal of baking is done, the cooking and baking areas can be placed close together in order that they can share kettles, ovens and mixers. Both should be located close to the pot-washing area.

Where cooks and bakers expect to use the same equipment extensively, employee work times can be staggered to ensure full utilization of equipment without employees getting into each other's way. Bakers, for example, might work at night preparing the following day's pastries and breads.

A well-thought-out layout would have a proof box, an oven, and a landing table next to each other to handle the baking of bread. Baker's tables tend to be centrally located to permit easy access to storage areas and frequently used equipment. Space has to be available for storage of baking supplies and finished items. Perishable items will have to be refrigerated prior to being moved to the serving area.

Principles of Cooking

Moist-Heat Cooking.   Cooking is done by one of two methods: moist-heat or dry-heat cooking. Meats contain collagen, a fibrous matter that makes it tough. A similar tissue in vegetables is cellulose. Moist heat dissolves both to render the meat and vegetable tender. This is the reason that tougher cuts of meat are cooked in liquid.

The liquid used might be water, milk, tomato juice, wine, broth, or stock [19]. The most common cooking methods using liquid are boiling, blanching, braising, poaching, simmering, steaming, and stewing.

Boiling involves immersing the item in water at a temperature of 212°F (100°C). Boiling tends to take valuable nutrients out of the food being cooked. They remain in the water, which can be used for soup, stock, or a sauce. Foods tend to be boiled for a short period of time. Vegetables may be undercooked by boiling and transferred to a steam table, where the cooking process is completed as they wait to be served. Meats are simmered rather than boiled, while the process is not recommended for eggs, poultry, or fish because of the harm boiling does to the nutrients contained in these items.

Blanching or scalding involves exposing the food to boiling water for a very short period. Some items are blanched to remove some of their strong flavor, while others are blanched to dislodge external membranes. Blanching makes it easier to remove the skin from some fruits and vegetables. The term *blanching* also refers to the cooking of vegetables in deep oil, almost to the point of doneness, prior to finishing just before service. Parboiling involves keeping the food in the water longer and is used to cook the item partially before finishing it with another form of cooking. Squash, for example, may be parboiled before baking.

The appearance and taste of cooked vegetables and fruits are influenced by the alkalinity or acidity of the liquid in which they are cooked. Thus green vegetables turn drab in an acidic liquid, while the color is intensified in an alkaline medium. The latter type of liquid, however, may negatively affect the structure and presence of vitamins in the vegetables. To maintain as many nutrients as possible, cooking should be kept to a minimum.

In braising, meat is cooked in a small amount of fat in a covered container. Meat may be browned before stewing—called brun—to give it color. Blond braising involves no searing. Searing the food, according to a number of studies, does not help seal in the juices. The juices in which the meat is stewed add to its flavor. Less tender cuts of meat can be made tender by simmering in a liquid for a long time at a low temperature. Stewing is closely related to braising. Whereas braising involves cooking whole or sliced foods, stewing involves chopped or cubed foods. Stewing uses more liquid compared to braising, the liquid covering the entire item being cooked. A heavy pot is used to ensure even cooking. Dishes may be browned (brun) first or not (blond). Thicker stews result from cooking without a lid over the pot.

Poaching is the term given to cooking in a liquid at a temperature below the boiling point of water. It is useful for foods that require gentle handing and low-temperature cooking, such as eggs and fish. Poultry, particularly bigger birds, are moister, more tender, and more flavorful when poached then when roasted.

Simmering involves cooking in a liquid whose temperature is between 185 and 205°F. When meat is placed in cold water and brought to a simmer, it has more flavor than when added to hot water and cooked. Chefs call simmering "let the liquid smile, not laugh out loud" [20].

Steaming food in the vapor of boiling-hot water is an excellent method for retaining nutrients in the food being cooked. Shrinkage is reduced and flavor maintained. Cereal products are typically steamed or boiled. Salt and a little oil can be added to the water for best results.

Dry-Heat Cooking.   Dry-heat cooking is used for the more tender foods and includes baking, barbecuing, broiling, grilling, ovenizing, roasting, and frying. Traditional barbecuing means roasting food in a covered pit, usually at a low temperature. The term now includes cooking over a grill or broiler and higher temperatures.

Broiling is usually reserved for the best cuts of meat. Thick pieces of meat will produce uniformly cooked meat with minimum shrinkage. Food is dipped in or brushed with oil to prevent it from sticking to the cooking surface. Meats are cooked on both sides for best results. Temperature is best between 300 and 350°F. The internal temperature should be 140°F for rare, 160°F for medium, and 170°F for well done. Grilling is similar to broiling and is usually reserved for steaks and hamburgers.

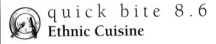

quick bite 8.6
Ethnic Cuisine

A report by the National Restaurant Association on Ethnic Cuisine reached the following conclusions:

1. Americans are becoming more interested in ethnic cuisines.
2. Most consumers indicate that flavorful food is more important than authenticity.
3. Italian, Mexican, and Cantonese-Chinese dominate the market.
4. The "second wave" of ethnic cuisines include Tex-Mex, Chinese (Hunan, Mandarin, or Szechuan), German, Greek, Japanese, and Cajun–Creole.
5. The fastest-growing segments are Italian, Mexican, Thai, and Chinese (Hunan, Mandarin, or Szechuan).
6. The popularity of a cuisine is related directly to a consumer's familiarity with the cuisine's culture.
7. Restaurants are the primary source of ethnic-cuisine education for diners.
8. People also learn about ethnic cuisines by preparing dishes at home, attending potlucks, growing up with it at home, watching TV cooking shows, and traveling.
9. Seventy percent agreed with the statement: "I hate it when a menu only gives a foreign name without explaining the ingredients or preparation."
10. Diners are either culture oriented (30 percent), seeking out new cultural experiences; restaurant oriented (40 percent), motivated by the need to eat and seeing ethnic restaurants as an eating alternative rather than a cultural experience; and preparation oriented (30 percent), where the interest is in the cooking method and ingredients used.
11. The six ethnic appeals are:
    - *Exotic-authentic* (Indian, Thai, Japanese): dishes that are authentic and difficult to make at home.
    - *Festive* (Mexican, Tex-Mex, and Cajun–Creole): hot and spicy and served in a festive atmosphere.
    - *Traditional* (Greek, Scandinavian and German): mild pleasant flavors and relates to people's country of origin.
    - *Fine dining* (French and Italian): where dining is seen as a special occasion.
    - *Basic family-style* (basic Italian, Mexican, and Chinese Cantonese): good for eating with children and for carryout.
    - *Adult-sophisticated* (complex Mexican and authentic Italian): relatively inexpensive and less appropriate for children.

Source: Heather Papadopoulos, "The Dish on Ethnic Cuisine—It's Hot," *Restaurants USA*, vol. 15, no. 3, March 1995, pp. 40–42. *Note:* The report is *Ethnic Cuisines: A Profile* and can be ordered from the National Restaurant Association at (800) 424-5156, ext. 5375.

In ovenizing, food is placed on greased pans and fat dribbled over it frequently while it bakes in the oven. The finished product resembles fried or sautéed food.

Ideally, roasting is done at lower temperatures (250 to 350°F). In this way, shrinkage is reduced while flavor is enhanced. Because roasts will continue to cook after removal from the oven, they should be taken out before the desired internal temperature (the best guide to doneness) is reached. The roast should then "rest" for 15 to 20 minutes before it is sliced. This makes slicing easier.

Foods are fried when they are cooked in fat or oil. The result is a pleasant, nutty flavor. Sautéed items are shallow fried; deep frying involves complete immersion of the food into the fat or oil. In the latter case it is important to ensure that grease does not penetrate the item being cooked. This is accomplished in one of two ways: Either the food is coated with a protective covering or the food is cooked at a temperature high enough that the food emits a barrier of steam to prevent the fat from penetrating the food.

The major ingredients used in baking are:

- *Flour.* All-purpose flour consists of 20 percent soft wheat flour and 80 percent bread flour. Soft, weak, or pastry flour should be used for making pastries; hard-wheat flour is used for making bread.
- *Shortening.* Hydrogenated fats, oils, butter, and lard are used as shortening to produce a tender finished product.
- *Leavening agents.* Air, steam, and baking powder are examples of leavening agents, all used to add texture and volume. Heat helps in the process.
- *Yeast.* Added to water before being stirred with other ingredients, yeast gives off carbon dioxide and alcohol in the baking process.
- *Eggs.* Eggs can be added for flavor, color, or to act as a binding agent.

Salads. Salads consist of a base, body, garnishes, and dressings [21]. The base typically consists of salad greens, is used for visual effect, and is usually not eaten. The body of the salad consists of the items that make up the salad. Garnishes are also added for eye appeal and include such things as croutons, nuts and fish. Finally, garnishes add flavor and help keep the salad moist. It is difficult to maintain consistent quality because fresh vegetables are used in salads. They are also labor intensive and difficult to keep for extended periods. However, they are easy to make, the ingredients can be changed at the last minute, depending on what is available, they are nutritious, and they add a different taste and texture to other items on the menu.

Salads should be made up shortly before serving, as they are highly perishable. Stainless steel equipment is required for their preparation. Fruits such as apples and bananas will brown when exposed to the air. This can be prevented by dipping the fruits in lemon juice.

Control

One important key to controlling costs is to use standardized recipes. Standardized recipes ensure that "when the specified conditions are followed in them, the result is always a product which is similar in all respects" [22]. Standardized recipes should contain "(1) the name of the menu item; (2) the pan size; (3) the temperature; (4) yield; (5) the portion size; (6) the portion utensil; (7) the cooking time; (8) a sequential list of ingredients; (9) the quality of each ingredient; (10) the method; and (11) the special equipment needed" [23].

To prepare a standardized recipe, the following steps should be followed [24]:

1. Prepare the recipe according to the original source and evaluate according to acceptability for the operation.
2. Multiply the recipe to meet the number of portions needed and evaluate again as to acceptability, making any adjustments necessary to improve the dish. For example, the amount of seasonings required is not a simple multiple of the recipe.
3. Prepare the enlarged recipe and have it evaluated by a taste panel for suitability.
4. Prepare the recipe a minimum of three additional times, testing the popularity, preparation cost, and yield.
5. Standardize the recipe relative to ingredients and preparation methods and list all relevant information on a recipe card.

SERVICE

Service Styles

Over the years a variety of service styles have evolved, some more formal than others. Good service is more than following various rules of service. Good service is that which pleases the customer, which adds to the customer's enjoyment of the meal. Where the choice is between slavishly following rules and pleasing the customer, the choice should be the latter.

Family-Style Service. In family-style service, sometimes called English service, food is brought to the table in bowls or on platters and placed before the host. Traditionally, the host plates the food and, if necessary, carves the meat and hands it to the server, who lays the plate before the guest. Less formally, guests may help themselves from the serving dishes placed on the table. This style of service requires fewer servers and is particularly useful for serving large numbers of people in a short period of time, as at a banquet.

Plate Service. Plate or American service involves plating the food in the kitchen and serving it in the dining room. Solids are served from the left and beverages from the right. Designed to be quick and efficient, this service allows for close control of portions.

Table-Side Service. Table-side or French service requires a *chef de rang* (waiter) and a *commis de rang* (assistant). Food is plated and served in the dining room from a *gueridon* (rolling cart). Final cooking may also be done on the gueridon by means of a small stove warmer or *rechaud*. The waiter takes the order, which is delivered to the kitchen by the assistant. The assistant will bring

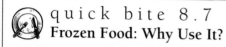
the food from the kitchen to the gueridon, where it is finished and plated by the chef de rang. The assistant serves the plates to the customers. The waiter is responsible for serving drinks and presenting the check.

In French service everything is served from the customer's right except for bread, butter, and salads, which are served from the left. Finger bowls, containing warm water with rose petals or lemon slices, are often provided for rinsing fingers.

Because side tables are required for this style of service, fewer dining tables can be located in a given area. This limits the revenue-producing ability of the restaurant. Due to the heavy use of employees and equipment, table-side service is the most costly of all service styles and therefore tends to be used in restaurants that can command a high average check. It is very dramatic and personal.

Platter Service. In platter, sometimes called Russian, service the food is prepared and portioned in the kitchen, where it is placed on platters. Plates are placed in front of each customer from the right of the guest and the food served from the platter to the plate by the server, serving from the customer's left and working counterclockwise around the table. Plates are removed from the right.

Buffet Service. In buffet service customers choose their meals from items laid out on a serving table. They either plate their own dishes or are served by employees standing behind the table. Silverware can be provided either on the buffet table or at the individual eating tables.

Space Requirements

Table service operations need pickup areas next to the cooking area to hold items prior to service. Salads, beverages, and desserts are picked up separately from cooked items. Rolls, bread, butter, and water are stored at server stations throughout the dining area.

In self-serve operations a variety of serving-line configurations are possible. Straight-line arrangements allow for easy access and a clearly defined flow of traffic. However, this layout limits the number of people who can be served within a set period of time. The greater the amount of linear space available for serving food, the greater the capacity of the system.

For most table service restaurants space requirements for serving areas are estimated as part of the main cooking area. Cafeterias, however, are different, in that separate areas are needed for serving. Space is required for the serving counter, for customers, and for servers. The amount of space needed depends on the number of customers to be served and the time allotted for service. Straight-line cafeteria counters can serve anywhere from 2 to 10 people a minute, depending on the number of choices and the number of servers. The more choices and the fewer the servers, the lower the number of customers who can be served per minute.

In recent years the traditional straight-line cafeteria counter has given way to island counters that are accessible to customers from all sides. These so-called shopping-center arrangements can accommodate up to 20 customers per minute.

Straight-line counters require 10 to 15 square feet of floor space for each linear foot of counter. The linear length of the counter depends on the number of items to be displayed. Shopping-center counters require 18 to 20 square feet of floor space per linear foot of counter. In both cases this space takes into account the counters, customer aisles, room for servers, and back-bar equipment.

The size of the serving area for cafeterias should be based on the dining room capacity. Ideally, the rate of people entering the dining room from the serving area—the flow rate—should equal the rate of people leaving the dining room having completed their meals. The number of usable seats needed in the dining room can be determined as follows:

$$N_d = \frac{N_m + N_{sa}}{(T_m/T_d) - 1}$$

where N_d is the number of persons in the dining room or the number of usable seats, N_m the total number of persons to be fed, N_{sa} the number of persons in the serving area, T_m the meal period, and T_d the time a person spends in the dining area.

Cafeteria counters are placed as close to the cooking area as possible. This allows for speedy replacement of food items as they become depleted. Deserts and salads are placed at the beginning of the line; hot foods are located at the end of the line. This minimizes cooling of the hot items while increasing the sales of cold items. Having loaded up with an entree, a customer may be reluctant to add a dessert. If the dessert is located before the entree, however, the customer may be more inclined to select it.

The flow of many cafeteria lines breaks down as customers leave the line to pay. Additional cashier stations may be required to take care of this problem.

Portion Control

The last step in the control process is to ensure effective portion control. The easiest way to ensure this is to use standard utensils when measuring and/or serving food. This can be done using such things as standard-sized pans, ladles, serving spoons, scoops, portion scales, cutting markers, meat slicers, egg slicers, and individually weighed, measured, and packed items (for example, sandwiches) [25].

DISHWASHING

Dishwashing facilities are typically separated from other functions in an area that requires high levels of ventilation and illumination. Acoustical tile is useful in reducing the high noise level associated with this activity. Machines can be purchased appropriate to the number of dishes to be washed.

Often, separate facilities are used for washing glasses. Satisfactory results can be obtained with the use of additives or by washing glasses shortly after the water has been changed.

Design of this area depends on how much has to be washed and the time available for this function. Some operators carry a large inventory of flatware and store the dirty dishes, washing them over a longer period of time, taking advantage of off-peak energy rates while spreading employee workload. In other situations, management reduces inventory cost but requires that soiled dishes be washed immediately and put right back into service during the course of a meal period.

The sequence of tasks during dishwashing is sorting, scraping or preflushing, stacking, loading, removal, and loading. Equipment should be arranged accordingly. Consideration has to be given to the movement of dishes in and out of the dishwashing area. Commonly, bussers bring dirty dishes into the area in bins. Clean dishes will either go to the kitchen, where the cooked food will be plated, or the dining room, where tables will be reset. Mobile plate and cup racks can be provided to move dishes to these areas.

Pot and Pan Washing

The amount and type of space required for pot and pan washing will depend on the volume to be washed and when it is to be done. Where the same person washes dishes as well as pots, storage space for the pots will be required, as the dishes will have a higher time priority. Larger facilities may use machines rather than the typical sink for this purpose.

quick bite 8.8
Road to the Top: Marian and Michael Ilitch

Secretary-Treasurer and Chairman, Little Caesars Enterprises

A high school graduate, Michael Ilitch quit minor league baseball because of a leg injury. He went on to sell dinnerware and aluminum awnings door to door until he had saved the $10,000 needed to open a restaurant in Garden City, Michigan. Wife Marian suggested the name "Little Caesars." Says Marian, "we were just married, and he was my hero, my Caesar. But he hadn't accomplished anything yet, so he was my little Caesar." That was in 1959. Today the company is a $500 million food, sports, and entertainment enterprise. Michael handles the marketing, while Marian, named number 1 in *Working Woman* magazine's 1994 "Top Women in Business," controls accounting and finances.

Little Caesars Enterprises Inc. is now the country's second-largest chain, with 4700 units worldwide and annual sales of $2.3 billion. In addition to pizza the Ilitches own sports teams and manage theaters. After a slow start—it took 10 years to grow to 50 stores—when women started entering the workforce in large numbers in the 1970s the need for fast food and takeout increased.

Michael says he wants to be remembered for "teaching America how to eat two pizzas." Indeed, the theme "Pizza! Pizza! Two great pizzas! One low price" is heralded by marketing specialists. Others, such as Michael Scruggs, who began as a manager trainee in 1978 and is now a group vice president, credit the Ilitches' ability to motivate employees. "They capture the magic of getting people to perform at a high level. They recognize when they've got someone they can grow with, and they give that person the authority to get the job done." They also give back to the community, getting involved in urban development in the 1980s by purchasing and renovating the historic Fox Theatre. Actually, says Michael, "we got involved in urban development to combat a competitor who opened a new arena in the suburbs." Since 1982, their investment in downtown Detroit has surpassed $200 million. Whether opening a subsidized day-care center or talking to the teenager making the dough, the Ilitches intend to stay in touch with the customers and employees of the future.

Source: Suzanne Kapner, "Marian and Michael Ilitch," *Nations's Restaurant News,* January 1995, pp. 105–106.

WASTE DISPOSAL

Waste disposal requirements depend on the total relative amounts of paper, plastic, cans generated, the cost of removal, and the prevailing laws regarding disposal.

Various disposal options are compaction, incineration, grinding, and pulping [26]. Compactors are useful when handling large amounts of waste. They reduce large volumes of waste into smaller amounts. Both volume and weight are concentrated. Care must be taken that the resulting package can be handled easily. Incineration involves burning the waste. Local pollution regulations may make this option cost prohibitive.

While most municipalities allow grinding as a way of disposing of waste, some communities have experienced problems with non-biodegradable materials and have placed restrictions on the use of this method. In waste pulping a liquefied waste is produced through the use of heavy-duty rotary grinders using recirculating water. The water is extracted and the resulting semidry pulp is stored in bins prior to removal. This system cannot accommodate glass or metal.

ENDNOTES

1. Mahmood Khan, *Foodservice Operations* (Westport, CT: AVI Publishing Company, 1987), pp. 254–257.

2. Lewis J. Minor and Ronald F. Cichy, *Foodservice Systems Management* (Westport, CT: AVI Publishing Company, 1984), p. 100.

3. Khan, *Foodservice Operations*, pp. 148–149.

4. Ibid., p. 175.

5. Ibid., p. 197.

6. Ibid., p. 163.

7. Ibid., pp. 164–165.

8. Ibid., p. 148.

9. Ibid., p. 148.

10. Ibid., pp. 209–211.

11. Edward A. Kazarian, *Foodservice Facilities Planning*, 3rd ed. (New York: Van Nostrand Reinhold, 1989), p. 11.

12. Khan, *Foodservice Operations*, pp. 211–215.

13. Ibid., p. 214.

14. Kazarian, *Foodservice Facilities Planning*, p. 12.

15. Ibid., p. 13.

16. Khan, *Foodservice Operations*, p. 218.

17. Ibid., p. 220.

18. Minor and Cichy, *Foodservice Systems Management*, p. 33.

19. John B. Knight and Lendal H. Kotschevar, *Quantity Food Production, Planning, and Management*, 2nd ed. (New York:Van Nostrand Reinhold, 1989), p. 173.

20. Ibid., p. 275.

21. Khan, *Foodservice Operations*, p. 267.

22. Ibid., pp. 252–253.

23. Minor and Cichy, *Foodservice Systems Management*, p. 130.

24. Khan, *Foodservice Operations*, pp. 254–257.

25. Ibid., p. 283.

26. Kazarian, *Foodservice Facilities Planning*, p. 17.

chapter nine

KITCHEN EQUIPMENT AND INTERIORS: SELECTION, MAINTENANCE, AND ENERGY MANAGEMENT

learning objectives

By the end of this chapter you should be able to:

1. Identify the considerations involved in the selection of kitchen equipment.

2. Identify the basic types of equipment found in kitchens.

3. Compare and contrast the relative advantages of the various materials used in kitchen interiors and equipment construction.

4. Identify the most important concepts in cleaning and maintaining kitchen equipment.

5. Design a comprehensive energy management program.

EQUIPMENT SELECTION

Basic Considerations

Several basic considerations are involved in the selection of kitchen equipment [1]. Management should consider capacity, need, cost, functional attributes, and sanitation and safety.

Capacity. Determination of the capacity of each type of equipment to be used in an operation is critical before deciding how many pieces of which equipment to purchase. If the capacity calculation is too low, bottlenecks and slowdowns will occur; if it is too high, the restaurant will spend too much money on equipment that will not be used to its capacity.

Required equipment capacity can be determined as follows [2]:

1. Analyze each food item on the menu to estimate the number of portions to be prepared for every meal period. If menus are changed daily, it will be necessary to use a sample of dishes to be served.
2. The portion size for every menu item is then determined.
3. Multiplying the projected number of portions by the portion size will give the total volume of food to be prepared at each meal period.
4. The method of preparation and production is selected next for each item on the menu. Depending on the style of operation, items may be prepared individually to order, in small batches prior to the order, in large batches prior to service, or partially prepared in batches and finished when an order is received. The processing time has to be taken into account, together with when the preparation can be done. It may, for example, be possible to use the same piece of equipment at different times during the day to prepare more than one item.
5. The batch size is then determined for those items to be prepared in batches. The smaller and more frequently prepared the batches, the less equipment capacity is needed and the fresher the end product.
6. For items prepared to order, the number of portions to be prepared at any one time is estimated based on the projected number of customers, which items they are likely to order, and their arrival patterns.
7. Equipment catalogs can then be consulted to determine the number of pieces of equipment to be ordered. Some types of equipment are selected on the basis of the number of pans they can hold. In this case it is necessary to divide the number of portions to be prepared by how many can fit into a standard-size pan to get the capacity of the equipment in "number of pans required." For example, ovens hold bake pans that are 18 by 26 inches. Identifying how many portions can fit into a pan 18 by 26 inches and dividing that into the number of portions required will give the number of pans required and, consequently, an estimate of the size of the oven needed.

Need. Equipment should not be bought or leased unless it is needed. But what, exactly, does this mean? A piece of equipment is "needed" if it improves the quality of the food being prepared, produces product and/or labor cost savings; results in increased quantity of finished product, and/or contributes to the profitability of the operation [3].

The need for a particular piece of equipment should be classified as either essential, high utility, or basic [4]. In this way, priorities can be established in the event of a cash shortage.

Cost. There are various costs involved in the purchase of a piece of equipment [5]. In addition to the initial purchase price, the equipment must be installed, insured, maintained and repaired, financed, and operated.

Part of the cost analysis involves inclusion of the labor costs involved in

Courtesy Rock Bottom Restaurants, Inc.

preparation. The cost of buying preprocessed vegetables should be compared with the cost of a vegetable peeler plus the labor cost of peeling the items in-house.

Khan suggests the following formula as a method of calculating the value of a piece of equipment [6]:

$$H = \frac{L(A + B)}{C + L(D + E + F) - G}$$

where H is the calculated value; L the expected life of the equipment in years; A the savings in labor per year; B the savings in material per year; C the cost of the equipment, including installation; D the cost of utilities per year; E the cost of maintenance and repair of the equipment per year; F the annual projected interest on the money in C, if invested elsewhere for the life of the equipment; and G the turn-in value at the end of the life of the equipment.

If H is greater than 1.0, the equipment should be purchased. The higher the value of H, the more attractive the purchase becomes. This equation requires an estimate of the expected life of the equipment. The normal life of kitchen equipment varies from 9 to 15 years.

Functional Attributes.   It is important that equipment do what it is intended to do. Performance relative to cost and compared to the performance

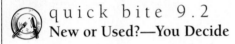

quick bite 9.2
New or Used?—You Decide

Here are some considerations involved in purchasing used equipment:

1. In renovating an existing operation, check to see whether kitchen equipment was purchased new and was well maintained. It may only need a good cleaning to keep it operating efficiently.
2. Using old equipment is risky if it must be moved to a new location. Without the original packing, pieces may break loose.
3. It is risky to rely totally on used equipment.
4. There is less risk when purchasing used nonmechanical equipment. However, check for the NSF logo and make sure that it meets local codes. Georgia, for example, requires four-compartment pot sinks.
5. Buy new if the equipment is "menu critical," if the food items need critical temperatures or finish, if there is any question of employee safety, if the equipment is "mechanically or electronically complex, if you don't have someone you trust to check it out beforehand, or if the manufacturer is out of business.
6. Used refrigeration equipment should be priced at no more than 10 to 20 percent of the cost of new equipment.

Source: Foster Frable, Jr., "Is Purchasing Used Equipment a Wise Decision?" *Nation's Restaurant News*, October 3, 1994. pp. 36, 61.

of other equipment should be examined carefully. Consideration should also be given to likely changes in the menu that may render an expensive piece of equipment obsolete. Quietness of operation, availability of parts, and ease of maintenance are also important. Finally, the type of energy used must be noted as part of the cost consideration.

Sanitation and Safety. The National Sanitation Foundation (NSF) certifies equipment that meets the sanitary standards required for foodservice operations. NSF-approved equipment should be a consideration in making equipment purchases.

Safety is also an important consideration. All materials used should be nontoxic. Parts should be easily disassembled for easy cleaning, moving and sharp parts need to be protected, and safety locks are desirable on all equipment.

Materials Used

The cost of a piece of equipment is directly related to the type of material used to construct it. The following are the most common materials used in constructing kitchen equipment.

Wood.   The disadvantages of wood-constructed items outweigh the advantages. Because wood absorbs moisture it tends to crack, thereby making it unsafe from the viewpoint of sanitation. It is, however, light in weight, can be designed into various shapes, cushions noise, is attractive, and is relatively inexpensive. Today, its use is limited to areas where there will be no contact with food.

Metals.   Although a variety of metals are used in foodservice equipment, the most common metals in use are alloys. An alloy is a combination of one or more metals, commonly stainless steel (iron and carbon), brass (copper, zinc, and other metals), and Monel (nickel and copper). Pure copper is almost never used because it needs constant polishing, is heavy, and reacts with some food items.

Stainless steel is easily cleaned, is attractive, resists rust and stain formation, and can, because its surfaces show dirt easily, be kept sanitary. Two important considerations in purchasing stainless steel are thickness and finish. Thickness is important because stainless steel is fairly expensive. Selection is done through gauge numbers, which indicate the thickness of the steel. The thicker the steel, the lower the gauge. Gauges 8, 10, and 12 are good supports; 12 and 14 can be used for tabletops. Cost is also a function of the amount of polishing desired. The more polishing required, the higher the cost. The amount of polishing done on the equipment is a function of the finish number; the higher the number, the more polishing was done and the higher the cost. In production areas, finish 4 is common. In serving areas, a higher number would be appropriate.

Nickel is often found on equipment trim, railings, and counters. Aluminum is popular for utensils, equipment both inside and out, and steam-jacketed kettles. It is light, is a good conductor of heat and electricity, does not corrode easily, and is durable.

---

 quick bite 9.3
Underbar Design

Despite the fact that underbar equipment determines bar productivity, it is usually the last part of the bar to be constructed. Here are appropriate construction standards:

1. *Stainless steel.* Nickel keeps steel from rusting. The best quality is 18/8 (the ratio of steel to nickel) series 300.
2. *Gauge.* The lower the gauge, the thicker and longer lasting the metal. An 18-gauge stainless is needed for the more substantial parts of the system, while front aprons can be constructed of gauge as high as 24.
3. *Insulation.* This should be foamed-in-place polyurethane.
4. *Construction.* The most common method of construction is spot welding. The best method is heliarc welding, a process by which metal is heated to a temperature sufficient to fuse pieces together.

Source: Michael W. Sherer, "Underbar Design," *Top Shelf,* July–August 1992, pp. 42–45.

Cast iron is used in places that do not come into contact with food, such as stands and equipment supports. Iron is used in pots, pans, griddles, and gas burners, while brass is favored in faucets and shutoff valves.

Steel ovens, range interiors, frames, and supports are common. When steel and iron are treated with acid, they are galvanized. Galvanized steel and iron are common in dishwashing machines, sinks, and equipment legs.

Plastics.   Various plastics are being used increasingly in foodservice operations. They are very versatile, durable, and capable of being molded into different shapes. Acrylics are used in food covers; melamine can be used for dishes and glassware; fiberglass trays are common; nylons are used for mobile parts; storage bowls and containers are made of polyethylene; dishwashing racks are commonly made of polyproplyene; polystyrene is used in cups and covers.

Coatings.   Coatings are placed on the interior surfaces of equipment to give it additional properties. For example, silicone makes a nonsticking surface; Teflon aids in the release of food from a pan. For surfaces that come into contact with food, the coating should be smooth, corrosion resistant, nonabsorbent, as heat resistant as possible, and easily cleanable. There should be no interaction between the food and the coating such that the taste, color or smell of the food is changed.

Energy Sources

Because of the rising cost of energy, the source used to power the equipment is becoming an increasingly important consideration in selecting equipment. Electricity, gas, steam, and oil are all used as energy sources in kitchens.

In foodservice operations the form of energy used most commonly is electricity. Two voltage systems are used; 110–120 volts and 220–240 volts, the latter being more powerful. It is important that the correct voltage be available for a particular piece of equipment.

Fuses are used to prevent the entire electrical system from "blowing." The fuses used must be appropriate to the task. A simple equation is useful in determining the type of fuse required (7):

$$W = V \times I$$

where W is the measure of electricity in watts, V the force behind the electrical current, and I the amount of electricity flowing.

For 2000 watts of electricity on a 110-volt line, the amount flowing, I, is W divided by V, or 2000 divided by 110, or 18.2 amperes. Adding in a 25 percent safety factor means that this circuit should be protected by a 25-ampere fuse. Electricity costs are expressed as a certain number of cents per kilowatthour, the cost of 1000 watts of electricity running for 1 hour.

Specifications

It is vital that exact specifications be used when purchasing equipment. These should include [8]:

1. The title or name of the piece of equipment
2. The scope or intended use
3. Classification: the type, model, size, and style
4. Specific requirements to include such things as:
    -   Dimensions and temperature ranges
    -   Materials used in construction and finish
    -   Electrical requirements
    -   Control regulations and displays
    -   Performance criteria
    -   Certification by various agencies [such as the Underwriters' Laboratories (UL), National Sanitation Foundation (NSF), National Electric Manufacturers Association (NEMA), American Gas Association (AGA), and the American Society of Mechanical Engineers (ASME) for steam equipment]
    -   Types of warranties
    -   Parts and labor numbers and costs for maintenance and repair
    -   Number of manuals required
5. Quality assurance: inspection and performance tests
6. Delivery and installation dates
7. Payment terms and dates
8. Drawings and illustrations
9. The name of the contact

EQUIPMENT TYPES

Dry-Heat Cooking Equipment

Ranges.   Ranges, either gas or electric, are the most basic piece of cooking equipment for most foodservice operations. Generally, they are mounted on the floor, with the cooking done in pots directly on the range top. A heavy frame is preferred because of the heavy use that ranges receive. Ideally, they should have reflectors and removable drip pans for ease of cleaning. While the number of ranges required will vary depending on the type of menu served, the following guidelines can be used as a guide [9]. For a restaurant serving fewer than 300 meals a day, one range would be sufficient, two ranges would be needed to cook between 300 and 400 meals a day, three could handle 400 to 500, while four could cope with 500 to 1000 meals daily.

Hot tops require from 20 to 30 percent more energy than open burners because the heating plate must be heated before the pan is heated. While burners are limited to one pan each, hot tops offer more flexibility by providing an area for several pots and pans.

It is important that grease traps be easily removable for both cleaning and maintenance.

Conventional Ovens. Because conventional ovens are used a great deal, durability is important. The ease of cleaning and energy conservation should also be considered. Four to five inches of insulation (fiberglass, rockwool, or vitreous fiber) is desirable to help cut energy losses. Ovens may be stacked one on top of the other to cut down on space needs. The same guidelines for range requirements can be used to estimate oven needs. A more sophisticated formula is [10]:

$$\text{required no. ovens} = \frac{\text{no. servings}}{\substack{\text{no. servings} \\ \text{per pan}} \times \substack{\text{no. pans} \\ \text{per oven}} \times \substack{\text{no. batches} \\ \text{per hour}}}$$

---

quick bite 9.4
New Technology in Equipment

Advances in kitchen technology are helping operators do a better job of running their businesses. Here are some examples:

1. Convection ovens that vent rearward rather than from the top, thereby freeing up storage space. According to Michael Langley, senior engineer for Arrow Industries, "it gives you back the top of the oven for sheet pan storage."

2. Equipment that is engineered to handle more than one task at the same time. Langley notes a combination oven that bakes bread and steams fish in the same area with no crossover of odor or moisture. This is particularly important for operations where cooking goes on 24 hours a day, such as cruise ships.

3. Rapid heat recovery, which minimizes heat loss when moving food items in and out of combination ovens.

4. Combination gas and electric "slow cooker" units that act as smoking, slow-roasting, and temperature-holding units to produce everything from mesquite-barbecued chickens to ribs and briskets. Sandy Davis, executive chef at the Cowgirl Hall of Fame, loads briskets into his cooker at night and programs it for a 10-hour cycle. "The smoker switches itself into a 'hold' phase—168°F—after the timer shuts down the cooking." The briskets are ready the next morning, at which time the chickens are put in for a 2-hour cycle and the ribs for 2-1/2 hours.

5. Better fans in convection ovens, making for more even cooking.

Source: Jack Hayes, "The Kitchen Quest: Versatility and Simplicity," *Nation's Restaurant News*, September 19, 1994, pp. 124, 128, 132, 164.

Convection Ovens. Placement of the heating element(s) in a conventional oven does not allow for the consistent distribution of heat inside the oven. Convectional ovens are designed to eliminate this problem. The forced-air model uses a fan to distribute heat in a uniform manner, thus allowing more internal space to be used.

In the roll-in type, carts or racks can be rolled into a large oven, thereby allowing heat to reach all the racks equally. Another model, the pulse-type, alternates hot and cold air. The hot air cooks the food and the cold air prevents overcooking.

In general, convection ovens require less labor, space, and energy, cook at lower temperatures, and enhance quality by allowing for an even distribution of heat. On the other hand, soft foods or batters may suffer visually from the circulation of air in the oven.

Infrared Ovens. The relatively new infrared ovens take up less space than conventional ovens while using less energy because they cook at higher temperatures for relatively short periods.

Mechanical and Pizza Ovens. The major differences between conventional and mechanical ovens are that the latter are larger and have mechanical parts inside that help move the food while inside the oven. A reel oven has trays that move vertically in the oven. Glass doors allow for inspection of the food as it is being cooked. Rotary ovens, on the other hand, have circular shelves that rotate horizontally around a central axis. Traveling tray ovens are large ovens that allow food items to travel through the oven on trays. Pizza ovens are deeper than the other types and allow for the horizontal placement of pizzas.

Microwave Ovens. Microwave ovens use radiation to cook food. Because of this, food is cooked faster and the surrounding air is not heated. These ovens are particularly useful for reheating items and thawing meats. They cannot handle large quantities of food nor can they brown food items. To eliminate the latter problem, a combination convection/microwave oven has been developed.

Deck Ovens. Deck ovens are decked or stacked to save on floor space. They may be either roasting or baking ovens. Capacity can be estimated by identifying the number of batches per hour that can be handled. Roasting times vary from 15 to 18 minutes per pound for a cooked ham to 30 to 50 minutes per pound for fresh pork. Baking times vary from 15 to 20 minutes for rolls to 50 to 60 minutes for fruit pies.

The two-deck arrangement is the maximum height for safety in a deck oven. In a three-deck arrangement the top oven is too high while the lower deck puts a strain on workers' backs because of the bending that is required for loading and unloading.

Broilers. Broiling produces a charred or smoked flavor to meats by cooking the meat on a grid, which allows the fat to drip down and partially burn, thereby imparting the smoked flavor.

Broilers are commonly included into the range area in one of three ways [11]. Either the broiler is at the same height as the range top, or it is purchased as a central component with an overhead oven heated by the burners in the broiling compartment, or it is mounted on a conventional range-type oven with or without an overhead oven.

A small broiler—a salamander—can be mounted on top of a heavy-duty range for smaller operations that do not require much broiling. Broiler capacity is a function of the size of the broiler grid and the type of food to be cooked. For example, a 1-inch steak will take 15 minutes to be cooked rare, while a half chicken will require 30 minutes of cooking. The number of portions to be prepared at any one time will determine the number and size of broilers needed. For example, the cooking time for various items on a griddle will range from 1 to 2 minutes for a grilled cheese sandwich to 8 to 10 minutes for a ham steak.

Griddles. A griddle offers a heated surface particularly useful for short-order cooking. Space should be provided near the griddle to hold supplies and other equipment necessary for its operation. Griddle capacity is determined as suggested above for broilers.

Steam Equipment

Steam-Jacketed Kettles. Steam-jacketed kettles are indispensable in most restaurant kitchens. They are excellent for foods that do not require high temperatures. The steam in the jacket heats the metal, which, in turn, heats the food inside the kettle—the steam does not come into contact with the food, so, the nutritional loss is low. If there is no steam supply, a special generator must be purchased, adding to the cost of the equipment. A water faucet over and a drainage line near the bottom of the kettle are important considerations.

The capacity of the kettle needed is calculated as follows [12]:

$$\text{capacity of kettle} \atop \text{(in gallons or liters)} = \frac{\text{no. servings} \times \text{portion size} \times \text{\% headspace}}{\substack{128 \text{ oz (1 gal)} \times \text{ no. batches} \\ \text{[or 1000 ml (1 liter)]}}}$$

Fifteen percent is usually allowed for the headspace to prevent overflow, spillage, and/or spattering.

Steamers. Steamers are capable of cooking large quantities of food quickly while retaining nutrients and maintaining quality. Once food is placed in the steamer, even from a frozen state, it can be left alone. Although useful for vegetables, rice, pasta, and special desserts such as custard, other types of food cannot be successfully steamed. In addition, adjustments are necessary to get the food quality to where it should be.

Fryers

Deep-Fat Fryers. In purchasing deep-fat fryers it is important that they be made of noncorrosive material and that the temperature controls be placed such that they can be reached safely without exposure to spattered fat. A convenient system should be in place to drain the fat and a mechanism should be in place for the removal of food particles from the fat.

The capacity of a fryer depends on the pounds of fat in the fry kettle, the heat input, and the cooking time required. Typically, fryers are designed on a fat-to-food ratio of 6:1, indicating that 6 pounds of fat is required in the kettle for each pound of food to be fried. Conventional fryer capacity ranges from 15 to 130 pounds. A useful rule of thumb is that a fryer can prepare 1.5 to 2 times its weight of fat per hour. Thus a 130-pound-capacity fryer can cook from 195 to 260 pounds of food per hour.

Pressure fryers have lids that can be sealed, thus allowing frying under pressure. As a result, cooking time is shorter and at a lower temperature. Because of this the fat does not break down so quickly. In addition, there is less moisture loss, resulting in food that is crispy on the outside and juicy on the inside.

The continuous-type fryer moves food continuously through the fat on a conveyer belt. An automatic basket-lift or a timer bell allows cooks to attend to other tasks while frying food without the danger of it being overcooked.

Tilting Skillets. A tilting skillet or tilting fry pan is fastened to the floor by brackets. Its versatility makes it very desirable: It can substitute as a griddle, deep-fat fryer, poacher, or holder of food.

Small Equipment

Food Cutters. Able to handle meats, vegetables, and fruits, food cutters can cut, dice, and shred. Food is placed in a bowl that rotates and exposes the food to high-speed rotating blades.

The capacity of the machine is a function of the size of the bowl and the amount of food that can be processed per minute. Cutters can be either bench or floor models.

Slicer. The essential elements of a food slicer are a circular knife blade and a carriage that passes under the blade. These allow for strict control of the thickness of slices of food.

Mixer. Every kitchen needs some blenders and mixers. The major purchasing consideration is the horsepower of the motor. It is preferable to purchase a larger model over a smaller one that requires several batches. The variety of attachments available make mixers very versatile pieces of equipment.

Through the use of a variety of attachments, a mixer can do much more than mix food. Adapters are available to allow chopping, dicing, shredding, and juice extraction. The smaller bench model comes in sizes from 5 to 20 quarts, while the larger models are sized from 30 to 400 quarts.

Vertical Cutter/Mixer. Consisting of a stationary bowl with high-speed horizontal blades, the vertical cutter/mixer has a greater capacity than that of other food cutters.

Vegetable Peelers. Vegetable peelers consist of a cylindrical tank that has a revolving disk in the bottom. There is an opening above the disk for loading the potatoes and one below for removing the peels. As the disk revolves, the vegetables are peeled by being thrown against the abrasive-coated walls.

Dishwashers

Dishwashers come in a variety of types. The most common are the immersion dishwasher, which submerges racks of dishes; the single-tank, stationary-type dishwasher, which wash racks of dishes with jets of water within a single tank; the conveyer-rack machine, which carries racks of dishes on a conveyer belt through the dishwasher; the flight-type dishwasher, which has a continuous rack conveyer on which dishes are placed on pegs or bars for transportation through the machine; and the carousel-type dishwasher, which features a closed-circuit conveyer for loading and unloading dishes.

Dishwasher capacity is stated as the number of pieces that can be washed per hour or the number of meals to be served per meal period. A single-tank dishwasher can handle from 50 to 600 meals per meal period; two-tank machines are capable of handling from 1500 to 2000 meals per meal period; three-tank machines are suitable for 2500 meals per meal period.

Refrigeration Equipment

Refrigerating equipment may be either mobile or fixed reach-ins, specialized units, or ice-making equipment [13].

Reach-ins.   Reach-in units may be of either refrigerated or low- temperature type. Whether the door opens to the left or right is an important consideration when considering traffic flow throughout the kitchen. Doors, which may be of full or half length, should have strong catches. Adjustable shelving allows maximum storage flexibility.

Low-temperature reach-ins may be of upright or chest type. The former cost a little more and will lose more refrigerated air than the latter, but they are easier to defrost, require less floor space, and allow for easier storage and removal of items.

Specialized Equipment.   Specialized equipment consists of such items as fountains, salad or cold pans, display refrigerators, and walk-ins.

Because fountains must provide for different refrigeration needs, two or more condensing units may be required. For example, drinking and carbonated water, whipped cream, and other foods should be kept at about 40°F, while ice cream must be slightly colder than 10°F for dishing.

Salad pans or cold pans are commonly used in cafeteria counters for display of salads and other cold items. Some are designed to be flooded with water, which is then frozen and the display items placed on the ice.

Walk-ins are used to store large quantities of food in central storage areas. Typically, a large operation uses three walk-ins: one for fruits and vegetables, one for meats, poultry, and fish, and one for diary products.

Ice-Making Equipment.   Electricity, cold water, and drainage facilities are necessary for ice-making equipment. Ice can be made in blocks, cubes, or crushed/flake form. Flake machines produce more ice per day than do cube machines. Block ice can be sculpted into decoration pieces. Cubes can be from 1/4 to 1 inch. Cube ice lasts longer in drinks and is, therefore, used in takeout and for drinks to be held before being consumed. Flake ice, on the other hand, cools the drink faster but melts faster as well. Small cubes or flakes make a drink look larger in the glass than do large cubes.

INTERIOR SURFACES

Materials

Selection of materials for interior walls, floors, and ceilings has to take into account not only attractiveness to customers, but also such things as ease of cleaning, ease of maintenance, and safety.

Flooring. The most important factors to consider when selecting floor coverings are the resiliency and porosity of the material. Resiliency refers to the ability of the material to withstand shock. Asphalt, linoleum, vinyl, and sealed wood are examples of resilient floors.

Porosity identifies the extent to which the material can be penetrated by liquids. Absorption of liquids can damage a floor, in addition to making it difficult to get rid of microorganisms on or below the surface.

A variety of materials can be used for floor coverings [14]. Asphalt is tough, inexpensive, and resistant to water and acids. However, it tends to buckle under heavy weight and does not wear well under exposure to grease or soap.

Good carpeting holds its shape. It absorbs both sound and shock and has a good appearance. It should not be used in food preparation areas because of the difficulty in keeping it clean and hygienic in an area where spills are common.

Ceramic tiles are nonabsorbent. They are useful for walls but are much too slippery for use on floors. Concrete, a mixture of cement, sand, and gravel, is inexpensive. However, because it is porous, it should not be used in food preparation areas.

Although it retains its shape, linoleum is nonabsorbent and is unable to withstand weight. Marble has a good appearance, is nonresilient, nonabsorbent, expensive, and slippery. Plastic is the most resilient of all the materials listed. It is, however, nonabsorbent and cannot be exposed to alkalines or solvents.

Rubber helps prevent slips and is resilient. It can be slippery when wet unless an abrasive is added. Although resilient and resistant to water, grease, and oil, water seepage can cause vinyl tiles to lift, causing a safety and sanitation hazard.

Terrazzo, a mixture of marble chips and cement, offers a good appearance if sealed properly. However, it is nonresilient and nonabsorbent, and is slippery when wet. Additionally, the installed cost is approximately six times that of vinyl. However, because of its longer lifespan, over a 40-year period the cost of terrazzo is only 12 percent higher than that of vinyl.

Wood is absorbent, can be fairly inexpensive, and offers a good appearance. It should not be used in food preparation areas, as it offers a breeding place for dust and insects. Properly sealed, wood can be used in serving areas.

Kitchen floors need to be nonslip, sanitary, and able to handle spills and constant cleaning. Preferred materials are marble, terrazzo, natural quarry tile, asphalt tile, or sealed wood. Poured seamless concrete can be used if it has been sealed adequately.

Carpeting can only be used in serving areas. Carpets that are closely woven are easier to clean. Medium to dark colors with patterns tend not to

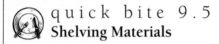

quick bite 9.5
Shelving Materials

New codes and regulations will reduce usable space in production and storage areas by as much as 30 percent. Manufacturers of storage equipment have made improvements in storage equipment to help address this problem.

1. High-impact polymer shelving is lighter in weight than traditional shelving and is available in low-, medium-, or high-flexibility forms with prices that range from much less to slightly higher than that of metal shelving. Low-flexibility systems are suitable for use in warewashing or for chemical or linen storage. Polymer dunnage racks have the advantage over wood pallets that they can be pressure washed and steam cleaned. The medium- and high-flexibility systems allow for such features as adaptable shelves.
2. Cantilevered shelving systems are easily adjustable and offer more space than do to conventional systems. They are finished in corrosion-resistant aluminum or epoxy-coated steel.
3. Wall storage systems can be custom-designed to store food preparation items as well as to provide fold-down work surfaces.
4. High-density active aisle systems "combine stationary units along with mobile units which are guided by an overhead track to create a 'floating' aisle and a high-density storage system." Having the track overhead increases accessibility and means that no special floor preparation is needed, while safety and sanitation maintenance are easily accomplished.
5. Extrawide and special-use shelving.

Source: Foster Frable, Jr., "Storage Equipment Helps Manage Shrinking Space," *Nation's Restaurant News,* November 7, 1994, p. 34.

show spots. They do, however, require vacuuming on a daily basis in addition to periodic shampooing. Because bar areas suffer from dropped cigarettes and spilled drinks, they can use marble or tile to advantage.

Coving is a useful technique that improves sanitation by providing a curved sealed edge between floor and wall. Sharp corners or gaps that would be difficult to clean are thus eliminated.

Walls and Ceilings.   In selecting wall and ceiling materials, four things are particularly important: cleanability, location, noise reduction, and color. Often materials are chosen without regard to future maintenance time and costs. For example, ceramic tile, which is a popular wall covering, should have its grouting smooth, waterproof, and sealed to help in keeping it clean.

Stainless steel is a favorite material for kitchen locations because it is durable and moisture resistant. This is important in an area such as a kitchen, which involves a great deal of traffic and has a high humidity level. On the other hand, painted plaster or cinder-block walls, if selected properly, can be used successfully in dry areas. They would not, however, be suitable in areas where food or grease could splash on the wall.

Older people tend to touch the wall for support, especially on stairs and in corridors. Wall surfaces in these areas should be easy to clean. Smooth sealed plastic, plastic-laminated panels, and plastic-coated tiles are excellent ceiling choices for their ability to spread light and absorb sound.

In food preparation areas it is desirable to have light-colored walls and ceilings to help distribute light and to make dirt easier to see (and, therefore, to clean).

EQUIPMENT MAINTENANCE

The cost of equipment maintenance, which is largely a function of labor, should be determined when purchasing equipment. Planning the maintenance function will help assure lower operating costs through reduced maintenance while ensuring continued high sanitation standards throughout the life of the equipment.

The following are the most important concepts involved in cleaning and maintenance [15].

---

 quick bite 9.6
Getting It Repaired

Before calling for equipment repair, make sure that you have the following information:

1. Equipment brand
2. Model number
3. Serial number
4. Current operating problem

According to service manager Randy Finley, "95 percent of the calls we receive do not contain this basic information." The more details that can be given over the phone, the easier it is to diagnose problems before arriving at the restaurant site. Calling a service representative rather than the factory will speed the repair process. Many repairs can be "made" over the phone if the service representative is trained to ask the right questions. Finally, before calling, check the basics: Is the appliance plugged in? Did a circuit-breaker trip? Is the gas on?

Source: Kat LaMons, "When It Has to Be Repaired—NOW!" *Restaurants USA,* vol. 15, no. 1, January 1995, pp. 37–38.

---

1. Minimize soil, dirt, and food buildup.
2. When buildup occurs, make it easy to remove.
3. Avoid as many soil-collecting surfaces and recesses as possible.
4. Select smooth, nonporous surfaces.
5. Provide easy access to areas that have to be cleaned frequently.
6. Streamline electrical, gas, and plumbing connections.
7. Use coved corners on equipment and building surfaces.
8. Provide adequate drains and cleanouts.
9. Use automated cleaning and sanitizing systems.

Stainless Steel Surfaces

Stainless steel surfaces are subject to staining. It requires contact with air to keep the layer of oxide that gives it its shine, and thus it must be cleaned regularly. On a routine basis the surface should be cleaned with a hot detergent solution, rinsed, and wiped dry with a soft clean cloth. Periodic deep cleaning consists of a paste of water and a nonabrasive scouring powder. The paste is rubbed in the direction of the polish lines to prevent scratches. The surface is then rinsed and dried.

Stainless steel, wood, or plastic scrapers—but not steel wool, steel scrapers, or knives—can be used to remove heavy deposits of food and/or soil. A vinegar and water solution, followed by rinsing and drying, is appropriate for removing hard water deposits.

Equipment

Broilers. Broiler grates and other movable parts should be cleaned daily. With gas broilers it is important to check the flame. A yellow-tipped flame indicates insufficient air. The burners can be adjusted to give a blue flame. Gas ports should be kept clean. With electric broilers heating elements can be replaced when they burn out.

An energy management program would ensure that [16]:

1. Burner orifices are checked and cleaned.
2. Pilot lights are cleaned and adjusted.
3. Air shutters are checked to ensure that the air–gas mixture is correct.
4. Ceramic and metal radiant units are checked for deterioration and replaced with new chips if blackened or cracked.

Coffee Urns. Two problems with coffee urns can ruin the taste of the coffee. First, minerals in the water can be deposited. Second, deposits will accumulate on surfaces that are exposed to brewed coffee or coffee vapors.

The solution is to clean the urn after making every batch of coffee. This is done by rinsing the urn out to remove any remaining coffee and deposits, adding a gallon or so of hot water, and brushing the interior of the urn, then rinsing the urn. Twice a week the urn can be cleaned with a manufacturer-recommended product to remove stubborn deposits.

Thermostats should be checked periodically to ensure that the correct serving temperature is being maintained. Weekly checks for leaks should also be made.

Dishwashers.   The power should be turned off before cleaning a dishwasher. Tanks have to be drained and cleaned, wash arms removed, and lime or hard-water deposits eliminated from the rinse jets.

The exterior can be cleaned with a detergent solution, rinsed, and dried. Periodic checks are necessary for leaks, and belts and conveyors are examined for wear and lubricated.

On a regular basis [17]:

1. Spray nozzles, tanks, and heater coils are cleaned with a wire when lime deposits are detected.
2. The temperature of the final rinse is checked to ensure that it is at 180°F on high-temperature machines and at 140°F on low-temperature machines.
3. Feed and drain valves and pumps are checked for water leakage.
4. Speed reducers on conveyor-type washers are examined to ensure proper lubrication.
5. The insulation of water lines in the recirculation loop is noted.
6. The power rinse is examined to ensure that it turns off automatically.
7. Thermometers are checked and adjusted.

Fryers.   Fryers should be cleaned daily or at least twice weekly, depending on use. The fat must be removed and the interior wiped out and filled with water and a fryer cleaner solution. The interior is then rinsed and dried after removal of the cleaning solution.

Tilting fry pans should be cleaned daily. Food residue is scraped from the surfaces, which are then washed down with warm water and the pan rinsed.

An energy program would ensure that [18]:

1. Fat containers are inspected for grease leaks.
2. Thermostats are calibrated.
3. Gas burners and pilot lights are cleaned and adjusted.
4. Flues are examined for possible obstructions.
5. Gas valves are lubricated.

Fat is the most costly part of the frying process. During frying the food absorbs fat, which must constantly be replaced. Fat should be strained daily and 15 to 20 percent of the kettle capacity added as fresh fat.

Fat breakdown can be minimized by [19]:

1. Switching the fryer to "standby" during slack periods.
2. Never adding seasonings to foods during frying.

3. Keeping all metal components in contact with the fat free of carbon, food crumbs, soap, and moisture.
4. Ensuring that the fat level not be topped up with lard, meat drippings, or other fatty substances.

Griddles.   At a minimum, griddles should be cleaned once a day. A griddle stone rather than steel wool should be used on the griddle surface, always rubbing with the grain of the surface. The surface is then seasoned prior to the next use.

It is also important that [20]:

1. Thermostats are calibrated.
2. Pilot lights are adjusted to the lowest possible flame.
3. The air–gas mixture is checked to ensure a blue flame. Cold spots should be checked for on a periodic basis.

Ovens.   Similar maintenance procedures for griddles should be evident in the operation of ovens. On a daily basis, burned-on particles of food should be removed from the decks and the interior of the oven brushed out. Hardened food can be removed by sprinkling with salt and running the oven at 500°F for half an hour. The charred food is then removed with a spatula.

Ovens and oven racks need to be level for even cooking. Door crevices need to be kept clean to ensure proper closure, which keeps the heat in.

The interior of convection ovens may be porcelain, stainless steel, aluminized steel, or Teflon coated and should be cleaned following the recommendations of the manufacturer. Clean doors will help ensure minimum heat loss. Fan blades that are dirty will reduce airflow and can be cleaned with a detergent solution.

Microwave ovens require less maintenance that do other types. As before, special attention should be paid to the door to ensure a tight fit.

After cleaning ranges a light coating of cooking oil is applied to help prevent rusting.

Food Cutters, Choppers, and Slicers.   Choppers and cutters should be rinsed after each use. They should be unplugged before cleaning. Special care must be taken with slicer blades, which should be sanitized and allowed to dry after cleaning.

Mixers.   As above, mixers should be cleaned right after use.

Tables.   Tabletops can be scrubbed with a hot detergent solution before being rinsed, sanitized, and allowed to dry. Drawers should be emptied and washed weekly.

Refrigerators.   The inside of reach-in refrigerators should be cleaned once a week. Shelves are removed and cleaned at the pot sink or run throughout the dishwasher.

Condenser coils need to be watched for dirt buildup, which cuts down on the transfer of heat and causes the unit to run excessively. Coils are dusted or wiped free of dust and dirt.

Walk-ins should be cleaned at most once a month, depending on use, following the procedures outlined above. A comprehensive program would ensure that [21]:

1. Worn or damaged compressor belts are replaced.
2. The refrigerant level is checked if a short cycle or loss of temperature control is noticed.
3. The fan, condenser fins, plates, and blower coils are cleaned.
4. Gaskets, seals, and hinges on doors are checked for a tight fit.
5. Defrosting is done monthly.
6. Thermostats are properly calibrated.
7. Hinges and latches are lubricated with food-grade oil.
8. Outside walls are felt for cold spots that would indicate insulation failure.
9. The defrost cycle is set such that freezers will defrost during off-peak hours.
10. Compressors are checked for leaks and refrigerant levels.
11. The condenser is brush cleaned.
12. Coils are examined to ensure that they are not clogged with dirt or grease.
13. All service motors are inspected regularly.

Steam Equipment.   Steam-jacketed kettles are cleaned after the steam is turned off and they have been allowed to cool. The kettle is flushed, filled with a detergent solution, and soaked for 30 to 60 minutes. The kettle is then drained, rinsed, and sanitized.

Ventilating Hoods.   Filters should be cleaned at least once a week. Clogged filters reduce airflow and significantly reduce the efficiency of the ventilation system. As a result, droplets can fall onto food that is being prepared. A more serious danger is that posed by the threat of fire due to grease buildup.

ENERGY MANAGEMENT

It is estimated that a comprehensive energy management program can save the average foodservice company 20 percent of its energy bill. One of the major problems in controlling energy costs is that a significant part of the cost is fixed. Refrigerators and fans are in operation regardless of sales volume, and most appliances are designed for high-volume operation. A reduction in number of meals prepared will not result in a corresponding reduction in energy costs. To get costs under control it might be possible to plan less energy-intensive meals—prepared foods and salad plates—during low-business periods.

Comprehensive Program

A comprehensive approach to handling energy costs involves several steps [22].

Top Management Commitment.   Employees pay attention to what management pays attention to. Getting the support of top management is an essential first step in a successful program. Top management's responsibilities are to define the goals and standards for the program. Basic goals might include [23]:

- Reduce the consumption and cost of energy and water utilities by 20 percent per year.
- Improve the quality of the operation such that guest satisfaction is increased.

Standard methods to track and summarize energy consumption must also be developed to monitor the program. A base level should be established to serve as a measure of progress made. Usually, this figure is developed from the 12-month period prior to the implementation of the program.

Base measures should be established for each month. The total water consumption in gallons and water consumption per customer should be noted.

For electricity, gas, and other energy sources the various units of energy, as reported on utility bills, must be converted into a standard measure, usually the British thermal unit (Btu). The following factors are used to convert energy use into a Btu value [24]:

Source	Measure	BTU
Electricity	kWh (kilowatthour)	3,413
Natural gas	Cubic foot	1,000
Oil	Gallon	140,000
Steam	Pound	1,000

From these sources total annual water and energy use can be determined, broken down by month and per meal served. This will serve as a base for comparing consumption before and after the program is implemented.

Energy Coordinating Committee. Management will not, however, have the time to oversee every detail of the program. Responsibility must be placed in the hands of someone to ensure accountability. The committee should be made up of a representative from each major department. This committee is responsible for tracking energy consumption and implementing improvements.

Energy Audit. Once a base level has been established the coordinating committee can conduct an audit to determine where energy waste is occurring.

Revise Operating Procedures. The audit should have revealed areas for improvement. Based on the findings of the audit, the committee can develop revised operating procedures for presentation to management. A new procedure might require ovens to be turned on 30 minutes prior to use rather than at the beginning of the shift.

A list of operating procedures can be developed and new policies implemented and explained to employees. Employees may need to be trained in the new procedures, and incentives may have to be developed to ensure compliance.

Analyze Alternatives. Some energy-saving suggestions will require the modification of existing or the purchase of new equipment. Detailed analysis will be required to determine the costs and benefits of a suggestion. The following recommendations can assist in reducing energy consumption [25].

How to Cut Utility Costs

According to Edison Electric Institute, restaurants consume twice as much energy per square foot than does any other business. Here are some ideas on how to cut utility costs:

1. Turn off unneeded equipment during slower periods.
2. Routine maintenance can cut up to 10 percent from energy bills.
3. Turn employees on to conservation.
4. Take advantage of the time-of-use rate. Under this option energy used during off-peak hours (evenings and on weekends) is much cheaper than energy used during peak times.
5. Have someone devote 100 percent of their time to energy issues.
6. Switch to energy-efficient equipment if it is right for your menu and you can get it repaired locally.
7. Monitor your energy use monthly.
8. Purchase insulated cooking equipment.
9. Preheat cooking equipment no longer than the manufacturer's guidelines.
10. Use cooking equipment to capacity.
11. Change heating, ventilation, and air-conditioning filters quarterly.

Source: Sarah Hart Winchester, "Putting Energy into Cutting Utility Costs," *Restaurants USA*, vol. 15, no. 5, May 1995, pp.12–14.

Lighting

1. Washing walls and ceilings to help maximize light reflection.
2. Removal of decorative lighting in the dining room.
3. Cleaning all lamps and light fixtures.
4. Replacing several small-wattage light bulbs with one large one.
5. Removing all unnecessary light bulbs.
6. Changing extended-life lamps to standard-life lamps; reflector floor lights to parabolic floodlights; and older-model fluorescent lights to high-efficiency fluorescent lights.
7. Replacing lamps installed more than two years previously because of the decrease in light output.

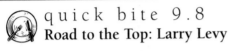

quick bite 9.8
Road to the Top: Larry Levy

Chairman and Chief Executive, Levy Restaurants

In the 18 years since Larry Levy opened his first unit, he has lived by what continues to be the company's mission statement: "Being passionate about our products and services while having fun in our work." The company has annual revenues exceeding $110 million in sales from 23 restaurants and 17 specialty stadium and convention center concessions.

Levy is proud of operating restaurants that are the best in their class. He says, "I think . . . we . . . have come close to perfecting midwestern hospitality. We treat people like guests in our home." He also talks about midwestern frugality. "Fifty percent of the restaurant experience might be the way you are treated. So service really influences the value perception."

According to associates, Larry is successful because "he's a go-getter and very sensitive to the public's needs and wants. He and Mark [his brother] have intense pride in what they do: . . . It's our life." Former manager Larry Huber credits Levy's accessibility to his unit managers as an admirable trait. Levy is also accessible to the community, serving on a variety of civic boards. He attempts to combine the rigors of work and family by getting together with his wife, four sons, and mother in company restaurants.

Source: Carolyn Walkup, "Larry Levy," *Nation's Restaurant News*, January 1995, pp. 117–118.

Water

1. Replacing washers immediately in dripping faucets.
2. Draining and flushing hot water tanks every 3 to 6 months.
3. Checking the steam trap on steam water heaters regularly.
4. Checking insulation on water heaters by feeling for hot spots.
5. Having burners adjusted if the exhaust is smoky or high in CO_2 emissions or if the stack is extremely hot.
6. Insulating all hot-water pipes.
7. Using a lower water temperature for nonsanitizing areas.
8. Reducing water pressure at the intake valve.

Heating, Ventilation, and Air-Conditioning (HVAC) System

1. Turning off the heating and cooling in seldom-used spaces.
2. Removing obstructions from heating and cooling vents.
3. Replacing caulking and weatherstripping around doors, windows, and ventilating units.
4. Clean or replace all filters in exhaust hoods and the HVAC system.

5. Checking heating and cooling ducts and exhaust hoods for cleanliness, insulation, and leaks.

6. Use natural gas rather than electricity as the energy source for the booster heater for dishwashers.

ENDNOTES

1. Mahmood Khan, *Foodservice Operations* (Westport, CT: AVI Publishing Company, 1987), pp. 112–116.

2. Ibid., pp. 164–166.

3. Ibid., p. 112.

4. Lendal H. Kotschevar and Margaret E. Terrell, *Foodservice Planning: Layout and Equipment*, 3rd ed. (New York: John Wiley & Sons, 1985), p. 330.

5. Khan, *Foodservice Operations*, pp. 112–113.

6. Ibid., p. 113.

7. Ibid., p. 119.

8. Ibid., p. 138.

9. Ibid., p. 126.

10. Ibid., p. 126.

11. Edward A. Kazarian, *Foodservice Facilities Planning*, 3rd ed. (New York: Van Nostrand Reinhold, 1989), p. 171.

12. Khan, *Foodservice Operations*, p. 113.

13. Kotschevar and Terrell, *Foodservice Planning: Layout and Equipment*, 3rd ed. (New York: John Wiley & Sons, 1985), p. 447.

14. Kazarian, *Foodservice Facilities Planning*, pp. 112–113.

15. Kazarian, *Foodservice Facilities Planning*, p. 219.

16. Lewis J. Minor and Ronald F. Cichy, *Foodservice Systems Management* (Westport, CT: AVI Publishing Company, 1984), p. 242.

17. Ibid., p. 242.

18. Ibid., p. 241.

19. Kazarian, *Foodservice Facilities Planning*, pp. 223–224.

20. Minor and Cichy, *Foodservice Systems Management*, p. 241.

21. Ibid., p. 242.

22. Robert E. Aulbach, *Energy and Water Resource Management*, 2nd ed. (East Lansing, MI: The Educational Institute of the American Hotel and Motel Association, 1988), p. 99.

23. Ibid., p. 101.

24. Judy Ford Stokes, *Cost Effective Quality Food Service: An Institutional Guide* (Rockville, MD: Aspen Systems Corporation, 1985), p. 258.

25. Minor and Cichy, *Foodservice Systems Management*, pp. 243–244.

chapter ten

SANITATION
AND FOOD SAFETY

By the end of this chapter you should be able to:

1. Identify the role of the restaurant manager in sanitation.

2. Identify the major sanitation problems in a restaurant.

3. Show how to establish proactive sanitation and safety programs.

4. Develop procedures for preventing foodborne diseases.

5. Build effective employee hygiene habits.

ROLE OF THE MANAGER

Management is responsible for serving food that is nutritious, appeals to the senses, and is safe to eat [1]. According to the National Assessment Institute, a restaurant manager is responsible for [2]:

- Identifying health hazards in the daily operation of the restaurant.
- Developing and implementing policies, procedures, and standards to prevent foodborne illnesses.
- Coordinate training, supervision, and direction of food handling and preparation while taking corrective action as required to protect the health of customers and employees.
- Inspecting the operation periodically to ensure that policies and procedures are being followed correctly.

---

 q u i c k   b i t e   1 0 . 1
Hot Concepts: Quizno's

Quizno's attempts to position itself between quick service and full service and aims for a more upscale market than do its competitors, Subway and Blimpie. Emphasizing the quality of its ingredients and the atmosphere in the 60-seat dining rooms, it charges 40 cents more per sandwich than does the competition and refuses to discount.

The resultant $5 average check translates into annual sales of $361,000 per unit. The menu features 18 sandwiches, prepared salads, some pastas, soups, desserts, and beverages. The best-seller is the Italian club of meat and mozzarella in three sizes on a white or whole-wheat baguette with sesame seeds. Cold sandwiches are heated in a conveyor toaster oven to melt the cheese and enhance the flavors of the meat before adding the cold accompaniments.

The units serve eat-in and carryout with a 50–50 split between the options. Inside the stores have both booths and tables with padded seats, pine furnishings with oak trim, carpeting and black-and-white-tiled floors and Italian posters. The open kitchen is decorated with Italian foodstuffs.

President and chief operating officer Richard E. Schaden bought out the original franchisor in 1991 and increased the company's size from 17 units to 82 units by 1995, with 70 more in various stages of development. High growth is expected through area development agreements. The companies' priorities are to cluster stores in major markets to achieve economies of scale in advertising, achieving more operating efficiencies, and training franchisees on how to make a profit.

Source: Carolyn Walkup, "Quizno's: Serving a High-Class Hero," *Nation's Restaurant News*, May 16, 1994, pp. 104, 122. *Note:* By mid-1997, the Quizno's Classic Subs restaurant chain had grown to nearly 200 restaurants operating in 28 states and Canada and had agreements with Area Directors in place to develop more than 70 markets across the country.

QUIZNO'S IS WORTH A SHORT WAIT!
Good Food made Fresh to your order may take a little longer.

CLASSIC SUBS

	Sm.	Reg.	LG.
CLASSIC ITALIAN	3.39	4.79	6.99
BEEFEATER	3.39	4.79	6.99
BEEFEATER ITALIANO	3.39	4.79	6.99
TURKEY & HAM CLUB	3.39	4.79	6.99
CAPICOLA	3.39	4.79	6.99
BAR-B-QUIZNO	3.39	4.79	6.99
SAUSAGE	2.99	4.49	6.99
MEATBALL	2.99	4.49	6.99
VEGGIE	3.39	4.79	6.99
TRADITIONAL	3.39	4.79	6.99
TURKEY	3.29	4.69	6.99
CHEESE	2.99	4.49	6.99
GENOA SALAMI	3.29	4.69	6.99
HAM	3.29	4.69	6.99
TUNA	2.99	4.49	6.99
TURKEY BACON GUACAMOLE	3.39	4.79	6.99
BACON LETTUCE TOMATO	2.99	4.49	6.99
ADD BACON TO ANY SUB	.59	.79	.99
ANY LARGE SUB		6.99	

SALADS

ITALIAN CHEF SALAD	3.99
TRADITIONAL CHEF SALAD	3.99
TUNA CHEF SALAD	3.99
TURKEY 'N CHEESE SALAD	3.99
TURKEY TURKEY SALAD	3.99
LARGE GARDEN SALAD	2.59
SMALL GARDEN SALAD	1.39
DELI SIDE SALAD	.59

SIDES

Chili	cup	1.89
	bowl	2.39
Soup	cup	1.59
	bowl	2.19
Chips		.59

DRINKS

Courtesy Quizno's Classic Subs.

To assist them in taking a proactive stance in assuring sanitary procedures, managers should have some knowledge of the following [3]:

1. *Properties of food:* the amount of available moisture and the pH level that strengthens or represses the growth of bacteria together with a list of potentially dangerous foods.
2. *Food processing/preparation:* processes the food will undergo.
3. *Volume of food prepared:* the larger the quantity of food to be fixed, the greater the potential danger.
4. *Type of customer:* acknowledging the fact that certain people (the very old, very young, infirm, and those who are sick) are more susceptible to foodborne illness than the rest of the population.

MAJOR SANITATION PROBLEMS

Foodborne Illnesses

According to the Centers for Disease Control (CDC), foodborne illnesses occur because of [4]:

1. *Inadequate cooling and cold holding* (63 percent). Storing food in large containers more than 4 inches deep, means that the food in the center of the container will not cool fast enough to prevent bacterial growth. Putting tight lids on containers in which hot foods are stored will slow cooling when the product is refrigerated. Similarly, stacking food containers one on top of the other and arranging cooler racks such that air is prevented from flowing freely around all surfaces of the containers will also slow down the cooling process.

2. *Preparing food ahead of planned service* (29 percent). Food should not be prepared more than a day ahead of time.

---

 quick bite 10.3
FDA Food Code, 1993

The Federal Drug Administration has released a 400-page food code. This is not a federal law or regulation; however, local authorities can choose to adopt all or part of it.

Here are some of the changes from prior codes:

1. Standards for time and temperature.
   - Poultry: 165°F for 15 seconds
   - Pork: 150°F for 60 seconds or 145°F for 3 minutes
   - Ground beef: 155°F for 15 seconds
   - Cold holding: 41°F
2. Provides a two-step cooling process (140°F to 70°F in 2 hours and 70°F to 41°F in 4 hours) for potentially hazardous foods.
3. Requires that employees wash their hands twice and use a nailbrush after each rest room use.
4. Requires food workers to use gloves when handling ready-to-eat foods.
5. Requires that consumers who order raw or partially cooked foods of animal origin must be informed of the increased risk to especially vulnerable populations.
6. Requires that the person in charge demonstrate to the regulatory authority a knowledge of foodborne disease prevention and the requirements of the 1993 code.
7. The definition of "potentially hazardous food" is expanded to include cut melons and garlic–oil mixtures.

The full report can be ordered through the National Technical Information Service at (703) 487-4650. It costs $23 for a spiral-bound copy and $17 for a diskette.

Source: Kim Austin, "FDA Releases New Food Code," *Restaurants USA*, vol. 14, no. 4, April 1994, p. 7.

---

3. *Inadequate hot holding* (27 percent). Contaminated food will come from holding food at temperatures between 120 and 70°F for more than 4 hours; using hot-holding units for uses other than intended; improper operation of hot-holding units, such as turning the thermostat too low or failing to turn on the fan; and combining new and old food items.

4. *Poor personal hygiene/infected persons* (26 percent). Inadequate handwashing and food contact with employees who have infectious diseases are major problems in this area.

5. *Inadequate reheating* (25 percent). It is important that temperatures be brought to 165°F and kept there for a time sufficient to kill any microorganisms.

6. *Inadequate cleaning of equipment* (9 percent). It is especially important to sanitize sinks and cutting boards, ensure that water temperature is above the safe level, and that sanitizing agents are strong enough to reduce bacteria.

7. *Cross-contamination* (6 percent). Cross-contamination can come from such things as touching raw foods, then handling cooked foods before washing hands, inadequate cleaning of raw food items, and improper sanitizing of surfaces and utensils between use with cooked and raw food items.

8. *Inadequate cooking or heat processing* (5 percent). Of particular concern would be the undercooking of poultry, pork, and eggs. Checking the internal temperature of food is essential to ensure adequate cooking.

9. *Contaminated raw materials* (2 percent). Serving food raw means that there is no chance to reduce the level of microorganisms once the initial preparation has occurred.

10. *Unsafe sources* (1 percent). It is vital that approved suppliers be used and that fish be certified as having come from clean waters.

(*Note:* Figures add up to more than 100 percent because more than one factor is usually involved in an outbreak.)

Foodborne illnesses occur from one of three sources [5]: biological, chemical, and physical.

Biological Sources

Bacteria. Biological contamination can come from bacteria, viruses, and parasites. Most foodborne illnesses are caused by microorganisms, the most significant group of which are bacteria. Bacteria are transmitted by wind, moisture, dust, and direct contact with other living things. They reproduce two to three times an hour, depending on the available moisture, pH, temperature, oxygen, and food levels present. Bacteria prefer high-protein food products. Thus items with high protein—poultry, meat, gravy, eggs, salads, fish, and so on—are particularly susceptible to bacterial growth. They also require a certain amount of moisture. Dry products such as cereals, flour, rice, and sugar do not contain enough moisture for bacteria to multiply.

The U.S. Public Health Service defines the temperature danger zone as being between 45 and 140°F. Most bacterial growth occurs within this range.

The amount of time that food products remain within this temperature range should be minimized. Certain bacteria actually prefer cold temperatures as low as 19°F and can even reproduce in refrigerated storage. Freezing or drying foods will delay the growth of but not kill organisms.

Some bacteria require oxygen to reproduce, while others can multiply even without it. Neutral pH is 7.0. As the pH value moves closer to zero, food becomes more acidic and the conditions for bacterial growth lessen. The preferred range for bacterial growth is 6.5 to 7.5.

The best way to limit bacterial growth is to control time and temperature—the time that foods are within the temperature danger zone. It is impossible to eliminate all bacteria; it is only possible to limit the growth of harmful bacteria to levels considered safe.

Viruses. Viruses are spread to food by employees infected with the virus. This can occur through such means as failing to wash hands after going to the bathroom, coughing, sneezing, or wiping a runny nose with a hand. Hepatitis A is one common illness transmitted by a virus. The most likely foods to cause illness through viral transfer are those which are not heated after handling: salads, cold sandwiches, raw or uncooked oysters, and so on.

Parasites. Parasites live within or feed off another organism. Parasites with their eggs can be contained in such foods as pork and fish. Parasites can be destroyed by cooking the food to a high enough level. Trichinosis and dysentery are the result of parasites in pork and water, respectively.

Fungi—molds, yeasts, and mushrooms—can be poisonous. Certain molds can produce toxins that have been associated with foodborne illness. Freezing will retard the growth of molds but will have no effect on those already present. Molds will be destroyed by heating to 140°F for 10 minutes but will not get rid of any toxins already present. Cooking at the correct temperature is the best way to prevent fungi growth.

While yeasts are not known to cause illness, it will cause certain foods and beverages to spoil. They can be killed by heating items to 136°F for 15 minutes and controlled with cleaning and sanitizing.

Chemical Contamination

Chemical contamination occurs when substances such as cleaning compounds or pesticides get into food. Food additives and preservatives are used to enhance food flavor and keep the product fresh longer. Some, however—such as nitrites, sulfites, and MSG—can be harmful. Although the use of sulfites is prohibited by restaurants, it is allowed in food processing under tight regulations.

Pesticides, used to control insect damage on crops, can lead to poisoning if the residue is not removed completely. Chemical contamination can also come from toxic metals such as copper, brass, cadmium, lead, and zinc. Zinc galvanized containers can make acidic foods such as fruit juice and pickles poisonous. Care should also be taken that items used for cleaning purposes be stored properly in a manner that will not bring them into contact with food.

Physical Contamination

Physical contamination occurs when hair, dirt, and similar items come into contact with food. Poor ventilation and maintenance can contribute to objects or moisture coming into contact with food.

Cross-contamination occurs when there is contact between safe and contaminated foods: for example, when raw food comes into contact with food that has been cooked. Cleaning and sanitizing of equipment should occur between use with different foods and between the same cooked and raw foods. As an example, raw chicken might be trimmed on a cutting board and then cooked. The cooked chicken should not be placed back on the cutting board until the board has been cleaned and sanitized.

The symptoms of bacterial food infection are nausea, vomiting, diarrhea, and intestinal cramps.

TAKING A PROACTIVE STANCE: HACCP

The objectives of a food sanitation program are to protect food from contaminating substances and to minimize the effects of any contamination that does occur [6]. The Hazard Analysis Critical Control Points (HACCP) system, developed in the 1960s to ensure the safety of food prepared for astronauts, is set up to maximize food safety. The system combines three elements—principles of food microbiology, quality control, and risk assessment—and emphasizes a movement away from the inspection of facilities to one that centers on the process of preparing and serving safe food [7].

The HACCP system consists of six steps [8]:

1. Identify hazards and assess their severity and risks. This involves examining the menu and recipes to identify potentially hazardous foods. Reducing the number of steps involved in preparing menu items will reduce the risk of contamination [9].
2. Determine critical control points. Four important control points are good personal hygiene, avoidance of cross-contamination, cooking, and cooling [10].
3. Implement control measures and establish criteria to assure control. Procedures must be observable and measurable. For example, the directions for fixing a baked chicken breast should include: "1. washing hands; 2. washing, rinsing, and sanitizing the cutting board and knife that are used for slicing the chicken breast; and 3. the actual product temperature of 160°F (73.9°C" [11].
4. Monitor crucial control points and record data. After receiving turkey and checking that the temperature is lower than 45°F, it is important to check that after storing it, the temperature in the refrigerator is 40°F or lower and that the raw turkey is not stored above cooked food.
5. Take appropriate action when control criteria are not met. You might find, for example, that the chef is preparing turkey breasts all at one time. The

It is generally agreed that effective safety programs require that operators analyze past accidents to identify areas of concern, inspect the facility to identify problem spots, and develop a plan to make employees more aware of the problem.

Here are some specific steps to take:

1. Give someone the responsibility to oversee the implementation of safety procedures. When Southwest Cafe, Inc. hired Randy Conner as director of risk management, he instituted procedures that saved the company $250,000 in the first six months of the program.

2. Get free or low-cost advice from insurance companies, many of whom have a loss-prevention service. Liberty Mutual conducts safety audits of Red Lobster and Olive Garden restaurants to advise on safety.

3. Check internal claims records and get accident-loss records from insurance carriers. When Godfather's Pizza found out that the leading cause of Workers' Compensation claims was "cuts," they had employees use a cut-resistant glove, reducing cuts by 68 percent and claims from $246 to $141.

4. Utilize free or inexpensive training methods. The local fire department will teach fire-extinguishing techniques and the Heimlich maneuver, and the American Red Cross covers basic first aid.

Source: Slyvia R. Somerville, "Safety Is No Accident," *Restaurants USA*, vol. 12, no. 7, August 1992, pp. 14–18.

turkey is within the temperature danger zone for longer than it should be. Corrective action is required that will reduce the amount of time the turkey is within the danger zone. New procedures have to be developed such that turkey breasts are prepared in smaller batches and returned to the cooler immediately upon completion.

6. Confirm that the system is working as planned. For each step in the process of receiving through reheating for service, four areas are determined: the critical control point, the potential hazard, appropriate standards, and whatever corrective action is needed if the standards are not met. For example, the first control point is in receiving beef and vegetables. Contamination and spoilage are potential hazards in both cases. Receiving standards should be set such that the temperature of the beef is at 45°F or lower, packaging on both products is intact, there is no odor, stickiness, or cross-contamination from other foods on the truck, and there are no signs of insect or rodent activity. If any of these conditions are present, the proper corrective action is to refuse delivery. A similar procedure is spelled out for each step in the process.

PREVENTIVE PROCEDURES

Purchasing

The key to effective procedures in purchasing is to use reliable suppliers.

Receiving

Deliveries should be scheduled during slow periods so that time can be devoted to careful inspection. Check the condition of the delivery truck for signs of improper storage during transit. Temperatures should be checked to make sure that refrigerated foods are below 45°F and frozen foods are below 0°F. Cartons that are damaged should be rejected.

Glass thermometers or those filled with mercury should not be used, as they can break. Select thermometers at least 5 inches long and insert at least 2 inches into food when taking a reading. The thermometers should then be cleaned and sanitized after every use.

Meat products must be inspected by a federal or state regulatory program. If they pass the inspection, they are given a circular identification stamp indicating where the meat was processed. Suppliers can be asked for written conformation that individual cuts have been inspected. Check the appearance and smell—aged meat will be darker in appearance than fresh; slimy, sticky, or dry meat should be rejected, as should products with a sour smell.

Poultry must also be inspected under a federal or state program. Operators should use only Grade A poultry. Signs of aging are purple or greenish color, bad smell, darkened wing tips, soft flabby, and sticky flesh.

Since there is no mandated inspection program for seafood, it is particularly important to buy from suppliers you trust. Fresh fish should be delivered in crushed ice at a temperature between 32 and 45°F. Fish is safe if it has bright skin, moist, red gills, eyes that are clear and bulging, and scales that are firmly attached. The flesh should be firm and elastic to the touch and should not separate easily from the bone.

Fluid or frozen liquids in cartons of frozen foods or large ice crystals in the product itself are indications that it has been thawed and refrozen. Such items are not acceptable.

Carefully check the expiration date on milk and dairy products. All products must be Grade A pasteurized. Once milk has been taken from a container, it should never be returned to that container.

Eggs can be spot-checked by breaking one or two open to check that the temperature is below 45°F, there is no noticeable odor, the yolk is firm, and the white clings to the yolk.

It is now possible to purchase certain items in packaging from which air has been removed. Gases may be added to help preserve the item. Vacuum-packed foods must be kept at temperatures below 45°F, fish below 38°F. *Sous vide* refers to products that are vacuum packed and then fully or partially cooked. Products must be stored at temperatures from 32°F to 38°F. Plants that sell sous vide products must be certified by the Federal Drug Administration (FDA).

Storage

The six most significant reasons for food spoilage are [12]:

1. Incorrect storage temperatures
2. Excessive storage time
3. Inadequate ventilation in storage areas
4. Failure to segregate foods in storage
5. Unacceptable sanitation standards
6. Excessive delays between receiving and storing functions

The National Restaurant Association recommendations for storing food are shown in Table 10.1. Food products should be used in the order in which they have been received. This concept is known as FIFO: first in, first out. Items should be dated and newer stock placed behind older stock to help ensure the integrity of the process. Ideally, purchases will be kept in their original containers. If not, care must be taken that the items are kept in containers that are clean

Table 10.1 Recommended Conditions for Storage

Storage Area	Temperature (°F)	Relative Humidity (%)
Dry storage	50–70	50–60
Refrigerated storage		
Dairy products and eggs	38–40	75–85
Red meats and poultry	32–40	75–85
Fresh fish	30–34	75–85
Live shellfish	35–45	75–85
Fresh vegetables and fruit	40–45	85–95
Frozen storage	< 0	

Source: Applied Foodservice Sanitation, 4th ed. (New York: John Wiley & Sons, 1992), p. 121.

and nonabsorbent. Metal containers can be dangerous when they come into contact with foods with a high acidic content.

Different types of meat should be kept separate from each other, as should raw and cooked items. Items should be stored at least 6 inches off the floor and away from pipes that might drip onto the food. Allow for air circulation around all surfaces between packages. Before opening cans, wipe them with a clean cloth to prevent contamination from the outside the cans. Cleaning supplies should be stored separately from food items.

Going back to the beef stew example, we can see that the potential hazards are due to cross-contamination and bacterial growth and spoilage. Appropriate standards would be to store the raw beef on a lower shelf with the vegetables above it, label, date, and use FIFO rotation, and ensure that the beef temperature remains under 45°F. Corrective action would involve moving the beef to a lower shelf and discarding either beef or vegetables if they have been kept longer than they should have.

Preparation and Serving

The highest risk for contamination is when food is being prepared and served. There are three concerns [13]: employee hygiene, time and temperature control, and the cleaning and sanitizing of utensils, equipment, and surfaces with which food comes into contact. Employee hygiene is dealt with later. As far as time and temperature are concerned, the major goal is that the time that a product is in the danger zone, between 45 and 140°F, be minimized. One particular problem for operators is the procedure for thawing frozen food. To minimize time in the danger zone, frozen food should never be thawed at room temperature but can, instead, be thawed under refrigeration, by cooking as a continuous process, in a microwave oven, or under water at about 70°F for a maximum of two hours.

Cross-contamination becomes a potential problem during preparation. As noted earlier, cross-contamination occurs when cooked food comes into contact with raw food. Similarly, surfaces that have had contact with raw food must be sanitized before coming into contact with cooked food.

In cooking, it is especially critical that the internal temperature of food items be checked in several places to ensure that cooking is complete. As noted before, thermometers with stainless steel stems should be used. They should be sanitized between uses and allowed to return to room temperature before being used again. The following minimum temperatures are recommended [14]:

- 45°F or below: steak tartare
- 130°F: beef
- 145°F: potentially hazardous foods
- 150°F: pork and pork products
- 155°F: ground beef
- 165°F: poultry and meat containing stuffing
- 165°F: all foods previously served and cooled that are reheated
- 170°F: pork and pork products cooked in a microwave

Holding equipment should never be used to heat food. The equipment itself should be able to maintain a temperature of at least 140°F and hold the food at the required temperature at all times. A food thermometer will be necessary to check that temperatures are maintained. Chances for contamination can be reduced if holding time is kept to a minimum, if foods are stirred periodically, and if covers are used over containers.

Milk, egg, and egg products should be stored at temperatures below 45°F. After cooking, eggs should be held at a minimum of 140°F.

Ice should be treated and handled with the same care as for food. Using hands, cups, or glasses to handle ice is to be avoided; hands carry germs, and glasses can break in the ice bin.

In self-service areas, customers, who probably have less sanitation background, are the people who come into contact with the food. The key is to set up the system such that contact with food is minimized. This will mean such things as providing individually wrapped portions wherever possible, supplying food or "sneeze" guards, furnishing enough utensils so that each dish has its own utensil and changing them periodically for fresh, sanitized items, and constantly monitoring the temperatures of the various items.

Reheating

If food has been cooked and held under sanitary conditions, it can be reused. Great care must be taken that it has not been exposed to contamination. It is estimated that up to 20 percent of usable food in the United States is thrown out. Various agencies have been set up to collect restaurant leftovers and distribute them to the needy. The major rule of thumb, however, is: If in doubt, throw it out [15].

If the decision is made to keep leftovers, the food must be chilled to reach an internal temperature of 45°F as quickly as possible. This can be done by dividing large quantities of food into smaller portions prior to chilling, placing food in containers with a depth no greater than 2 inches, stirring the contents of the container; giving the containers an ice-water bath (placing them in larger containers filled with ice), and using specially designed refrigeration units.

Stored leftovers should be covered and sealed, stored above raw foods, and labeled clearly. Reheated foods must reach an internal temperature of 165°F.

Bars

The National Restaurant Association has published a list of 12 effective bar sanitation tips [16].

1. Wash glasses in a high-temperature dishwasher with a chemical sanitizer.
2. Air-dry all glasses.
3. When using the three-sink method, have the first sink filled with a detergent solution at a temperature of at least 110°F; the second sink filled with clean water at a temperature of 120°F, and sanitize the glasses by immersing them in water at 170°F for 30 seconds.
4. Have employees use racks or baskets when using the three-sink method, to avoid burning themselves.
5. As a sanitizing alternative to hot water, use a chemical sanitizer at a temperature of at least 75°F.
6. Test the sanitizing water with a test kit.
7. Store glasses upside down.
8. Store bar utensils such that they will be picked up by their handles.
9. Check local regulations on the frequency of cleaning of beer lines; it may have to be done once a week.
10. Use different cloths for wiping down bottles and wiping down the bar.
11. Do not use scented or oxygen bleaches as sanitizers. The label will say whether or not it is registered with the Environmental Protection Agency (EPA).
12. Store glasses a minimum of 6 inches from the ground protected from soil and condensation.

Equipment

Various equipment manufacturers have developed standards for equipment designed for sanitation. Operators should look on equipment for designations from Underwriters' Laboratories (UL) or NSF International, for assistance in purchasing.

Cleaning. To reduce bacteria to safe levels, kitchen equipment must be sanitized. Sanitizing equipment means going beyond cleaning with detergent and hot water; it means using heat and chemical agents after cleaning.

A variety of factors must be considered before cleaning begins [17]:

- *Type and condition of soil.* Soil can be protein-based (for example, blood or egg), grease or oil, dissolved in water (for example flour), and acid or alkaline. Whether it is fresh, ground-in, soft, dried, or baked-on will influence how easy it is to remove.

- *Type of water.* Hard water makes cleaning more difficult and leaves a scale or lime deposit on equipment.
- *Temperature of water.* The higher the temperature, the faster the cleaning.
- *Surface being cleaned.* Aluminum can darken in highly alkaline or chlorinated cleaners; abrasive cleaners may be needed for hard, baked-on soils.
- *Type of cleaning agent.* Soap can leave a film; abrasives can scratch the surface being cleaned; acid cleaners may be needed from time to time to remove lime buildup from equipment.
- *Agitation or pressure to be applied.* The more agitation, the more effective and faster the cleaning.
- *Length of treatment.* The longer the cleaning agent is exposed to the object, the more effective the cleaning.

There are three main types of cleaning products [18]: detergents, acid cleaners, and abrasive cleaners. Detergents are used with water to loosen dirt. They are very effective, inexpensive, and can be used on food-contact surfaces. Acid cleaners are used on dirt that alkaline-based detergents cannot remove. Used incorrectly, they can damage surfaces and cause chemical burns on the skin. Abrasive cleaners work by using finely ground minerals that scour the surface to remove soil that is crusted on. Soft plastic surfaces can be easily scratched, thereby making them less effective to bacteria prevention. After using abrasive cleaners, care must be taken to rinse away any residue.

Sanitizing occurs after cleaning and rinsing to kill bacteria. It involves the use of hot water or chemical compounds. Sanitizing should occur after every use. To sanitize using hot water, equipment and utensils must remain under water at a minimum temperature of 170°F for at least 30 seconds.

Chemical sanitizers are used more often than hot water for the purpose of destroying microorganisms. They include chlorine, iodine, and quaternary ammonium. Chlorine compounds work well in either hard or soft water and do not irritate when used properly. However, they can cause damage to metal equipment. Water should be used to thoroughly rinse away any trace of detergents prior to the use of the chlorine compound, which should be at a temperature of 75°F. Iodine compounds work well in hard water and, being less corrosive than chlorine, do not irritate the skin or harm metal or rubber surfaces. Water temperature should be between 75 and 120°F. Quaternary ammonium compounds (quats) are skin safe and do not damage equipment, but their effectiveness can be reduced in very hard water. At a temperature of 75°F they work well in both acid and alkaline solutions.

Combination detergent–sanitizers are available. They must be used twice, once to clean and a second time to sanitize. Equipment and utensils should not be rinsed after sanitizing. The cycle is wash–rinse–sanitize.

Rodent and Insect Control

The most frequent pest problems in a restaurant come from rats, mice, flies, and cockroaches. A good pest control program uses both environmental sanitation and chemical or blockage control [19]. Control for rats and mice begins with disposing of garbage in a sanitary manner. Rodents must have access to food. Removing the trash and keeping storage areas clean will eliminate hiding places. Rodents can be killed with poison—mice are more susceptible—or trapped. Slow-killing poisons are best because they allow rodents to leave the premises before they die. Rodent-proofing the building consists of ensuring that doors are tight-fitting, with the bases flashed with metal; screening all windows less than 3 feet from the ground with hardware cloth screening; having concrete rather than wooden basement and ground floors; and closing all holes in foundations.

Control of flies begins with eliminating potential breeding places. This entails not allowing food to accrue and spoil and removing garbage quickly. Screens will help keep flies out. Sprays, insecticides, and poisons will eliminate flies, but their use should be monitored carefully to ensure that food will not be affected by them. An electric fly catcher draws flies to an electric element, which kills them.

Cockroaches need moisture to survive. Most commonly, they enter an operation from deliveries. Hence crates and boxes should be inspected and disposed of as soon as possible. Frequent cleaning will reduce the number of new cockroaches. Once their hiding places are known, a qualified exterminator can lay poison to kill them.

In general, the following practices will help prevent problems [20]:

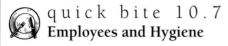

quick bite 10.7
Employees and Hygiene

The National Restaurant Association has unveiled a comprehensive program designed to develop hygiene-conscious employees: SERVSAFE. Foodservice units whose managers and supervisors have been trained, tested, and certified in the SERVSAFE program in the past five years can become a participant in the Industry Council on Food Safety. Participants receive:

1. A recognition plaque that is to be posted in a prominent place in the restaurant
2. A window decal
3. A council logo slick that can be used on letterheads or menus
4. A sample press release suitable for sending to the consumer press
5. A slick sheet of consumer food-safety tips than can be printed on fliers or takeout boxes for customers
6. Crisis-management steps to take in the event of an outbreak

Source: "Food Safety," *Restaurants USA*, vol. 14, no. 4, April 1994, pp. 11–15.

- Use a reputable supplier.
- Dispose of garbage properly and promptly.
- Store recycleables as far away from the premises as is allowed.
- Store all foods and supplies properly.
- Dispose of mop and cleaning water properly, mopping up spilled water at once.
- Clean and sanitize the operation thoroughly.

Crisis Management

Crisis management is " the organized and systematic effort of an operation to prevent, react to, and learn from crises" [21]. The development of a crisis management plan is one mark of a proactive rather than a reactive management. There are three steps involved in such an effort: preparation, management, and evaluation [22]. In the first stage a crisis team is formed. This team develops procedures and policies to be undertaken in case of a crisis. It is important that one and only one spokesperson be appointed to speak for the operation.

To manage the plan, a standardized complaint form should be developed and used to get information from complaining customers. Once it has been determined that the complaint is justified, the company decides whether to deal with the situation internally or whether outside help is needed. If the problem is

Employee hygiene is very important. *Source:* Robert Christie Mill.

small—the food was served cold—it can be settled in-house with a refund or small gift. Bigger problems, such as food poisoning, require outside assistance. It is important to communicate effectively with regulators, the public, employees, and the media.

Afterward, evaluation begins. Whatever caused the problem has to be identified and corrected. Employees should be involved in giving their reaction to what happened, how it was handled, and how it can be prevented in the future. Finally, a copy of the complaint should be kept.

EMPLOYEE HABITS

Employee Health

Employees who have symptoms that suggest they are susceptible to passing along bacteria should not be allowed near food. If they have a fever or are sneezing, coughing, or have oozing burns or cuts, they are prime candidates for spreading harmful bacteria. Blood contaminates food and any surface with which it comes into contact. If food is exposed to an employee's blood, it must be discarded immediately. Employees who have cuts can continue to work as long as the cut is protected. Water-resistant bandages, changed often and covered with water-resistant material or plastic gloves, will serve as protection. The same procedures should be followed for burns.

The HIV microorganism that causes the AIDS virus is not spread by food. Service workers infected with AIDS can safely work around food unless they are cut or have other infections or illnesses.

Personal Hygiene. The first step to staying healthy is to practice good health habits. This involves:

- Bathing daily with soap and water
- Covering one's mouth when coughing or sneezing, then washing hands immediately afterward
- Avoiding such things as scratching the head or touching the mouth or nose
- Not eating, drinking, chewing gum, or smoking when food is being prepared or cleaned

- Avoiding the dropping of sweat onto food or equipment
- Using disposable towels to wipe away sweat and washing the hands before working with food
- Using hair restraints
- Keeping nails short and clean

Hand Washing.   Bacterial contamination occurs primarily when microorganisms are spread to food from the hands of employees. For this reason the best way to prevent contamination is effective hand washing. Hand sinks should be readily accessible and be used exclusively for this purpose. Warm water, soap, and disposable towels or an air-drying machine are required for effective hand washing. Hands must be washed after any act that might cause contamination—using the toilet, eating or drinking, handling raw food, and so on. Similarly, hands should not be dried or wiped on aprons.

Clothing.   Employee changing rooms should be kept separate from food preparation areas. Uniforms should also be clean and changed when necessary to prevent contamination.

Safety and Accident Prevention

The Industrial Commission of Ohio's Division of Safety and Hygiene identifies six acts that often result in accidents [23]:

1. Failing to look where one is going
2. Failing to observe surroundings
3. Failing to handle knives and tools with care
4. Reaching too high or too low; lifting a weight that is too heavy, or lifting incorrectly
5. Failing to pay attention when using knives, grinders, or other cutting tools
6. Failing to protect hands from hot pans, pots, and plates

Restaurant employees are particularly susceptible to falls, burns, cuts, and improper lifting. Falls can be minimized by keeping floors dry and in good repair, wiping up spills immediately; rinsing after cleaning to remove any detergent or grease film; using slip-resistant shoes and floor coverings; and using signs indicating when a floor has just been cleaned.

Burns can be prevented by removing lids slowly to let steam escape; by using dry, flameproof potholders; by turning pot handles inward on the range; and by keeping stove tops and hoods free from grease.

Cuts can be avoided by keeping knives sharp, always cutting away from the body, having knives with built-in guards or shaped handles, and storing knives in a rack or knife holder. Improper lifting accounts for 25 percent of lost-time accidents [24]. Most injuries occur when putting down objects rather than picking things up. People should lift with their feet rather than with their back. This means [25]:

quick bite 10.8

Road to the Top: Christopher Sullivan and Robert Basham

Chairman and Chief Executive; President and Chief Operating Officer,
Outback Steakhouses, Inc.

The success of Outback Steakhouses cannot be denied—almost $1 billion in annual sales from 350 restaurants. The reasons for the success are attributed to Sullivan and Basham's tendency to break the rules: They insist on serving dinner only (in part to keep their employees fresh), the kitchen is larger than the dining room, and they have an "equity-sharing" philosophy, which gives them their pick of managers and operating partners. Says Basham: "The thing we keep trying to avoid is becoming too corporate." They learned from mentor Norman Brinker (who developed Steak & Ale, Chili's, and Bennigans) the importance of passing responsibility down the ladder.

Growing up with five brothers and sisters, Christopher Sullivan got a job as a line cook with Bonanza Steakhouse to pay for his college tuition. Later he paid for his final two years of school by bussing and waiting on tables at Steak & Brew in Fort Lauderdale. With one semester left, he dropped out to join Steak & Ale as a management trainee, completing his degree as a correspondence student.

Robert Basham was raised by a married sister after his mother died when he was five. His older brother ran a restaurant and got Basham involved. Shortly thereafter, the same brother fired his younger sibling for taking off to be in a wedding without arranging for someone to handle his responsibilities. Says Basham: "It was a kick in the ass I'll always remember."

The two got together in the mid-1970s at Steak & Ale and rose together in positions with Chili's and Bennigans. Taking on Gene Knippers as a real-estate partner, they put together a joint-venture deal to get 17 Chili's up and running. In 1987 they sold their company back to Chili's, making $1.5 million each in Chili's stock. Twenty years after their first meeting, their combined net worth is estimated at $262.5 million.

Source: Jack Hayes, "Christopher Sullivan and Robert Basham," *Nation's Restaurant News,* January 1995, pp. 199–200.

- Getting a good footing
- Placing the feet shoulder width apart
- Bending the knees before grasping the weight
- Keeping the back straight
- Getting a firm hold
- Lifting gradually by straightening the legs

The Occupational Safety and Health Act (OSHA) was passed in 1970 to assure safe and healthy conditions in the workplace. They lay out guidelines for the work environment and inspect to ensure that businesses are in compliance. OSHA checklists can be used as a guide to whether or not the restaurant is safe for employees. A comprehensive program involves four things: inspecting all equipment and physical facilities, examining the physical fitness of employees to perform their jobs safely, reviewing operational practices and personnel activities as they do their jobs, and checking compliance with safety and health regulations.

ENDNOTES

1. Lewis J. Minor and Ronald F. Cichy, *Foodservice Systems Management* (Westport, CT: AVI Publishing Company, 1984), p. 161.

2. National Assessment Institute, *Handbook for Safe Food Service Management* (Upper Saddle River, NJ: Regents/Prentice Hall, 1994), p. 8.

3. Ibid., p. 42.

4. Ibid., pp. 11, 39–41.

5. Mahmood A. Khan, *Concepts of Foodservice and Management*, 2nd ed. (New York: Van Nostrand Reinhold, 1991), p. 208.

6. Minor and Cichy, *Foodservice Systems Management*, p. 162.

7. National Assessment Institute, *Handbook for Safe Food Service Management*, p. 35.

8. Ibid., p. 37.

9. National Institute for Food Service Industry, *Applied Foodservice Sanitation*, 4th ed. (New York: John Wiley & Sons, 1992), p. 86.

10. Ibid., p. 87.

11. Ibid., p. 89.

12. Minor and Cichy, *Foodservice Systems Management*, p. 181.

13. *Applied Foodservice Sanitation*, p. 67.

14. Ibid., p. 135.

15. Ibid., p. 176.

16. "Twelve Bar Sanitation Tips," *F&B Business*, December 1989, p. 55.

17. *Applied Foodservice Sanitation*, pp. 188–189.

18. National Assessment Institute, *Handbook for Safe Food Service Management*, p. 96.

19. John Knight, p. 47.

20. *Applied Foodservice Sanitation*, pp. 228–229.

21. Ibid., p. 279.

22. Ibid., p. 280.

23. Knight, p. 52.

24. Ibid., p. 51.

25. Ibid., p. 53.

The two fundamental accounting statements are the statement of income and the balance sheet. The former indicates the profitability of the business over a period of time. The various costs of operating the business are subtracted from the revenue generated to show either a profit, if the revenue is greater than the costs, or a loss, if the costs are greater than the revenue. The balance sheet indicates the financial condition or value of the business at a particular point in time. Typically, December 31 is used as that point.

---

quick bite 11.2
The Rugged Entrepreneur and the Cautious Executive

A survey of 74 foodservice professionals indicated that self-defined executives and entrepreneurs place similar value on measures of success. The most important profit measures to both groups are:

1. Net profit
2. Cash flow
3. Return on investment
4. Gross profit
5. Return on assets

Cost measures were considered to be more valuable than financial measures. The most important cost measures, in order of importance, are:

1. Direct materials cost
2. Direct labor cost
3. Overhead cost
4. Indirect labor cost
5. Administrative cost
6. Indirect materials cost

The most important financial measures are:

1. Operating ratio
2. Current ratio
3. Price/earnings ratio
4. Earnings per share
5. Payout ratio
6. Debt/net worth ratio

Source: Lothar A. Kreck and Denney G. Rutherford, "Measures of Foodservice Operational Success: Entrepreneurs vs. Executives," *Hospitality Research Journal*, vol. 14, no. 3, 1991, pp. 43–52.

Statement of Income

A representation of where the average restaurant dollar comes from and goes to is shown in Table 11.1. Following the standard format for an income statement, averages are shown for four types of restaurant: full-menu table service; limited-menu table service; limited menu, no table service; and cafeteria.

Revenue and other income for the period are listed. All expenses incurred during the period in question are then subtracted from total revenue to determine the profit (if any) before taxes.

The Uniform System of Accounts for Restaurants has been developed by the accounting firm of Laventhol and Horwath and accepted by the National Restaurant Association as a blueprint for categorizing revenues and costs and laying out a statement of income. By following this guide, individual operations can compare their operating figures with those of similar restaurants in the industry. Annual figures and ratios for this purpose are produced by both the National Restaurant Association and Deloitte & Touche. In analyzing statements of income it is useful to consider not only the dollar figures but also the amounts as a percentage of revenue. Such a procedure allows for a more reliable comparison of, for example, management's effectiveness in controlling labor costs relative to the volume of sales.

Revenue.   Revenue is primarily from sales of food and sales of beverages. Other revenues—for example from room rental—would be shown later as other income. The relative proportions of food to beverage revenue is important because the cost of sales for beverages is less than the cost of sales for food. An operation with a high percentage of beverage to food revenue is thus typically good for bottom-line profit.

Cost of Sales.   Cost of sales is the cost of the food and beverage items that have been sold. To determine the food and/or beverage cost for an operation, beginning and ending inventories must be made. The ending inventory for period 1 becomes the beginning inventory for period 2. Because inventories can vary from day to day, a physical inventory should always be taken on the same day of the week. If an operation deliberately avoided ordering food until the day after a physical inventory was taken, the food cost would be uncharacteristically low; similarly, an unusually high inventory would increase the cost of food and a corresponding lower profit. Inventories are normally taken once a month.

The cost of food sales is calculated as follows:

inventory of food
at beginning of period (dollars) + purchases of food during the period

= total value of available food − inventory of food at end of period

= value of food used during the period

A similar calculation is made to determine the cost of beverage sales. Food and beverage cost percentages will be different. It is, therefore, desirable to compare the cost of food to food revenue and the cost of beverage to beverage revenue and express them as percentages.

Table 11.1   Statement of Income

	A	B	C	D
Sales				
Food sales	82.6	97.6	100.0	100.0
Beverage sales (alcoholic)	20.0	14.7		1.6
Total sales	100	100	100	100
Cost of sales				
Food cost	34.5	35.7	33.8	35.0
Beverage cost (alcoholic)	27.9	27.2		27.8
Total cost of sales	33.2	34.7	33.8	34.5
Gross profit on sales	66.8	65.2	66.2	65.3
Other income	0.4	0.2	0.0	0.9
Total income	68.0	65.8	66.5	67.0
Controllable expenses				
Payroll	29.4	26.1	24.6	27.8
Employee benefits	4.5	2.8	3.3	4.5
Direct operating expenses	5.6	4.7	4.8	3.8
Music and entertainment	0.1	0.0	0.0	0.0
Marketing	1.9	2.3	4.5	1.9
Utilities	3.2	3.2	3.8	2.9
Administrative and general	3.1	3.0	1.2	3.0
Repairs and maintenance	1.7	1.5	1.6	1.4
Total controllable expenses	51.0	45.6	44.7	49.1
Income before occupancy costs	16.2	20.5	22.1	16.3
Occupancy costs				
Rent	5.4	5.9	6.9	4.8
Property taxes	0.6	0.4	0.7	0.5
Other taxes	0.3	0.3	0.6	0.0
Property insurance	1.2	0.9	0.7	1.0
Total occupancy costs	7.0	7.7	8.3	5.9
Income before interest and depreciation	8.3	11.6	14.3	9.2
Interest	0.6	0.5	1.2	0.2
Depreciation	2.1	2.2	2.6	2.6
Restaurant profit	5.5	9.2	10.8	7.1
Corporate overhead per restaurant	1.8	1.6	4.7	5.5
Other deductions		Insufficient data		
Income before income taxes	3.8	6.8	7.3	4.6

Source: Restaurant Industry Operations Report, 1992 (Washington, DC: Deloitte & Touche and the National Restaurant Association, 1992), pp. 23, 53, 79, 102. *Note:* (1) All figures are medians and based on 1991 data. (2) All ratios are based on a percentage of total sales except food and beverage costs, which are based on their respective sales. (3) Columns do not total when medians are involved becasue each line is analyzed separately. A, full-menu table service; B, limited-menu table service; C, limited menu, no table service; D, cafeteria.

quick bite 11.3
How to Cut Costs

Here are some ways to cut costs:

1. *Maintain tight inventory control.* Ronald Allcorn, owner of the Hilltop Cafe & Pizzeria in Pittsburgh, found that one of his cooks was putting an extra pinch of cheese on every pizza. That one pinch was costing the operation $30 a day, which, Allcorn pointed out; "was $30 I wouldn't be able to put toward a raise for him."

2. *Check various suppliers' prices once a month.* George Lamb, general manager of the Greystone Restaurant in Edmond, Oklahoma, recommends talking to four different suppliers.

3. *Make prepared items in-house.* Jacqueline Canter, manager of Canter's in Los Angeles, finds that it is cheaper and the food is fresher.

4. *Reduce staff expense.* Stephen Jais, coowner of Sweetwaters Grille & Bar in Hyannis, Massachusetts, has a three- rather than four-person prep line by cross-training employees. Staggering the times at which employees work can also save on costs.

5. *Watch energy costs.* Jais uses low-cost fluorescent bulbs and double doors in the entry so that cold air doesn't come in.

6. *Lease rather than buy.* Lamb finds it cheaper to lease three ice machines than to own one and pay maintenance on it.

Source: Sarah Hart Winchester, "Cutting Costs without Cutting Quality," *Restaurants USA*, vol. 15, no. 3, March 1995, pp. 11–13.

Gross Profit.   Gross profit is the profit after taking the cost of sales—food and beverage—from total revenue.

Other Income.   As noted above, the principal sources of revenue for a restaurant will come from sales of food and beverages. Other income would cover any other revenue taken in the sale of nonfood and nonbeverage items, such as candy, room rental, and concessions.

Controllable Expenses.   Management has direct responsibility for and can influence controllable expenses. They include such things as:

- *Salaries and wages :* employee payroll
- *Employee benefits:* employee meals, Social Security taxes, medical insurance costs, workers' compensation insurance, etc.
- *Direct operating expenses:* costs involved in the operation of the business, such as uniforms, laundry, and decorations
- *Music/entertainment:* live or canned music
- *Marketing:* promotion, advertising, etc.
- *Energy and utility service:* cost of fuel, water, waste removal, etc.

Controllable Expenses

The top controllable expenses at restaurants are:

Type of Operation	Rank	Expense Category	Median Amount per Seat	Median Percentage per Seat
Full-menu	1	Payroll	$1580	29.9
table service	2	Direct operating	307	5.7
	3	Employee benefits	178	4.0
	4	Utilities	175	3.2
	5	Administrative and general	156	3.0
Fast food	1	Payroll	$1786	25.0
	2	Direct operating	317	4.8
	3	Marketing	248	3.3
	4	Utilities	236	2.9
	5	Employee benefits	178	2.5

At full-menu table service restaurants, paper and cleaning supplies are the top direct operating expenses, while linens are the top direct operating expense at higher-check establishments.

Source: National Restaurant Association, *Restaurant Industry Operations Report*, 1993, reported by Hudson Riehle, "Managing Direct Operating Expenses Is Key to Profits," *Restaurants USA*, vol. 14, no. 5, May 1994, pp. 42–43.

- *Administrative and general:* overhead costs not directly connected with providing customer service, such as telephone, postage, and office supplies
- *Repairs and maintenance:* cost of repairing and maintaining the building and equipment

Total Controllable Expenses. Managers have control over both the controllable expenses listed above and the food and beverage costs noted earlier. Any costs listed later are fixed in the short run and usually cannot be influenced by the unit manager.

Income before Rent and Other Occupation Costs. This figure is obtained by subtracting total controllable expenses from total income. Companies often use this figure as the basis for determining management bonuses.

Rent and Other Occupational Costs. These costs are those associated with getting the property operating and include rent, real estate taxes, and property insurance. This overhead is fixed and cannot be changed in the shortrun. These figures depend on the agreement negotiated and will be in effect for the term of the agreement.

Depreciation.   Depreciation is a noncash, tax-deductible expense. Since the building, equipment, and other assets wear out, an allowance is given to indicate the cost involved as the assets are used. Various methods can be used to depreciate assets in accordance with guidelines as to how long the assets are expected to last. The expense reduces taxes due and is available as positive cash flow to the operation.

Interest.   When bank loans are used to finance a business, the cost of borrowing the money is charged as interest. Depending on how a building is financed, the operation may have rent costs (if the building is leased) or interest costs (if it is purchased).

Income Tax.   Businesses pay taxes on their profits just as individuals pay taxes on their income. Net income is what is left after taxes have been subtracted.

Balance Sheet

The balance sheet shows the financial situation for the business at a particular point in time, usually December 31. The fundamental equation is

assets = liabilities + equity

The assets are what the business owns; the liabilities are what is owed by the business; the difference is the net worth or equity of the business.

Assets.   Assets are either short-term or fixed. Short-term assets are those that can be or are liquidated within a year. This includes cash on hand, accounts receivable (money owed to the operation), inventories of food, beverage, and other items (china, cutlery, etc.), and any expenses that have been prepaid.

Fixed assets are those items that have a life longer than a year. This includes such things as land, building, and equipment and uniforms. If the building is leased and the operator has made improvements, the improvements would be listed here as leasehold improvements. Note that although the value of the building and furniture and fixtures is reduced by the amount depreciated, the value of the land (although it can change in value) is not changed by depreciation.

Liabilities.   Current liabilities are those payable within the year. Most of this is made up of accounts payable, bills owed by the operation to various people. Long-term liabilities are those that will be paid off over several years. The total amount of the outstanding mortgage (less the current portion, which is included under current liabilities) tends to be the largest part of this item.

Shareholder's Equity.   As noted above, the difference between assets and liabilities is the equity or what the business is worth. Profits are either distributed to the owners as dividends or kept in the business. The latter are referred to as retained earnings.

ANALYZING FINANCIAL STATEMENTS: STATEMENT OF INCOME

Financial statements will be analyzed by various people for different reasons [1]. Bankers will look at the numbers in evaluating a loan proposal to determine the likelihood of repayment; an investor will use the statements to estimate a return on the investment; a supplier may look at the books before deciding whether or not to extend credit; management analyzes the numbers to determine the profitability or efficiency of the operation.

The figures mean little unless they are compared to something. Statements of income may be compared to forecasted or budgeted figures, to industry averages, or to previous results of the operation. Similarly, with the income statement, the dollar figures are not as meaningful as when they are expressed as a percentage of sales. A large operation will have food costs, in dollars, much higher than those of a smaller operation. For people evaluating the operation, the key is how well the costs have been controlled compared to sales. Looking at percentages allows an analyst to compare one operation to another.

Systematic Approach

A systematic way to analyze the statement of income is to begin with the bottom line, working upward in an attempt to zero in on problem areas. In this approach, the first step is to compare net income as a percentage of total revenue to a standard. As noted above, that standard may be a forecast, the previous year's figures, or an industry average. If the ratio is acceptable, management will presumably be pleased. This is not to say that the way the business is run cannot be improved; it merely indicates that the operation is "on target."

If, however, the bottom-line ratio is not acceptable, the second step is to move to the next major level, total controllable expenses. Here again, the approach is to compare the ratio of total controllable expenses to total revenue. If this figure is "acceptable" but the bottom-line figure is not, the problem lies somewhere in between the two ratios, in this case with the uncontrollable fixed costs, such as rent, interest, and other occupation costs. We have an indication that management is able to keep the controllable expenses in line but is still not having an acceptable bottom line. The problem in this case is that total revenue is not sufficient to produce enough income before rent and other charges to cover the fixed uncontrollable expenses. The task for management is to increase sales volume while continuing to control costs, thereby generating enough income to cover the fixed costs.

If the ratio of total controllable expenses is not acceptable to management, the problem is somewhere above this line on the statement of income.

This, in essence, is the systematic method of analyzing the statement of income:

1. Compare ratios at two levels.
2. If the lower level (closest to the bottom line) is acceptable and the higher one is not, the problem is with some figures in between the two.
3. If the ratio at a particular level is not acceptable, the problem is with one or more of the figures above this level.

Continuing this analysis, let us assume that the ratio of total controllable expenses to total revenue is not acceptable. As noted above, the problem lies somewhere above this line. We would then go to the next major level on the statement of income—total income—in an attempt to isolate the problem. If this ratio of total income to total revenue is acceptable, the problem lies somewhere in between total income and total controllable expenses. Each line under controllable expenses would be analyzed to determine which figures are over budget or out of line with competing ratios.

The analysis would continue using the method outlined above. Using this method management can isolate problem areas systematically.

Three-Part Method

According to Keiser [2], a statement of income can be divided into three parts: sales, expenses, and profit. He recommends analyzing each part separately.

Sales. In looking at sales, management basically wants to know three things:

1. Are sales increasing or decreasing?
2. Why is this happening?
3. Is the level of sales appropriate to the value of the business, the size of the operation, and/or the amount invested in it?

To answer these questions it may be necessary to break sales figures down by product category and/or by meal period. The former is germane to profitability, as the profit potential on beverages is greater than that on food. In making comparisons it is important to ensure that the comparison base is the same. Figures can be compared for the same month or week of the year compared to previous years as well as year-to-date.

Since revenue is a product of the number of covers (customers) times the average price of a meal, an increase in sales is due to one or both of these reasons. A sales increase might reflect an increase in menu prices. This may, in fact, camouflage a reduction in the number of covers served. It is important that the average cost of a meal cover, at a minimum, any cost increase the business incurs. If the cost of doing business increases by 8 percent, for example, the average price of a meal should be at least 8 percent more.

The laws of supply and demand indicate that other things being equal, as price goes up, the number of customers will go down. A price increase that results in fewer customers may actually generate less revenue, than previously. This concept is known as elasticity of demand. A menu item is price elastic if an increase in price produces less revenue due to reduced demand. Similarly, a price reduction will result in more demand and more revenue. Price elasticity means that the demand is sensitive to changes in price.

The item is price inelastic if the price increase generates more revenue. In this case the market is less sensitive to changes in price. An increase in price has not caused sufficient customers to stop ordering the item such that total revenue—the product of price times number of customers—increases. Similarly, a price cut will not generate enough additional customers to generate more total revenue in a price-inelastic situation.

To fully understand the reasons for a decrease in sales, each meal period, and each menu item, should be analyzed separately. It is only by doing this that management can pinpoint the meal period and/or menu item(s) causing the problem.

Several ratios are important when analyzing sales:

$$1. \text{ Average check } = \frac{\text{revenue}}{\text{number of customers}}$$

If the average check is less than "normal," prices may have to be increased or promotions put into effect to "push" the sale of more expensive items or to package appetizers and/or desserts with entree items to increase the average amount spent.

For full-menu table service restaurants the median check (the middle value of all amounts) was $10 in 1991. [All figures quoted in this section are taken from *Restaurant Industry Operations Report, 1992* by Deloitte & Touche and the National Restaurant Association (Washington, DC, 1992).] This figure was greater for establishments that served alcohol, were open for dinner only, were located in hotels or clubs, and had a menu theme that was either steak or seafood, Continental, or regional.

The median check for limited-menu table service restaurants was $6.48 in 1991. This amount was greatest for operations that served alcohol, were open for dinner only, and featured an Italian theme.

The median check drops to $3.80 for limited-menu restaurants without table service. This amount was also enhanced by serving alcohol and serving lunch and dinner, as distinct from serving breakfast and lunch.

Cafeterias reported a median check of $5.39. This was greater for those serving alcohol and located as the sole occupant of a building, as compared to being located in a shopping center or mall.

$$2. \text{ Seat turnover} = \frac{\text{number of customers}}{\text{number of seats}}$$

This ratio demonstrates how well the facility is being utilized. A low turnover indicates poor utilization—more customers can be accommodated; a high turnover may be a sign to expand.

Average daily seat turnover for full-menu restaurants was 1.6. This figure was greater for those operations that only served food, were located in a shopping center or mall, were open 24 hours, and had an average check of less than $5 with an American theme.

The median daily seat turnover for limited-menu table service restaurants was 1.8 and was greatest for establishments serving food only, open for all three meals, located in shopping centers or malls, with a lower average check, and serving Italian food.

For limited-menu restaurants without table service the median figure of 6.4 was greatest when operations served no alcohol, were the sole occupant of the building, were open for all three meals, and specialized in American food.

Cafeterias reported a median daily seat turnover of 2.0, a figure that was greater when only food was sold, the average check was less than $4, and the operation was located in a shopping center or mall.

$$3. \text{ Sales per square foot} = \frac{\text{sales}}{\text{number of square feet}}$$

This ratio is useful when comparing alternative uses for a particular space. What, for example, would the sales per square foot be for sit-down versus take-out service?

Full-menu table service restaurants reported median sales per square foot of $190.65. This figure is greatest for those serving alcohol, having a Continental theme, having an average check in excess of $15, and located in an office building.

The median figure of $164.79 for limited-menu table service operations is greater when food only is served featuring an Italian theme, with an average check of less than $5.

For limited-menu operations with no table-side service, the median figure of $233.33 per square foot is greater when there is no alcohol served and an American theme is featured in a building where the restaurant is the sole occupant.

The $149.41 median figure for cafeterias is enhanced when the operation is the sole occupant and the average check is greater than $6.

Expenses. Expenses are either variable, semivariable, or fixed. Variable expenses are those that vary proportionately with volume. Food and beverage costs fall into this category. If selling one hamburger costs 35 cents in product cost, selling two will cost 70 cents.

Semivariable expenses contain both a fixed and a variable component. They will change with volume but not directly. Employee wages is a good example. As volume increases the number of employees needed will increase and the wage bill will go up. An operation must be staffed in advance of customers coming in and a certain minimum number of employees must be present. As volume increases, the number of employees can be increased. However, sales forecasting is very difficult and there will be times when there is an imbalance between the number of customers and the number of employees needed to cook for and serve them.

Fixed expenses are those that do not vary as volume varies. The rent must be paid when one customer or 1000 customers are served. According to Keiser, "The more variable the expense, the more significant its percentage figure as related to sales" [3].

The three most important, because they are the largest, controllable ratios are:

1. Cost of food sales $=$ $\dfrac{\text{cost of food sold}}{\text{food sales}}$

2. Cost of beverage sales $=$ $\dfrac{\text{cost of beverage sold}}{\text{beverage sales}}$

3. Labor cost (%) $= \dfrac{\text{cost of labor}}{\text{total revenue}}$

It should be noted that an operation can offset a high cost in one area with a low cost in another. For example, a restaurant that uses convenience products will have a higher food cost than one that prepares items from scratch. The latter, however, will have higher labor costs.

For full-menu table service restaurants the median prime cost is 66.8 percent of sales. Operations selling food only are better able to control food cost while labor costs are essentially the same whether or not alcoholic beverages are sold.

Multiunit company-operated and multiunit franchise-operated units are better able to control food and payroll costs compared to independent operations. However, company units do a better job of holding down beverage costs than do the other two.

In general, the higher the sales volume generated, the better the median percentages. Also, the larger the metropolitan area in which the restaurant operates, the lower the median food and beverage costs. Labor costs are essentially the same, irrespective of city size.

The median prime cost for limited-service table service restaurants is 63.8 percent and is lowest for those places operating in a shopping center or mall and highest for clubs. As before, operations serving food only are better able to control food cost while payroll costs are essentially the same whether or not alcohol is served. Multiunit operations are better able than independents to con-

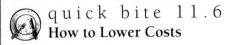

quick bite 11.6
How to Lower Costs

According to Jim Sullivan, managers have direct responsibility for only 3 percent of daily controllable costs, while hourly employees "control" the other 97 percent. Here are his ideas on how to lower monthly costs:

1. Audit your garbage for items that should not have been thrown out.
2. Recycle paper. Notepads can come from computer-generated reports.
3. Play safety bingo. Every day that the operation runs without an accident, post a bingo number. Whenever there is an accident, clear the numbers and start again.
4. Recycle edible garbage to cut down on solid-waste collection costs.
5. Use shallow bus tubs to reduce breakage from overstocked bus tubs.
6. Publicize and track daily waste.
7. Tell employees: "Never go into the dining room or kitchen empty handed."
8. Keep backup employees on call.
9. Move silverware soaking solution away from trash cans.
10. Offer employees 1 percent of the savings of any ideas they come up with.
11. Double-check point-of-sale orders.
12. Train employees to sell.

Source: Jim Sullivan, "A Dozen Good Ideas to Lower Monthly Costs," *Nation's Restaurant News*, February 13, 1995, pp. 38, 70.

trol costs, company-operated restaurants doing the best job with food costs and franchises doing the best job with labor costs.

Food cost remains essentially the same irrespective of sales volume, although beverage costs decline as sales volume, increases. Control over payroll is seen only as sales volume goes over $1 million a year. Both food and beverage median costs are lower as the size of the metropolitan area increases, but labor costs become more expensive in areas greater than 2 million people.

The median prime cost of 60.8 percent of sales for limited-menu restaurants with no table service is greater for units in office buildings and less for those in a shopping center or mall. Independents are not able to control food cost as well as multiunit operations, with franchise operations doing the best job of all. The median payroll cost is the same irrespective of affiliation.

As sales volume increases, operators are better able to hold down food cost. There is no clear pattern for labor costs and sales volume. The larger the metropolitan area, the higher the median food cost and the lower the median labor cost.

Cafeterias have a median prime cost of 67.6 percent of sales. Food cost for units having a sales volume below $750,000 a year is greater than those above that figure, whereas the reverse is true for payroll cost. Median food and labor costs also increase as the size of the metropolitan area increases.

Although the three items noted above are the most important—or prime—costs, every controllable expense should be tracked on a regular basis. It is also vital when comparing ratios that the same type of restaurant be used. The ratios for a fast-food unit will be much different from those for a full-service operation. Figures can also be compared on a cost-per-seat or cost-per-meal basis.

Profit. How much is "enough" profit? In the final analysis the profit generated must be sufficient to keep the owner(s) pleased with the investment. A restaurant may produce profit, but if the owners feel they could get a better return on their investment from another investment, the level of profit generated may not be enough to keep the operation open.

Three ratios are particularly important:

1. Operating ratio $= \dfrac{\text{net income before taxes}}{\text{net sales}}$

This ratio is also referred to as net profit to net sales, earnings ratio, operating margin, or profit ratio. Obviously, the higher that ratio, the better.

In full-menu table service operations the median operating ratio is greater for units serving only food (5.7 percent) compared to those also serving alcohol (3.3 percent). Franchise-operated multiunits produce more (5.7 percent) than either company operated multiunits (4.9 percent) or independents (2.9 percent).

Operating profit increases once the $1 million sales barrier is surpassed. It also increases as the size of the metropolitan area grows to a population of 2 million people. Beyond that figure the upper quartile (top 25 percent) figures are better while the median figure is lower. The median operating profit for multiunit company operated stores (12.7 percent) far exceeds that for independents (6.0 percent) and for franchise operations (5.3 percent).

The upper quartile operating profit goes down as sales volume increases. The median figure for units with a sales volume of between $500,000 and $1 million is less than for those having a sales volume of less than $500,000 and less than for units with a sales volume greater than $1 million. Profit percentages are greater for units in a metropolitan area of less than 500,000 than for those in an area of between 500,000 and 1 million people.

For limited-menu units with no table service, multiunit company-operated restaurants have a greater median operating profit (9.9 percent) than either multiunit franchise operations (6.6 percent) or independents (6.1 percent). The median figure is significantly better at a sales volume of between $400,000 and $600,000 a year and in a metropolitan population greater than 2 million people.

Full-menu cafeterias serving alcohol do not have as good an operating ratio as those serving food only. Sales volume and the size of the surrounding metropolitan area have little impact on median operating profit.

2. Net profit to net equity $= \dfrac{\text{net profit after taxes}}{\text{net equity}}$

This ratio measures the owner's return on her or his investment. As noted earlier, the equity is the difference between assets and liabilities. The higher the risk involved in the investment—and restaurants can be very risky investments—the higher the return that is expected.

Some businesses—for example, fast-food units—make a relatively small profit on each item sold. However, they rely on a large volume with a relatively small investment compared to sales to produce a modest operating ratio but a good net profit to net equity.

3. Management proficiency ratio $= \dfrac{\text{net profit after taxes}}{\text{total assets}}$

This ratio is an indication of what management does with the assets it has. The higher the ratio, the better job that management is doing.

ANALYZING FINANCIAL STATEMENTS: BALANCE SHEET

Current Assets

As noted above, current assets are those that can easily be liquidated.

Cash. Sufficient cash must be available to meet current expenses. Any remaining cash can generate interest from a bank. Cash is kept on hand for change and petty cash, and is also maintained in a bank account to pay expenses.

Accounts Receivable. Accounts receivable are what customers owe. A business that is strictly cash will have no accounts receivable. On the other hand, an operation that has a large banquet business and bills customers after the event may have a substantial accounts receivable.

The time between providing the service and being paid for it represents the restaurant "allowing" the customer use of the restaurant's money. Thus the shorter the average collection period or the greater the turnover, the better for the operation. At the same time, extending credit may be necessary to attract the customer. The important point to note is that there is a cost involved in providing credit.

1. Accounts receivable turnover $= \dfrac{\text{total sales}}{\text{average accounts receivable}}$

2. Average collection period $= \dfrac{365 \text{ days}}{\text{accounts receivable turnover}}$

3. Number of days tied up $= \dfrac{\text{accounts receivable}}{\text{daily sales}}$

The third ratio shows how many days' sales are tied up in accounts receivable. The figure should be as low as possible.

Inventories.   Inventory turnover will vary depending on the type of operation and will vary from twice a week for fast-food units to three to five times a month for full-service operations.

The restaurant must balance the need for it to have sufficient supplies on hand so that it will not run out of items with the fact that inventory costs money. The more items on hand for a period of time, the more money the restaurant ties up. Slow turnover indicates that inventory levels are too high. In addition to the money tied up, the longer items are kept, the greater the chance of spoilage.

On the other hand, a particularly high turnover may indicate that the business is, in essence, using the cash from day 1 to purchase supplies for day 2. Some balance must be found.

$$\text{Food inventory turnover} \; = \; \frac{\text{value of the food inventory}}{\text{cost of food sold}}$$

$$\text{Beverage inventory turnover} \; = \; \frac{\text{value of the beverage inventory}}{\text{cost of beverage sold}}$$

Current Ratio.   The current ratio is a measure of how strong the business is in its ability to pay off short-term debts.

$$\text{Current ratio} \; = \; \frac{\text{current assets}}{\text{current liabilities}}$$

Analysts want to see a ratio approaching 2:1 ($2 of assets for every $1 in liabilities), although in the restaurant business, the ratio is closer to 1:1. This is due to three factors [4]: a lack of accounts receivable, small inventories, and fast inventory turnover.

The difference between current assets and current liabilities is working capital. There should be enough working capital to allow the business to get through a financial crisis.

Fixed Assets

Comparing operations on the basis of fixed assets is difficult because of the variety of ways in which operations can be financed. One useful technique is to use a "cost per seat" figure as the basis for determining how much can be spent on the operation.

Liabilities

The major short-term liabilities are employee wages and payments to suppliers. The average monthly payment to suppliers can be determined by dividing cost of goods sold by 12. An accounts payable figure much higher than this average indicates an operation that is slow to pay.

Liabilities are often looked at relative to the net worth of the operation. Creditors will feel more secure when the ratio of debt to equity is low. Such a ratio indicates that the owners are heavily involved financially in the business compared to the amount of outside or debt financing. Lenders feel that the more owners are involved in the business financially, the greater their commitment to the business. A low ratio will increase the chances that the operation will get more credit.

COST–VOLUME–PROFIT ANALYSIS

Cost–volume–profit or break-even analysis is a graphical representation of the relationship between sales volume, fixed and variable costs, and profit. Management can determine what sales volume is required to show a profit as well as determining the level of costs and profit or loss at specific levels of sales.

Break-Even Chart

The horizontal axis of a break-even chart (see Figure 11.1) consists of the number of meals sold or customers served; the vertical axis represents both sales volume and costs in dollars.

Sales. A sales volume line can be drawn by multiplying the number of meals served by the average price of a meal. Thus if the average check is $9, $6300 in sales volume will result when 700 meals or customers are served. This is represented by point A on the chart.

Costs. For the purpose of break-even analysis, costs must be defined as either fixed or variable. Fixed costs are those that do not vary as volume varies. The amount of interest to be paid is the same whether one meal is served or 1000 meals are served.

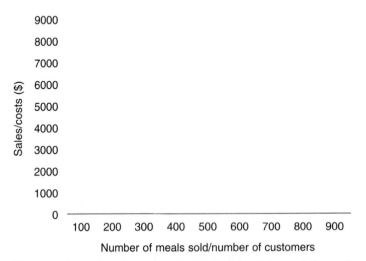

Figure 11.1 Break-even chart. *Source:* Adapted from James Keiser, *Controlling and Analyzing Costs in Foodservice Operations*, 2nd ed. (New York: Macmillan Publishing Company, 1989), pp. 410–411.

Thus fixed costs can be represented by a line parallel to the horizontal axis. Variable costs are those that, by definition, vary *proportionately* with volume. That is, if sales volume doubles, variable costs double. The obvious variable costs are food and beverage costs.

Many costs are semivariable. Labor costs are a good example. A certain number of employees are necessary to open the doors for business. If sales volume increased by 30 percent, the operation would need more employees but labor costs would probably not increase by 30 percent. Existing employees could pick up some of the slack by producing more.

Three methods for breaking costs into their fixed and variable components are [5]:

1. Maximum/minimum calculation
2. Multipoint graph
3. Regression analysis

Using the labor cost as an example, it is necessary to identify the sales volume in terms of meals sold or dollar sales volume together with the appropriate labor cost by month. In the maximum/minimum method the months with the lowest and highest labor costs are separated out and the lower labor cost is subtracted from the higher labor cost.

For example, assume that the highest and lowest sales volumes were in July and February, respectively.

	Sales Volume	Labor Cost
July	$40,000	$12,500
February	15,000	8,000
Differences	$25,000	$ 4,500

The variable cost per unit is obtained by dividing the wage difference by the difference in sales volume. In the example above, $4500 is divided by $25,000 to give 0.18, the variable cost per dollar of revenue. At $40,000 sales volume the labor variable cost is $40,000 × 0.18, or $7200. This figure is then subtracted from total costs to obtain the level of fixed costs. Monthly fixed costs are $12,500 minus $7200, or $5300.

The same type of analysis can be plotted on a graph. Assume the following daily figures for a restaurant [6]:

Number of meals sold	300	900
Average check	$9.00	$9.00
Revenue	$2700	$8100
Fixed costs	$1000	$1000

(Determined by dividing the fixed costs of the operation for the year by 365)

Administrative and general	$ 850	$1320
Labor cost	1750	2350
Food costs	945	2835
Profit or (loss)	$(1845)	$ 595

It can be seen that if 500 meals are sold a day, the restaurant will lose $1845 per day and will have a profit of $595 if 900 meals are served. Plotting these figures on a chart will show the profit or loss at various levels of sales volume.

The daily fixed costs of $1000 are represented by the horizontal line FC in Figure 11.1. At a volume of 500 meals the remaining costs—administrative and general, labor, and food—of $3545 is added to the fixed costs and charted (point B). At a volume of 900 meals a day, the variable and semivariable costs of $6085 are added to the fixed costs and plotted (point C). A line is then drawn joining points B and C. The break-even point is where total revenue equals total costs (point D). By extending lines to both the horizontal and vertical axes we can see that this restaurant breaks even when 750 meals are sold. The resulting sales volume of $6750 (750 × the average check of $9) will exactly equal the costs incurred. When fewer than 750 meals are served, costs are higher than revenue and a loss will result; when more than 750 meals are served, revenue is greater than costs and the result is a profit.

Similar charts can be prepared to show the impact of changes in price on profit. If, for example, a 5 percent increase in price is being considered, the impact on the number of meals served can be forecast and a new chart prepared to determine the impact on profit. Of course, the analysis is only as good as the impact forecast.

Because this method requires only two sets of figures it is simple to use. However, these two sets of figures may not be representative of sales volume and labor costs levels.

A multipoint graph improves on this by plotting on a graph monthly figures for an entire year. The horizontal axis would be the sales volume and the vertical axis would be the labor cost. The result is called a scatter graph: "a number of points scattered around a line that has been drawn through them" [7]. The resulting line is the one that seems to be the best fit through all the monthly points. The spot at which the line hits the vertical axis represents the level of fixed labor costs.

Regression analysis takes this process one step further by using an equation to determine fixed costs. For each month of the year four figures are listed: the sales volume or number of meals served, the appropriate level of labor cost, the product of these previous columns, and the sales volume or number of meals served squared:

$$\text{fixed costs} = \frac{(\Sigma Y)\,(\Sigma X^2) - (\Sigma X)(\Sigma XY)}{n(\Sigma X^2) - (\Sigma X)^2}$$

where ΣY is the sum of the monthly labor costs, ΣX is the sum of the monthly sales volumes, ΣXY is the sum of the monthly (X times Y) columns, and n is the number of periods (12 months).

Break-Even Point. The break-even point can also be arrived at arithmetically. When a customer orders a meal for $9, the variable costs associated with producing that meal are subtracted immediately. The remainder contributes toward paying off the fixed costs. When all of the fixed costs have been paid off, the restaurant breaks even. (Remember that variable costs are paid after every sale.) Thus the contribution margin is the selling price of a meal minus the variable costs associated with its production.

Once the break-even point has been reached, the contribution margin becomes profit. Thus if the variable costs associated with the $9 meal are $5.50, each time a meal is served the restaurant takes in $9, pays out $5.50 in variable costs, and "contributes" $4.50 toward paying off the fixed costs. Once they have been paid off, the restaurant gets $4.50 profit for each meal sold beyond that point.

The break-even point can be determined by dividing fixed costs by the contribution margin:

$$\text{break-even point} = \frac{\text{fixed costs}}{\text{contribution margin ratio}}$$

where the contribution margin is the unit selling price minus the unit variable cost, or

$$\text{break-even point} = \frac{\text{fixed costs}}{\text{contribution margin}}$$

where the contribution margin ratio is contribution margin/sales volume.

Earlier we noted that many costs are semivariable. In calculating the break-even point, some authors recommend that costs be classified as either fixed or variable. If we revisit the example above, the drawbacks of allocating costs in this manner can be seen.

The only "true" variable cost in the example above is food cost, which is 35 percent of revenue. The contribution margin ratio would, therefore, be 65 percent of revenue. The remaining costs when serving 300 and 900 meals are $3600 and $4670, respectively. If these are classified as fixed costs, it is obvious that different break-even points will result.

Using the cost structure for 300 meals, we find that

$$\text{break-even point} = \frac{\text{fixed costs}}{\text{contribution margin ratio}}$$

$$= \frac{\$3600}{0.65} = \$5539 \quad \text{or} \quad 616 \text{ meals}$$

This is the sales volume necessary to break even. The number of meals that must be sold to break even is this figure divided by the average check of $9, or 616. (All figures are rounded up.) Using the cost structure for 900 meals yields

$$\text{break-even point} = \frac{\text{fixed costs}}{\text{contribution margin ratio}}$$

$$= \frac{\$4670}{0.65} = \$7185 \quad \text{or} \quad 799 \text{ meals}$$

To get more precise it is necessary to attempt to classify how much of any one cost is fixed and how much is variable. Working with historical data, it would be possible to derive graphs plotting the various categories of cost against volumes and extrapolate the line back to determine the fixed component of that cost.

Referring to Figure 11.1 and extrapolating line BC back to the vertical axis, it can be seen that at zero volume $3050 is incurred in costs. This, then, becomes the "true" level of fixed costs. Using the previous example:

Number of meals sold	300	900
Average check	$9.00	$9.00
Revenue	$2700	$8100
Fixed costs	$3050	$3050
Variable costs (administrative and general and labor)	550	1620
Food costs	$ 945	$2835
Total variable costs	$1495	$4455
Contribution margin (revenue minus variable costs)	$1205	$3645
Contribution margin ratio (contribution margin divided by revenue)	45%	45%
Break-even point (dollars) (fixed costs divided by contribution margin ratio)	$6778	$6778
Break-even point in meals [break-even (dollars) divided by average check]	753	753

The sales volume necessary to produce a given level of profit can be calculated as follows:

$$\text{sales revenue required} = \frac{\text{fixed costs plus desired profit}}{\text{contribution margin ratio}}$$

Useful as it is, break-even charts can be only a rough approximation of profit. This is, in part, because assumptions must be made regarding allocation of costs. In Figure 11.1 we assumed that the line CB could be extrapolated back. Cost allocations are good only over short ranges of sales volume. When they are extrapolated beyond that range, the analysis is less exact. In addition, this analysis works best when there is only one product. In a restaurant where there are

quick bite 11.7
Find the Break-Even Point

Given the following information, find the daily break-even point for Bubbles restaurant.

1. Forecasted annual sales: $178,500
2. Number of days of operation per year: 255
3. Projected annual costs:

Fixed

Labor	$36,720
Payroll tax	3,672
Insurance	700
Rent	8,400
Accounting	500
Bank service charge	180
Utilities	6,000
Telephone	1,200
Interest	812
Advertising	900
Dues/subscriptions	120
Business personal property tax	280
Cleaning expenses	480
Donations	200
Depreciation	1,800
Miscellaneous	1,000

Variable

Food and paper products	71,400

Solution

1. Separate fixed and variable costs.
   - Total fixed costs: $62,964
   - Total variable costs: $71,400

2. Divide total variable costs by total sales:

   $$\frac{\$71,400}{\$178,500} = 0.40$$

(continued)

3. Subtract total variable costs as a percent of sales from 1:

$$1 - 0.40 = 0.60$$

4. Divide the result into total fixed costs:

$$\frac{\$62,964}{0.60} = \$106,940$$

5. Divide by the number of days the store is open:

$$\frac{\$104,940}{255 \text{ days}} = \$411.52$$

Source: Michael J. Strausser, "How to Figure Your Break-Even Point," *Restaurants USA*, vol. 14, no. 2, February 1994, pp. 15–17.

many items on the menu, markups will vary and an average will have to be used. This limits the accuracy of the analysis.

CAPITAL BUDGETING

Capital budgeting is defined as "the planning of expenditures whose returns are expected to extend beyond one year" [8]. Funds can come from depreciation, retained earnings or profit, additional debt, or additional equity from investors and are used for the replacement of existing equipment or facilities or expansion of the operation.

Determining Priorities

Typically, the amount of funds available is not enough to meet the number of projects available. Some method or methods are necessary to allocate scarce resources (money) to desirable projects. Four methods can be used [9]:

1. *Economy study:* a financial analysis comparing two or more proposals
2. *Rate of return:* a comparison of the savings or additional income generated to the amount invested
3. *Net present value (NPV):* the value in the present of future returns, discounted at the cost of capital less the cost of the investment
4. *Internal rate of return:* a rate of return that equalizes the present value of the return and the investment

Economy Study. An economy study might be used to compare the long-term costs and returns on the purchase of a new piece of equipment compared to keeping and maintaining existing equipment.

Future costs, both fixed and variable, need to be forecast and become part of the analysis. The annual fixed expenses would include such things as interest, depreciation, and taxes and insurance.

There are several methods to calculate depreciation. The simplest method estimates the salvage value of the equipment at the end of its useful life, subtracts this amount from the initial cost of the equipment, and divides this by the number of years the equipment is expected to be in operation. For example, if an oven were to cost $20,000 and have an expected life of eight years, at which time it could be sold for $1000, the annual depreciation expense would be

$$\frac{20,000 - 1000}{8} \quad \text{or} \quad \$2375$$

Annual operating expenses would include labor, power, supplies, and repairs and maintenance.

Many firms will use the amount of time it will take for the expenditure to pay for itself to judge whether to make the capital expenditure. The shorter the payback period, the better. Payback periods can range from a matter of three years for a small piece of equipment to much longer for a building. The formula for estimating the payback period is [10]

$$\frac{\text{pay-back}}{\text{period}} = \frac{\text{cash outlay for project}}{\text{annual net income or savings before depreciation but after taxes}}$$

Although it is fairly easy to estimate future costs, it is much more difficult to calculate changes in sales brought about by capital expenditures. Redecorating the dining room may be justified if the project will bring in more business. A reliable estimate of the new business due entirely to the redecoration is difficult at best.

Rate of Return. The rate of return on a project is the average additional income of savings after taxes and depreciation divided by the average investment in the project.

The rate of return can be determined annually as well as over the lifetime of the equipment. Annual savings of $500 on an investment of $4000 will give an anticipated rate of return of $500/$4000, or 12.5 percent.

The average value of the equipment is the initial investment minus the salvage value divided by 2. If we assume for this example that there is no salvage value and the equipment will last five years, the average value is $2000. The rate of return on the average value of the equipment over its lifetime is $500/$2000, or 25 percent.

Net Present Value. One problem with the methods described above is that they do not take into account the fact that the value of a dollar today is greater than its value in the future.

The desired rate of return on the investment must be determined and an analysis carried out over the life of the project to determine cost savings in present value terms. A piece of equipment might cost $3000 today and will result in annual savings of $1000 for four years.

Net present value calculates the present value of a return in the future. The formula is

$$PV = \frac{FV}{(1 + i)\,n}$$

where PV is the present value of a future return, FV the amount received at the end of n years, i the desired return on the investment, and n the number of years before the future return will be received

Tables have been formulated to indicate the net present value of money at specified interest rates. Using the figures above, the cash savings would be calculated as follows:

Year 1	$1000	×	0.893	=	893
Year 2	$1000	×	0.797	=	797
Year 3	$1000	×	0.712	=	712
Year 4	$1000	×	0.636	=	636
Year 5	$1000	×	0.567	=	567
Total					3605

Thus, over five years, the cash savings in present terms would be $3605. Proceeds from the sale of the piece of equipment to be replaced and any tax advantages resulting from a loss from that sale would also be considered as part of the cash inflow to be compared to the cash outflow of $3000.

Internal Rate of Return. The discounted or internal rate or return considers the time value of money and determines the rate of return that would result when the present value of the return equals the initial investment. Management could then determine whether or not this rate of return was acceptable to them in making a decision on the project.

When the cash savings are the same per year, the net investment can be divided by the annual savings to give a factor that can be compared to figures in tables of net present value to give the internal rate of return. Such tables can be found in capital budgeting texts.

Using the figures above—a $3000 initial outlay with nothing from the sale of the old equipment and no resulting tax savings—and such a table, the internal rate of return is 19 percent.

ENDNOTES

1. James Keiser, *Controlling and Analyzing Costs in Foodservice Operations*, 2nd ed. New York: Macmillan Publishing Company, 1989), p. 335.

2. Ibid., pp. 335–347.

quick bite 11.8
Road to the Top: Jackie Shen

Owner, Jackie's

When Jackie Shen came to the United States from Hong Kong in 1981, she was 17, had $125, and wanted a career in hotel management. Today she is the owner of Jackie's, a French–Oriental restaurant in Chicago.

Starting out at a small college in Iowa, she worked at McDonald's, babysat, and cleaned houses to supplement the scholarship she had been awarded. Between semesters she was working as a museum guide when she also began waitressing at a deli. From then on she continued to waitress all through college, first in Iowa, then in Houston. Returning to Chicago after graduation, she worked for the Ritz and washed pots and pans at the Park Hyatt before opening a hot dog and hamburger stand, Uncle Pete's. Frustrated by her cooking skills, she went to work in various kitchens, watching the chefs, then going home to practice French cooking.

Taking the $20,000 in profits from the sale of Uncle Pete's, she bought a bar, renamed it "Jackie's," and added the French–Oriental theme. She has given back to the community as an organizer of Chicago's Taste of the Nation, a nationwide fundraiser for the homeless.

Says Jackie, "I'm a big believer in the personal touch. I like to see personal relationships in business, where we get to know each other and are able to help each other through our crisis periods."

Source: "Women in Foodservice: Three Success Stories," *Restaurants USA,* vol. 13, no. 9, October 1993, pp. 28–31.

3. Ibid., p. 339.

4. Ibid., 349.

5. Michael M. Coltman, *Cost Control for the Hospitality Industry* (Boston: CBI Publishing Company, 1980), pp. 16–25.

6. Keiser, *Controlling and Analyzing Costs in Foodservice Operations,* p. 410.

7. Coltman, *Cost Control for the Hospitality Industry,* p. 21.

8. Keiser, *Controlling and Analyzing Costs in Foodservice Operations,* p. 381.

9. Ibid., p. 410.

10. Ibid., p. 385.

chapter twelve

EMPLOYEE SELECTION

learning objectives

By the end of this chapter you should be able to:

1. Identify the work groups that management will increasingly turn to for employees in the next decade.

2. Discuss the major laws and regulations affecting employee hiring.

3. Identify the steps involved in staffing the operation, outlining important principles at each stage of the process.

4. Develop guidelines on how to conduct a hiring interview.

SUPPLY OF LABOR: THE CHANGING PICTURE

An examination of major demographic trends identifies the hiring environment in which management will operate. Consider that [1]:

- A slowdown in the growth rate of the workforce—21 percent in the 1970s, 12 percent in the 1980s—has led to predictions of labor shortages.
- Service industry employment is projected to increase, but at a slower rate.
- More than two-thirds of all labor force growth will come from women.
- Minority labor force growth will be twice that of the white labor force.
- The pressure of immigration, whether legal or illegal, will grow, particularly from Latin America.

The restaurant industry has traditionally relied on the 16 to 24-year-old age group for many of its employees. The number of 16- to 19-year-olds dropped 25 percent between 1979 and 1992, but by 1997, will regain almost half the numbers lost earlier. In contrast, the number of 20- to 24-year-olds will decline until 1997, when the numbers in the workforce will begin to increase [2].

As a result of these trends, to meet their future needs, operators will have to turn increasingly to sources of employees they have previously not considered.

---

quick bite 12.1
Hot Concepts: Wolfgang Puck Cafe

Wolfgang Puck, "chef to the stars," has gone casual! With wife and business partner Barbara Lazaroff, he has developed a chain of moderately priced cafes, a combination of full-service and counter-service operations. The couple's goal is to have 100 units by the turn of the century.

With an average check of $12 for lunch and $14 for the dinner, annual per unit sales range from $2.2 to $4.5 million, with express units averaging $1.5 million. The cafes cost approximately $250 per square foot and seat between 88 and 200 customers. New units will be in the 6500- to 7000-square foot range.

Despite attempts by bankers to have the company go public, the principals are committed to remaining private in addition to staying a "nonchain chain." Menus are modified at each location to appeal to regional tastes, and items are prepared from scratch.

The cafe menus rely on such Wolfgang signature items as smoked salmon pizza and Chinois chicken salad. Puck is intent on transferring his trendsetting in food to the way he treats employees. Combined food and labor costs approach 60 percent, in part because "we give paid vacations, health and dental plans, everything."

Source: Richard Martin, "Wolfgang Puck Cafe," *Nation's Restaurant News,* October 14, 1996, pp. 144, 146.

Women

At this time more than five of every eight foodservice employees are women. According to the Bureau of Labor Statistics, women will make up two-thirds of labor force growth by the year 2000. More than one-third of them will be black or Hispanic. In fact, by 2000, black women will outnumber black men in the workforce, in contrast to the pattern among whites, where men outnumber women 3:2 [3].

To attract and keep female employees, companies may have to develop more "female-friendly" policies. Flexible work schedules, assistance with day care, and medical benefits aimed at women are some of the ways that companies can demonstrate their interest in attracting and keeping female employees.

A female-friendly atmosphere is one that does not tolerate discrimination or sexual harassment. Discrimination on the grounds of sex has been prohibited since 1968. Sexual harassment—increasingly regarded as a form of sexual discrimination—is an area of increasing importance to employers. The Equal Employment Opportunity Commission defines sexual harassment as:

> Unwelcome sexual advances, requests for sexual favors, and other verbal or physical conduct of a sexual nature constitute sexual harassment when (a) submission to such conduct is made either explicitly or implicitly a term or condition of an individual's employment, (b) submission to or rejection of such conduct by an individual is used as the basis for employment decisions affecting such individual, or (c) such conduct has the purpose or effect of unreasonably interfering with an individual's work performance or creating an intimidating, hostile, or offensive working environment [4].

Management has a duty to create and maintain an atmosphere that does not tolerate sexual harassment on the part of supervisors, employees, customers, and suppliers.

Minorities

By 2000, one of every four people living in the United States will be a member of a minority group. This will be a significant change from past decades [5]. Non-Hispanic whites, who made up 79 percent of the workforce in 1990, will account for a lower 65 percent of entrants into the labor pool between 1990 and 2005. Hispanics will account for 16 percent of entrants, due largely to high levels of immigration. Thirteen percent of workforce entrants between 1990 and 2005 will be black and 6 percent will be Asian [6].

For Hispanics the cultural and language barriers make their success in the workplace more difficult. Among many Hispanics the tradition of a male-dominated, traditional society can place significant pressures on Hispanic women as they seek the security and independence that working outside the home can bring. This is particularly evident for female managers supervising employees with such an orientation.

Businesses can require that English only be spoken under very narrowly drawn guidelines. Taking a proactive approach and realizing that it is difficult to

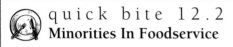

quick bite 12.2
Minorities In Foodservice

A larger proportion of women, African-Americans, and Hispanics are employed in foodservice than in all other types of employment.

Occupation	Percent of Total		
	Women	African-Americans	Hispanics
All employees 16 and older	46	10	8
Food preparation and service occupations	58	12	12
Supervisors	68	10	7
Bartenders	53	4	3
Waiters/waitresses	80	5	8
Cooks	44	19	14
Food counter/fountain (fast food)	69	13	8
Kitchen/food preparation workers	75	15	11
Buspersons	44	11	18
Miscellaneous	47	17	20

Source: U.S. Department of Labor, Bureau of Labor Statistics, reported in "Foodservice Trends," *Restaurants USA,* vol. 14, no. 7, August 1994, p. 40.

manage someone if it is impossible to communicate with that person, some companies are teaching English to their employees while supervisors are encouraged to learn Spanish.

To attract and keep employees it is important to understand what motivates them and to develop an atmosphere that reinforces these things. At the risk of generalizing, it is true that most Hispanics place a high value on the family. Because unemployment rates in Hispanic areas are high, regular work is valued and contributes to the self-esteem and status of adult males.

Urging employees to have families visit the operation can make the employee feel that the family is assimilated into the workplace, thereby heightening the importance of the employee's work.

Immigrants

It is estimated that a minimum of 450,000 immigrants a year enter the United States legally, while an additional 100,000 to 300,000 come in illegally every year [7].

California, Texas, and New York account for more than half of all foreign-born residents, 20 percent of all recent immigrants living in the Los Angeles area [8].

Under the Immigration Reform and Control Act of 1986 it is unlawful for an employer to knowingly hire any alien not authorized to work in the United States. Irrespective of legal issues, hiring illegal aliens begins the employer–employee relationship with a lie.

"Illegals live in a world of lies. They are not liars, but theirs is a world of lies. They have to live–to eat–and to eat they have to say things that others want to hear. If a boss asks if they are here legally, they say they are. But they know that the boss knows they are lying and the boss is lying when he acts like he believes him" [9].

Restaurateurs have to ask themselves whether or not this is the best way to begin a relationship.

Older Employees

In 1982 about one in every five persons was 55 or older. This ratio will be one in four by 2010 and almost one in three by 2030. Older employees represent a marketing tool for companies faced with increasing numbers of older customers. More than half of all working adults indicate a desire to work beyond the standard retirement age.

Advances in medicine have resulted in greater numbers of healthier older people. Older people tend to be "more dependable, have lower absenteeism, are punctual, . . . show good judgment based on their past experience, interact

---

quick bite 12.3
Bias Against the Elderly?

A survey of 151 management and nonmanagement workers employed in school foodservice throughout Pennsylvania indicated some bias against older employees. Specifically, the percentage of participants who either agreed or strongly agreed with these statements is as follows:

- Older employees are harder to train for jobs: 19 percent.
- Older people are more dependable: 76 percent.
- Older workers usually turn out work of higher quality: 47 percent.
- Most older people can't keep up with the speed needed in the hospitality industry: 19 percent.
- Supervisors find it hard to get older people to adopt new methods on the job: 55 percent.
- Older employees make better employees: 23 percent.

In general, the older the respondent, the more favorable the attitude toward older employees.

Source: Fred J. DeMicco, "Attitudes toward the Employment of Older Foodservice Workers," *Hospitality Education and Research Journal,* vol. 13, no. 3, 1989, pp. 15–30.

---

well with others, and show greater motivation due to increased job satisfaction and less job-related stress" [10]. They are not as adaptable and creative as younger employees.

An outreach program is necessary to attract older employees. Although most national studies indicate that they tend to prefer part-time employment and flexible work schedules, this finding is not supported by studies in the food-service industry. Older people identify with people younger than themselves. Advertisements showing people about 10 years younger than the age group sought are more likely to be successful.

Seniors are motivated by the desire for social interaction followed by having a purpose in life. Stressing the importance of interacting with customers and other employees and letting them know that their experience is appreciated are important factors in attracting this employee group. The fast-food companies—led by McDonald's and KFC (the former Kentucky Fried Chicken)—have done a particularly good job of reaching out to older employees.

According to the American Association of Retired Persons, to be successful, training should be related directly to the job for which the person is being trained, should be given only for jobs that the employee has a chance of getting, should be active rather than passive, should be self-paced and individualized, and is more effective if short-term rather than a longer-term program.

Part-Timers

A major reason that many companies like to hire part-timers is that they typically do not pay them benefits. Benefits may add as much as one-third to the labor bill. The importance of benefits was noted in a recent survey of restaurant operators. The most frequently mentioned changes in benefits mentioned by operators were establishing a 401(K) program, improving health insurance, providing profit sharing, instituting a pension plan, and increasing employees' share of benefit costs. More than half provided meals free of charge, while an additional 12 percent paid partially for them. Ninety percent of the hourly employees at foodservice companies with sales of $1 million or more a year receive meals and paid vacations, while more than 80 percent of the companies offered medical/surgical coverage. Forty-four percent gave Christmas bonuses, while one in eight offered maternity leave [11].

Part-time employees tend to be less loyal to the company, have higher turnover rates, and must be trained more often and supervised more closely. However, they can be laid off with less risk of lawsuits and/or unemployment compensation claims. They can be more eager to work, as they work fewer hours per day than do full-time employees. They may also be more willing to perform any job given to them. It is important to hire people who really want to work part-time. Employees will often say they are happy with part-time hours in order to get a start with a company. If the manager accepts this and continues to give few hours, the employee may become dissatisfied.

The orientation and training programs for part-time employees should be the same as those for full-timers. Although they only work for a few hours a day, those hours tend to be when the business is busiest. They do not have the luxury of slack business periods to get accustomed to the operation. It is therefore important that the training they receive be given during those slack periods and also be sufficiently rigorous to allow them to perform when business is busiest. Finally, they should be treated like full-time employees. People who are treated as second-class employees will act accordingly.

Disabled

In 1990 the Americans with Disabilities Act was signed into law. This law guarantees civil rights protection to persons with disabilities. For example, it is illegal to treat a disabled employee differently than any other employee, refuse to hire or promote qualified individuals because of a disability, put disabled employees into lower-paying jobs, or pay them at a different pay level [12].

The ADA defines a person with a disability to be one who has "a physical or mental impairment that substantially limits one or more major life activities" [13], who has a history of such an impairment, and/or who is perceived as having a disability. Individuals with disabilities, who may be customers or employees, are entitled to "reasonable accommodation" from a restaurant. Reasonable accommodations include the removal of barriers in the workplace, such as rearranging furniture to provide access aisles; provision of auxiliary aids and services, such as an adapted computer or occasional assistance; and modification of policies such as dress codes or flex-time and job restructuring. If the operator can show that the accommodation will create an "undue hardship"—it will be a significant hardship or expense—the change is not required.

Barriers present in the operation must be removed if this can be done without much difficulty or expense. This might include such things as [14]:

- providing a minimum of one accessible marked parking space per 25 parking spaces in the lot
- Providing the accessible spaces closest to the accessible entrance
- Ensuring an unobstructed path of travel from the on-site parking to the restaurant entry
- Having continuous handrails at both sides of all stairways
- Having flashing lights and audible signals on all alarms
- Ensuring that pathways to foodservice areas are free of stairs
- Ensuring that service is available at accessible tables or counters within the same area
- Ensuring that the same menu is available in an accessible space as is served in a mezzanine or raised or sunken dining area
- Ensuring that all rest rooms, and some telephones and drinking fountains, are fully accessible

Table 12.1 contains reasonable accommodations made by Hardee's in the development of their Creatively Applying People's Abilities (CAP) program in an attempt to employ 2000 persons with disabilities by 1996.

Table 12.1 Reasonable Accommodations: Hardee's CAP Program

Disability	Job Duty	Accommodation
Auditory hallucinations	Maintenance	Job coach, flexible schedule, management education on disability
Emotional disability	Cashier	Knowledge of medication effect
Hearing and speech impairment	Maintenance	Sign language, job restructure
	Host/hostess	Job restructure, job reassignment
Mental disability	Fried chicken preparation	Job coach, group training, transportation during inclement weather
	Host/hostess	Restructured job, additional training time, color-coded bar towels
Orthopedic impairment (arms)	Crew	Flexible schedule
Alcohol abuse		Supervisor meetings and counseling, Alcoholics Anonymous
Physical disability Paraplegic (legs)	Front-line cashier	No heavy lifting, curb cut, flexible schedule

Source: William F. Jaffe, "Integrating the Disabled Employee into the Quick-Service Restaurant: The Enclave Model," *Hospitality & Tourism Educator*, vol. 6, no. 2, Spring 1994, p. 19.

There may be more than physical barriers to overcome in hiring the handicapped. There may by resentment and apprehension from existing employees. A communications program to orient new *and* existing employees to each other will help the transition into the workplace.

The number of people with disabilities employed as restaurant employees increased from 14,000 in 1980 to 19,000 in 1990 [15]. In 1991, over 25 percent of operators employed people regarded as retarded or learning disabled, while nearly one-fourth employed persons with a physical disability such as sight or hearing impairment. About 5 percent employed persons with an emotional disability.

McDonald's, KFC, Hardee's, Pizza Hut, and Friendly's are just some of the companies that have taken the lead in organizing programs aimed at employing the disabled. The McJobs program at McDonald's, for example, has graduated more that 1000 employees since 1989 from their training program.

About nine in 10 of these restaurateurs rated the dependability of their employees with disabilities as excellent or good compared to employees who were not disabled. About seven in 10 rate the productivity of disabled employees as excellent or good compared to those without disabilities [16].

The Friendly Restaurant Company has a four-step process to help ensure a successful program. This program involves:

- Identifying company needs
- Identifying community resources
- Establishing a mutual relationship
- Building the relationship and understanding the pitfalls

Many jobs within the company are routine, repetitive, mechanical, and/or tedious. They are also the jobs that account for much, if not most, of the turnover in the business. The mentally handicapped or restored person may be perfectly satisfied to handle these types of jobs which the company has the hardest time keeping filled. Dishwasher, stock clerk, bus help, kitchen help, sorter, janitor, and truck help may be particularly appropriate.

The employment options used most in integrating employees with disabilities into the workplace are individual worksites, enclaves, and work crews [17]. In an individual work site a person with a disability works at a community site with a support person. A group of no more than eight people working within a regular industry comprises an enclave, while groups of no more than eight people who perform specialized contract services are termed work crews. There is no consensus as to the most effective method of integration. A Marriott study of the three methods concluded that the individual worksite was most beneficial, while the enclave approach was of marginal benefit and sometimes harmful to the employee. Other studies outside the hospitality field have found the enclave to be the most effective method.

To build the relationship, management must first evaluate the employee to determine the type of work that he or she is best suited to handle. The employee may need the manager's help in overcoming uncertainties in interacting with others. Orientation and training techniques may have to be adapted to the disability of the employee. It is important that the manager, rather than another employee, supervise the training directly. Many handicapped employees adjust better to a new job situation if they feel they have the full support of the manager. Direct supervision of training is one way to demonstrate this.

A continuous schedule of positive reinforcement may be required to develop a new behavior. Meals, drinks, and verbal praise will, in many cases, be more effective than money in motivating mentally handicapped persons if they lack a realistic conception of the worth of money.

A variety of community organizations are available to assist in finding and placing handicapped employees. Contact with one or more specialized agencies to find out what they do will help establish the mutual relationship necessary for a successful hire.

THE REGULATORY ENVIRONMENT: EQUAL EMPLOYMENT OPPORTUNITY

In hiring employees, managers have to operate within an environment of laws and regulations that have been developed by government. In recent decades equal employment opportunity has received more attention than any other in the field of human resource management. Equal employment opportunity involves the "employment of individuals in a fair and unbiased manner" [18].

Federal Laws

A variety of federal laws have been enacted that affect equal employment opportunity. The major ones are [19]:

- Equal Pay Act of 1963, which requires employers to pay equal pay for equal work regardless of sex. Jobs are considered equal when they entail essentially "the same skill, effort and responsibility under similar working conditions and in the same establishment" [20].
- Title VII of the Civil Rights Act of 1964 (amended 1972), which prohibits discrimination in employment on the basis of race, color, religion, sex, or national origin.
- Age Discrimination in Employment Act of 1967 (amended 1986), which prohibits discrimination against people 40 years or older in areas of employment because of age.

---

 quick bite 12.4
Immigration Law

Here are some commonly asked questions about immigration law:

1. When do I fill out the employment eligibility verification form?
   - Up to three days after the employee starts work.
2. Am I responsible for determining if the documents are real?
   - No, if the documents "on their face" appear to be genuine.
3. How long do I need to keep the I-9 forms?
   - Three years. If employees stay longer than three years, you must hold on to the I-9 form for one year after he or she leaves.
4. What if INS finds an illegal worker?
   - If you complete and retain all I-9 forms, you cannot be penalized unless INS can show that you knew about the illegal status of the worker.
5. What are the penalties?
   - Fines range from $100 to $1000 per violation. Fines for knowingly hiring an unauthorized worker range from $250 to $10,000 per incident.
6. How can I get more information?
   - Call the Immigration and Naturalization Service at (800) 255-8155.

Source: Pat DiDomenico, "Immigration Crackdown Targets Restaurateurs," *Restaurants USA*, vol. 15, no. 4, April 1995, pp. 8–9.

- Pregnancy Discrimination Act of 1978, which prohibits discrimination against pregnant women in employment if they are capable of performing their job.

These laws cover all private employers engaged in interstate commerce who have a minimum of 15 employees working 20 or more weeks a year.

In addition, companies that are agencies of or contractors with the federal government are subject to various laws and executive orders. Such companies might be foodservice operators who have the contract to provide foodservice at a government facility. The more important regulations are [21]:

- Vocational Rehabilitation Act of 1973 (amended in 1974), which prohibits federal contractors from discriminating against handicapped individuals and requires them to develop affirmative action plans to hire and promote such people.
- Vietnam Era Veterans Readjustment Assistance Act of 1974, which prohibits discrimination against Vietnam era veterans for contractors with government contracts of $10,000 or more and requires affirmative action programs to advance such people.

Various other executive orders have been created to extend the same protection indicated above to employees of contractors to the federal government.

In addition to federal laws, most states and many other local governments have passed laws prohibiting discrimination in employment. Managers are advised to check with local and state agencies to determine the specific laws applicable to them.

Bona Fide Occupational Qualification

If an employer can show that discrimination on the basis of age, religion, sex, or national origin is justified by nature of the job itself, they can claim a bona fide occupational qualification (BFOQ). Claiming that, for example, hiring a woman instead of a man is a business necessity has been defined very narrowly by the courts. It would be appropriate, for example, to have males only as attendants in a men's bathroom.

Sexual Harassment

Sexual harassment is defined by the Equal Employment Opportunity Commission as "unwelcome advances, requests for sexual favors, and other verbal or physical conduct of a sexual nature." It is illegal when it is determined that such conduct interferes with the work performance of an employee or when it creates a hostile work environment. Although there have been some reported cases of sexual harassment of a male by a female, the vast majority of problems occur when a male supervisor, employee, customer, or supplier is accused of harassing a female.

The employer is held responsible for sexual harassment when he or she knows or should have known about it and did not prevent it or take corrective action. An effective sexual harassment policy should include the following [22]:

1. Develop a comprehensive company-wide policy announced to all employees and indicating that sexual harassment will not be tolerated.
2. Provide training sessions for all supervisors to explain the legal requirements and the company policy.
3. Establish a formal complaint system indicating how employees can make charges without fear of retribution and how charges will be investigated and resolved.
4. Take immediate action on receipt of a complaint.
5. Take immediate and consistent disciplinary action once a charge has been substantiated.
6. Follow up on all cases to assure a satisfactory resolution.

Affirmative Action

Affirmative action programs require employers to institute programs and to correct past discriminatory practices. To comply, employers must make an affirmative effort to find, hire, train, and promote employees of protected groups. Employers who have federal contracts greater than $50,000 are required to have affirmative action programs.

The basis steps in developing an effective affirmative action program are [23]:

1. Develop an equal employment policy and affirmative action program in writing.
2. Assign responsibility and the authority to go with it to a senior manager to implement the program.
3. Publicize the program.
4. Identify the number of minority and female employees by department and job classification.
5. Develop goals and timetables to increase, where necessary, the number of minorities and females.
6. Develop and implement specific programs to meet the set goals.
7. Develop an audit program to monitor and evaluate progress.
8. Develop programs to support the effort.

RECRUITMENT OF EMPLOYEES

Job Analysis

A job analysis, a periodic analysis of every distinct job in the operation, is crucial to a successful human resources management program. Figure 12.1 illustrates the relationship and importance of a job analysis to other personnel-related tasks. Before managers can hire an employee, they need to know what they should be looking for. A listing of the knowledge, skills, and abilities required to perform a job is known as a job specification.

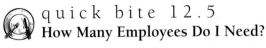

quick bite 12.5
How Many Employees Do I Need?

Average Number of Employees Utilized by Restaurants

	Number of Employees per Restaurant			Annual Employee Turnover	
	Full-Time	Part-Time 20–35 hours	Part-Part-Time Under 20 hours	Salaried	Hourly
Full menu	15	15	8	20%	102%
Limited menu table service	7	10	7	—a	107%
Limited menu, no table service	5	6	5	25%	122%
Cafeterias	10	10	20	—a	107%

aInsufficient data.

Source: Restaurant Industry Operations Report, 1992 (Washington, DC, National Restaurant Association, 1992), pp. 19, 20, 49, 50, 75, 76, 100, 101.

The job specification for a particular job comes from a document that lays out the purpose, scope, and major duties and responsibilities of a particular job. This document is called a job description. The job description is developed as a

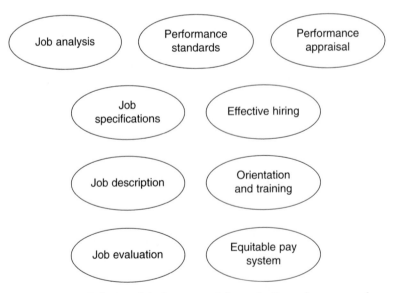

Figure 12.1 Relationship between job analysis and personnel-related functions.

How many smiling faces does a company need? *Source:* Robert Christie Mill.

result of a job analysis. The analysis of a job is the basis for the development of performance standards for that job. In fact, performance standards for the job cannot be developed until and unless a job analysis has been completed.

Performance standards tell the employees "how well they are expected to perform" [24]. They are job descriptions translated into measurable form. The standards of performance expected for the job set the stage for appraising the performance of the employee performing that job. In other words, there is no foundation for firing an employee for not performing the job unless clear performance standards have been developed. These standards can only come from having conducted a job analysis.

An orientation program will include an introduction to the important facets of a job while training seeks to develop the employee's ability to perform that job. Neither can be done unless the manager can identify the important aspects of the job. This knowledge comes after analyzing the job.

One facet of a motivated workforce is one that feels they are being treated in a fair and equitable manner relative to their pay. Many suggest that the more important the job to the company, the more someone who performs in that job should be paid. Job evaluation evaluates the relative worth of every job in the operation. Job evaluation typically uses job descriptions as the basis for determining job worth. As noted above, job descriptions are the outcome of a job analysis program.

Analysis Process

There are several ways that a job analysis can be carried out. First, the manager can observe the employee performing the job. While necessary as part of the process, it is not a good idea to rely solely on this method. The employee may adjust the speed of her or his work if they are aware that they are being watched. The result may be a distortion in the number of employees needed. Direct observation does not reveal the mental processes used to perform a job. Some additional input is necessary.

An interview with the person doing the job is usually used as a supplement to direct observation. Employees may be asked to list, in chronological order, everything they do as part of their job. There may also be distortions with this type of review. The worker may exaggerate the importance of the job, or a poor attitude may diminish the importance of the tasks performed. Employees may forget parts of the job or may be performing tasks that should not be part of the job but were inherited from past jobholders.

An interview with the employee's supervisor might take care of any potential problems faced in the methods mentioned above. There is the possibility that the supervisor might be unclear about what should be done, but generally speaking, supervisory input will round out the picture supplied by personal observation and employee interview.

Tasks. The first step in the job analysis is to develop a job list, an inventory of the tasks associated with the job. These are limited to "how to" items.

For a garde-manger or cold-meat chef, a job list might indicate that the employee should be able to [25]:

1. Plan future meals
2. Carve cold meats
3. Prepare various dishes
4. Prepare sandwiches

The job list for a food server might read [26] as follows:

A food server must be able to:

1. Greet and seat restaurant guests
2. Serve water; light candles
3. Take beverage orders and serve drinks
4. Present the food menu and beverage list
5. Assist customers in making food and beverage selections
6. Place orders in the kitchen
7. Serve food and beverage items ordered and clear table between courses
8. Present bill
9. Perform other duties as assigned

Job Breakdown. For each item on the job task list, there will be a detailed job breakdown indicating what is to be done, how it is to be done, and why each step is important. A fast-food operation may need 40 to 60 job breakdowns, each one to three pages in length. The time required initially is well worth the effort.

The completed job breakdown serves as a listing of standard operating procedures for the restaurant in addition to being the basis for training new employees in how to perform in the way that management wants.

Job Description.   As noted above, the job description lays out the purpose, scope, and major duties and responsibilities of a particular job. As a minimum it should include the following [27]:

1. Job title
2. Title of immediate supervisor
3. Job summary: 20 to 30 words identifying the purposes of the job
4. Essential functions: what should be done; percentage of time spent on each; equipment used; types of materials handled
5. Reporting relationships: to whom jobholder reports; who reports to jobholder
6. Qualification standards: personal and professional qualifications; skills, education, and experience required; physical and mental demands; amount of responsibility; personal characteristics for job success

A job analysis should be updated periodically. Often, a restaurant will initiate a change of theme or menu without updating the job descriptions required to perform the work. As the operation changes, so will the jobs and the type of employees needed to perform them.

A job analysis may pave the way for a restructuring of employees. It may turn out that some employees are performing jobs that can be done by others. Some may be performing tasks that have been made redundant. Although this is not the major reason for conducting a job analysis, it is probably the reason many employees are fearful of such an effort—they think management will use the results to eliminate jobs. It is important that whoever conducts the job analysis realize the potential concerns of the employees and the impact they might have on their willingness to participate honestly in the process.

THE HIRING PROCESS

A television advertisement for oil filters features an auto repairman who examines a car and finds that because the oil filter was not replaced on a regular basis, the car needs a new engine. The tag line is "You can pay me now, or you can pay me later." The message is that investing a little time and effort up front will save money in the future. The same can be said about hiring employees. Managers who invest little time or effort in selecting employees are likely to have more problems in the future: problems such as absenteeism, high turnover, pilfering, and low productivity. There are many potential steps in the hiring process. Each step taken costs time and money but reveals more information about potential employees. That, in essence, is the cost-benefit decision that each employer must make when determining a hiring process. Will the cost of taking this action result in a better hire that will bring the operation cost savings or increased sales sufficient to justify the cost of hiring? If the answer is "yes," take the time and effort to collect the additional information; if the answer is "no," forgo that step in the process.

Next we outline a variety of steps in the hiring process. For many operators this list will seem too costly both in terms of time and money. Others will willingly spend the time and money up front in the belief that careful hiring will produce better profitability in the future. The steps are [28]:

- Preliminary interview
- Completion of application form
- Employment tests
- Interview in human resources department
- Background investigation
- Medical examination
- Preliminary selection in human resources department
- Supervisory interview
- Realistic job preview
- Hiring decision

Preliminary Interview

Very often, prospective applicants will call or come into the restaurant wishing to know if there are any openings. The preliminary interview might be no more than a first impression as to what job the person is interested in, whether there are openings, and whether the applicant seems like a good fit for such a job.

While it is true that first impressions mean a lot, it is probably wise to err on the side of including rather than excluding candidates. The fact that someone is willing to inquire about jobs shows a certain amount of initiative.

Completion of Application Form

In reviewing a completed application there are certain cues that will indicate whether or not a candidate should be considered further. Some of the red flags to consider are:

- Has the candidate had too many jobs in the past? A history of job hopping may indicate someone who cannot be happy at any one thing or someone who cannot keep a job.
- Lack of progress in previous jobs. Employees who have not been promoted and/or who have not received pay increases over time may lack the ambition and/or skills to perform at higher levels.
- The reasons for gaps in employment history need to be explored. The rea-

sons may be legitimate—a return to school—or questionable—spent time in prison.

- Questionable reasons for leaving jobs.
- Inconsistency in career path. People who have worked in a variety of food-service sectors (fast food, fine dining, cafeterias) may not really know what they want to do.
- A messy application with misspellings and erasures can indicate an employee whose work habits are equally messy and undisciplined.
- Illegible handwriting that goes above or below the lines may indicate physical problems.
- Does the handwriting on the application match the signature? Some applicants get friends to complete the application for them if they feel they cannot do it themselves.

Employment Tests

Selection tests are used to provide an objective means of measuring abilities or characteristics. In the restaurant business, because of ready access to cash and supplies, there are potential problems with employee theft; other customer-contact positions require employees with empathy and an outgoing personality. Many argue that properly constructed tests can identify employees who have the characteristics necessary for specific positions.

Various laws and regulations governing tests used in the United States have been developed at three levels:

- At the federal level most of the laws are embodied in Title VII of the Civil Rights Act of 1964 and related EEOC regulations, in particular the Uniform Guidelines for Employment Selection Procedures.
- Regulations at the state level tend to follow federal guidelines but may add other, more stringent requirements.
- Professional standards are established by the American Psychological Association, American Guidance of Personnel Association, and the National Measurement Association.

The purpose of these regulations is to ensure that job applicants are not subject to discrimination or unfair, arbitrary rejection.

To be useful a test must be:

- Sensitive, so that it distinguishes between people who possess the characteristics and those who do not.
- Standardized, so that benchmark scores have been identified on a representative and sizable sample of people for whom it is intended and against whom an applicant's scores will be compared.
- Reliable, so that it always measures the same thing.
- Valid, so that it measures what it is intended to measure.

quick bite 12.6
Can You Self-Monitor?

A useful test to identify service-oriented employees is the Self-Monitoring Scale. Developed by Mark Snyder of the University of Minnesota, someone who is defined as a high self-monitor, having picked up cues in the environment, can control and modify his or her behavior and expressions successfully based on the behavior and expressions that are most appropriate. Such a person would be better able to adjust his or her behavior to meet the needs of customers. In addition, high self-monitors have a higher level of persuasive communications skills.

With use of the scale, Snyder reports a 70 percent correlation in identifying self-monitors. Following is the 18-item Self-Monitoring Scale together with the typical replies of high-self-monitoring individuals. (Some observers suggest using a Likert-type scale rather than a simple true–false.)

1. I find it hard to imitate the behavior of other people.   (F)
2. At parties and social gatherings, I do not attempt to do or say things that others will like.   (F)
3. I can only argue for ideas which I already believe.   (F)
4. I can make impromptu speeches even on topics about which I have almost no information.   (T)
5. I guess I put on a show to impress or entertain others.   (T)
6. I would probably make a good actor.   (T)
7. In a group of people I am rarely the center of attention.   (F)
8. In different situations and with different people, I often act like very different persons.   (T)
9. I am not particularly good at making other people like me.   (F)
10. I'm not always the person I appear to be.   (T)
11. I would not change my opinions (or the way I do things) in order to please someone or win their favor.   (F)
12. I have considered being an entertainer.   (T)
13. I have always been good at games like charades or improvisational settings.   (T)
14. I have trouble changing my behavior to suit different people and different situations.   (F)
15. At a party I let others keep the jokes and the stories going.   (F)
16. I feel a bit awkward in public and do not show up quite as well as I should.   (F)
17. I can look anyone in the eye and tell a lie (if for a right end).   (T)
18. I may deceive people by being friendly when I really dislike them.   (T)

Source: William W. Samenfink, "Identifying the Service Potential of an Employee through the Use of the Self-Monitoring Scale." *Hospitality Research Journal*, vol. 15, no. 2, 1992, pp. 1–10.

Validity can be either concurrent or predictive. To establish concurrent validity, existing employees are tested and their test scores recorded. Their job performance is also evaluated and noted. The test score of each employee is then compared to how well the person performs on the job to determine whether or not there is a significant relationship between the two. If there is a significant relationship—those who score well on the test perform well on the job, and vice versa—the test is valid and can be used on future applicants as a predictor of future job success.

With predictive validity all applicants are tested and the test scores noted but they are not used to determine whether or not to hire. Applicants are hired on the basis of other methods, such as an interview. After a period of time the performance of each employee is evaluated and the person's job performance is compared to his or her test scores. If there is a significant relationship between test score and job performance, predictive validity exists and the test can be used on future applicants as a predictor of job success.

Although written integrity tests are controversial, the American Psychological Association has given them qualified support, indicating that most of the evidence supports the idea that some of the tests do work. Tests are more likely to work if they meet the four criteria noted above.

Three companies—London House, Reid Psychological Systems, and Stanton—account for 70 percent of the integrity test market and tend to have the strongest research support. Reid Psychological Systems, for example, claims reliability coefficients of 0.90 on internal consistency and 0.78 on test–retest reliability. Concurrent reliability has been measured in four studies at 0.43 (twice), 0.62, and 0.39. This compares favorably with average validity scores over several thousand studies for personality tests of 0.30. Predictive validity scores have also been impressive.

According to Reid, people who possess integrity [29]:

- Value their self-concepts and personal reputation as honest persons
- Value integrity in their friends and associates
- Avoid thoughts or situations related to theft, deceit, or inappropriate behavior
- Are willing to discipline other people or themselves for violating socially accepted standards of honest conduct

In addition to the integrity attitude test, others are available, including:

- Substance use attitudes
- Substance use history
- Sales productivity
- Service relations
- Numerical skills
- Social conduct history
- Work/education history

These tests vary in price from $16.50 to $25.00 each, the unit cost getting progressively smaller as the number used increases. (This section should not be taken as an endorsement of Reid Psychological Systems. It is published as an example of what one company offers in the area of employee testing.)

Interview in Human Resources Department

Where a foodservice company has a corporate human resources department, the individual manager can expect assistance in interviewing employees. The basic breakdown of responsibility is that whoever is better able to do the job should do the job. Human resource professionals have specialized knowledge in the area of selecting qualified applicants within the existing regulatory environment. Managers would do well to utilize that expertise. A typical breakdown of responsibilities regarding interviewing is that the personnel or human resource manager would:

- Develop legal, effective interviewing techniques
- Train managers in selection interviewing
- Provide interview formats and tests
- Send qualified employees to managers who want to do the final interview

The line manager or supervisor, on the other hand, would typically:

- Decide whether or not to do the final interview (most will, rightly, want to)
- Do the actual final interviewing and hiring where appropriate
- Provide feedback to personnel on hiring decisions and reasons for not hiring

The interview is the most widely used and probably the most subjective method used in selecting employees. It has been demonstrated, for example, that [30]:

- Negative information brought out during the interview is weighed too heavily and positive information not weighed heavily enough.
- A favorable–unfavorable information sequence of information resulted in better applicant ratings than did an unfavorable–favorable sequence.
- Interviewers have an "ideal" stereotypical candidate against which they compare candidates. This ideal is a composite of the interviewer's perception of the characteristics of successful jobholders.
- Visual cues are often regarded as more important than verbal cues in reaching conclusions.
- The interviewer's rating of candidates is, in part, dependent on the quality of the other candidates being interviewed at the same time.

The interview is the best method for determining whether or not candidates possess certain characteristics, such as self-confidence, effectiveness in

The interview is the best suited and most widely used selection method in the restaurant industry. Structured interviews are one way to improve the reliability and validity of an interview. A structured interview is a "face-to-face encounter where the interviewer uses an identical set of predetermined questions with each applicant." The following questions were found to be useful in selecting swing managers for fast-food operations:

1. Tell me about two or three people you work with at _____ with whom you have to interact "differently." Perhaps these people were new to the organization, older workers, or disabled.
2. Tell me about two or three situations where you had to deal with a difficult customer. How did you know they were unhappy? How did you handle them?
3. Tell me about some problem situations (other than unhappy customers) that you've encountered on the job. How did you handle them? Would you handle them the same way again?
4. Have you been able to make any parts of your job easier or more rewarding? How?
5. Describe some of the times you tried to persuade or influence other crew members or members of the management team. What did you do? How did it turn out?
6. Describe some situations where you did more than was expected on the job.

Source: Michael T. MacHatton and Lynne E. Baltzer, "Quality Personnel Selection: Using a Structured Interview Guide to Improve Selection of Managers," *Hospitality Research Journal,* vol. 18, no. 1, 1994, pp. 77–99.

expressing oneself, and sociability, factors that are especially important in customer-contact positions. For this reason it is recommended as part of the hiring process. However, there are ways to improve its effectiveness.

There are three steps in preparing for the interview [31]. The interviewer should be selected, the place where the interview will take place must be identified, and time should be planned to preview the application.

In a corporation human resource managers may be responsible for an initial screening of candidates. However, line management should have the responsibility for making the final hiring decision. Whoever conducts the interview should have a complete understanding of what the job entails, in addition to the skills, knowledge, and abilities required to perform that job. The former comes from a job description, the latter from a job specification. In addition, the interviewer must be objective, an excellent judge of people, a good listener and an excellent representative of the operation. The interview is not only an opportunity to select employees; it is a way to represent the restaurant to people in the community. Even if an employee is not hired, the person interviewed will leave with some kind of an impression about the company based on the type of interview that he or she had. That impression can be positive or negative. Some people have left interviews indicating that "Not only would I never work for that restaurant; I would never eat there and will tell all my friends to avoid eating there."

Care should be taken in selecting a time and place conducive to making an objective decision on whether or not a candidate is a proper fit for a job. Interviews should be scheduled when the interviewer can devote her or his time exclusively to the task at hand without interruptions. Sitting at a table in the restaurant can be a good idea as long as the manager makes it clear that they are not to be disturbed. This setting gives the interviewee a chance to see part of the operation.

The application form and additional screening information should be reviewed before the interview begins. A list of appropriate questions should also be developed prior to the interview. Many companies have found that a structured interview is most effective. In a structured interview questions are developed based on the most important and most time-consuming duties of the job, and all candidates are asked those questions. Questions might be situational ("What would you do if . . . . ?"), cover job knowledge ("How is a 'rusty nail' made?"), consist of a simulation ("Show me how you would clear this table"), or deal with employee requirements for the position. The interview may be part oral, part written, and part physical, and sample answers to the questions to be asked should be developed beforehand.

Developed along the lines suggested above, a structured interview is more likely to be objective and nondiscriminatory compared to unplanned interviews. Questions focus on what is important in performing the job. Writing the questions down together with sample answers ensures that everyone is asked the same questions and that the interviewer has thought about the answer that is preferred. Inexperienced interviewers will often ask a question and fail to listen to the candidate's answer, as they have to formulate the next question in their mind while the candidate is answering the first.

One problem with a structured interview is that the structure itself can mean that potentially good candidates can be lost because of the lack of flexibility of the interview itself. Responses that do not conform to the sample answers developed should not be discarded if, in fact, they are good and legitimate.

First impressions are very important. It is often a mistake to judge someone based only on appearances and first impressions. However, someone who comes to an interview late, lights a cigarette without asking for permission, and has dirty shoes and/or messy hair certainly does not seem too interested in the job.

Some small talk is useful to get the interviewee relaxed. The application form should have been reviewed immediately prior to the interview but should not be consulted during the interview, to avoid a stilted question-and-answer session.

During the body of the interview the objective is to get the person being interviewed to do most of the talking. The interviewer has an idea (from the job description and job specification) of what is needed. By listening to the respons-

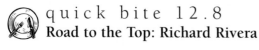

quick bite 12.8
Road to the Top: Richard Rivera

Chairman and Chief Executive, Longhorn Steaks, Inc.

In 1971, Richard Rivera became acquainted with Steak & Ale and switched career ambitions from becoming a lawyer to being a restaurateur. Beginning as a management trainee, he embarked on a successful career with several chains. In 1994, after five years as chief executive of TGI Friday's, he joined Longhorn, an $88 million annual sales company, for the opportunity to run an independent corporation rather than a division of another company. His personal maxim: "You learn as much from the people who work for you as from the people you work for."

He credits much of his success to the self-reliance he learned from his upbringing. At the age of 2 he left the United States with his family to live in Argentina. Later he lived in several South American countries and became fluent in Spanish. Traveling to and from the United States at an early age helped create his self-confidence.

Rivera believes that in a business where so many employees are Hispanic, being able to speak Spanish is a tremendous asset: "It changes the way you think about things. . . . It opens up your mind to more ways of looking at a problem or looking at a people situation." Associates say that his love of sailing mirrors his ideas on business: "He does have a sense of adventure, but he's very pragmatic and methodical about how he goes about it; he enjoys himself while he's doing it."

Source: Ron Ruggles, "Richard Rivera," *Nation's Restaurant News,* January 1995, pp. 173–174.

es of the interviewee, the interviewer is better able to evaluate whether or not that person is the right one for the job.

People can perform a job if they have the skills and the motivation. Many positions in a restaurant are not highly skilled jobs or require skills that can be taught readily on the job. The manager must decide whether it is more important to hire attitude and train skills rather than vice versa. Particularly for front-of-the-house jobs, it is better and easier to hire attitude. It is difficult to identify the basic values, ethics, and motivation of someone rather than the extent to which the person possesses specific skills. Here are some questions that will help [32].

1. Ask people about their first job. When a person started work can be a good indication of their work values and motivation. It does not matter so much whether or not the job was restaurant related. What is important is the reason they went to work and what they got out of the experience.
2. Ask younger people about their class schedule while in college. The restaurant business is one that is physically demanding. People who had

trouble getting up before an 11 o'clock class may not have the energy level needed for your business.

3. Ask about the first time they sold something (for server positions).
4. Ask about their experiences as a *customer* in your operation or those of the competition. Their response will indicate what they think of customer service and what is required to satisfy a guest.
5. Ask who their heroes (or best friends) are and why. We tend to look up to people we admire. The answer to this question will indicate what the interviewee's values are.
6. When hiring someone who will take reservations over the phone, interview them over the phone. That way you will find out how they really sound to potential customers. If they pass this test, interview them in person.
7. "What were customers like in the last place you worked?" Again, this will indicate true feelings about the importance of customers.
8. "Who was the best (and worst) manager you ever had, and why?" This will give an indication of how well or how poorly this person works with people in positions of authority.
9. "If you could have improved anything about your last job, what would it have been?" Exceptional employees are those who express their interest in the job by continually seeking ways to improve it and others within the operation.
10. "Why should we hire you?" Some employees feel that the world owes them a living. Others, the kind you want, believe that they can contribute something positive to the operation.

Once the interviewer's questions have been exhausted, it is time to ask the applicant if she or he has any questions. It is doubtful that everything could have been covered to the interviewee's satisfaction, so some kind of response should be expected. In fact, if the applicant has no questions, it probably indicates a lack of interest in the job. The number and type of questions asked can also give a clue as to what is important to this person.

Questions can be either direct or indirect. Direct questions are those that require a one- or two-word answer ("When did you leave your last job?"). They are useful for collecting large amounts of information very quickly. However, for a real evaluation, indirect questions (for example "Why did you leave your last job?") are better, because they require that the applicant talk more to answer the question completely. Remember, the objective is to get the applicant to talk.

It may be necessary to probe the answer to a question. A probe is an attempt to elicit more information from the interviewee if the initial answer to a question is considered vague. If it is to work, the probe should seek to confirm, clarify, and/or promote further discussion. Probing can come only if the interviewer actively listens to the initial response to learn that it does not give a complete answer to the question.

There are certain questions that employers cannot lawfully ask. Topics should be avoided that could discriminate against employees on the basis of federally protected categories. Businesses cannot discriminate on the basis of race, ethnic background, origin, color, gender, age (over 40), handicap, military experience, and religion. Additional state and local laws have been enacted to protect additional groups of people. Basically, it comes down to this: Ask questions that deal solely with a person's ability to do the job—and nothing else. A person may be asked whether or not they have the legal right to work in the United States; they cannot be asked whether or not they or their parents are naturalized citizens. They can be asked which high school they attended but not when they went there. They can be asked if they have ever been convicted of a crime but not whether they have ever been arrested for a crime.

Background Investigation

The value of a reference check is the belief that past experience on the job is the best predictor of future job performance. It is, however, increasingly difficult to get worthwhile feedback about prior job experience. Applicants will only give the names of people who might be expected to give glowing references. The best source of past performance is to check with previous supervisors. There are two potential problems. First, because of the high turnover in this business, it may be difficult to locate references from even several months back. Second, previous employers may be reluctant to give detailed information on previous employees. There have been cases where employees who did not get a job have turned around and sued previous employers for giving a negative reference. People who are familiar with the law may be reluctant to do more than give the former employee's date of hire, date of departure, and job title.

Because of the usefulness of a reference from a previous supervisor, it is recommended that managers continue to give honest evaluations of their past employees. This advice is given in the hope that the manager who gives evaluations will receive them from others when requested.

There are some guidelines that, if followed, will help keep managers out of trouble from disgruntled employees [33].

- Don't volunteer information; respond only to specific requests. Before responding, telephone the inquirer to check on the validity of the request.
- Direct all communications only to persons who have a specific interest in that information.
- State that the information being given is confidential and should be treated as such.
- If possible, obtain written consent from the employee.
- Provide only information that relates to the job and job performance in question.
- Avoid vague statements (such as "She was careless at times").
- Document all released information.
- Clearly label all subjective statements based on personal opinions and feelings.

- When providing information negative to the employee, give the reasons why and specify the incidents.
- Avoid answering questions "off the record."

When requesting a reference, the most important things to check are [34]:

- Employment dates
- Job title
- Primary job duties and responsibilities
- Applicant's performance compared to others
- Attendance and lateness records
- Applicant's ability to get along with fellow employees and managers
- Amount of supervision required
- Quality of applicant's work
- Motivation and enthusiasm toward the job
- Starting and final pay
- Reason for leaving
- Anything else of significance

It would also be useful to find out if the previous employer would rehire the person. It is worth asking this question, although if the person giving the interview knows anything about the law, he or she will probably answer "It is against company policy to rehire previous employees." In addition to reference checking, employers may wish to check criminal records, driving records, Workers' Compensation records, federal court records, and educational records if it is deemed important.

Specialized companies will check these types of records for a fee, but it is possible to obtain a great deal of information yourself simply by using public records. Criminal records at the county or state level can be checked over the telephone. The state motor vehicle office will provide driving records. Workers' Compensation records, available through the state, will indicate past job injuries together with whether or not an employee has been cleared to return to work. Such records cannot be used to discriminate against an applicant who has made compensation claims at other places. Federal court records can also be accessed, while educational records are checked through the appropriate educational institution. Information from such background checks can be used as part of the selection process only if it is job related and is applied to every candidate.

Medical Examination

State agencies require medical clearances for all food handlers. An increasing number of companies will test new employees for drug use. Although controversial, drug testing has generally been upheld by the courts as long as it is applied to every job candidate for every position.

Preliminary Selection in Human Resources Department

At this point it would be appropriate for the personnel department, having screened prospective employees, to make a preliminary cut of employees deemed inappropriate. The remainder would be cleared for interviews with line managers who would make the final decision.

Supervisory Interview

The guidelines given above for interviewing with people from the personnel department are equally appropriate for interviewing with line management.

Realistic Job Preview

Often, the manager will be interviewing an excellent candidate, someone who will really make a difference to the operation. At other times she will be in somewhat of a panic to fill a position. In either or both cases, there is a tendency to sell the job to the applicant as something better than it really is. In such a situation the initial job expectations are set too high. The applicant might be told that no more than a 45-hour week will be required and that two days off a week are standard. The job will be viewed as attractive and there will be a high rate of job acceptance.

Once on the job, however, the newly hired employee realizes that all is not as promised. The employee becomes dissatisfied, less motivated, and may quit. In the short run a body has been found; in the long run, there is increased turnover.

A realistic job preview, on the other hand, presents an accurate picture of the job and its conditions as part of the hiring process. The job may or may not be attractive to applicants and there will probably be a lower rate of job acceptance than that described above. Of the smaller percentage of applicants who do accept the job, however, a greater number will find that the job is, in fact, as represented. They will tend to be more satisfied, more motivated, and will stay longer than the group discussed above.

Hiring Decision

It is important that the hiring decision be made in a timely manner and that applicants be made aware of that date. If an applicant is well qualified for the job, any delay in making the decision may mean that the person will find employment elsewhere.

Informing both those who will receive job offers and those who will not makes for good public relations and keeps those who did not get the job interested in applying for other opportunities within the operation for which they might be better suited.

In making a job offer the following elements should be covered [35]:

- Position title
- Person to whom to report
- Salary or pay

- Shift
- Starting date
- Starting time
- Ending time
- Days off
- Equipment needed
- Clothing required
- Meal arrangements
- Parking
- Wen to come for processing of personnel forms

The working relationship will be easier if it begins on the right foot. This means making the new employee feel welcome and preparing existing employees for the new arrival. Involving existing employees before a new worker shows up will help ease the difficulties associated with getting to know and work with the new person.

ENDNOTES

1. Robert Christie Mill, *Managing for Productivity in the Hospitality Industry* (New York: Van Nostrand Reinhold, 1989), p. 11.

2. National Restaurant Association, *Foodservice Manager 2000,* Current Issues Report (Washington, DC: National Restaurant Association, 1992), p. 19.

3. William B. Johnston, and Arnold H. Packer, *Workers for the 21st Century* (Indianapolis, IN: Hudson Institute, 1987), p. 89.

4. Karen Eich Drummond, *Human Resource Management for the Hospitality Industry* (New York: Van Nostrand Reinhold, 1990), p. 230.

5. Johnston and Packer, *Workers for the 21st Century,* p. 89.

6. National Restaurant Association, *Foodservice Manager 2000,* p. 19.

7. Johnston and Packer, *Workers for the 21st Century,* pp. 92–93.

8. Ibid., p. 92.

9. Paul Ehrlich, Loy Bilderback, and Anne H. Ehrlich, *The Golden Door* (New York: Ballantine Books, 1979), p. 242.

10. Mill, *Managing for Productivity in the Hospitality Industry,* p. 19.

11. National Restaurant Association, *Foodservice Manager 2000,* p. 28.

12. William F. Jaffe, "Integrating the Disabled Employee into the Quick-Service Restaurant: The Enclave Model," *Hospitality & Tourism Educator,* vol. 6, no. 2, Spring 1994, p. 15.

13. National Restaurant Association, *Americans with Disabilities Act: Answers for Foodservice Operators* (Washington, DC: National Restaurant Association, 1992), p. 2.

14. Ibid., pp. 8–18.

15. National Restaurant Association, *Foodservice Manager 2000,* p. 27.

16. Ibid., p. 27.

17. Jaffe, "Integrating the Disabled Employee into the Quick-Service Restaurant," p. 19.

18. Arthur W. Sherman Jr., George W. Bohlander and Herbert J. Chudren, *Managing Human Resources*, 8th ed. (Cincinnati, OH: South-Western Publishing Co., 1988), p. 63.

19. David Wheelhouse, *Managing Human Resources in the Hospitality Industry* (East Lansing, MI: Educational Institute of the American Hotel and Motel Association, 1989), p. 67.

20. Ibid., p. 66.

21. Ibid., p. 71.

22. Ibid., p. 79.

23. EEOC, *Affirmative Action and Equal Employment: A Guidebook for Employers*, vol. 1 (Washington, DC: Equal Employment Opportunity Commission, 1974), pp. 16–17.

24. Lewis C. Forrest, *Training for the Hospitality Industry* (East Lansing, MI: Educational Institute of the American Hotel and Motel Association, 1983), p. 56.

25. Donald Lundberg, *The Management of People in Hotels and Restaurants*, 5th ed. (Dubuque, IA: Wm. C. Brown Company, 1992), p. 85.

26. Forrest, *Training for the Hospitality Industry*, p. 41.

27. Ibid., p. 53.

28. Sherman et al., *Managing Human Resources*, p. 160.

29. Reid Research Report, unpublished promotional booklet, undated.

30. Sherman et al., *Managing Human Resources*, p. 172.

31. Wheelhouse, *Managing Human Resources in the Hospitality Industry*, pp. 176–183.

32. Bill From and Len Schlesinger, *The Real Heroes of Business* (New York: Doubleday, 1994), pp. 323–333.

33. J.D. Bell, J. Castagnera, and J. P. Young "Employment References: Do You Know the Law?" *Personnel Journal*, vol. 63, no. 2, February 1984, pp. 32–36.

34. Karen Eich Drummond, *Human Resource Management for the Hospitality Industry* (New York: Van Nostrand Reinhold, 1990), p. 33.

35. Wheelhouse, *Managing Human Resources in the Hospitality Industry*, p. 119.

chapter thirteen

TRAINING
AND DEVELOPMENT

learning objectives

By the end of this chapter you should be able to:

1. Design an effective orientation program.

2. Compare and contrast the various training methods.

3. Design, implement, and evaluate an effective training program.

4. Develop the skills necessary to become an effective trainer.

5. List the elements of a strong employee and management development program.

EMPLOYEE ORIENTATION

Orientation is "the formal process of familiarizing new employees with the organization, their job, and the work unit" [1]. Conducted properly, orientation will give employees the knowledge necessary for them to be successful in an operation.

It is generally recognized that a well-run orientation program will help [2]:

- Lower turnover
- Increase productivity
- Improve employee morale
- Lower recruiting and training costs
- Facilitate learning
- Reduce the level of anxiety of new employees

As noted above, a comprehensive orientation program should cover three major areas: the organization, the job, and the work unit. The following elements are typical of a comprehensive program [3]:

---

 quick bite 13.1
Hot Concepts: Dive!

News that the first Dive! restaurant in Los Angeles was bringing in 2000 covers a day convinced owners Levy Restaurants, Stephen Spielberg, and Jeffrey Katzenberg to consider a chain of submarine-themed restaurants. The second, built at a cost of $10 million, is in Las Vegas and features a perpetual waterfall, an hourly dive sequence, "depth charges," and other computer effects. Porthole monitors feature seascapes from around the world.

Merchandise is sold in addition to food, the latter featuring gourmet submarine sandwiches or, as Larry Levy calls them, "entrees on baguettes." Items include a "Parisien" with grilled chicken marinated in Pommery and Dijon mustards with smoked Gouda and artichoke, and a vegetarian with goat cheese, roasted yellow peppers, sauteed spinach, and sundried tomato salsa, in addition to the "traditional" Sicilian sub. Other subs include Portobello mushrooms, roasted peppers, Romano cheese, arugula, and rosemary aoli, a tempura-fried soft-shell crab with watercress, plum tomatoes, and Chinese tartar sauce, and a Tuscan steak item with sliced tenderloin, fresh rosemary, cracked pepper, lemon juice, and extra-virgin olive oil.

The average check is $12.50 at the $7.5 million, 11,000-square foot Los Angeles operation, which also features salads, burgers, and oven-roasted chicken, shrimp, and vegetable entrees.

Source: Richard Martin, "Dive!" *Nation's Restaurant News,* May 22, 1995, pp. 148, 150.

The organization:

1. Description of the operation's history, size, and objectives
2. Company standards regarding job behavior and performance
3. Conditions of employment regarding such things as hours of work and pay periods
4. Key management and the chain of command

The purpose of this segment is to let employees see the "big picture" of what the company stands for. In so doing, employees will get a feeling for how their job fits into the entire operation and realize the history and tradition behind what the operation does.

The job:

5. Detailing of the duties and responsibilities of the job and its importance to the entire organization
6. Explanation of the training to be given
7. Explanation of how performance will be evaluated
8. Sanitation and safety regulations

The objective of this segment is to let employees know what a "normal" workday looks like.

The work unit:

9. Introductions to fellow employees
10. Immediate contact in dealing with problems
11. Tour of the entire operation
12. Rules, regulations, and policies

The Old Spaghetti Factory includes the following items in their orientation program [4]:

- Brief history of the company and store
- Customer philosophy
- Names of managers
- Name of trainer
- Schedule and scheduling
- Where to park
- Attendance and tardiness
- No-solicitation rule (prohibits employees from selling any products or services or from distributing literature on the premises without prior approval from the employer; designed to prevent unions from distributing union literature in the restaurant)
- How to sign in

Orientation Manual

Many operators are providing workers with an employee manual as part of their orientation. Here is an example of an outline for such a manual:

A. Operational Procedures

1. Clock-in	2. Smoking
3. Horseplay	4. Phone calls
5. Answering the phone	6. Solicitations
7. Paychecks	8. Advances
9. Absences/tardiness	10. Personal property
11. Personal business	12. Age requirements
13. Accidents	14. Customer complaints
15. Employee meals	16. Breaks
17. Parking	18. Scheduling
19. Dress code	

B. Personal Hygiene

1. Hair	2. Clothing
3. Face	4. Hands
5. Fingernails	6. Washing hands

C. Employee Benefits

1. Insurance	2. Promotions
3. Training	4. Uniforms
5. Vacations	

D. Menu Breakdown

E. Greeting, Seating, and Table Service

F. Abbreviations

G. Employee Agreement

Source: A. Dyal Bailey, "The Quick Way to Produce an Employee Manual," *Restaurants USA*, vol. 12, no. 8, September 1992, pp. 16–18.

- Meals
- Wage and raise policy
- Payday and paycheck procedure
- House and safety rules
- Grooming and uniform standards
- Other store rules

- Training schedule
- Handwashing and sanitizing

It is as important to prepare existing employees for the new hire as vice versa. Employees may be suspicious of new hires and will wonder if and how a new employee will affect them and their job. This important section aims to make new employees feel like they belong.

There is a danger in exposing the new hire to too much information over a short period of time. For a new employee, the first day is especially stressful: dealing with a work environment, employees, supervisors, and customers who are different. In such a situation the employee may be unable to absorb much additional information. Nevertheless, the first few days of contact between the employee and the company will set the tone for the longer-term relationship.

To combat potential problems of information overload, employees are given much of the information in writing in the form of an employee handbook. They are then asked to sign a declaration indicating that they have received this information. In this way the company protects itself against future employee claims that they were not told certain information. This is particularly important for those employees who have to enforce company rules.

The final part of an orientation program is the evaluation and follow-up. Too often the assumption is made that because employees have been through the program, they have absorbed the information. The objective is, in fact, to have them absorb certain information deemed important by management. Some companies will test employees several weeks after the orientation to determine whether or not the information has been taken in.

EMPLOYEE TRAINING AND DEVELOPMENT

Importance of Training

There are some in the industry who see training as a cost rather than an investment. When sales drop, any training that is currently being done is stopped altogether. They argue that given the turnover rate in the industry, there is little point in training employees who will invariably leave. They argue that they are, in essence, training employees for others.

This argument fails to recognize that employees may be leaving, in part, because management has not invested the time, money, or energy in them, the employees. A well-trained group of employees should result in a reduction of costs, stress, turnover, and absenteeism and a corresponding increase in efficiency and customer satisfaction.

Responsibility for Training

The person responsible for training will depend on the size of the organization and how it is structured. For a restaurant that is part of a chain or a unit part of a

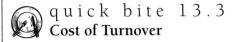

quick bite 13.3
Cost of Turnover

Here are the costs directly related to turnover:

1. Advertising and recruiting
2. Time spent on recruiting
3. Orientation and training
4. Overtime for existing employees
5. Support items such as uniforms and wine openers

Here are the indirect costs of turnover:

1. Lack of productivity in new employee
2. Loss of reputation and goodwill
3. Waste and breakage
4. More accidents
5. Lack of teamwork
6. Decreased motivation among existing staff

Here are the figures: The National Restaurant Association estimates median turnover rate at about 100 percent. In 1990 the average cost for turning over one hourly employee in the restaurant industry was between $2900 and $4100. It costs an Applebee's $10,000 to replace a "shift-ready" manager.

Source: Loret Carbone, "Less Employee Turnover: The Hidden Key to Profitability," *Nation's Restaurant News*, March 20, 1995, p. 50; Theresa Howard, "New Strategies for Tomorrow's Workforce," *Nation's Restaurant News*, March 20, 1995, p. 63.

---

larger organization, line managers will be supported by staff people in a human resource department with specialized expertise in training.

Such staff people can be called upon to [5]:

- Assist line managers in developing training programs
- Conduct general training programs focusing on such general topics as supervisory techniques and time management
- Coordinate various elements of training, such as the use of outside speakers and seminars and directing programs of succession planning and cross-training
- Research, monitor, and evaluate training

Even if there is staff assistance, the unit manager bears the ultimate responsibility for training new employees. At the independent unit level the unit manager does not have the benefit of specialized staff assistance. The general manager of a restaurant will not necessarily carry out the actual training. The training itself is best done by someone who understands the performance standards required for the job and is able to pass those skills on to others. Often, that person is the department manager.

TRAINING PROCESS

Training can be defined as "any procedure initiated by an organization to foster learning among organizational members" [6]. Training is done initially to bring new hires up to the standards required by the company. Beyond this, as the job or the market changes, there will be a need to establish training programs to adjust operations to the new situation.

There are several steps involved in developing a training program [7]:

1. Conduct a needs assessment.
2. Determine learning objectives.
3. Develop the overall training program.
4. Develop individual training lessons.
5. Conduct the training.
6. Evaluate.
7. Follow up.

Needs Assessment

The purpose of a needs assessment is to determine what types of training are needed. Assessment can be done at three levels [8]: organizational analysis, task analysis, and person analysis.

The organizational analysis looks at the company as a whole and in light of company goals, resources, and the external environment in which it operates, suggests where the training emphasis should be. For example, there has been increased attention in the courts on the topic of sexual harassment. In light of this environmental influence, an organizational analysis might suggest supervisory training in this area.

A task analysis involves designing the content of a training program based on the duties involved in a job. A job description is one document that results from having conducted a job analysis. The job description will indicate the most important and time-consuming tasks involved in performing that job. Performance standards will then be developed for every important part of the job. These performance standards represent the level of performance required for that job. A person analysis then determines what knowledge, skills, and attitudes are required to perform the job successfully. People hired for that job must either possess these skills or must be trained in them. The need for training can also come from accident records, personal observation, exit interviews, customer complaints, and employee evaluations.

Learning Objectives

Learning objectives should be SMART: specific, measurable, achievable, realistic, and time-bound. Both manager and employee will then know up front what is to be done, the level of performance that is to be achieved, and when it is to be accomplished.

Training Program

The complete training program can then be laid out. The training necessary for a specific job comes from an analysis of that job. A job analysis will identify the important tasks that make up that job. This is what people performing the job must be able to do. If an employee is hired without the ability to perform one or more of these tasks, the task must be taught to the employee. The program will identify what is to be taught, when, where, how, and to whom it is to be taught, together with an estimate of the cost involved.

Earlier, the process for conducting a job analysis was identified. The process involves developing [9]:

- A job list
- A job breakdown
- A job description
- A job specification

A job list is an inventory of all the tasks that must be performed as part of that job. For example, a job list for a food server might include the following, among others [10]:

- Greeting and seating restaurant guests
- Serving water; lighting candles
- Taking beverage orders and serving drinks
- Presenting the food menu and beverage list
- Assisting guests in making food and beverage selections

A job breakdown is then prepared for each task on the job list. The job breakdown indicates how the task should be performed. It comprises four parts: what is to be done, what materials are needed, how it is to be done, and why that step is important.

The task of "assisting guests in making food and beverage selections" might involve six steps [11]:

1. Approach the table.
2. Take cocktail order.
3. Serve cocktails.
4. Check back for a second cocktail.
5. Take the food order.
6. Take the wine order.

Each item would then be described in more detail as to the procedures for performing the task, any materials that might be needed, and why the specified procedures are important. The first step might look like this [12]:

WHAT TO DO
Approach the table.

HOW TO DO IT
Stand erect. Look at the guest, smile, and greet them pleasantly. Introduce yourself. If you know their names, use them when you greet them. Be courteous.

---

 quick bite 13.4
Moving on Up

As managers move from managing a single unit to overseeing multiunits, they shift their management emphasis in the following ways:

1. From technical trainer to manager developer.
2. From receiver of information to communicator of information
3. From a structured to an unstructured environment
4. From a doer to a delegator
5. An increased understanding of motivation techniques and how their management skills affect other people
6. More knowledge about financial analysis, business precision and accuracy, computer applications, personnel management, the analysis of operating results, and how to provide solutions to problems identified in their review process

They identified what they did to make their restaurants more successful than others in the region as follows:

1. Supporting managers and allowing them to manage their own restaurants
2. Letting managers establish their own goals
3. Developing managers, assistant managers, and crews
4. Motivating and establishing pride and team spirit
5. Modeling the work ethic

Source: W. Terry Umbreit and Don I. Smith, "A Study of Opinions and Practices of Successful Multi-unit Fast Service Restaurant Managers," *Hospitality Research Journal*, vol. 14, no. 2, 1990, pp. 451–458.

WHY IT IS IMPORTANT

You "win" the table by your first contact when you are pleasant and personable.

From the job breakdown a description of the job can be developed and used to write a job specification: a list of the knowledge, skills, and abilities needed by someone to perform the job. When employees are hired, their existing knowledge, skill, and abilities can be compared to those in the job specification to identify shortcomings. These items form the basis for the tasks that employees have to be trained to perform. The specifics are to be found in the job breakdown. These will also serve later as the performance standards to determine the extent to which employees are performing up to the level required by the restaurant.

Training Lessons

The entire training program is then divided into segments and a lesson plan developed for each segment. Typically, classroom training sessions should last from 15 to 30 minutes. The training lesson will identify a learning objective for that session and suggest which techniques should be used to meet that objective.

Conducting the Training

At this point it is necessary to select someone to do the training. Typically, that task is left to the immediate supervisor or a fellow employee. Just because someone knows how to perform a job or has responsibility for seeing that the job is performed well does not mean that the person will be effective in training another person to perform the task effectively.

According to Wheelhouse [13], effective trainers are:

- Good judges of people
- Objective
- Aware of, understand, and accept the differences in people
- Good at listening and communicating
- Good role models for the department
- Optimistic and enthusiastic about the job, the department, and the company

If a fellow employee is asked to take on the role of trainer, that person should be compensated financially and given positive recognition within the operation. A server acting as trainer will be able to serve fewer customers and will have fewer tips. Extra pay and recognition should be given to make up for this shortfall.

Evaluation

This next step in the process determines the extent to which the training objectives have been met. The success of the training can be measured at various levels [14]. At the first and most basic level the trainee's reaction can be measured: Did they like the program? Next, their knowledge level can be measured: Did they learn the new information? Even better is to evaluate behavior and/or attitude: Do the employees demonstrate new behaviors and/or attitudes on the job that can be traced to the training received? Finally, and most important, was the training cost-effective: Was the cost of the training outweighed by a resulting increase in employee productivity?

Follow-up

Follow-up is necessary to ensure that the skills taught are used constantly. Supervisors can follow up through coaching—checking that the results of a training program are improving employee performance and either giving positive feedback when it is happening or correcting that performance, when necessary, in a way that will improve the performance of the employee.

PRINCIPLES OF LEARNING

There is a difference between training and learning. Often, it is assumed that because training takes place, the trainees have learned. Learning does not take place until and unless the information that was part of the training program was received, understood, and internalized. Thus for training to be effective, it has to be designed such that it helps trainees learn. By identifying how people learn and designing training programs with these principles in mind, trainees will be more likely to learn.

Intention to Learn

People will not learn unless they want to. The trainer's role is to help supply that motivation by letting the trainee know the importance of the information about to be presented. Employees need to know what's in it for them. It may be that learning how to perform a new task will increase tips, help the employee get a promotion, or give them more status within the operation. The task is to find out what is important to the employee and to show how actively participating in the training will help the employee satisfy that need.

Whole Learning

Learning is improved if the entire job or task is shown in relation to other jobs and the task to be taught is then broken down into its constituent parts. Known as whole or Gestalt learning, the idea is that a trainee will better comprehend the task if she or he knows where that task fits into the entire operation. When training a dishwasher, for example, one would first explain how and where the dirty dishes come from, how they are cleaned, and what happens to them once they leave the dishwasher's control. By adding an explanation as to the importance of having clean dishes, the person being taught the job now has a frame of reference for learning the specific steps involved in producing clean dishes.

Reinforcement

People act in ways that are rewarding to them. Rewards can be external—pay increase, promotion, verbal praise—or internal—a feeling of accomplishment. Trainers should find out what rewards are important to the trainee and reinforce positive behavior using these rewards to get more of the same behavior.

Positive reinforcement—a reward for doing something right—is more effective than punishment—an action to punish the person for doing something wrong. Reinforcement is improved when the reward is given as soon as possible after the action. Praising a hostess immediately after she helps a family calm a child fretting at the dinner table is more effective in reinforcing the behavior than waiting until the end of the shift.

Practice

The saying goes: "Practice makes perfect." Some would adapt this to say: "Perfect practice makes perfect." The point, however, is that repeating the newly learned skill will improve the performance of that skill. Further, active practice is more effective than reading or listening.

Spaced versus Massed Practice

Retention is improved when new material is spread out over several sessions rather than being condensed into fewer, longer sessions. If, for example, it is estimated that a new job will require 8 hours of training, the trainee will learn better if there are 2 hours of instruction in the new job each day for four days rather than one 8-hour day of new material.

Learning Curve

People learn at different rates. There appear to be three patterns by which learning takes place. The learning of most routine jobs follows a decreasing returns pattern, wherein there is a rapid increase in the skill level followed by a tapering off in the rate of improvement as the trainee's rate of performance stabilizes at a "normal" rate.

When someone is learning a completely unfamiliar job, the increasing returns pattern is common. This learning curve starts out very slowly and increases with more instruction and practice.

The S-shaped curve is one where the trainee's performance starts out slowly, improves rapidly, then tails off. It is common with difficult tasks that also require the trainee to become familiar with the basics of the job.

With all three patterns, trainees will have periods of growth and times when performance seems to have flattened. This leveling off of performance can be discouraging for many trainees unless they are told that this is normal. Positive encouragement at these times is necessary for long-term growth in job performance.

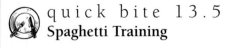

quick bite 13.5
Spaghetti Training

The manager training program for the Old Spaghetti Factory consists of the following:

Orientation	2 days
Host/hostess training	4 days
Bus training	4 days
Wait training	10 days
Bar training	8 days
Kitchen training	20 days
Office training	5 days
Floor operation training	5–10 days
Department assignment	beginning at week 14
Management effectiveness seminar	6 days

A variety of off-the-job options also exist. Some companies will pay for employees to attend classes—or even to get degrees—related to their careers. Industry certificate programs are available through the National Restaurant Association. There is an incentive to perform when trainees are paid for classes that they pass rather than just take. Other techniques involve such things as simulations, formal human relations training, or leaves of absence.

Source: Vincent H. Eade, *Human Resource Management in the Hospitality Industry* (Scottsdale, AZ: Gorsuch Scarisbrick, Publishers, 1993), p. 190.

Behavior Modeling

One of the most effective ways in which people learn is through behavior modeling: watching other people perform the task and copying their behavior. It is particularly good for situations where trainees have to learn specific information and then apply it in practice.

TRAINING METHODS

There are three general types of training: learner-controlled, individual, and group instruction [15].

Learner-Controlled Instruction

In learner-controlled or self-instruction programs, employees learn individually, at their own pace. It is training without a trainer. Whether a videotape presentation, a programmed instruction manual, or a computer-interactive program, trainees use them at times convenient to them. Because the training message is consistent, they are considered to be the best method for training standardized routines to employees.

Such programs are particularly appropriate for teaching repetitive tasks, when there are many employees doing the same job, where turnover is high, and/or when there are large numbers of temporary employees who must be trained [16]. There is a downside, however: that the initial cost is high in terms of time and dollars to develop the program. When procedures change, the program is out of date and must be redone.

According to Forrest, there are nine characteristics of learner-controlled instruction [17]:

1. Self-direction
2. Performance-based expectations
3. Contract learning
4. Learning environment
5. Printed resource materials
6. Demonstration of mastery
7. Feedback
8. Self-pacing and sequencing
9. Challenge and bypass

Self-Direction

The process of learner-controlled instruction is controlled by the trainee. The objective is to learn the material efficiently and effectively. Some take the view that this type of program can only be effective with trainees who are self-directed. These companies prescreen employees to eliminate any who are not. The advantage to the trainee from this process is that not only are the tasks learned but employees identify how to make solid, responsible decisions while managing their time.

Performance-Based Expectations. In a typical training schedule, trainees spend a period of time on one job before moving on to another. In learner-controlled instruction, trainees move on to other tasks after they have mastered the performance of that task. They need to be told what tasks they will have to perform and what level of competence defines mastery. The performance standards for a particular job could double as the competency level for that job.

Contract Learning. A learning contract serves as an agreement between the employee and the trainer and is a record of employee performance. The trainer, by signing the document, agrees to assist the employee in achieving the competencies defined. Once the trainer is convinced that the competencies have been developed, the contract is signed to that effect. A written contract formalizes the process and helps ensure that both trainer and trainee take it seriously.

A typical contract will contain [18]:

- *A competency statement:* a learning objective, what the trainee will be able to do
- *Learning activities for developing the competence:* knowledge that must be developed and skills acquired by the trainee
- *Evaluation guides:* minimum performance standards for each competency
- *Resources:* printed information available to the trainee
- *Agreements and certification:* places for trainer signatures

Learning Environment. Learner-controlled instruction takes place on the job during actual working conditions.

Printed Resource Materials. As noted above, the trainee must be supplied with written materials indicating the standard operating procedures and company standards for performing the job for which he or she is being trained. In this way any observed deviations between the way the job is supposed to be done and how it is actually being performed can be noted and corrections made.

Demonstration of Mastery. Trainees show that they have met the expectations laid out earlier when they show that they have mastered the tasks or competencies in the learning contract. Then, and only then, can they move on to learn other parts of the job. In a program where employees spend a certain amount of time in a department, they may have learned the task but must stay in that department until it is time to move to the next stage.

Feedback. When the trainer signs off on a specific competency the trainee is given specific, timely, and positive feedback on his or her performance. This type of feedback has been shown to aid in learning and performance.

Self-Pacing and Sequencing. Trainees learn at their own speed and construct the training in a way that makes sense to them. Because of this element of control, it is argued, they will learn faster and will remember better what they have learned.

Challenge and Bypass. Because employees learn at different speeds, a time-based training program is designed to accommodate slower learners. For an employee who has had significant experience or who can learn faster than others, such a program can mean they will spend time on a task that they have already mastered. Learner-controlled instruction allows them to move quickly through tasks they already have experience with and move on to competencies that are new to them. They are thus less likely to be bored by "old" material.

Individual Training

The most commonly used individual training method is on-the-job training. It is fast, flexible, and inexpensive. Four steps are involved: preparation, presentation, practice, and feedback.

Preparation. Preparation includes the development of what is to be taught, how it is to be taught, why it is important, and the standards to be achieved. The job is broken down into its parts, which are then listed in terms of importance. For example, the job of a restaurant cashier might be described as [19]:

Ensures that each guest leaves the restaurant satisfied by being friendly, fast, accurate, and helping other employees if needed, while maintaining a pleasant appearance and a clean work area. Accountable for all cash, guest checks, charges, and related reports for the restaurant during the shift.

The elements or parts of the job are:

- Friendliness
- Appearance
- Teamwork
- Opening duties
- Operating duties
- Closing duties
- Reports
- Equipment

Each element can form the basis for a separate training module.

Presentation. A good presentation consists of several steps. The trainee will probably be experiencing some stress as a result of having to learn something new. It would, therefore, be a good idea to say or do something to put the employee at ease. The trainer should introduce himself or herself, giving enough background to justify why he or she is qualified to be doing the training. The trainer would then explain what is to be taught and why it is important. These two items are intended to motivate the employee to learn what is to be taught. Next, the trainer should find out what the trainee already knows about the task at hand in order to communicate at a level appropriate to the trainee.

The entire job would then be explained with a description of how and where it fits into the entire operation. This gives a context for the task to be covered. When people know how their job relates to the overall organization, they are more likely to understand its importance. The job is then demonstrated at normal pace, then more slowly. As this is happening, the trainer explains what is being done and why it is important that the job be done in this way. The trainee can be asked specific questions as this is going on, to determine whether she or he understands.

Practice. When the trainee practices the new task, the objective is to concentrate first on accuracy, then on speed of completion. The trainee performs the job, explaining what he or she is doing and why each step is important. By having the trainee articulate the steps in this way, the trainer tests that the employee does, in fact, understand the importance of what is being done.

Feedback. Feedback is necessary to ensure that the employee continues to perform the job the way it should be done. People perform better and learn more effectively with positive feedback than with negative feedback. A word of praise works better than a rebuke. When an employee does something wrong it is important to focus on *what* went wrong rather than on *who* did something amiss.

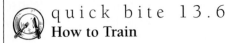

quick bite 13.6
How to Train

Answer these questions to determine how good a trainer you are:

1. Do you spend as much time in preparation as in instruction?
2. Have you prepared job breakdowns for what you will teach?
3. Do you explain to employees how they will benefit from the training?
4. Before training, do you find out what the employee already knows?
5. Do you lay out a timetable for the training?
6. Do you accept that there will be times when you will notice no progress?
7. Do you expect that employees will learn at different rates?
8. Do you show and tell how to do the task?
9. When mistakes are made, do you point out what the employee did right before correcting their mistakes?
10. Do you give clear instructions?
11. Do you ask the employee to attempt the task while explaining it to you?
12. Do you praise frequently?

Note: The answer should be "yes" to all these questions. What skills and attitudes are necessary to adopt these behaviors? Do you have them?

Source: Lewis C. Forrest, Jr., *Training for the Hospitality Industry* (East Lansing, MI: Educational Institute of the American Hotel and Motel Association, 1983), p. 107.

Some trainers will work with an employee to perform a task, then once the employee has demonstrated the job correctly will move on to work with other employees. When feedback goes from continuous reinforcement to no reinforcement it is likely that the behavior will stop or that performance will go down. To maintain that performance, periodic reinforcement is required. This will probably be the task of the employee's supervisor. The same principles regarding the importance of positive feedback hold when supervising the employee as when training that person.

Group Training

Group training is particularly effective for teaching human relations skills. It can be used when a number of employees are to be trained in the same task. A common mistake that trainers make when dealing with groups is to rely on a lecture format. Because this is the format they have been exposed to themselves as students, they feel most comfortable with it as trainers. However, especially when working with adults, participation increases motivation and learning.

A variety of participatory techniques are available to increase both trainee motivation and learning. Brainstorming gets trainees involved in coming up with new ideas or in providing solutions to problems. In small groups, participants attempt to come up with as many ideas as possible. Initially, there is no criticism of ideas. Once a list of ideas has been developed, the ideas are explored as to their feasibility.

Case studies are situations taken from real life. The situation is explained in writing and, through discussion, trainees identify the problem and attempt to come up with a solution. The actual solution is less important than the process the group went through in arriving at it.

In a role-play situation, trainees are given background information and asked to act out a situation. It may involve such things as responding to a situation where the customer complains about the food.

A simulation is the practice of skills in the work area itself. Prior to the official opening of a new restaurant, the staff may have a preopening in which an invited list of customers eat at the restaurant as a trial run to the actual opening.

CAREER DEVELOPMENT

Employee Development

One answer to the problem of employee turnover is a career development program. Such a program involves assisting employees at all levels to determine their career goals and working with them to achieve such goals. To the extent that employees leave an operation because of the lack of opportunities to advance, such a program should help provide opportunities for growth.

A career development program should apply to all employees, not just managers. Too many managers assume that someone who washes dishes for a living has no desire to anything but that for the rest of his or her life. There are people who are good at what they do and have no desire to be moved or promoted to another job. They should not be looked down on but, as long as they are solid contributors to the operation, should be rewarded and appreciated. For those employees at all levels who do want something better or different for themselves, a career development program will help them get there. At the same time, such a program can serve as a motivational device for existing employees that can help increase productivity while reducing turnover.

A career development program consists of [20]:

- Identifying the objectives and needs of the business
- Identifying the personal goals and needs of employees
- Developing an action plan to match the employees' needs with those of the organization
- Providing feedback and guidance to carry out the plan

Management Development

It is important to offer training for management as well as for employees. A typical management training program revolves around three things [21]:

- Training existing managers
- Promoting people from within
- Developing programs for management trainees

Succession Planning.   Many companies use succession planning to identify what type of training is required. Succession planning is "a formal process in which plans are developed to ensure that replacements can be readily identified to fill key positions in your organization" [22].

Such a program involves tracking the key positions with the operation and identifying the feeder jobs for each of these key positions. A feeder job is one from which the jobholder can be promoted into a key position. The short- and long-term staffing needs of the operation are then determined to identify how many managers are needed and when they will be required. Those people in the operation who are potentially capable of being promoted into management are then identified and, for each, an estimate of promotion potential is made. For each person an evaluation is made as to whether or not they are promotable and, if so, when. For each key position two or three alternative successors are identified in case of turnover.

For each employee identified as promotable, a list of needed skills is drawn up and a timetable established for the development of these skills. This list, updated every six months, forms the basis for the type and amount of management training to be done. The list also lets management know the extent to which additional management will have to be found outside the organization.

At the same time that the company is evaluating its managers, each individual should be developing a personalized career development plan. The questions to ask are these [23]:

- What are my career goals?
- What are my options for career development?
- What skills and abilities do I need to acquire?
- What plans do I need to make to move toward my goals?
- What will be my implementation steps and timetable?

Methods.   The methods used to develop managers can be done on or off the job. It is imperative that whichever methods are chosen, they be planned rather than left to chance. The oldest method of development is that of coaching. This term refers to the ongoing, daily instruction provided by a superior. Some people are better than others at developing subordinates. Managers need training in how to develop their staff effectively. Job rotation is another common tool for developing management talent. This involves moving an employee into different positions in a planned manner to allow the trainee to develop additional skills and knowledge. Larger organizations have the option of giving managers committee assignments or positions as "assistant to," to encourage their development.

quick bite 13.7
Road to the Top: Elizabeth Terry

Owner, Elizabeth on 37th

At the age of 16, Elizabeth Terry entered a sewing contest in an attempt to win a sewing machine to be able to make her own clothes and "be a little more stylish." She didn't win the sewing machine. Instead, she won first prize, a trip to Europe. Says Elizabeth: "I think that was the beginning of knowing I was going to be part of a bigger world."

Putting herself through college, she graduated in 1966 with a degree in psychology and began work as a probation officer. After moving with her husband to Atlanta, she started giving wine-and-cheese lectures, fell in love with food, taught herself to cook, and opened a small deli in a wine-and-cheese store. Here she learned that "a restaurant is not a retail business; it's a small manufacturing business. Everything that comes into the restaurant must be changed before it goes out."

In 1981 they moved to Savannah, plunged their savings plus a $100,000 bank loan into an old mansion, and opened "Elizabeth on 37th." The cuisine is based on historically accurate Savannah cooking from the eighteenth and nineteenth centuries. The success of the restaurant—named one of the nation's top 25 restaurants by *Food and Wine* magazine— does not come in the way of community involvement. Once a week the restaurant takes a meal to the soup kitchen. In addition, Elizabeth and her husband are involved in environmental issues in the region.

Source: "Women in Foodservice: Three Success Stories," *Restaurants USA*, vol. 13, no. 9, October 1993, pp. 28–31.

ENDNOTES

1. Arthur W. Sherman, George W. Bohlande, and Herbert J. Chudren, *Managing Human Resources*, 8th ed. (Cincinnati, OH: South-Western Publishing Co., 1988), p. 194.

2. Ibid., p. 194.

3. Ibid., p. 197.

4. Vincent H. Eade, *Human Resource Management in the Hospitality Industry* (Scottsdale, AZ: Gorsuch Scarisbrick, Publishers, 1993), p. 180.

5. David Wheelhouse, *Managing for Human Resources in the Hospitality Industry* (East Lansing, MI: Educational Institute of the American Hotel and Motel Association, 1989), pp. 146–147.

6. Sherman et al., *Managing Human Resources*, p. 199.

7. Karen Eich Drummond, *Human Resource Management for the Hospitality Industry* (New York: Van Nostrand Reinhold, 1990), pp. 68–78.

8. Sherman et al., *Managing Human Resources*, p. 201.

9. Lewis C. Forrest, *Training for the Hospitality Industry* (East Lansing, MI: Educational Institute of the American Hotel and Motel Association, 1983), p. 40.

10. Ibid., p. 41.

11. Ibid., pp. 45–46.

12. Ibid., p. 45.

13. Wheelhouse, *Managing for Human Resources in the Hospitality Industry* pp. 148–149.

14. Mary L. Tanke, *Human Resources Management for the Hospitality Industry* (Albany, NY: Delmar Publishers, 1990), p. 75.

15. Wheelhouse, *Managing for Human Resources in the Hospitality Industry,* p. 154.

16. Ibid., p. 154.

17. Forrest, *Training for the Hospitality Industry,* pp. 112–116.

18. Ibid., pp. 113–114.

19. Wheelhouse, *Managing for Human Resources in the Hospitality Industry,* p. 155.

20. Tanke, *Human Resources Management for the Hospitality Industry,* p. 198.

21. Wheelhouse, *Managing for Human Resources in the Hospitality Industry,* p. 176.

22. Tanke, *Human Resources Management for the Hospitality Industry,* p. 80.

23. Ibid., p. 193.

chapter fourteen

MOTIVATING
THE EMPLOYEE

learning objectives:

By the end of this chapter you should be able to:

1. Suggest what causes employees to behave the way they do.

2. Suggest how management can channel and maintain employee behavior through the implementation of various process theories of motivation.

3. Identify the six dimensions of organizational climate outlined below.

4. Describe how to implement successfully the following in a restaurant operation:
    • Management by objectives
    • Job redesign
    • Positive reinforcement
    • A climate of trust

5. Summarize the major theories of leadership, indicating how they can be applied to a restaurant situation.

EMPLOYEE MOTIVATION

The Role of Managers

Managers cannot motivate employees—motivation comes from within. However, managers are responsible for providing a climate within which employees are motivated to perform. Many managers do not agree that it is their responsibility to motivate employees. They believe that it is the responsibility of employees to "bend" to the needs of the company. If they do not, they are fired. From a purely economic viewpoint this approach is bad management. Treating employees in an arbitrary, inflexible manner will guarantee that the operation will suffer high turnover as increasing numbers of employees decide that they cannot put up with such treatment. Even if they stay, there is a good chance that productivity will go down and absenteeism and pilfering will rise as employees seek to "get even" with the company for perceived slights.

When an employee joins a company there is an implied, and sometimes an explicit, contract. The employee puts forth time and effort in order to receive pay; the company gives the security of a job in return for that effort.

Although every person is an individual, the operation cannot adapt to each employee. There has to be a middle ground wherein management is flexible to employee needs while realizing that the objective is to run a profitable operation. At the same time, employees must sacrifice some of their independence and the satisfaction of their individual needs to the good of the company. An understanding of what motivates employees is critical to getting employees to perform in a productive manner.

We begin the chapter with a survey of the major theories of motivation and propose an inclusive model of organizational climate that builds on these theories. Utilizing this model, managers can implement a comprehensive approach to developing and maintaining a motivated team of employees.

Theories of Motivation

A complete discussion of motivation must cover the following:

- What causes behavior?
- What channels behavior?
- How is behavior sustained?

Content Theories.   Content theories are concerned with what causes behavior. Four such theories that have gained acceptance to one degree or another are Maslow's need-hierarchy theory, Alderfer's ERG theory, Murray's acquired needs theory, and Herzberg's two-factor theory.

Maslow.   Psychologist Abraham H. Maslow focused on a person's basic needs and the relative order of their importance. He identified a hierarchy of needs as follows:

quick bite 14.1
Hot Concepts: Panda Express

According to former president and chief operating officer Joseph Micatrotto, the reason for the phenomenal growth of Panda Express is "the five types of restaurants we can open." Units in the chain vary from 400 to 2000 square feet, with annual volumes ranging from $350,000 to $1.5 million. Operations are located in a variety of places, from malls and supermarkets to universities and fast-food rows.

Spun off from the full-service Panda Inn in 1983 by cofounders J. C. Cherng and his father, Chinese master chef Ming-Tsai Cherng, the chain had 125 units in 1994 and is scheduling an aggressive expansion. Says Micatrotto, "It's obvious when you're this dynamic that one of two things happens: You either go public, or you're acquired." It's success is that it is a "quick-service environment with a full-service kitchen." It faces challenges in finding the right sites and the right people as it continues to grow east and diversify from malls and supermarkets.

With an average check of $5.75 and food and labor costs of 29 and 18 percent of sales, respectively, the company is looking for ways to streamline costs by seeing "how much we can introduce in prep and pre-prep—what comes in the back door."

Source: Richard Martin, "Panda Express: Bullish about the Bear," *Nation's Restaurant News,* May 16, 1994, pp. 86, 88.

1. *Physical:* the need for food and shelter.
2. *Safety and belonging:* the need for protection from people and/or the environment. This person would be cautious, avoiding risk and planning for the future.
3. *Social:* the need for love and belonging. This person will have high social needs, like people, wish to be a team player, and want to be accepted.
4. *Esteem:* the need for self-respect and the respect of others. People seeking the respect of others would seek attention and thrive on publicity and praise. They would be aware of status symbols and desire material things.
5. *Self-actualization:* the need to meet one's potential. Such people are interested in making creative contributions and want a challenging work environment.

Maslow's hierarchy of needs suggests that lower-level needs must be satisfied for the most part before a person can be concerned with the satisfaction of higher-level needs. A corollary of this is that once a need has primarily been satisfied, it ceases to motivate the person.

It is difficult to identify where money comes into this picture. For some, money is necessary to satisfy basic needs and is regarded as crucial to meeting physiological needs. For others, money is seen as a status symbol. The problem

Courtesy Panda Express.

for those using this theory to identify needs is that it may be thought that money no longer motivates a person making a considerable salary, as their basic needs have been taken care of. For the person who sees money as a way of keeping score with the world, money will continue to be important as a motivator long after basic needs are taken care of.

Managers should attempt to determine what needs employees are seeking to satisfy and create an environment that gives employees opportunities to satisfy them. Consider the restaurant that hired Sarah as a bookkeeper. Sarah had been a stay-at-home wife for 25 years, raising the children. Bored at home, she decided to get a part-time job. After only a few weeks at work, management noticed that Sarah was forever venturing out of the office to visit with the servers and cooks. The result was that the work of the other employee was interrupted while Sarah's job duties were left unfinished. Management could have fired Sarah. Instead, a thoughtful discussion with her indicated that the main reason she took the job was the desire to interact with others. Her husband was doing well financially, so money was not a prime factor in her decision to reenter the job market. Management gave Sarah a job as hostess and now has a personable greeter, a satisfied employee, and customers who are delighted with the service they receive.

Alderfer. Alderfer proposed three need categories: existence, relatedness, and growth. The first—existence—similar to Maslow's physiological and safety needs; the second—relatedness—involves relationships with others and is simi-

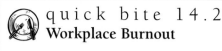

quick bite 14.2
Workplace Burnout

An investigation of 532 foodservice managers of five hotel chains indicated that 28 percent of the respondents reported strong feelings of emotional exhaustion, while 20 percent reported strong feelings of depersonalization, two symptoms of the burnout syndrome. Restaurant (35 percent) and catering sales (32 percent) managers reported the highest frequency of emotional exhaustion; restaurant managers (28 percent) also reported the highest depersonalization ratio. Women reported greater burnout than did men. As the average number of hours worked per week increased from 50 to 80, so did the reported frequency of burnout and increased personal accomplishment.

Source: Christopher Krone, Mary Tabacchi, and Bonnie Farber, "A Conceptual and Empirical Investigation of Workplace Burnout in Foodservice Management," *Hospitality Education and Research Journal*, vol. 13, no. 3, 1989, pp. 83–91.

lar to the safety, social and ego-esteem needs of Maslow; and the third—growth—is similar to self-esteem and self-actualization. According to Alderfer, more than one need can operate at a time. He also proposes that in addition to a hierarchy effect, people who are frustrated in their ability to satisfy a higher-level need may regress to become more concerned with the fulfillment of lower-level needs.

Murray.   Murray suggests that a large part of performance can be explained by a person's need for achievement. People with a high achievement motivation prefer moderate risk, are persistent, take personal responsibility for their performance, need feedback on how well they are performing, and are innovative [1]. Conversely, people with low achievement needs take high risks.

David McClelland, a student of Murray's, sees motivation as a function of three needs: the need for affiliation, the need for power, and the need for achievement. Those with a high need for power want to control, dominate, or otherwise have an impact on others. Power can be individualized power or socialized power. In the former situation, people want power for its own sake. They desire the emotional feelings they get from applying power. Socialized power comes from using one's influence to attain objectives that will benefit everyone. Obviously, the latter behavior makes for a more effective manager.

These motives are developed through learning. In other words, people learn to behave in ways rewarding to them.

Herzberg.   Herzberg identified two aspects affecting the work of an employee: hygiene factors and motivators. The absence of hygiene factors will result in employee dissatisfaction, but their presence will not result in a motivated employee. The most important hygiene factors are [2]:

- Company policy and administration
- Supervision

- Salary
- Interpersonal relations
- Working conditions

Motivators are the factors whose presence will act to motivate the employee. The most important motivators are [3]:

- Achievement
- Recognition
- The work itself
- Responsibility
- Advancement

Herzberg believes that the key to motivating employees is to enrich jobs such that they provide employees with work that is interesting and meaningful. The content theories described above would indicate that [4]:

1. Individuals prioritize needs and act in an attempt to satisfy them.
2. More than one level of need may be operable at any one time. If higher-level needs cannot be satisfied, the satisfaction of lower-level needs takes on greater importance.
3. Much of an employee's performance can be explained by the need for achievement.
4. Certain factors—motivators—motivate people; others—hygiene factors—do not. However, the absence of the latter will result in dissatisfaction.

Process Theories.   Process theories are concerned with what channels behavior and how that behavior can be sustained. Four theories will be discussed: equity theory, expectancy theory, reinforcement theory, and goal-setting theory.

Equity Theory.   Equity theory considers that people look at what they put into the job relative to what they get out of the job and compare both to others. If they perceive that there is an inequitable situation, they will work to reduce the inequity. The greater the inequity, the stronger will be the motivation to reduce it.

There are a number of ways to reduce a perceived inequity. People can [5]:

- Reduce what they put into the job
- Seek more rewards for their effort
- Delude themselves into believing that the situation is equitable
- Leave or be absent from a job
- Get others to lower their efforts
- Change the basis of comparison

People will choose the course of action easiest for them.

The key points in this theory are that people make comparisons; that what they *perceive* or believe (rather than what may actually exist) is what is important; and that their reaction can be one of several.

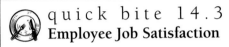

quick bite 14.3
Employee Job Satisfaction

A survey of 310 part-time and 310 full-time nonmanagement restaurant employees found few differences between the two groups in the following areas of job satisfaction: work, pay, promotion opportunities, supervision, co-workers, and the job in general. Full-time employees were more satisfied with promotion opportunities and their work than were part-timers.

Source: Richard F. Tas, J. B. Spalding, and Juliet M. Getty, "Employee Job Satisfaction Determinants within a National Restaurant Company," *Hospitality Education and Research Journal,* vol. 13, no. 3, 1989, pp. 129–136.

Expectancy Theory. According to expectancy theory, employees are motivated to produce to the extent that they believe they will receive a reward important to them. They will put forward more effort, leading to greater productivity, for which they will receive a reward important to them. The effort is diminished if:

1. The reward is unimportant to them.
2. They do not believe that they will get the reward.

This means that the manager needs to know what is important to the employee and must also convince the employee that he or she can be trusted to provide the reward.

Tying expectancy theory into Herzberg, hygiene factors such as working conditions are seen as less motivating than such things as a promotion. We can speculate, therefore, on the relative impact on performance of employees or promising to improve working conditions compared to the promise of a promotion. The latter, it is suggested, would act as a greater motivating factor.

Expectancy theory can also be examined relative to Maslow. Effort on the part of the employee will lead to the employee performing if he or she believes that there will be a reward important to the employee, a reward that will, to some extent, satisfy needs important to the employee.

Reinforcement Theory. Reinforcement theory is based on the idea that performance improves when it is rewarded or reinforced. This idea of modifying people's behavior says that people behave in ways that are rewarding to them. By rewarding existing behavior, that behavior will be encouraged and repeated.

Something in the environment (antecedent) stimulates behavior for which there is a consequence. Behavior can be "managed" by managing antecedents and providing the appropriate consequences. Managing antecedents can be done by removing barriers that hinder the completion of a good job or by providing aids that help employees do a good job [6]. Barriers might be such things as training deficiencies or confusing policies or rules. Factors that help get the job done might include clear plans and instructions and realistic deadlines.

There are four types of consequences to a particular behavior: positive reinforcement, negative reinforcement, extinction (no consequences), and punishment. Positive reinforcement—"catch somebody doing something good and reward them"—is generally accepted as the most potent consequence in shaping future behavior.

Goal-setting Theory. Goal-setting theory states that setting or accepting more difficult goals will result in higher performance than the setting or acceptance of easier goals. Employees will set goals for themselves if management does not. Therefore, management should get involved in raising employee goals.

The foregoing theories would indicate that [7]:

1. People compare what they put into their work and what they get out of it to the inputs and outputs of others.
2. People will expend effort to the extent that they believe they will receive rewards important to them.
3. Behavior can be shaped by a system of rewarding desired behavior and punishing undesirable behavior. Positive reinforcement of desirable behavior is a stronger motivator than is punishment of undesirable behavior.
4. Having a specific goal will increase performance; having a difficult (yet attainable) goal will result in higher performance than will having an easy goal.

ORGANIZATIONAL CLIMATE [8]

Bearing in mind the various theories as to what motivates employees, the manager's role is to provide the climate within the organization that will motivate employees to perform. The organizational climate is how it "feels" to work there. The organizational climate:

1. Consists of a set of properties of the work environment.
2. Is based on the perceptions of the people who work there.
3. Influences the motivation and behavior of employees, depending on how they perceive the climate [9].

These points indicate that it is possible to describe and measure the climate within an organization in terms of a number of dimensions. In this chapter we will go on to suggest six dimensions of climate. The point is also made that it is the perception of the employees, not management, that is important in defining climate. The employees' perception of what exists within a company may be the same or different from what is actually occurring in the company. However, it is the employees' perception, right or wrong, that is important. Finally, it is the employees' perception that will influence to what extent employees are motivated as well as how they behave. If, for example, an employee perceives that management does not set high service standards (even if the standards actually are high), she or he may decide: "If management does not care about the service, why should I?"

Dimensions of Climate

Research has resulted in descriptions of climate in anywhere from four to seven dimensions. One well-respected model is that of the Forum Corporation [10]. In this model the climate of an organization is described in terms of six dimensions: three dealing with performance, three with development. The performance dimensions are clarity, commitment, and standards. The development dimensions are responsibility, recognition, and teamwork.

Performance Dimensions.   The first performance dimension is that of clarity. Clarity refers to how well employees understand the goals and policies of a company, in addition to how clear they are about their own jobs. It is the feeling that things are organized and run smoothly. For example, when employees are not given a written job description but are told to "watch Joe and learn from him," they are probably unclear about what they should be doing and would give the climate a low score on this dimension.

Many managers do not tell employees enough about the overall goals of the operation. They may feel that employees do not care. However, many employees do care. The result is that these employees do not know what is important to the company. If they do not know what is important, they will not know how to act in certain situations. For example, if a customer complains about the way a steak is cooked, what should the employee do? A restaurant that is concerned primarily with customer satisfaction would want the employee to correct the situation in favor of the customer. A company more concerned with cost control might have the employee try to convince the customer that the steak was prepared the way the customer ordered it.

Commitment, the second performance dimension, is the extent to which employees continually feel committed to achieving the goals of the company, the extent to which they accept goals as being realistic, the extent to which they are involved in the setting of such goals, and the extent to which their performance is continually evaluated against the goals of the organization. Companies have certain goals, such as profitability, return on investment, customer satisfaction, and cleanliness. These goals are achieved (or not achieved) by the efforts of the employees. The goals of the restaurant can be met only if employees are committed to achieving them. The greater the commitment, the more likely it is that the objective will be achieved.

The final performance dimension is standards. Standards measure the degree to which employees feel that management emphasizes the setting of high standards of performance and the extent to which they feel pressure to continually improve their performance. Employees may have higher standards than does the company. For example, in a restaurant that is very bottom-line oriented, concessions may be made in the areas of customer service, equipment maintenance, and employee training. Management may think that their standards—low costs and high profits—are high.

Employees may feel that company standards—cut back on service, maintenance, and training—are low. This will influence how they feel toward the company and may well affect their performance. In *In Search of Excellence*, the

quick bite 14.4
What Influences Graduating Seniors?

A survey of faculty and graduating seniors of hospitality management programs at five universities concluded that:

1. The recruiter plays a significant role in the student's decision about whether or not to join a company.
2. Faculty and students view the same aspects of the selection process differently. Students' top influences on whether or not to accept a position were: personal experience, employees of the employer, the employer's recruiters, the faculty, and the student's coop position. For students, the five job-related factors having most influence on the employment decision were: the way the company treats its employees, the degree of interesting work, the amount of responsibility given the student, the reputation of the company in its field, and the growth potential of the company.
3. The sources of influence on whom to interview with are different from those that influence which job to accept. In choosing with whom to interview, students were most influenced by their personal experience, the employees of the company, the faculty, a representative of the company as a guest speaker, and job fairs. The following sources of influence were of less influence when the job acceptance decision was made: a representative of the company as a guest speaker, the news media, campus placement office, professional societies, friends outside school, and student organizations.
4. The student's perceptions of the job decision are changed by going through the process. This can be seen clearly from the findings reported above.

Source: Dennis R. Laker and Susan R. Gregory, "Attraction and Influence on the Employment Decision of the Recent Hotel and Restaurant Graduate," *Hospitality Education and Research Journal*, vol. 13, no. 3, 1989, pp. 31–42.

authors compared the bottom lines of companies that emphasized financial objectives such as profit and return on investment with those that stressed non-financial objectives such as customer satisfaction or quality [11]. They found that the latter actually produced better bottom-line results than did the companies that stressed financial objectives. One explanation is that fewer layers of employees can relate to the financial objectives of the operation; they are unlikely to be personally involved in getting a return on investment or participating in a profit-sharing program. Many more layers of employees can relate to something like customer satisfaction: When they go out as customers, *they* know what it means to be satisfied.

Development Dimensions. Responsibility, the first development dimension, is the feeling employees have that they are personally responsible for the work they do, that supervisors encourage them to take the initiative, and that they have a real sense of autonomy. The employee who has to check with the boss before he or she can do anything does not have this.

The second development dimension is recognition, the feeling that employees are rewarded for doing good work rather than receiving criticism and punishment as the predominant form of feedback. In a climate such as this, rewards and recognition outweigh threats and criticism, there is in place a promotion system that helps the best person get promoted, and the restaurant has a reward structure related to excellence of performance. When we hear "the boss wants to see you," most of us immediately think, "What did I do wrong?" A major reason for this is the idea of management by exception. Under this accounting term, targets are set and, if met, the business is on target and no remedial action need be taken. If sales or cost projections are out of line, however, a red flag goes up to initiate corrective management action. Similarly, in dealing with employees, if employees are performing the way they should, the manager—with many demands on her time—will pass over that employee to concentrate on those who are not performing up to standard. The result is that the only time employees hear from management is when things go wrong. Under this type of climate, employees may actually perform negatively in order to receive some feedback, even if it is criticism. An absence of feedback is even more punishing than is punishment.

Teamwork is the third development dimension. This is the perception of belonging to an organization that is cohesive, one where people trust one another, where employees feel personal loyalty and the sense that they belong to the company. It is the feeling of *us* working together, rather than *us versus them*, whether that be management versus employees or kitchen versus dining room.

DEVELOPING A PRODUCTIVE ORGANIZATIONAL CLIMATE

There is a problem within the operation when employees are dissatisfied enough with their jobs that the dissatisfaction affects their job performance. That dissatisfaction comes when there is a gap between what employees want in terms of clarity, commitment, standards, responsibility, recognition, and teamwork and what they perceive they are getting in terms of those dimensions.

It is suggested that a four-pronged approach to dealing with employees will produce an organizational climate that will motivate employees to perform. The four guiding principles of this system are management by objectives, job redesign, positive reinforcement, and the development of trust. In the following sections we look at how these concepts relate to employee motivation.

Management by Objectives

Properly implemented, a philosophy of management by objectives should take care of situations where there is a discrepancy between what employees want relative to clarity, commitment, and/or standards and what they feel they get.

Management by objectives (MBO) can be defined as a managerial process in which managers and employees join in pursuit of specific, mutually agreed upon goals of limited duration, through a plan of action that is monitored in appraisal sessions following mutually determined standards of performance [12]. The definition above indicates that:

1. Manager and subordinate agree on company and personal objectives for the subordinate.
2. The objectives are for a specified period of time, usually a year.
3. Objectives should be specific and measurable.
4. The subordinate prepares a plan of action that is reviewed by the manager.
5. At the end of the time period there is a formal appraisal process to indicate the extent to which the objectives have been met.

The evidence is mixed as to whether or not MBO works. Conceptually, the idea appears sound. Objectives should be set; manager and employee should agree as to what the important objectives are; manager and employee should agree on what is to be measured; the plan of action designed to achieve the objectives should be monitored; and there should be a session at the end of a specified period at which the employee's efforts are evaluated. Despite mixed results regarding the overall effectiveness of the concept, there is general agreement that the mere setting of goals improves performance. MBO also assumes that people will work toward goals to which they are committed. That commitment comes from being involved in the process of setting the objectives.

Implementing the Concept

A program of management by objectives is most appropriate when there are problems with clarity, commitment, or standards. Clarity, it will be recalled, indicates how well employees understand the company's goals and policies and feel that things are organized and running smoothly.

Commitment indicates how strongly employees feel about achieving company goals. To what extent do they accept these goals, see them as realistic, get involved in setting them, and have their performance evaluated against them?

Standards indicates the emphasis that management puts on a high quality of performance. How much pressure exists to improve performance?

Clarity. How will a properly implemented program of MBO improve these three dimensions of climate? When management involves employees in the objective-setting process it becomes *clear* to employees what objectives are important and the role that they, the employees, play relative to management in achieving these objectives.

In many cases, management has done a poor job of communicating the objectives that are important to a company. The manager or supervisor is the key link between the company and the employee. The objective of the company is to make a profit; the employee is seeking satisfaction from the job. How are these brought together? To maximize profit, the company must determine the key result areas that must be emphasized; what employee behavior is necessary in those key areas; whether employee performance matches the behavioral objectives set; and how to communicate to employees the results of their efforts, following up with praise, coaching, or remedial actions.

At the same time, the employee has several questions: What is really expected of me? How far am I expected to go? How good is good? How am I doing? It seems that the best performance and highest degree of goal attainment exist when there is agreement between manager and employee as to the content of the employee's job.

Objectives can be set in a variety of ways. The manager could come in one morning and say "We've had a number of complaints about the quality of service in the restaurant. From now on, I want you to pick up the pace to improve the job that you do." Will employees know what is expected of them? On the other hand, the manager could hold an employee meeting, announce that there are problems with the level of service, and solicit ideas from the employees about what is causing the complaints and how they can be resolved. In one situation in which the author was involved there were numerous complaints about slow service in a lounge bar that was part of an airport hotel. Examination of the situation indicated that the staff was well trained and motivated to perform. The reason that service was slow was that management, seeking to keep inventory costs down, stocked only 12 highball glasses behind the bar. When there was a heavy demand for highballs, servers had to wait for customers to finish a drink, clear the table, and have the glasses washed and rinsed before another drink could be poured and served. The result? Slow service. When asked, employees were able to explain what caused the service breakdown and to suggest a solution. It became clear to management and employees alike that reducing inventory costs was less important than satisfying customers. The point is that when management and employees discuss in specific terms what they should focus on, employees are clear about what they should do and what they can expect from management.

Standards. But what about the level of standards that would be set when employees are involved? A fair amount of research indicates that participative rather than assigned goals leads to the setting of higher goals and, in turn, to higher performance. In particular, some studies indicate that participative goal setting has produced higher goals among minorities and the less educated.

If we assume that most employees want to do a good job, it is fair to say that when involved in the setting of objectives, most employees, will set objectives they can be proud of. Thus, involving employees may very well produce standards higher than if management alone had set them.

Commitment. Generally, employees resist making commitments to goals for two reasons: They do not feel that they are capable of reaching a goal because they lack confidence, ability, or knowledge, or because they see no personal benefit or gain in terms of money, promotion, personal pride, recognition, or whatever is important to them. This relates to the concept of expectancy theory.

By allowing employees to participate, it gives employees a feeling of control over the process that they might not ordinarily have had in their lives. Steak & Ale has found that commitment is improved when [12]:

- Decisions are made as far down the company ranks as possible.
- People are told the whys and hows of change.
- People are informed about how well the company is doing.
- Employee input is sought.
- Employees' individuality is respected.
- The focus of leadership styles is on helping people perform.

Although management has to take primary responsibility for determining the key results areas, employees can be involved in helping set objectives for these key areas.

Let us return to the earlier problem with service. A manager might ask: "What would a server do that would have you say 'That is excellent service?' What would a server do that would have you say 'That is terrible service?'" Employees could easily come up with a list of specifics. They might say that excellent service includes such things as:

- Calling regular customers by name
- Seating customers right away
- Smiling at customers

Terrible service might include such things as:

- Forgetting who ordered what
- Not making eye contact
- Being slow to bring the check

Management can go on to ask for input on how long it should be before a customer's presence is recognized, before they should be given a menu, before they receive the drinks and the meals they ordered, which customers should be smiled at (everyone!), who should get eye contact, and so on. The result will be a series of objectives—employees should make eye contact with and smile at every customer, drinks should be delivered within 4 minutes of being ordered, and servers should always remember who ordered what—that employees are committed to achieve *because they have been involved in setting them*. Ideally, the standards set will be high (who is going to suggest low service standards?), and they will be clear as to exactly what they are expected to do.

Evaluating Employee Performance. Once set, the objectives become the performance standards against which employee performance will be evaluated. Next, management will monitor employee performance.

In deciding which method to use, various criteria should be kept in mind. First, the method should validate the selection techniques used. If an effective selection method is in place, an appraisal method should show a significant percentage of employees meeting the performance objectives of the job. If this does not happen, it indicates that the selection method is faulty and/or the appraisal method is poor.

Another purpose of an appraisal method is to provide a rationale for making personnel decisions. It is important that the method selected be legally defensible. In this regard it should be based on an analysis of job requirements. Ratings should be documented and employees have a formal appeal procedure.

A variety of methods are commonly used. Performance can be evaluated through direct indices or personal traits against set objectives or behaviorally anchored rating scales. Direct indices are objective and can be well documented. Servers may be evaluated on the basis of number of appetizers sold, for example. Direct indices, however, cannot take into account how well employees deal with customers and fellow employees.

In the personal trait method, characteristics are identified that are considered to be an important part of the job—such as creativity, dependability, and initiative—and the employee is evaluated on the extent to which he or she possesses them. A major problem here is the subjectivity involved. The extent to which a person is creative is open to a great deal of interpretation and argument.

Behaviorally anchored rating scales (BARS) are very compatible with a program of MBO. Whereas management by objectives focuses on the end result, BARS stresses the means to reach the end. In a BARS program the behavior necessary to reach the set objective is specified and the employee evaluated on the extent to which the behavior is displayed. Take, for example, the objective of selling more appetizers. Employees may be unable to sell a customer on buying an appetizer because they lack the training or because the customer is just not that hungry. Thus, through no fault of their own, the objective is not met. BARS identifies whether or not the employees do what they should, within their power, to get the sale.

The behaviors necessary for successful suggestive selling need to be identified. Success in selling probably comes from displaying a knowledge of items on the menu, suggesting items to every customer while maintaining eye contact and smiling, and describing those items using language that paints a desirable picture. This is another area in which employee involvement can be sought. Given a few minutes and some encouragement, employees can come up with several types of behavior that would encourage or discourage the sale of extra items. These behavioral objectives or anchors become the behavioral standards against which employees will be measured.

The ratings scale is typically displayed on a single page with various scale points, ranging from excellent to unacceptable. For each scale point there are behavioral statements representing the behavior that will probably lead to that level of performance. By observing the behavior, a manager can determine whether the employee behaved in a way that would lead to the objective being met.

BARS are useful for several reasons. They focus on behavior, what employees actually do in their jobs. They stress only those things over which an employee has control. Employees have no control over whether a customer buys dessert; they do have control over whether they ask the person to buy. Specifying behavior tells employees what to do to be given a rating of excellent; employees can then adjust their behavior accordingly. If they do not perform as desired, managers can also be specific about what the employees did wrong.

Although this method is time consuming and costly to develop, BARS makes it easier for managers to implement the last part of the MBO process, providing employee feedback.

Providing Employee Feedback.   Employees need to know how they are doing. Many managers view the appraisal session with as much trepidation as does the employee. It may be especially difficult and uncomfortable if the subordinate is older or has more experience than the manager.

Most people enjoy giving good feedback (although they may not do enough of this). However, it can be difficult to tell employees they are not doing so well. One reason is that the manager has little or no objective data on which to base an evaluation. With BARS the manager can indicate the specific objective things that the employee did or did not do.

Having employees evaluate themselves prior to the appraisal interview with the manager provides a basis for discussion of any differences in the ratings. In some cases, managers may be surprised that employees are regarding

---

quick bite 14.5
Building Employee Morale

It's not the big problems that cause problems with employees—it's the little things. Here are some ideas on how to improve employee morale by concentrating on the little things:

1. Listen attentively to your employees.
2. Don't use "cute" names such as "Hon" and "Dear."
3. Build an atmosphere of trust by acknowledging their ideas even if you don't take action on them.
4. Be honest with employees.
5. Show flexibility in scheduling.
6. Remember the basics—provide comfortable uniforms and keep the bathrooms stocked.
7. Train employees to give them the confidence to handle problems.
8. Make sure that everyone knows the goal and the rules.
9. Treat your employees like family. Bill Fromm says, "If you want the customer to be treated like a king, treat your people like royalty."
10. Find and utilize all of your employees' talents for things outside their specific jobs.
11. Put a simple, sincere note in with the paycheck.
12. Publicize letters of appreciation.

Source: Robert Liparulo, "Building Employee Morale," *Restaurants USA*, vol. 12, no. 8, September 1992, pp. 12–14.

---

their own shortcomings. It is also a good idea to give the employee the manager's basic evaluation one to three days prior to the appraisal interview. This allows the employee to get over the initial defensiveness that comes from a negative appraisal and to approach the interview more objectively.

It can be argued that a formal annual evaluation is of questionable value. Some research is available to show that in annual interviews, praise has no effect, while criticism brings on defensive reactions that in some cases result in decreased performance in the future. For this reason it is suggested that coaching be a day-to-day activity, not once a year.

The actual interview can take one of several formats. In the tell-and-sell interview, the objective is to communicate the manager's evaluation of the employee and persuade the employee to improve. The manager acts as judge. This approach is most likely to work when the employee respects the manager and feels that the manager is, in fact, qualified to pass judgment on his or her performance.

A second approach is the tell-and-listen interview. The task is to communicate the evaluation while giving the employee an opportunity to react to it. The manager still plays the role of judge but spends time listening to the employee and attempting to summarize the employee's reactions.

In the problem-solving interview, the approach is to stimulate growth and development within the employee rather than focus on past behavior. In the role of helper, the manager uses exploratory questions to identify new ideas from the employee on how performance can be improved. This does not mean that performance is not evaluated. It does mean that the focus is not on how the employee has failed, but rather, on why the employee has failed and what has to change for her or him to succeed.

While the potential for change is great, the interview is unsuccessful if the employee is unable or unwilling to bring forward ideas. Additionally, the interview may not go the way the manager thought it would. The employee may identify changes the employer is unwilling or unable to consider.

Job Redesign

When employees rate their job low on "responsibility," they are saying that they do not feel personally responsible for the work that they do, that supervisors do not encourage them to take the initiative, and that they do not have a real sense of autonomy. When the level of responsibility felt is less than the level desired, there is a problem. The answer lies in redesigning the "problem" jobs.

Definition.   The classical approach to designing jobs held that productivity would be increased by task specialization. Additionally, by simplifying jobs, costs would be reduced because management could avoid paying for a difficult skill that was used only sparingly in the performance of a piece of work.

More recently, with a workforce that is increasingly educated and demanding, there has developed the thought that low-skill, monotonous jobs will lead to boredom and job dissatisfaction, which, it is argued, will lead to lateness, absenteeism, and reduced performance on the job. Thus the move to job redesign to accomplish two things: task efficiency and human satisfaction.

The objectives of a program of job redesign are to design jobs to help the company get work done in the most productive way possible while helping satisfy employee needs for a good-quality work life by fashioning jobs that are interesting, challenging, and provide opportunities for employee accomplishment.

Job redesign, then, assumes that employees want jobs that are interesting, challenging, and provide opportunities for employee accomplishment. Employees who cannot or will not handle such a job are likely to become confused and frustrated at being asked to think rather than just perform. When employees feel that they are being given insufficient responsibility, when they are in a job that they feel is monotonous, segmented, and routine, the job is a good candidate to be redesigned.

There are two common redesign strategies: job enlargement and job enrichment. Job enlargement—horizontal job loading—involves adding more tasks to the individual job to provide a greater variety of tasks for the person doing the job. Adding one meaningless task to another meaningless task is like adding zero to zero. The answer is still zero.

Job enrichment—vertical job loading—enriches the job by taking some of the tasks performed by management and adding them to the job of the employee. Traditionally, management has planned the work, the employee performs it, and management decides whether or not it has been performed correctly. Vertical job loading seeks to build into people's jobs some of the planning and/or control functions usually performed by managers.

A program of job enrichment fits in well with a number of the motivational theories noted above. Herzberg's work indicates that 80 percent of job satisfaction comes from achievement, recognition, and responsibility. Job enrichment can be seen as an outgrowth of this model.

Behavioralists believe that reinforcement is the key to achieve performance. They view job design as a way of making the job more intrinsically rewarding, thus leading to higher levels of performance. Others feel that cues received from the environment are diffused over areas of the brain to arouse and activate the person. The greater the variety and stimulation in a job, the higher the state of arousal and the greater the motivation.

As noted above, expectancy theory holds that a person will behave in a certain way if he or she believes that such behavior will result in an important outcome. This theory indicates that the worker perceives that an enriched job will lead to an intrinsic reward, so the employee is committed to the job and performs better *if such rewards (challenge, responsibility, etc.) are regarded as important by the employee.*

Implementation.   The manager's task is to organize the tasks involved in performing the job and the relationships between the person doing the job and the supervisor, any subordinates, and all fellow employees, to produce jobs that will be performed in an efficient manner while contributing to employee satisfaction.

Employee Satisfaction.   Behavioral scientists have found that three factors are critical to satisfaction and motivation on the job. Employees must feel that what they are doing is meaningful in terms of their own set of values, they must feel personally responsible for the outcome, and they must learn how well they are performing.

If, for example, a server feels that serving food is demeaning, the person is unlikely to feel good about the job, the company, or himself. It is difficult for a person to give good service when feeling this way. In a kitchen organized such that several cooks are involved in the preparation of a particular dish, the fact that no one has total responsibility for the outcome will diminish the rewards of the job. Finally, consider the typical relationship between kitchen and dining room. Cooks prepare the meal and hand it over to servers to give to the customer. If they get no feedback from either the customer or management, their job satisfaction will go down. Brian Watts, managing director of the catering facilities at the Bank of England, found that the quality of food improved noticeably when he redesigned the cooks' job to serve customers the food they had cooked in the kitchen.

Throughout this segment there has been talk of employee job satisfaction and motivation. No links have been established between job satisfaction and productivity. However, there are links between job satisfaction and such things as absenteeism, lateness, and turnover. These things cost the operation money. It can be safely assumed that anything that will improve job satisfaction will reduce costs in terms of the items mentioned above. Additionally, it is not hard to accept that employees who feel a level of dissatisfaction with their jobs will be unable to give truly hospitable service to customers.

Basic Job Dimensions.   Every job has five basic dimensions that affect whether or not the job produces any of the three factors noted above. How meaningful the job appears to the person doing it depends on three of these dimensions: the variety of skills used, task identity, and task significance. The more skills that are used in performing a job, the more meaningful the job appears to the employee performing it. The job seems more important because it requires more skills. It is also less boring because of the variety of skills required. Skill variety can be improved by such things as combining tasks and/or adding customer contact to a job that did not require such contact previously. For example, instead of one person washing dishes for an 8-hour shift, perhaps they could wash dishes for 4 hours and bus dishes for 4 hours. This enlargement of the job adds variety while allowing the dishwasher to get to the front of the house and interact with the customers.

Such a technique also relates to task identity, the extent to which the job entails doing something from beginning to end. The more that employees are involved in a job from beginning to end, the more motivated they are about what they are doing. The busser who takes dirty dishes into the kitchen does not see what happens to them after they are left with the dishwasher. By doing both jobs, the flow of dishes from use to reuse is seen in its totality. This technique may also improve relations between two employees who bicker over who should do what in the interaction of their jobs. Bussers can make the dishwasher's job easier or more difficult, depending on how they arrange the dirty dishes as they are cleared from the tables. Dishwashers, on the other hand, do not see the hectic pace in the dining room. Seeing the job "from the other side" can produce more-understanding employees.

Task significance refers to the way a job affects others in a substantial way. The more employees feel that what they are doing affects the overall goal of the restaurant in a substantial way, the more satisfaction they get from what they are doing. Before Disney employees are allowed to sell popcorn or clean Main Street, they must undergo a training program that emphasizes what they do in relation to customer satisfaction. The street cleaners are very visible to visitors and therefore, they are asked numerous questions. They are told that an important part of their job is acting as a Disney "Ambassador" in addition to their crucial role of keeping the place clean. On the other hand, what message does a manager send to back-of-the-house employees when she or he spends little or no time behind the scenes, preferring to be out front with customers?

What is said, or communicated, nonverbally is also important. Saying such things as: "I don't know how you can stand this job for 8 hours a day" lets the employee know exactly what is thought about the job. If the job is so bad, what does that say to the employee about the person doing the job? If employees are told: "You start as a hostess and if you work out and when we get an opening, we'll move you into a server's position," they learn that much is thought of the hostess position. It is better if they are told: "We have found that you will benefit from starting out in this position. You will have a chance to work with all of our servers and see how this operation works. You set the tone for the customer's experience because you make that first impression. When you get your own station, you'll have a better understanding of the way the restaurant operates." Taking those who burnish the silverware up to see the banquet room when it is set up for a party allows them to see how the silverware adds to the look of the room.

The fourth basic characteristic of a job is the amount of autonomy involved in it. The more autonomy that workers experience, the more personal responsibility they will feel for the outcome of the work. Employees in highly autonomous jobs know that they are responsible for success or failure. The management trainee who has to consult the manual for the answer to problems is taught to use the book as a crutch for judgment and initiative. The employee is not responsible for customer satisfaction; the manual is. When employees are given the responsibility and the autonomy to solve customer problems, they feel more responsible. This concept of *employee empowerment* pushes decision making down to the lowest possible level. Suppose, for example, that a customer complains about the length of time that he or she waits for the order to come. Many restaurants have a policy by which employees refer all complaints to a manager who seeks to appease the customer. When employees are empowered, they have, within certain boundaries, the latitude to take care of the problem. Whoever receives a complaint has ownership of it until it is solved. The server may offer to discount the meal or give a complimentary dessert to appease the customer. The feeling of control over the satisfaction of the customer will, for most employees, translate into more positive feelings about the job.

The last job dimension is feedback. The more feedback employees receive, the better they know how they are performing. For employees in tipped positions feedback comes regularly in terms of the amount of tips they receive. Management must pay more attention to nontipped employees who get little or no customer feedback.

quick bite 14.6
Improving Performance

Here are some ways to get better performance from employees:

1. Hire the values you are looking for.

2. Find out why employees are not performing and ask what you can do to help them do a better job.
3. Tell employees in writing what you expect.
4. Give employees clear performance standards.
5. Make sure that employees have the tools to do the job.
6. Get employee input on what behaviors they (the employees) should be engaged in.
7. Have employees come up with 10 "house rules."
8. Train, coach, evaluate, and reward the behaviors identified above.
9. Improve your feedback by dealing with the problems that are within an employee's control, think through what you will say and how you will say it, and be specific about behaviors rather than attitudes.

Source: Bob Losyk, "How to Improve Employee Work Performance," *Restaurants USA,* vol. 15, no. 2, February 1995, pp. 12–14.

Employee Growth Needs. Research results on the relationship between job satisfaction and the growth needs of employees have been mixed. Although some results show that the strength of growth needs moderates the amount of job satisfaction experienced, other studies show no effect. It appears that job satisfaction can be increased for all employees, but the increase is greater for those who have strong needs for growth.

Leadership Style. Managers can affect employee job satisfaction and performance through the style of leadership they adopt. The appropriate leadership style depends on the scope of the job and the growth needs of the employee performing that job [14]. When an employee has high growth needs and is performing a job high in variety (a high-scope job), participative management with a great deal of autonomy for the employee would be appropriate.

When a job is varied but the employee has a low need for growth, the manager should provide direction in planning, organizing, and controlling the work of the employee.

When an employee with high growth needs is performing a task that is not fulfilling, frustration and dissatisfaction will probably result. Supportive leadership will be necessary to produce a satisfied and productive employee.

When an employee with low growth needs is performing a dull and repetitive task, performance should be monitored but the manager need not supervise the employee closely. As long as the job is being performed to the level required, little or no interference from the manager is needed. This maintenance leadership style is appropriate until performance or satisfaction problems arise, in which case more direction or support can be given.

Positive Reinforcement

When employees rate a company climate low on "recognition," they are saying that they feel criticized and punished when they do something wrong rather than praised and rewarded when they do something right. The "solution"—positive reinforcement—assumes that people behave in a way that is most rewarding to them. Management can improve employees' performance by providing appropriate consequences to employee behavior. Research does seem to show that positive reinforcement works better than negative reinforcement in producing and maintaining behavior.

Punishment. Many managers have an overreliance on punishment as a means of shaping employee behavior. Punishment seeks the elimination of negative behavior by the application of negative consequences to that behavior. An employee comes in late. The employee is told: "If you come in late again this month, you will be fired." The negative behavior is the lateness; the punishment is being fired; the objective is to reduce or eliminate the negative behavior—to stop the lateness.

There are several problems with an overreliance on punishment. It may eliminate the behavior. However, it may, instead, result in avoidance behavior. Our tardy employee wakes up late. Instead of coming in late and being fired, the employee may call in sick and not come in at all. Or consider the chef who is told: "Don't let me catch you with your food costs this high again." Under his breath the chef may mutter: "Don't worry, you won't catch me." The result may be actions that suppress rather than eliminate the negative behavior. There is also the problem that if employees hear from management only when things go wrong, a negative climate results.

Positive Reinforcement. Positive reinforcement seeks to increase the occurrence of positive behavior by providing desirable consequences for that behavior. Let us return to our tardy employee. Positive reinforcement occurs when the employee is told that at the end of each week, all employees who have a perfect attendance record will be eligible for a prize drawing. The idea is to reward the desired behavior.

Implementation. The staring point is an audit of existing performance in behavioral terms. We may note, for example, that servers do not suggest dessert after customers are finished with the entree.

Next, management identifies what objectives it wishes to see accomplished. Carrying the dessert example through, a goal may be set of having servers sell 10 dessert a shift.

The next step is to identify the behaviors necessary to achieve the objectives. To sell desserts it is necessary to:

- Know what desserts are being offered.

- Suggest to every customer that they have a dessert.
- Describe the desserts accurately and in a way that is likely to induce purchase.

If employees do these three things, it is more likely that they will sell desserts than if they do not do these things.

The fifth step is the key to the success of positive reinforcement—reinforcing the behavior. Several types of reinforcement are possible. Continuous reinforcement involves reacting to the behavior every time it occurs. This is the type of reinforcement received when we put coins in a soda machine. Every time the correct amount of money goes into the slot, a soda appears. Continuous reinforcement is necessary to establish a new behavior.

Related to this is the idea of fixed and variable or intermittent reinforcement. Fixed reinforcement involves getting feedback on a set schedule in terms of time or number of actions. The most obvious example of fixed reinforcement is the weekly or biweekly paycheck. Because that check comes once a week, it becomes expected and, as a consequence, can lose its effect as a motivator. Intermittent reinforcement is given on an irregular basis.

In terms of motivation, variable or intermittent reinforcement is more effective in sustaining already established behavior. Consider the soda machine compared to the slot machine. If you put coins in the soda machine and nothing happens, you may give up and leave, muttering under your breath; or you may kick the machine; or if you are thirsty enough, you may put more coins in the slot. But if nothing still happens, will you put more change in? Probably not. We are used to a continuous schedule of reinforcement. When we go from continuous reinforcement to no reinforcement, the behavior stops.

Management will often work with employees to improve their behavior. After lots of work, lots of coaching, and lots of reinforcement, an employee's behavior begins to improve. But then the manager goes to work with another employee whose behavior needs to improve. Getting no more reinforcement, the first employee's new behavior may disappear.

Consider the slot machine. We put in some coins but get no response. Do we put in more? Of course! The behavior is continued far longer than we would feed the soda machine because we know that at some time there will be a worthwhile payoff. The intermittent variable response of the slot machine keeps the behavior going.

As the fifth step in the process, employees are encouraged to keep a record of their own work. This self-assessment means that employees themselves continuously reinforce their own behavior. Every time the server sells a dessert, she or he makes a note of it. The reinforcement is immediate. In this way the server sees the relationship between the behavior and the consequence. The success interval, or the distance between the behavior and the measurement, is shortened.

Finally, the supervisor looks at the performance of the employee and praises the positive aspects. For reinforcement to work, the employee has to see the relationship between the behavior and the consequence. With continuous reinforcement, it has to be as immediate as possible. It also has to be meaningful to the employee. The priorities of a waitress struggling as a single parent to raise two children are different from those of a college student working for "fun money."

Development of Trust

The last of the six dimensions of organizational climate to be considered is teamwork. This is the feeling of belonging to an organization characterized by cohesion, mutual warmth, and support, trust, and pride. Such employees trust and respect each other while feeling personal loyalty and a sense of belonging to the company. When employees perceive teamwork to be low, it is management's responsibility to instill a feeling of trust and loyalty.

Organizational Commitment.   What factors determine whether or not an employee will be loyal to a company? There are various models of organizational commitment which determine the factors that influence how and why employees are tuned in to the needs of the company. In these models there are several common ideas. The main factors that influence a person's commitment are investments, reciprocity, lack of alternatives, and identification.

As people invest more deeply in a company in time, energy, and commitment, the less they are likely to leave as they accept future rewards—promotions, for example—for their contributions. If they leave the company, their investment will not be recovered.

The idea of reciprocity is based on the assumption that if employees feel they are getting more than they deserve—that the rewards of the job are more than expected—they will remain with the operation to repay this debt through future performance.

Lack of alternatives means that the more specific skills become to a company, the less opportunity is available to use those skills outside the operation. This is not very important, however, in the restaurant industry, where the job in one restaurant differs little from that in another.

Identification is defined as the linking of one's social identity to ones work. As identification increases, change becomes harder and commitment is strengthened.

Implementation: Management Style.   Management's task is to integrate the employee with the company in such a way that there is evidence of mutual warmth and support. In a climate where truth and respect are present, employee feelings of belonging and loyalty will result.

Managers can implement such a climate by the style and behaviors they adopt. Many contemporary managers have idealized models in their imagination akin to the *heroic manager:* the conquering leader who rescues helpless, disorganized employees from all problems and leaves only when all has been accomplished by his or her own courage, intelligence, and skill. The helpless subordinates continue with their mundane tasks until another problem arises and the hero returns.

It is the feeling of control over themselves, but primarily over others, that creates this vision. When crises arise at work and tough decisions are called for, many managers feel responsible for knowing what the problem is, developing the solution, and exerting control over the situation.

When managers perceive their employees to be helpless and incapable and take full control, they elicit reciprocal behavior from their employees. Subordinates retreat to a defense of their narrow interests as managers exert complete control.

The key is for managers to act as *developers*, people with a strong employee-centered image. Managers learn to have impact without exerting total control, to be helpful without having all the answers, and to be powerful without needing to dominate.

The developer–manager model consists of three components that must be nurtured to achieve productive excellence: interdependence, interpersonal skills, and commitment to an overriding departmental goal. Within the operation there is a high degree of interdependence among departments and a constant stream of changes, both internal and external. This is especially true in the restaurant industry, where the satisfaction of the customer depends on the performance of many people in many departments. Managers must develop a method to handle this interdependence.

The solution is to build a team that shares the responsibility for managing departments. It is a joint responsibility group that shares in making the basic decisions and influences each member to a high level of performance. Building such a team leads to greater subordinate commitment and motivation. Joint responsibility increases individual challenge and potential learning and growth. Development occurs in technical and managerial skills. Research has indicated that groups make better decisions than individuals do when the problem is complex.

The second component in being a developer–manager is the importance of interpersonal skills. Daily interaction can be used to encourage and enhance growth in subordinates. Coaching from the develop–manager helps build competence. In this way, behavioral problems can be turned into an opportunity for growth.

The third component is getting employees committed to the overriding goal of the department. The goal unites employees because it is a vision they can share and work toward. Employees do not work for money alone; the goal generates reasons that make the work worthwhile. It is the achievement made toward the goal and the appreciation of the extra effort that become rewarding to the employee.

Implementation: Management Behavior.   The day-to-day behavior of managers nurtures or destroys a climate of trust and loyalty. Employees are constantly looking to determine the extent to which they should be on their guard in dealing with management. The more they perceive management as being threatening, the more time they will spend on their own emotional defenses. The more they perceive an atmosphere in which they can grow, the more emotion they can devote to the job.

Certain behaviors that management can develop encourage trust on the part of the employee.

1. Encourage employees to express doubts, feelings, and concerns. In some companies, expressing doubt about a management course of action is

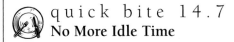

quick bite 14.7
No More Idle Time

Because of uneven demand, there will be times when employees are not working up to capacity. Here are some thoughts on how to make the most of all your employees' time:

1. Compress the schedule. Note when your first customer arrives and when the last one leaves and compare with your employees' work schedule. Can preopening activities be done by the closing staff?
2. Reexamine the hours of operation. Don't keep your employees hanging around if the business doesn't warrant it.
3. Keep a logbook that includes operational changes, customer comments, and inspirational thoughts. Have employees review it during downtimes.
4. Provide incentives for dull, repetitive tasks. Pay extra for the times when employees perform cleaning jobs.
5. Brainstorm new dishes, marketing ideas, or solutions to operational problems.

Source: Jay Solomon, "Making the Most of Idle Time," *Restaurants USA*, vol. 13, no. 7, August 1993, pp. 18–19.

liable to have that person labeled a traitor to the operation. In such an atmosphere, creative ideas are stifled.

2. Tell employees the reasons behind requests. When people understand *why* they are being asked to perform rather than just being told what to do, they feel that management has a greater respect for them. Consequently, they respect management more and perform better.
3. When something goes wrong, be more concerned about what happened and how to prevent it than in finding and punishing the guilty party. This does not mean permitting or encouraging slackness. It does mean that the focus is on problem solving, including the participation of the affected parties, rather than on assigning blame.
4. Encourage employees to come to you for assistance while helping them to develop independent judgment.
5. Be candid about the person to whom you are talking, but never gossip about anyone. Managers are never off the record.

LEADERS AND MANAGERS

Throughout this chapter we have referred to supervisors as "managers" while suggesting at times that they exhibit a "leadership" style. There is a difference between a manager and a leader. According to Benis and Nanus [15], most organizations are managed, not led. They, among others, promote the idea that what is increasingly needed are leaders, not managers. It is useful, therefore, to look at some ideas of what constitutes a leader and to relate these ideas to the task of motivating employees.

Leadership Theories

Leadership theories have evolved over the years. Trait theories, popular from the 1920s to the 1950s, focused on the role of personal characteristics such as intelligence and dominance. Beginning in the 1950s, we saw the development of behavioral theories which suggested that the effectiveness of leaders comes from what they do rather than the personal characteristics they possess. Another development is that of situational theories—the idea that the characteristics of employees and the situation the business is in must be considered when developing an effective leadership strategy.

Trait Theories. While early studies attempting to identify personal characteristics that made for successful leaders were inconsistent, later reviews have identified more consistent results. It appears that the following are important [16]:

- Vigor and persistence in the pursuit of goals
- Self-confidence
- Ability to influence others
- Ability to tolerate frustration

Taken together, they give a fuzzy picture of the personality of a leader. Although it is now felt that personality is part of being a leader, it is no longer accepted that the existence of various traits will make a person a leader, and vice versa.

Behavioral Theories. Because trait theories were unable to identify what made a leader effective, the focus turned to an examination of the behaviors that seemed to work.

Early studies at the University of Michigan found that production-centered supervision, where the focus was on getting the job done, actually produced less than did employee-centered supervision, where the accent was on developing high goals and focusing highly enthusiastic attention on the employees who did the work.

A research team at Ohio State University identified two similar dimensions of supervisory behavior—consideration and structure—which were popularized by Blake and Mouton as the managerial grid. Two dimensions—consideration for production and consideration for people—were place on a grid to form five possible supervisory styles [17]:

1. *Country club management:* where there is a high concern for people and a low concern for production. There is a friendly atmosphere at work and little pressure to perform.

2. *Impoverished management:* where there is a low concern for both people and production. Those in the organization put forth just enough effort to keep their jobs.

3. *Organization management:* where there is average concern for both people and production. There is a balance between getting out the work and keeping morale at a satisfactory level.

4. *Authority-obedience:* a workplace characterized by a very efficient workforce in which employees are expected to conform to the needs of the company.

5. *Team management:* where there is a high concern for both people and production. Employees see themselves as having a common purpose with the company and, as such, are committed to perform well.

In an attempt to synthesize earlier work, Gary P. Yukl identified the following measurable behaviors which, when used under specific conditions, will produce effective leadership [18]:

- Performance emphasis
- Inspiration
- Structuring reward contingencies
- Autonomy delegation
- Goal setting
- Problem solving
- Planning
- Work facilitation
- Interaction facilitation
- Criticism–discipline
- Consideration
- Praise–recognition
- Decision participation
- Role clarification
- Training–coaching
- Information dissemination
- Coordinating
- Representation
- Conflict management

Situational (Contingency) Theories. Aware that neither trait nor behavioral theories adequately explained what makes a leader, attention turned to the importance of situational variables. Basically, such theories say that there is no single style of leadership that will be effective in every situation. To be effective, leaders must adapt their behavior to changing situations.

Fiedler's contingency leadership model states that group performance is a function of both the leader and the leadership situation. The extent to which the leader is task or relationship oriented is a measure of the motivational system of the leader. The leadership situation consists of three things [19]:

1. Leader–member relations (the extent to which the group trusts and likes the leader and is willing to follow her or his instructions)
2. The extent to which the task is structured
3. Position power

The first factor is the most important. Fiedler's research has shown that task-oriented leaders are most effective where they have power by virtue of their

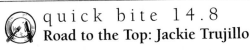

quick bite 14.8
Road to the Top: Jackie Trujillo

Vice Chairman and President, Harman Management Corp.

The day after she graduated from high school in 1953, Jackie Trujillo applied for a job with Leon W. "Pete" Harman, the first franchisee of "Colonel" Harland Sanders. Working as a carhop as she saved money for college, she postponed her education by making a loan to a relative who, she believed, needed the money more than she did. Harman Management is now KFC's largest franchisee, with 265 units in four states.

According to Marc Gordon, senior director of the National Restaurant Association Educational foundation, Jackie is "very intelligent and bright, but what comes through most of all is her genuine concern and dedication to her employees." Jackie explains: "We offer ownership to each of the restaurant managers. So the stores are run by manager-co-owners, and it's really their restaurant and customers."

Trujillo had an early introduction to work, shining shoes, mowing lawns, and working in an ice-cream manufacturing plant. She worked her way up through the ranks of Harman Management, starting as a tray setter, then working on the grill and in the bakery, washing dishes, and learning how to cook. She helped with openings and was then sent to observe the operations of other companies.

Eventually, she rose to division manager, executive vice president of operations, and in 1987, vice chairman. She has combined her career with a family life, her marriage of 34 years resulting in three children and three grandchildren.

Source: Robin Lee Allen, "Jackie Trujillo," *Nation's Restaurant News*, January 1995, pp. 209–210.

position, good relations with the group, and a job to be done that is well structured. Relationship-oriented leaders are most effective where the situation is moderately favorable or unfavorable to the leader. These might be situations where the leader is accepted but the job objectives are vague or where the task is structured but the leader is not accepted. The major lesson to be learned from this theory is that a style of leadership that is effective under one set of circumstances may not work under a different set of conditions.

The path–goal theory identifies two variables to be taken into account when deciding on an appropriate leadership style: employee characteristics and characteristics of the work environment. Preliminary finding indicate that [20]:

- A directive style of leadership is effective when the work situation is vague.
- Supportive leadership works best on employees who have jobs that are stressful, frustrating, or dissatisfying.

- Employees prefer a participative style of leadership in jobs that are not repetitive and which involve the ego of the employee.

Four points can be made regarding leadership theories [21]:

1. There is no universally accepted approach to studying leadership.
2. There are some personal characteristics that differentiate effective leaders from ineffective leaders.
3. There are two accepted dimensions of leadership:
   a. Employee-or relationship-oriented; or consideration
   b. Production- or task-oriented; or structure
4. Leadership effectiveness is some function of a leader's personal characteristics and behaviors, the feelings of the employees toward the leader, the type of job, relationships within the work group, and the organizational climate.

ENDNOTES

1. Craig C. Pinder, *Work Motivation: Theories, Issues and Applications* (Glenview, IL: Scott, Foresman and Company, 1984), p. 63; David C. McClelland, *Human Motivation* (Glenview, IL: Scott, Foresman and Company, 1985), pp. 595–596.

2. Auren Uris, *101 of the Greatest Ideas in Management* (New York: John Wiley & Sons, 1986), p. 26.

3. Ibid., p. 26.

4. Arthur W. Sherman, George W. Bohlander, and Herbert J. Chudren *Managing Human Resources*, 8th ed. (Cincinnati, OH: South-Western Publishing Co., 1988), p. 304.

5. Ibid., p. 299.

6. Ibid., p. 302.

7. Ibid., p. 304.

8. This material has been taken from Robert Christie Mill, *Managing for Productivity in the Hospitality Industry* (New York: Van Nostrand Reinhold, 1989), Chapters 6–10.

9. George H. Litwin, and Robert A. Stringer, Jr., *Motivation and Organizational Climate* (Cambridge, MA: Harvard University Press, 1968).

10. Forum Corporation, *The Language of Organizational Climate*, unpublished monograph, 1979.

11. Thomas T. Peters and Robert H. Waterman, *In Search of Excellence* (New York: Harper & Row, 1982).

12. M. C. McConkie, "A Classification of the Goal-Setting and Appraisal Process in MBO," *Academy of Management Review*, vol. 4, no. 1, 1979, p. 29.

13. Mill, *Managing for Productivity in the Hospitality Industry*, pp. 143–144.

14. Ricky W. Griffen, "Relationships among Individual, Task Design and Leader Behavior," *Academy of Management Journal*, vol. 23, no. 4, 1980, p. 667.

15. Warren Bennis and Burt Nanus, *Leaders: The Strategies for Taking Charge* (New York: Harper & Row Publishers, 1985), p. 218.

16. Marc G. Singer, *Human Resource Management* (Boston: PWS-Kent Publishing Company, 1990), pp. 353–354.

17. Ibid., p. 356.

18. Gary P. Yukl, *Leadership in Organizations* (Upper Saddle River, NJ: Prentice Hall, 1981), pp. 121–125.

19. Singer, *Human Resource Management*, pp. 356–357.

19. Ibid., p. 358.

20. Ibid., p. 359.

chapter fifteen

RESTAURANT MANAGER 2000

learning objective

By the end of this chapter you should be able to:

1. Identify the major skills and knowledge that will be required of restaurant managers by the year 2000.

THE STUDY

In 1991 the National Restaurant Association began a study to determine the skills needed for a foodservice manager in the year 2000. The methodology used was a Delphi study. A panel of experts was put together comprising the board of directors of the National Restaurant Association, the board of trustees of the Educational Foundation of the National Restaurant Association, human resources professional and training directors belonging to the Council of Hotel and Restaurant Trainers, educators belonging to the Council on Hotel, Restaurant and Institutional Education, state restaurant association executives, independent and chain operators, consultants, and other foodservice industry experts.

Panelists were asked to list any issues they believed would be important to foodservice managers at the turn of the century. Broad categories of topics were identified and a questionnaire sent to all panelists asking them to identify the importance of the various items discovered in the first phase of the project. The results are qualitative and subjective rather than quantitative and were published in 1992 [1].

---

quick bite 15.1
Hot Concepts: Landry's Seafood

The first Landry's restaurant opened in 1979. Despite many mistakes, it was grossing $1 million four years later when Tilman J. Fertitta "saw a great opportunity for a seafood chain." Today the high-volume units pull in annual sales volume of $3.3 million. The menu covers a wide range from red snapper, shrimp, and lump crabmeat to softshell crabs and oysters. Dishes have such signature toppings as mushroom wine sauce and lump crabmeat, brown roux with sauteed onions and crawfish tails, and a cheddar cheese sauce with shrimp and crab.

Combined lunch and dinner check averages are between $14 and $16, while the food cost is 33 percent of sales. Alcoholic beverages are 17 percent of sales. Although many operators are wary of specializing in seafood, Fertitta believes it to be very efficient "because of its seasonal flexibility. If something's not available or out of season, you simply use another species."

The plan is eventually to have a chain of 150 units nationwide. Fertitta prefers to enlarge the chain by acquiring independents and converting them to the 215-seat, 8000-square foot restaurants he desires. Although a casual-themed restaurant, employees are dressed in tuxedo shirts, bowties and black pants. They are supervised by a team of five managers: one general manager, two floor managers, and two kitchen managers.

Source: Bill Carlino, "Landry's Seafood: Not Just Another Fish in the Sea," *Nation's Restaurant News*, May 16, 1994, pp. 74, 78.

THE FINDINGS

The Manager's Job

In 1988 the National Restaurant Association identified the basic functional areas of a restaurant manager's job [2]. That report identified nine functional areas rank ordered in terms of importance as follows:

1. *Cost control and financial management:* monitoring, controlling, and reporting on store profitability indicators.

2. *Supervision of shift operations:* running each shift efficiently and effectively.

3. *Organizing and planning each shift:* preparing for the shift so that it will run smoothly.

4. *Unit coordination and control:* communication among and between managers, supervisors and other resources within the organization.

5. *Customer relations:* improving the dining experience for customers.

6. *Motivating employee performance:* improving the performance of employees.

7. *Employment and development of crew members:* obtaining, selecting, training, and keeping employees.

8. *Communicating with outside sources:* keeping in touch with corporate and community sources outside the unit.

9. *Monitoring and maintenance of facility and equipment:* keeping physical assets operational and in compliance with internal and external regulations and laws.

Three of these nine were found in the Delphi study as being of most importance: supervision of shift operations, employment and development of crew members, and motivating employee performance.

In the following sections we examine major findings in each of the following areas:

- Administration
- Finance
- Human resources
- Facility maintenance
- Sanitation and food safety
- Service
- Marketing
- Food and beverage
- Working conditions
- Background and education
- Industry trends

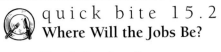

quick bite 15.2
Where Will the Jobs Be?

The following figures represent U.S. Department of Labor estimates of employment in foodservice using a medium scenario for economic growth.

Occupation	Employment (thousands)		
	1992	2005	Percent Change
Chefs, cooks, and other kitchen workers	3,092	4,282	38
Cooks, except short order	1,155	1,564	35
Bakers, bread & pastry	146	216	47
Cooks, institutional or cafeteria	406	470	16
Cooks, restaurant	602	879	46
Cooks, short order and fast food	714	971	36
Food preparation workers	1,223	1,748	43
Food and beverage service occupations	4,365	5,489	26
Bartenders	382	350	(8)
Dining room and cafeteria attendants and bar helper	441	572	30
Food counter, fountain, and related workers	1,564	1,872	20
Hosts and hostesses, restaurant, lounge, or coffee shop	222	301	36
Waiters & waitresses	1,756	2,394	36
All other food preparation and service workers	212	289	36
Foodservice and lodging managers	532	764	44
Total employment	8,201	10,824	32

Source: Renee Iwamuro, "Foodservice Employment to Top 12 Million by 2005," *Restaurants USA*, vol. 14, no. 2, 1994, pp. 43–45.

Administration

In the area of administration, the most likely development, according to panelists, is that managers will have to become computer proficient. As more operations move to comprehensive computer-based information, managers will have to be able to find, oversee, and use information from a variety of data bases on a regular basis. Managers will use computers to perform a variety of tasks, from scheduling employees and forecasting customer demand to collecting sales data and keeping inventories.

quick bite 15.3
Single-Unit to Multi-Unit Management

First-level multiunit managers employed by 10 fast-service organizations identified the importance of various dimensions of their jobs as (1) restaurant operations, (2) human resource management, (3) financial management, (4) marketing, and (5) facilities and safety management. The last two were perceived as being significantly less important than the other dimensions.

Managers had most trouble in human resource management in making the transition from single-unit to multiunit management. This was also the area in which they found themselves spending an increased amount of time. Specifically, managers suggested the following as problems:

- How to manage managers
- How to use different motivational techniques
- How to work with different personalities
- How to read behaviors
- How to communicate effectively
- How to solve problems through people
- How to coach and develop subordinates
- How to evaluate performance and take disciplinary action
- How to get unit managers to achieve high performance standards

They felt they needed more training in the areas of human resource management and marketing. The following marketing training needs were felt to be most important:

- Implementing local-store promotional programs
- Determining the effectiveness of promotional programs
- Identifying the appropriate products to promote
- Developing economic profiles of market areas and assessing competition
- Developing radio ads and buying media
- Developing in-house marketing and promotion programs

Source: Mark A. Mone and W. Terry Umbreit, "Making the Transition from Single-Unit to Multi-Unit Fast-Service Management: What Are the Requisite Skills and Educational Needs?" *Hospitality Education and Research Journal*, vol. 13, no. 3, 1989, pp. 319–331.

Second, managers will increasingly have to supervise a more culturally diverse workforce. Managers will have to become more sensitive to the characteristics of different cultures and customs. Many felt that managers who are bilingual will be at an advantage in communicating with, and therefore motivating, their employees.

A study of 19 general managers working for a restaurant company indicated that as a whole, they exhibited the following personality:

- "Can-do" attitude
- Acceptance of challenges
- Tendency to overestimate their abilities
- May come across as arrogant
- Unlikely to say: "I don't know," "I need help," or "I was wrong"

They have a high energy level and tend to overload their agendas, thereby making it difficult to attend to details. A highly competitive group, they take the initiative, keep score, and are rarely satisfied with a given level of accomplishment. They have a tendency to do everything themselves at the expense of delegating to others. They are outgoing and exhibit a need to control others. Rather disciplined and predictable, they tend to play by the rules. Their analytical ability dominates their skill in following through on their ideas. They are able to handle the countless pressures of the job by their ability to pay attention to what is going on under the most difficult of circumstances.

This group scored as high on confidence, extroversion, and ability to control their attention as any group of top executives in other industries and are as competitive as Olympic athletes and the Navy's SEALS.

Source: Robin W. Pratt and David L. Whitney, "Attentional and Interpersonal Characteristics of Restaurant General Managers in Comparison with Other Groups of Interest," *Hospitality Research Journal*, vol. 15, no. 1, 1991, pp. 9–24.

Third, managers will be more involved in teaching and training their employees. This will require them to develop better communication skills to enable them to do a better job of interacting with employees. Specific skills would include "public speaking, presentation, interpersonal skills and leadership abilities" [3]. More time will be spent training employees and less time dealing with paper.

Finance

The reason that managers will need more computer skills is that operations, primarily the chains, will increasingly have on-line computer-based financial systems. Point-of-sale systems and other electronic tools will "make the manager's more traditional accounting responsibilities more obsolete at the turn of the century" [4]. Managers who are able to perform spreadsheet analysis will be more effective in understanding and reporting on a unit's financial condition.

A second major thought is that managers are more likely to have their pay linked to performance through bonuses and incentives. Managers will continue to assume responsibility for achieving bottom-line results. In addition, however, they will be given more responsibility for managing costs as well as sales. As an example, they will be expected to take more responsibility in reducing Workers' Compensation claims.

Human Resources

Human resources will become increasingly important to tomorrow's managers. They will have to move from being authoritarian to becoming coaches and develop better people skills for dealing with employees as well as customers. It is expected that finding qualified employees will be more difficult.

More attention will be paid to reducing turnover and keeping qualified employees. The manager's task will be to create a climate within the operation that will foster team spirit and motivated workers. This will involve such things as paying on the basis of performance, and providing better fringe benefits, improved work schedules, ongoing training, extensive evaluations, and better retirement benefits.

Facility Management

Managers will get more involved in waste management and recycling. This will cover such things as ensuring that recyclable materials are properly sorted and helping encourage recycling by consumers. In this regard operators will have to become more familiar with government regulations regarding waste management.

Safety and security will also be a concern. Because of increasingly high liability costs, managers, with safety committees made up of employees, will be more aware of security issues both within and immediately outside their units.

Third, there will be a greater emphasis on the implementation of preventive maintenance programs as a way of reducing maintenance and repair costs.

Sanitation and Food Safety

By century's end restaurant managers will have to have a sanitation certificate. Most states will require sanitation testing. In addition, managers will have to communicate the importance of this topic to employees, who will receive more training in this area. It is expected that more natural cleaning agents will be developed as a consequence of restrictions on the use of pesticides and cleaners.

Service

As service increasingly becomes a method for differentiating one restaurant from another, managers will have to become adept at getting feedback from customers and providing service to an increasingly diverse customer base. To allow employees to deliver the level of service needed, managers will have to empower them, giving them the training to be flexible in dealing with customers as well as the authority to handle requests and complaints. This means that managers will spend more time on customer relations and on setting the stan-

quick bite 15.5
The American Restaurateur: Part One

The results of a survey of 18,000 owners and foodservice companies nationwide revealed a picture of the American restaurateur. Here are some of the findings:

1. How many hours a week do you work?

Work Hours/Week	Table Service[a]	Quick Service[a]
30 or less	3%	5%
31 to 40	5%	10%
41 to 49	9%	14%
50 to 59	16%	22%
60 to 69	27%	29%
70 to 79	21%	13%
80 or more	16%	3%
No answer	3%	5%

[a] Numbers may not round to 100% because of rounding.

Taking one day off a week (or none) is the norm and vacations are infrequent.

2. What was your first job in foodservice?

Position	Male	Female
Management	26%	23%
Back of the house (table service)	33%	16%
Front of the house (table service)	22%	43%
Crew person or supervisor	9%	9%
No response	10%	9%

According to 40 percent of the respondents, their first job was in foodservice; they are twice as likely as the general population to have begun in foodservice. They started as a dishwasher (16 percent), busperson (10 percent), cook (10 percent), or server (9 percent). Most owners worked their way to the top.

Source: Restaurants USA, vol. 11, no. 3, 1994, pp. 8–11, 17–24.

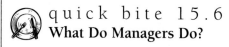
dards required to ensure that employees perform to the level needed to produce satisfied customers. They will spend more time talking to customers to get feedback on the service provided and giving that feedback to employees.

Marketing

Success in marketing will come from the manager's ability to understand and satisfy local tastes. To accomplish this, managers will have to understand the desires of neighborhood and local customers. They will be given greater latitude in implementing plans to accomplish this.

quick bite 15.7

The American Restaurateur: Part Two

Here are some additional results from the survey of 18,000 owners and food-service companies nationwide about the American restaurateur:

1. What activities do you especially like doing?

Leisure Activity	Restaurant Operators	General Public	Difference
Eating out in restaurants	61%	40%	+21%
Cooking	34%	22%	+12%
Traveling on weekends	41%	31%	+10%
Getting prepared for work	15%	6%	+9%
Spending time with family	80%	72%	+8%
Home repairs and improvement	22%	15%	+7%
Spending time by yourself	37%	32%	+5%
Spending time with friends	56%	53%	+3%
Going out for entertainment	42%	41%	+1%
Reading magazines	34%	33%	+1%
Reading books	36%	38%	−2%
Grocery shopping	8%	11%	−3%
Hobbies	35%	39%	−4%
Entertaining guests	29%	34%	−5%
Napping	14%	20%	−6%
Browsing in stores	14%	21%	−7%
Watching television	26%	36%	−0%

2. What is your favorite thing to eat?
   - Sandwich: hamburger
   - Entree: beef or veal
   - Ethnic: Italian
   - Appetizer: shellfish
   - Dessert: ice cream

(continued)

Within chain operations corporate staff will retain control over "creative development, market research, and media purchasing" [5]. However, managers will be given the lead in conducting local and in-store marketing efforts. This will include teaching employees to sell suggestively. Managers will require more expertise in advertising and public relations in order to reach their local target markets effectively.

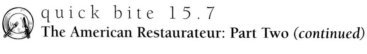

3.   Do you love your job?

Statement	Percentage Who Agree Or Strongly Agree
I am proud of my accomplishments	93%
I am satisfied with my career	79%
I am proud of the foodservice industry	73%
If I had to do it over again, I would choose a career in foodservice	54%
I would recommend a career in foodservice to my children	38%

Older restaurateurs are more likely than younger ones to recommend a foodservice career to their children. Quick-service operators are more satisfied than are table service operators with the tangible rewards of their jobs (income, hours worked, benefits, and job security). Table service operators, on the other hand, are more satisfied than quick-service operators with the intangible rewards of the job, such as interaction with staff and the satisfaction of making a contribution to society.

Source: Restaurants USA, vol. 11, no. 3, 1994, pp. 8–11, 17–24.

Food and Beverage

As consumers become more knowledgeable about nutrition, managers will have to develop more expertise about the nutritional content of ingredients and menu items. Quality control and product consistency will grow in importance. As a way of cutting down on costs, inventory control will become an even greater concern. In line with greater flexibility at the local level, managers will be given more authority to promote specific food and beverage items.

Working Conditions

Although the number of hours worked per week is not expected to decline, managers will have a better quality of life. Salaries and benefits will become more competitive and managers will have more formal education. The job will continue to be stressful, although training in how to deal with stress on the job may help managers deal with this issue.

Background and Education

To deal with a more diverse customer and employee base, managers will need better interpersonal and communication skills by the year 2000. A manager will

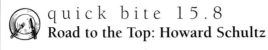

quick bite 15.8
Road to the Top: Howard Schultz

Chairman and Chief Executive, Starbucks Corporation

In 1975, Howard Schultz became the first member of his family to graduate from college. Today, he is chairman of the country's largest chain of specialty coffee and bean shops.

Joining the marketing department of Xerox right after graduation, he rose to become vice president of Hammarplast, a division of a Swedish housewares company. Starbucks, a customer of Hammarplast, hired him as director of retail operations and marketing in 1982. Taking the cue from Italy's widespread espresso bars, he persuaded the company founders to test espresso sales at one of the units in Seattle. Despite successful sales and Schultz's enthusiasm, the founders were reluctant to move into prepared coffee. Schultz left the company and started his own coffee-bar operation. The company expanded to three units and by 1987 was strong enough that Schultz was able to raise the $4 million needed to acquire the assets of Starbucks. His company, Il Giornale, was renamed "Starbucks" and the rest is history!

According to Larry Mindel, chairman of Il Fornaio America Corp.: "The real secret of Howard's success is that he put together an infrastructure of professional people who make every one of those stores operate like a Swiss watch. Starbucks is winning the battle not because its coffee is necessarily better than that of its competitors, but because Howard had the foresight to put together training programs, employee-stock-option programs and health-and-benefits packages—even for part-time employees. As a result, his stores run better, look better, and feel better than any of his competitors." As a result, his store turnover rate is about 60 percent a year compared to a rate of between 200 percent and 400 percent in typical fast-food operations.

Source: Alan Liddle, "Howard Schultz," *Nation's Restaurant News*, January 1995, pp. 183–184.

be more of a generalist and less of a specialist, creating the climate necessary to accomplish the profit objectives of the unit. Managers will have to become more democratic and flexible in dealing with employees and be able to "present an image of grace under pressure to both staff and customers" [6].

Industry Needs

More managers will be needed in casual dining table service, nursing care, and fast food, whereas fewer positions will be available in military foodservice and fine dining.

The Bottom Line

Managers who implement the principles and practices outlined in this book, paying special attention to the areas noted in this chapter, will lead the industry into the next century. Good luck in your efforts!

ENDNOTES

1. The entire report can be ordered from the National Restaurant Association, 1200 Seventeenth Street NW, Washington, DC 20036-3097; telephone (800) 424-5156 or (202) 331-5960.

2. "Job Analysis Report for Unit Manager and Assistant Manager," Educational Foundation of the National Restaurant Association, November 1988.

3. National Restaurant Association, *Foodservice Manager 2000*, Current Issues Report, (Washington, DC: National Restaurant Association, 1992), p. 5.

4. Ibid., p. 8.

5. Ibid., p. 14.

6. Ibid., p. 16.

INDEX